THE PLATFORM ECONOMY AND THE SMART CITY

MCGILL-QUEEN'S STUDIES IN URBAN GOVERNANCE
Series editors: Kristin Good and Martin Horak

In recent years there has been an explosion of interest in local politics and the governance of cities – both in Canada and around the world. Globally, the city has become a consequential site where instances of social conflict and of cooperation play out. Urban centres are increasingly understood as vital engines of innovation and prosperity and a growing body of interdisciplinary research on urban issues suggests that high-performing cities have become crucial to the success of nations, even in the global era. Yet at the same time, local and regional governments continue to struggle for political recognition and for the policy resources needed to manage cities, to effectively govern, and to achieve sustainable growth.

The purpose of the McGill-Queen's Studies in Urban Governance series is to highlight the growing importance of municipal issues, local governance, and the need for policy reform in urban spaces. The series aims to answer the question "why do cities matter?" while exploring relationships between levels of government and examining the changing dynamics of metropolitan and community development. By taking a four-pronged approach to the study of urban governance, the series encourages debate and discussion of: (1) actors, institutions, and how cities are governed; (2) policy issues and policy reform; (3) the city as case study; and (4) urban politics and policy through a comparative framework.

With a strong focus on governance, policy, and the role of the city, this series welcomes manuscripts from a broad range of disciplines and viewpoints.

The Platform Economy and the Smart City

Technology and the Transformation of Urban Policy

Edited by

AUSTIN ZWICK
and **ZACHARY SPICER**

McGill-Queen's University Press
Montreal & Kingston • London • Chicago

© McGill-Queen's University Press 2021

ISBN 978-0-2280-0673-2 (cloth)
ISBN 978-0-2280-0674-9 (paper)
ISBN 978-0-2280-0794-4 (ePDF)
ISBN 978-0-2280-0795-1 (ePUB)

Legal deposit third quarter 2021
Bibliothèque nationale du Québec

Printed in Canada on acid-free paper that is 100% ancient forest free
(100% post-consumer recycled), processed chlorine free

This book has been published with the help of a grant from the Canadian
Federation for the Humanities and Social Sciences, through the Awards to
Scholarly Publications Program, using funds provided by the Social Sciences
and Humanities Research Council of Canada.

We acknowledge the support of the Canada Council for the Arts.

Nous remercions le Conseil des arts du Canada de son soutien.

Library and Archives Canada Cataloguing in Publication

Title: The platform economy and the smart city: technology and
    the transformation of urban policy / edited by Austin Zwick
    and Zachary Spicer.

Names: Zwick, Austin, editor. | Spicer, Zachary, 1983– editor.

Series: McGill-Queen's studies in urban governance; 15.

Description: Series statement: McGill-Queen's studies in urban governance;
    15 | Includes bibliographical references and index.

Identifiers: Canadiana (print) 20210197102 | Canadiana (ebook)
    20210197188 | ISBN 9780228006732 (cloth) | ISBN 9780228006749
    (paper) | ISBN 9780228007944 (ePDF) | ISBN 9780228007951 (ePDF)

Subjects: LCSH: Smart cities. | LCSH: Cities and towns—Effect of
    technological innovations on. | LCSH: Gig economy. | LCSH: Disruptive
    technologies. | LCSH: Technology—Social aspects. | LCSH: Urban policy.

Classification: LCC TD159.4 P53 2021 | DDC 307.760285—dc23

This book was typeset by Marquis Interscript in 10.5/13 Sabon.

Contents

Figures and Tables

FIGURES

TABLES

Acknowledgments

This book is dedicated to all those people and places whose lives have been or will be transformed by technological change. As we make clear in the book, our cities are undergoing tremendous change. Disruption and displacement will be part of it. Our work was completed with those affected in mind. We hope the book will prove useful to those affected.

The editors would like to acknowledge and thank the contributions of the Syracuse University research and editing assistance team, including Kate Alexis Abogado, Médora Benson, Nina Carlsen, Canela Corrales, Alexandra Pastor, and Alexandra Peyton. We would also like to thank the publishing team at McGill-Queen's University Press, especially Jacqueline Mason, who was instrumental in guiding this book through to publication.

We would be remiss if we didn't thank our families for their ongoing support and patience as we spent many hours editing, reviewing, and fine-tuning every aspect of the book.

Finally, we would like to thank the authors. We are grateful for being able to bring together such a brilliant and interdisciplinary group of scholars. They engaged deeply in some of the most contentious areas in geography, political science, public policy, and science and technology studies today. They did so in creative and informative ways and we thank them for their contributions and patience as we brought the volume together.

THE PLATFORM ECONOMY AND THE SMART CITY

Introduction

Austin Zwick, Zachary Spicer, and Kate Alexis Abogado

Austin's one-year-old daughter unrelentingly finds smartphones around the house, even when they are seemingly well out of reach. Austin and his wife do their best to keep their phones away from her, but she learns new and ingenious ways to knock them off every countertop and discover them hidden between couch cushions. She scoops them up, entranced by the back lighting and moving images. Little does she know how much time she will spend in front of them as she grows older. Every facet of her life will be shaped by technology; she will never know a world without it. As parents, they are keenly aware how imperative tech literacy will be to her thriving in the world, but they also feel she is not yet ready for "screen time." Despite their attempts to determine her appropriate use of technology, she already discovering the world through a screen. What is the right balance?

Cities around the globe are feeling the same way. They understand the ubiquity of technology, but recognize that modernity is about to meet the next avalanche of innovation. Cities are looking for ways to harness technology to achieve their objectives while being wary of its potential wide-ranging harm. With the rise of the platform economy, as detailed in the chapters of this book, we recognize the promise of technology to some groups that holds peril for others. As cities shape technological solutions rather than merely respond to the latest innovations, questions of equity will take centre stage. This issue has become more pressing with the COVID-19 crisis as digital technologies have been key in connecting people and facilitating commerce through quarantines and safety precautions.

Our world is transforming at an unprecedented pace. Two trends intersect at the heart of this transformation: urbanization and technologization. In 1800, fewer than 2 per cent of the world's population lived in urban settlements. With the international benefits of the industrial revolution, that proportion grew to 35 per cent by 1950 (751 million people) and to 55 per cent today (4.2 billion), is predicted to reach 70 per cent by 2050 (7 billion), and will continue to grow into the foreseeable future.

At the same time, the rate of technological change has accelerated. Someone born in the twentieth century lived to see mass production of the car (1900s), the beginning of human flight (1910s), the rise of consumerism (1920s), the spread of telecommunications with radio and television (1930s), the destruction of the atomic bomb (1940s), the ubiquity of consumer appliances (1950s), the moon landing (1960s), the first computers (1970s), the eradication of smallpox and other diseases (1980s), the rise and spread of the internet (1990s), and now a smartphone in every pocket (2000s). What will the next century bring: autonomous vehicles? Virtual reality? Artificial intelligence? Space colonization? The possibilities are limitless.

These two phenomena – urbanization and technologization – are mutually reinforcing cycles. As technology freed human labour from the necessities of subsistence survival, people left the countryside for urban communities to seek new opportunities for employment. In cities they found an environment that valued specialized skills. These skills became specialized knowledge that was used to invent new machines that made more forms of labour superfluous. With the advent of industrial technologies, more forms of rural work could be done with fewer people, so they continued to flock to the city. This cycle has transformed human society to the point that now knowledge and creativity are the paramount drivers of economic growth. However, people – and their labour – are still a vital input to provision of goods and services, even if the tool of the job now requires a smartphone app instead of a shovel.

That's where our story begins. This book brings together a uniquely interdisciplinary group of authors to explore how technology has affected urban life, planning, and governance. This volume stems from a series of sessions on the platform economy held at a meeting of the Urban Affairs Association Toronto, Ontario (4–7 April 2018). During these panels, authors presented preliminary work on topics such as the growth of ride-hailing firms, the spread of labour precarity, regulatory and fee structures for platform companies, occupational health and safety in the platform economy, and more.

As we began to collect chapters for this book, we noticed the shifting ways in which cities were responding to technology. When platform economy firms started to infiltrate urban space, governments reacted (often slowly). UberX, for example, was disruptive to the taxi industry in 2012 because it caught incumbents and regulators by surprise. Now, however, governments have come to expect technological innovation and are finding ways to engage with it; attempting to channel technology toward different goals, including improving public transportation, attracting business investment, and improving liveability. In other words, cities are becoming "smart."

This transformation leads to a different set of societal problems that governments must now grapple with. In the platform economy, municipalities were tackling issues in policy areas that they were familiar with, including labour relations, land use, and transportation-for-hire. With smart cities, municipalities must now become experts in the application of information technology, data privacy, and regional economic change.

Before we go on, it is necessary to understand the answers to a few key questions:

FIRST, WHAT IS "THE PLATFORM ECONOMY"?

In what was once called "the sharing economy," digital platforms – from web interfaces to phone apps – began to "share" underutilized resources to improve efficiency under idealistic notions of equity and community. However, as the largest growth in this section quickly became technology start-ups that connected independent contractors to customers, with profit derived from serving as an intermediary rather than a traditional service provider, the term "platform economy" became more appropriate. This innovative business model completely disrupts how more traditional industries (e.g., taxis, hotels, etc.) operate. As the urban form has always reflected the needs of contemporary industries, the new reality of a digital economy has not only forced businesses to adapt but is reshaping cities as well. How are cities responding to this challenge of market and policy disruption? And how should they? Grisdale expands on this definition and provides an overview of common critiques in chapter 2.

SECOND, WHAT IS "THE SMART CITY"?

As the world has urbanized, demand for scarce resources in urban centres has become intense. Public administrators have looked to telecommunications, automation, digitalization – under the moniker of "smart cities" – to help address a wide variety of policy goals, from online integration of municipal social services to data-driven traffic optimization to online posting of key performance indicators. There is no agreed upon definition, but data have become the lifeblood of government decision making. Data will be necessary to power and to regulate new technologies, from blockchain encryption to autonomous vehicles. How should cities use technology to improve quality of life and governance, while also considering concerns about equity, privacy, and democracy? Hartt, Zwick, and Webb expand on this definition and offer critiques of the concept and implementation, in chapter 10.

As previously stated, we see the key difference between urbanization and technologization is that the former is led by private firms and the government reacts, while in the latter the government is proactive, often in partnership with the private sector. The platform economy was the first step of technologization of the urban environment and eventually led the way toward smart cities. This sea change in the local government's relation to technology, from reactive to proactive, will not happen overnight. A wide array of technologies – from installing sensors that measure utility usage to retrofitting infrastructure for autonomous vehicles – will take decades to plan, fund, and implement. Over time, as technology costs decrease and processes become routinized, every facet of the city will be embedded with microprocessors, routers, and other digital equipment. Municipal governance, too, needs to change with this trend, which will require time- and effort consuming bureaucratic reforms. Eventually, technology will become so engrained in urban planning that we will stop giving it a special label, and the term "smart cities" will become meaningless.

What we can take away at this point is that the type of technology integrating into urban life is becoming ubiquitous. The platforms we encounter provide us with mobility, food, goods, personal relationships, and short-term work, among other things. As made apparent by the COVID-19 crisis, tangible and intangible goods can be found, ordered, and delivered via platforms that are quickly reorienting our economy and our lives. At this point, the possibilities seeming endless, for good or for ill. Hundreds of firms compete across dozens of platforms for our business, our attention, our materials, and our labour. The authors included in this volume set out to determine what effect this has on our urban areas, and they have uncovered a mixed relationship, where technologization offers both promises and perils. Can we seize the opportunities while regulating the risks?

The sequence of chapters in this book follow this transition from the platform economy to the smart city. The twelve content chapters, excluding the introduction and conclusion, are then divided into three sections: Managing Platforms (chapters 2–5), Governing Platforms (chapters 6–9), and Cities as Platforms (chapters 10–13). The first section focuses on the societal costs and benefits of the platform economy, where market and policy disruption triggered government regulatory bodies to act. The second section focuses on how government is moving beyond regulation into a deeper understanding of the implications of these technologies for their cities' brands, partnerships, and regulatory frameworks. The final section focuses on how municipal government is becoming oriented to the future in technology and governance to achieve public policy goals. Each chapter begins with an outline of its contents highlighting the chapter's academic contribution, and ends with implications for governance and policy recommendations.

SECTION 1: MANAGING PLATFORMS

Chapter 2: Mobilizing the Platform Economy:
Regulating Short-Term Rentals in Toronto, by Sean Grisdale

As internet platforms such as Airbnb catalyze the expansion of short-term rentals, the industry has a growing impact on the urban economy. Because of this rapid shift facilitated by the platform economy, there is concern about the impact of short-term rentals on similar industries, such as the housing and hotels. Grisdale analyzes the city of Toronto as a case study to exemplify the speed with which legislators must now confront the ripple effects of emerging digital economies and spotlights the mobilization of coalitions in reaction to the growing short-term industry.

Chapter 3: Who's the Boss? The Impact
of Digitally Mediated Employment on Labour Markets
and the Nature of Work, by Andrew Wolf

The rapid growth of the "gig economy" has attracted attention to its disruption of the nature of work, as well as its incompatibility with urban labour regulations. Cities must fitting the square peg of a technologically mediated independent workforce into the round holes of employment status legality and consumerism. However, the single trend that carries on unabated, despite the shift, is the group that benefits from the gig economy – educated, white males with great assets – and leaves behind groups that have been historically marginalized within cities.

Chapter 4: Ride-Hailing Platforms Are Shaping the Future of Mobility, but for Whom? by Mischa Young and Steven Farber

Ride-hailing companies are industry disruptors that have thrived in the platform economy, as companies like Uber and Lyft change the patterns of daily life, from travel mode to car ownership. However, this chapter also explores the ripple effect of the industry, the continuation of inequity among marginalized groups, and the policies that can combat these ripples.

Chapter 5: Disrupting Stuff: Material Flows in the Platform City, by Clarence Woudsma

Everything you own had its own journey to get to you. But as technology and transportation has advanced, that journey – specifically the "last mile" – has transformed. Woudsma notes the platform economy's effect on urban freight, and the increase of unintended side effects that no one accounts or pays for. Despite the newfound ease of delivery that society knows today, this chapter asks whether the advancement of the platform economy is creating an unsustainable business model for delivery.

SECTION 2: GOVERNING PLATFORMS

Chapter 6: Ride Hailing in Canadian Cities, by Shauna Brail

In every city that welcomes ride-hailing firms as private partners, governments must swiftly write and carry out regulation for them. The digital technology of ride-hailing platforms may promise a lesser need for regulation, but in Canada more government attention was required. Brail looks at the new opportunities and benefits ride hailing has brought in Canada's thirty largest cities as well as the varying regulatory success within municipalities, and brings asks whether a digital economy creates more regulation, despite its seemingly innovative proposals.

Chapter 7: Taking Kingston for a Regulatory Ride? Uber's Entrance into Kingston, Ontario, by Betsy Donald, Morgan Sage, and Anna Moroz

As a country with a different regulatory structure for taxis and ride hailing in each province, Canada presents a unique challenge for companies to adequately assimilate into each separate municipality. Each local history and social dynamic heavily influences regulatory outcomes, and there is no better example than Kingston, Ontario. The small, public sector city does not regulate its taxi industry with police, and this chapter explores how Uber fits into Kingston's immunity from the heated politics surrounding transportation networking companies.

Chapter 8: A New Public-Private Partnership for the Platform Age? Uber as Public Transit, by Zachary Spicer

Uber's aggressive strategy to position its service as a public transit alternative has resulted in more North American communities welcoming its ride-hailing platform to complement and even replace public transit systems. The incorporation of Uber has taken different forms throughout the continent, but many cities have begun a public-private partnership with the company. Spicer examines the nature and legitimacy of Uber as a partner by spotlighting four North American municipalities and comparing their approaches.

Chapter 9: Regulatory Paradigms for the Coming Age of Autonomous Vehicles, by Austin Zwick and Eamonn Dundon

As the impending arrival of autonomous vehicles nears, governments must anticipate the work that will go into regulating this industry or be forced to react after AVs are available to the public. After discussing the key players and obstacles to autonomous vehicles before their emergence, Zwick and Dundon inspect autonomous regulation in the free-market "Smithville," United States, "Marxtown," China, and middle ground "Keynesport," Canada, to compare the implications of each paradigm for transportation governance.

SECTION 3: CITIES AS PLATFORMS

Chapter 10: The Promise and the Peril of the Smart City,
by Maxwell Hartt, Austin Zwick, and Brian Webb

What *is* a "smart city"? It is this million-dollar question that Hartt, Zwick and Webb answer through a review of the historical progression of the smart city concept to find a deeper definition of the term. From its inception to evolution, we find that the seemingly new idea of a smart city comprises data-driven, urban development fundamentals iterated throughout technological eras, yet its interpretations vary widely in form and practice. So the potential of the smart city is not all progressive and utopic, as societal problems – old and new – threaten to be propelled by the buzzword's applications, and it is this duality that this chapter seeks to explore.

Chapter 11: Seeing the City as a Platform: Is Canada's
Smart Cities Challenge a Good Step in That Direction?
by Pamela Robinson and Jeff Biggar

Current smart city efforts are commonly driven by the vendor – Uber and Airbnb serve as plain examples – but in Quayside, Toronto, the Sidewalk Lab "city-as-a-platform" project is uniquely driven by government. This contrast sets a precedent in the smart city landscape, especially for public-sector innovation – if it is even possible. In Canada, the Infrastructure Canada's Smart City Challenge presents municipalities with the opportunity to take a step further into transforming their cities into platforms. Robinson and Biggar highlight the s c c and its applicants to classify the potential innovation spawned by the challenge, and question whether it truly facilitates progress to the city-as-platform.

Chapter 12: A Smart City for Toronto: What Does
Quayside Tell Us about the State of Smart City Building?
by Zachary Spicer and Austin Zwick

The waterfront of Canada's most populous city is the focus of this chapter as Spicer and Zwick shed light on one of the first smart cities to be built "smart" from the foundation: Quayside. As Alphabet's Sidewalk Labs takes the wheel in the development of the project – not without controversy – we see a model of private smart city building unfold. Our authors shed light on the potential for the partnership to set precedent, both good and bad. Accordingly, this chapter focuses on how municipal and national governments must consider how the very technology that will consider their cities "smart" will affect community building, data privacy, and governance.

Chapter 13: From Processors to Platforms: Innovation and the Changing Nature of Space, by Nathan Stewart, Austin Zwick, and Eamonn Dundon

Cities invest in becoming "smart" to attract the jobs of the future. However, current regional industrial policy does not take into account the changing needs of innovative industries. Different approaches to economic geography – proximities and institutions, innovation systems, and externalities – are reviewed to show how information flows and social interactions are transforming ideas of space and place. Silicon Valley serves as a case study that exemplifies the perpetual innovation that stems from externalities derived from physical and social proximity that are needed to survive in this capitalistic era. The authors advocate for a marriage between place-making and industrial policy to help make cities smarter and more equitable.

Throughout this volume, the authors consider the type of society we want to live in. What societal trade-offs are we willing to make as technology integrates itself further into urban life? As the pace of the public sector's embrace of technology into all facets of policy and governance is only accelerating, this makes the open question of societal values more imperative than ever before. Despite these warnings of how technology can go awry, we believe that technology will create a better world if – and only if – we remember that it is not the technology alone that makes a city smart. Rather it is the residents. As Kresin (2013, 91) writes,

> We, citizens of all cities, take the fate of the places we live in
> into our own hands. We care about the familiar buildings and
> the parks, the shops, the schools, the roads and the trees, but far
> more about the quality of the life we live in them ... We need to
> know how decisions are made, we need to have the information
> that is at hand; we need to have direct access to the people in
> power ... While we can never predict the eventual effect of our

actions, we take full responsibility to make this world a better place ... [Government cannot] lose sight of the most valuable resource it can tap into: the Smart Citizen.

As for Austin's daughter, he can do his best to raise her to be one of these smart citizens.

REFERENCE

Kresin, F. 2013. "A Manifesto for Smart Citizens." In *Smart Citizens: Putting People First*, edited by D. Hemment and A. Townsend, 91–4. Manchester: FutureEverything.

SECTION ONE

Managing Platforms

2

Mobilizing the Platform Economy: Regulating Short-Term Rentals in Toronto

Sean Grisdale

- Building on previous critical research demonstrating the effects of short-term rentals on local rental markets, this case study documents the crafting of short-term rental policy in Toronto between 2016 and 2018. Addressing a qualitative gap in this emerging literature, this chapter offers a detailed critique of the claims made by pro-short-term-rental interests in their political efforts to persuade councillors, media, and the general public of the positive contributions of the digital short-term rental industry to the local economy.
- I argue that a significant focus on marketing and lobbying by digital short-term rental platforms like Airbnb arises primarily because they own no bricks-and-mortar assets. I show how the unique political imperatives and constraints that short-term rental platforms must navigate, as a consequence of their particular business model, force them to rely on public relations, community mobilization, public policy advocacy, and branding to fend off resistance from hotels and housing activists, while – as in the case of Airbnb – also working to ensure the maintenance of their monopoly in this sector.
- The case study of Toronto's regulation of short-term rentals also contributes to recent work in urban geography documenting the rise of technology industry coalitions and their increasing participation in and influence on urban politics.

INTRODUCTION

In late 2016, under pressure to address Toronto's ongoing housing crisis, Mayor John Tory's executive committee instructed city staff to speed up efforts to draft regulations for the quickly expanding digital short-term rentals industry – an industry synonymous with the likes of Airbnb and Vacation Rentals by Owner (VRBO). At the time, concerns with these new platforms were mounting. Reports of disruptions and safety issues in neighbourhoods and condos were topics increasingly discussed in the media, while the potential tax revenue lost in the absence of any regulation was also gaining traction as a policy concern (Gray 2016). At the same time, a coalition of activists, residents, researchers, and organizations argued that these platforms were repurposing limited rental stock for use by tourists rather than locals, and thereby exacerbating strained conditions of affordability in the city's already expensive rental housing stock (Grisdale 2019; Wachsmuth and Weisler 2018). After almost two years of research and consultation by city staff, and despite concerted lobbying led by Airbnb to resist and limit their scope, Toronto City Council passed a suite of regulations on 5 December 2017 (Gray 2017). However, while the new rules were set to come into effect in June 2018, three local short-term rental operators quickly advanced legal appeals to the province's independent planning tribunal[1] on the grounds that the regulations were unfair, infringing on their democratic right to use private property as they saw fit (Chhabra 2019). Even more, in September 2018, the tribunal announced that scheduling conflicts were forcing them to delay any decision on the matter until late August 2019 (Beattie 2018). At the time of writing, the intended regulations have yet to come into effect, meaning short-term rentals continue to operate and expand in this climate of uncertainty, while City Spokesperson Bruce Hawkins estimates the delay has already cost the city approximately $1 million in registration fees (Beattie 2018).

While short-term rentals are not a new phenomenon, their scope and extent has been massively expanded in recent years via internet platforms like Airbnb. However, research attending to this new era has only recently started to untangle their impacts on housing markets, tourism, and everyday city life (Slee 2015; Finck and Ranchordás 2016; Lee 2016; Schäfer and Braun 2016; Gurran and Phibbs 2017; Paulauskaite et al. 2017; Wachsmuth et al. 2017; Crommelin et al. 2018; Ferreri and Sanyal 2018; Wachsmuth and Weisler 2018;

Cocola-Gant and Gago 2019; Grisdale 2019; Combs et al. 2020). While these platform companies market themselves as small-time players whose business models operate adjacent to the mainstream hotel industry, the scale of lobbying for and against the short-term rental industry suggests these platforms are assuming a lucrative and significant role in the urban economy. Indeed, the exponential rise of this "sharing economy" industry owes much to the efforts of well-funded lobbyists and consultants concerned with advancing a vision of capitalism ostensibly premised on "innovation," "environmental sustainability," and "community building" (Martin 2016).

Toronto's case study provides a good example of the amazing pace with which legislators and policy writers are now expected to address the implications of these emerging digital and platform economies. Though one planner at the city acknowledged he has been aware of online private accommodation-booking platforms[2] since the turn of the millennium, he also noted it was not until January 2016, with the recognition that demand for these accommodations was increasing rapidly, that the City of Toronto started to respond to the growing concerns of housing and hotel advocates (personal communication 2017). However, this situation also set into motion the formation of new coalitions of interests pushing their regulatory visions for the sector. By the summer of 2017, as Toronto was researching and negotiating its short-term rental policy, its Lobbyist Registry recorded more than twenty different interest groups attempting to influence the ultimate framework for that regulation (City of Toronto 2017a).

Drawing on analysis of government reports, third-party policy and research briefs, deputation documents, and interviews with key actors involved in the negotiation and construction of short-term rental regulations in Toronto, this chapter contributes to a growing critical research agenda concerned with understanding the geography and mobility of urban policy creation (McCann 2011; Peck and Theodore 2015). Building on previous critical research demonstrating the effects of Airbnb on Toronto's housing market (Grisdale 2019), this case study documents the crafting of short-term rental policy in Toronto between 2016 and 2018. In a more qualitative register, this chapter offers a detailed critique of the claims and political efforts of the pro-short-term-rental coalition as they worked to persuade councillors, media, and the general public of the positive contributions of the digital short-term rental industry to the local economy. With this objective in mind, the chapter contributes to a qualitative gap in the critical research on digital peer-to-peer platforms through analysis of the economic and political contingencies structuring attempts to regulate, resist, and/or legitimize their practices. I find that the unique political imperatives and constraints that short-term rental platforms must navigate as a consequence of their novel business model forces them to rely significantly on public relations, community mobilization, public policy advocacy, and branding to both fend off resistance from brick-and-mortar hotels and housing activists, while Airbnb also works to ensure the maintenance of their monopoly in this sector. As such, it contributes to understandings of the increasing political and economic influence that technology companies appear to be exerting in Western urban economies like Toronto's (McNeill, 2016).

POLICY MOBILITIES

Drawing on an approach to critical policy studies called "policy mobilities" (McCann 2011; McCann and Ward 2011; Peck 2011; Peck and Theodore 2010, 2015; Prince 2012; Wiig 2015), this chapter recognizes that any process of policy creation is uniquely structured by different economic, geographic, political, and social factors. Though a given policy framework or model may be developed in one place, any model will always undergo change as it is negotiated and implemented in different geographic, social, and institutional contexts. For Peck and Theodore (2015), these realities call into question widely used "diffusionist" approaches to policy analysis that assume that policy models transfer intact from certain "capitals of innovation to [certain] hinterlands of emulation" (p. 7). In contrast, their 'policy mobilities' approach advocates a relational perspective that recognizes how policy travels in a multidirectional and hybrid fashion, across different scales of political power and jurisdiction.

For example, in Ward's (2018) historical study of the transnational development of "tax increment financing" (TIF), this relational framework is used to show how the very concept of TIF has taken on different meanings and served different purposes as it was adopted in different cities across the world. First conceived in the 1960s, TIF became widely adopted across North America, before more recently spreading to the United Kingdom. Ward documents how each city that subsequently took up TIF relied on precedents from elsewhere before applying its own version in a new context – leading to surprisingly different outcomes. As such, Ward argues urban politics is difficult to define as an object of scientific study, being better characterized as an ongoing set of processes, perpetually engaged in making and remaking, always generated and assembled in relation to particular historical and spatial conjunctures.

Thus, policy mobilities suggests that analysis of urban politics must go beyond conceiving the city as an isolated object of study. While research can, to a certain extent, foreground the city (as a bounded jurisdiction) and its suite of local interests and coalitions, the city and its actors must also be situated amidst their national and global contexts, recognizing connections between different cities, between the city and the state, and between the city and any globalized institutions and actors that influence or resist the formation of policy there (McCann 2011, 121; Peck and Theodore 2015).

Research on the short-term rental industry can benefit from and contribute to this research agenda in two key ways. First, this chapter considers how short-term rental policy changes as it travels between different institutional and socio-political contexts (Peck 2011). As such, a key contribution that studies of the platform economy can make to policy mobility studies might be understanding the dynamics of what Pasquale and Vaidhyanathan (2015) call "corporate nullification," which names an increasingly common dynamic whereby powerful corporations "nullify" laws or regulations with the justification that they offer a service whose contributions to the common good are so great that they outweigh the need for due process under legal norms. As such, I note the significant role that public relations plays in defending and normalizing disruptive and legally grey economic practices like home-sharing and ridesharing. The question here is how platform economies take advantage of the significant time it takes for cities to develop and enforce policy. While political responses to the activities of these new platforms have been largely reactive rather than proactive, different jurisdictions have chosen varying strategies and time frames with which to address their particular concerns. Thus, it is imperative we study how different places experiment with regulatory responses and how they learn from and reference one another, to understand how platforms like Airbnb and Uber attempt to influence and negotiate the immense diversity of political jurisdictions they operate in.

Second, Airbnb's "lean" business model (Srnicek 2017), which can operate globally by minimizing its ownership and responsibility over housing assets and labour, raises novel challenges for cities hoping to regulate local housing and real estate development and its use. Encompassing a range of business models, this "platform" economy leverages and mobilizes the increasing centrality (and ubiquity) of smartphones and internet connectivity in the everyday lives of big city residents (Botsman and Rogers 2010; Wiig and Wyly 2016). While not contractually tied to place through ownership of any brick-and-mortar assets, it is argued by Davidson and Infranca (2016) that the platform economy represents the information industry's move into "place-based" services. They note that while most technology and finance companies are best regulated nationally, the platform economy might be more beholden to municipal regulators. Leveraging the threat of capital flight is not an option for these firms because they have little fixed capital on their balance sheets and because they inherently depend on the infrastructure and culture of the city. The implication here is that in the absence of a competitive strategy premised on threatening to locate elsewhere[3] to secure the most desirable regulatory environment (Harvey 1989), their desire to extend to every corner of the globe creates an impetus to win over consumers, self-interested owners and renters, and municipal regulators by constructing discourses associated with increases in economic growth, efficiency, innovation, community, and sustainability.

McNeill (2016), notes that when "sharing economy" enterprises first entered cities, they were not interested in affecting urban governance; instead they preferred to market themselves as innovative alternatives to the mainstream. But now, after years of changing and often strained relationships between governments and platform companies, there has been a reversal, in which information and communication technologies and platform companies now exert powerful, self-serving influences on urban governance regimes through aggressive lobbying and public relation campaigns, backed up through the cultivation of technology industry coalitions (Keil 2017; Wiig and Wyly 2016). As such, Wiig and Wyly (2016) argue that similarities between discourses about the "smart city" and the "platform" or "sharing" economies express a new digital phase in the transformation and acceleration of the "city as a growth machine" (Molotch 1976).

Molotoch's concept of the "local growth machine" describes how local economic elites form political coalitions that are concerned primarily with growing or preserving the value of real estate in their locality, in a process that entails strategies to attract scarce international capital at the expense of growth coalitions in other jurisdictions. Given this tendency to form urban coalitions, Molotch argues critical urban scholarship must pay attention to how diverse actors organize, lobby, manipulate, and structure the governance and construction of cities to suit their locally contingent interests. However, while the impacts of digital technology platforms do not determine or produce predictable economic articulations, Wiig and Wyly (2016) argue there is substantial evidence to assume their "ongoing and inextinguishable" influence on urban politics (491). As such, the field of politics and criticism of these emerging forms of governance and policy remain wide open to contestation and interpretation (Wiig and Wyly 2016).

Especially in Toronto, a city eager to develop itself as a centre of technological innovation (Keil 2017; Pofeldt 2017; *Toronto Life* 2017), a critical understanding of how discourses of "smart governance" and "technological urbanism" influence popular perceptions of platforms like Airbnb and the extent of their regulation informs the conceptual framework of this chapter. This is an especially important discourse to unpack for anyone whose interests are not currently served by emerging technologies and platforms (Morozov 2013). Developing such a critique is necessary for unpacking those structural consequences of emerging technologies that may not be readily apparent amidst the more sensationalized micropolitics of Airbnb's local controversies.

METHODOLOGY

This study draws on twenty semi-structured interviews with key stakeholders identified as relevant to the discussion about Airbnb regulation in Toronto. The participant breakdown included four local politicians, three civil servants working on regulation of short-term rentals, five short-term rental hosts or Airbnb representatives, five activists or representatives of other interest groups or organizations, and three policy researchers or academics. Ninety-two key stakeholders were asked to participate by email, of whom twenty agreed to be a part of the study.

Potential participants were identified primarily from names listed on the Toronto Lobbyist Registry database on lobbying tickets related to Airbnb regulation, as well as through citations and authorship identified on grey literature documents, and from the list of individuals who participated in deputations before the June 2017 executive committee meeting on short-term rental regulation.

The purpose of the interviews was to reveal hidden assumptions, perspectives, and contingent knowledges not expressed through grey literature and other textual forms of discourse. These encounters revealed connections not easily derived from these documents, allowing the research to probe beyond the texts, often presented as expert findings rather than strategic documents, and thus designed to advance particular interests. Finally, as participants were asked to expand on many of the implications of short-term rentals that are either downplayed or absent in public discussion, these interviews were intended to open up space to showcase global points of connection in play, such as understandings of the channels of communication through which the policy is constructed.

NEW COALITIONS IN TORONTO

Between 2016 and 2017, two main interest coalitions were mobilized to negotiate the regulation of short-term rentals in Toronto (table 2.1). As Wachsmuth and Wiesler (2018) have noted, they are interesting because they cut across previously understood interest groups in the urban economy.

The accommodations industry is split between the brick-and-mortar hotel industry and short-term rentals. Short-term rental platforms ostensibly bring down accommodations rates, appropriate hotel revenues, possibly lower revenue accruing to the industry as a whole, and have the competitive advantage of not paying the same taxes or employing unionized labour that hotels do. Condominium communities are divided between short-term rental hosts and their disapproving neighbours and condo boards. This conflict has raised questions about the structure of what Lippert and Steckle (2016) call the "unofficial fourth level of governance"[4] that is embodied in condo boards, especially in those that did not anticipate ad hoc hotels operating in their building. While some owners of single detached homes favour Airbnb for the extra income they can generate by renting out a room in their house, entrepreneurs have also taken advantage of the platform to run larger accommodations outfits by renting multiple units across the city, while others have even developed cleaning, photography, or tourism services oriented towards the sector. Meanwhile, opponents have expressed frustration with noise and safety issues, as well as concerns that the platform drives neighbourhood change and distorts the local rental market.

Table 2.1
Breakdown of actors represented in the two main coalitions concerned with
short-term rental regulations in Toronto

Pro-short-term rental coalition		Anti-short-term rental coalition (Fairbnb)	
Organization	Industry	Organization	Industry
Airbnb	Home-sharing industry	ACORN	Tenants advocacy group
Airbnb hosts (approximately 70)	Home-sharing industry	Advocacy Centre for Tenants Ontario (ACTO)	Tenants advocacy group
Epoch Getaways	Travel start-up	Federation of Metro Tenants' Associations	Tenants advocacy group
Agreement Express	Financial technology	Friends of Kensington Market	Land trust/neighbourhood group
League Inc.	Financial technology	Silver Hotel Group	Hotel company
NetChoice Corporation	Financial technology	Condominium Owners Association	Condominium lobby
SheEO	Financial technology	City Institute at York University	Academic institute
Wealthsimple	Financial technology	Ontario Federation of Labour	Labour federation
Aviva Canada Inc.	Insurance	Unite Here Local 75	Hospitality union
Design Exchange	Design network	Local residents	Private citizens
Mildred's Temple Kitchen	Restaurant	Ontario Chamber of Commerce	Business lobby/network
North of 41 Tech Group	Technology lobby/network		
Sistering	Women's shelter		
UNIFOR	Hospitality union		
UrbanMetrics Inc.	Planning consultancy		

The Fairbnb Coalition

The Fairbnb Coalition was mobilized to represent a group of interests
pushing for stringent regulation of the short-term rental industry.
Although this group shared opposition to the practices of firms like
Airbnb, it is coloured by a range of concerns and ideological commitments. Indeed, in any other situation, an alliance of affordable housing

activists, unionized hotel workers, and the corporate hotel industry might be curious, considering the hotel industry's own interests in limiting the influence of hotel unions. The coalition has since expanded its activism nationally to fight for regulations in Ottawa and Vancouver, largely replicating the alliance of interests and countrywide scope of opposition to Airbnb in cities across the United States. For instance, the Share Better Coalition, which has been active in major cities across the United States, is a similar alliance of hotel and affordable housing interests.

The Pro-Short-Term-Rental Coalition

Opposing the proposed regulations is a coalition led by Airbnb and other short-term rental platforms, including their hosts, a range of local technology and finance interests, and some small businesses and free market policy think tanks (see table 2.1). The public relations narrative of this coalition is well summarized by a selection of thirteen letters sent to Toronto's executive committee ahead of a meeting discussing proposed regulations, that was held on 19 June 2017 (City of Toronto 2017b). These letters were generally scripted, as the majority exhibited similar formatting and flow, similar sentence structure, and repetition of three main points, suggesting a significant level of organization or influence by Airbnb.

The letters share three main claims. First, all the letters emphasize the importance of home-sharing as a means of enabling some homeowners to pay their mortgages or rent, often invoking very detailed accounts of the historical unaffordability of Toronto. Most letters cite a report with the same quote that "last year Airbnb brought more than 450,000 guests to Toronto who spent over $417 million in the city" (City of Toronto 2017b). It is important to note that this statistic comes out of a report commissioned by Airbnb and prepared by the real estate consulting firm UrbanMetrics Inc. that was submitted to the executive committee meeting on 17 June 2017. This study relies solely on self-reported data by Airbnb about guest spending and host activity and is not methodologically transparent, suggesting the study is potentially unreliable or biased.

The Claim to Biased Data

In fact, the mobilization and interpretation of different data constituted a key point of contention in developing and contesting Toronto's short-term rental policies. An interview with a senior City of Toronto planner confirmed that the interpretation of data, or the lack thereof, was a key problematic in determining proper regulatory measures, noting that Fairbnb and others

> took a lot of effort to try to critique the data that Airbnb provided and in some of the early days of our exercise, their critiques of information provided by Airbnb and other jurisdictions helped us to be aware of what to watch for in terms of information by Airbnb ... [W]e had to be cognizant that the information provided by the opposing groups – it was also slanted. So it's an interesting balancing act. But unlike a heck of a lot of other work we do, this exercise had all of these organizations coming out of the woodwork to help provide information.

Further, all interviews acknowledged the lack of data to adequately interpret the impacts of short-term rentals, offering different implications for different people. Generally, personal experiences, observations, or ideological assumptions coloured explanations in this absence. For those in opposition of Airbnb, the impacts on the rental market were obvious or estimable enough to confirm with the data. However, for Airbnb's coalition of interests, the lack of data was deployed as evidence of their vindication, and subsequently refuted with estimates they assembled themselves. Specifically, both Fairbnb and the Planning Department argued that as a consequence of Toronto's historically low vacancy rates, even a relatively small number of commercial hosts can have huge implications for rental availability in the city, especially when considering how geographically concentrated the phenomenon is (Grisdale, 2019). Thus, while Airbnb has been keen to express its willingness to be regulated, its curious silence on the service's impacts on rental markets is conspicuous.

The Claim to Disrupting Entrenched Corporate Interests

A second common claim is exemplified by a statement from Airbnb's global head of policy and public affairs in its *Policy Tool Chest 2.0*, who argues the only real opposition to home-sharing comes "from a hotel industry concerned about its ability to price-gouge consumers despite continuing to reap record profits" (Airbnb 2017, 5). This statement is a bold delegitimization of the significant role that housing affordability advocates and unionized hotel employees have played in the Fairbnb coalition. The statement is also a common narrative advanced by each host I interviewed. The contradictory framing of these documents is most interesting. They explicitly acknowledge the structural changes occurring in contemporary urban economies, and the affordability challenges they pose for everyday people, but also downplay the immediate importance of the private rental market for those who seek housing in the city, as well as the job security that unionized hotel work provides in a precarious service industry. Conversely, they emphasize the service's capacity to empower everyday people to confront precarity through entrepreneurial channels. Ultimately, the platform is framed as a cure for structural economic issues while its potential implication in exacerbating these issues is ignored.

The Claim to Attracting the Technology Sector

A final common claim made in the letters is that fostering a supportive environment for platforms like Airbnb will help to align the city with the needs and values of the city's burgeoning technology industry, adding weight to Keil's (2017) observation that technology interests are becoming an increasingly influential coalition influencing politics in Toronto. The legitimization of Airbnb in particular is thus equated with the empowerment of Toronto's "innovators" and entrepreneurs. It is also cited as a necessary platform to supply the "flexible" and "authentic" accommodations options increasingly expected by modern knowledge economy workers.

To better understand this claim, it is important to flag the key role played by one particular organization in developing Toronto's regulatory framework for short-term rentals. Founded in 2000, the Medical and Related Sciences (MARS) Discovery District is a major hub for the commercialization of publicly funded research in Canada. Self-described as an "urban innovation district" and "incubator," the organization's Solutions Lab seeks to link entrepreneurs with "corporations, investors, mentors, university institutions and labs" to test and implement their business ideas (MARS 2017). MARS is also the home of Airbnb's first Canadian office. In addition to hosting technology companies and supporting entrepreneurs, the MARS Solutions Lab advocates an approach to policy development premised on the leadership of private sector actors who can facilitate conversation between everyday citizens and institutional stakeholders (MARS 2017). While advocating for a collaborative approach to addressing social issues through conversations between "governments, foundations, corporations, non-governmental organizations, academia and the greater community," it also casts individuals as "users," and institutions as "platforms," in a bid to integrate a "start-up" ethos into the world of policy development. While collaboration across sectors is not inherently problematic, it is important to emphasize again how Airbnb's narrative seeks to delegitimize and silence the concerns of local renters and hotel union workers, suggesting the need for greater scrutiny over who is represented at the MARS Solutions Lab table.

This approach is not unique to the MARS Solutions Lab, which is one of many "social innovation" or "change labs" emerging in Western countries amidst economic austerity and entrepreneurial attempts by cities to attract technology jobs[5] (Joy et al. 2019; Public Policy Forum 2013). The Public Policy Forum notes that change labs "have evolved from a broad range of disciplines including group dynamics, group psychology and complexity theory, coupled with the addition of design theory," constituting a "change lab philosophy" that understands social problems primarily as technical problems (2). Conversely, in Canada, Joy et al. (2019) observe that this "social innovation agenda" now drives policy-making at all levels of government and in all sectors in the country, arguing the phenomenon has emerged primarily as a narrative justifying the need to do more with less in a post-financial-crisis environment marked by entrenched neoliberalism and austerity.

The MARS Solutions Lab has provided the key third-party forum for sharing economy policy in Toronto, with many of the interviewees in this study noting they had attended consultations facilitated by MARS. One condo board representative, frustrated with how Airbnb is disrupting her condo, noted she had attended every public consultation on the regulations, one of which was a working session at the MARS Institute. She added, this was "essentially how they devised the policy – is based on feedback from those sessions." The same senior planner also confirmed the city was "very in touch with MARS. Well, we funded work that they've done, you know? And so has the city. And we've done polling and we've done, as I say, literature reviews and jurisdictional reviews, so there's an emerging body of research around what governments around the world are doing."

The main document to emerge from this lab is "Shifting Perspectives: Redesigning Regulation for the Sharing Economy" (Steenhoven et al., 2016) a report produced by the MARS Solutions Lab in partnership with the province and the City of Toronto, which describes a range of stakeholder interests influencing regulatory measures for the sharing economy. However, in its holistic approach to policy-making, the document also outlines a framework for incubating the sharing economy more broadly, arguing many social and infrastructural issues in Toronto can be addressed by taking up a "sharing city" ethic. Therefore, this policy analysis (though well researched) is undergirded by an ideological argument that platforms must be at the centre of any modern city's approach to urban development.

While this brief discussion represents a provisional summary of the key arguments advanced by the two coalitions, the following section assesses the strategies of platforms like Airbnb as they continue to navigate their regulation in different cities. Specifically, this section aims to show how the form and substance of these strategies spring from the political economic imperatives and constraints particular to the digital platform economy.

POLICY MOBILITIES, PUBLIC RELATIONS, AND THE PLATFORM ECONOMY

Several themes stand out from responses to the regulation of short-term rentals in Toronto. First, there is the key role that lobbying, marketing, data analysis, and impression management play in influencing and participating in the direction of regulations. Second, there is the significant role that exercises in "*ex post* rationalization" (Langley and Leyshon 2016) and "corporate nullification" (Pasquale and Vaidhyanathan 2015) play in the narratives advanced by platforms like Airbnb. Third, the short-term rental industry has a dual commitment to legitimate their business models by willingly subjecting themselves to regulation, while simultaneously doing little to address their more controversial practices before those regulations are implemented. Specifically, many of these interviews identified a contradiction between Airbnb's stated willingness to be regulated, and the implications these regulations would have for the significant revenues the company accrues through its more commercialized hosts (Wachsmuth and Weisler 2018).

First, recent work on the platform economy notes how the success and quality of a given digital platform depends on its capacity to maximize "network effects" – a dynamic whereby a good or service becomes more valuable as more people use it (Srnicek 2017). It is well acknowledged by both critics and tech industrialists that maximizing the number of connections in the network necessitates an impetus to monopolization. For instance, PayPal founder and tech billionaire Peter Thiel has argued that in Silicon Valley, "competition is for losers" (Thiel 2014). In 2016, a City of Toronto executive committee report corroborates the platform's dominance, estimating Airbnb controlled approximately 85 per cent of the short-term rental market in the city. Similarly, while hosts acknowledged they used multiple platforms (like VRBO and HomeAway) to market their short-term rentals, there was general agreement that Airbnb was the most lucrative vacation rental platform because it had a strong brand presence in the public imagination as *the* home-sharing platform. As one host noted,

> Airbnb was getting a lot of traction as a platform, but prior to that we were always listed on other ones like VRBO, Homeaway, or on Canada Stays, Roomorama. Every year, there seems to be one or two new potential sources of leads ... [S]ince we started using Airbnb, we've gotten some very good clients. That's why we've continued to list and add more and more properties on it ... I always try and make sure people understand that it's a platform that I would say more and more travellers, business travellers included, are looking to Airbnb because they've had such widespread success of marketing their brand.

Second, while Airbnb owns no property, it depends on revenue flows leveraged through the city's physical infrastructure. As Davidson and Infranca (2016) argue, these platforms differ from previous enterprises in the information economy – e.g., internet companies like Google and Facebook, or issuers of securities and derivatives – in that their services are specifically "place-based." As such, the platform must convince locals to engage in the service, as hosts or guests, but also mobilize this local network to take political action on its behalf. In cities like New York, San Francisco, and Toronto, this has meant mobilizing hosts, citizens, and tech industry allies to petition for softer forms of regulation. Finally, these enterprises must attract and inspire socio-economic classes previously limited from travelling by the more expensive accommodation costs found in the traditional hotel industry. Part of this involves cultivating a culture of transnationalism and cosmopolitanism for "everyday people," a project exemplified in the company's democratizing rhetoric and narratives encouraging people to "belong anywhere" (Airbnb 2017).

This emerging literature on platform capitalism also acknowledges the significant role that evangelizing sharing-economy experts and consultants have played in producing the "sharing economy" as a cultural and economic norm (Langley and Leyshon 2017; Richardson 2015; Cockayne 2016; Martin, Upham, and Budd 2015; Martin 2016). However, one Airbnb employee noted the challenges faced by the organization in Toronto due to the negative public relations attending Uber's debut in the city. Appropriately, Airbnb has sought to distinguish itself from Uber by taking a more diplomatic approach to achieving legitimization. This strategy is largely the brainchild of their "global head of community and mobilization," Douglas Atkin, whose book *The Culting of Brands: Turn Your Customers into True Believers* (2005) investigates how brands can learn from the strategies employed by cults. In a 2004 interview with PBS, Atkin described the thrust of this approach:

> I believe that there is a very, very close relationship between cults and the best cult brands in the sense that people join and stay with cults for the exact same reasons as people join and stay with brands. The reason why is pretty obvious if you think about it: The desire to belong to something, to make meaning out of something, is universal. What's changed nowadays is, as we've become a more consumerist society, the institutions that become vessels for making meaning or venues for creating community have in turn become more consumerist, so the kind of functions that cults and religions used to perform years and years ago are increasingly being taken over by brands. (PBS 2004, para. 8)

Community building is central to Atkin's public relations strategy, which employs the same "snowflake model" of community organization employed in Obama's presidential campaigns (Slee 2015). In fact, Tom Slee (2015) has noted that some of Obama's former organizers have also worked for Airbnb in this capacity. Through this model, the organization's community organizers and mobilizers act as local nodes in the host community network, nudging them to take political action on behalf of the platform. As such, many employees carry job titles that might be found in any non-profit or community organization, from community organizers, to mobilizers, to public policy officers. The goal of the community organizer is not to manage or govern the community but to educate and politicize self-sustaining host networks that will then engage in grassroots campaigns on their own. This strategy leverages what Atkin calls the "commitment curve," an approach premised on nudging community members to take up increasingly time-consuming and difficult political actions that contribute to helping the platform achieve regulatory legitimacy. In a conference presentation at CMX Summit, a self-described "hub for the community industry," Atkin described a progression of increasingly hard "asks" that one can make of a community, which run from signing a petition, to showing up to a meeting, to tweeting a senator, to crowdfunding an advertisement, to writing an op-ed, to visiting a senator, and finally, to attending or even organizing a rally. The aim here is to become a "community-driven megabrand." As Atkin argues, "As far as I know, we're the only company that's doing it ... [I]t's sort of new" (CMX Summit 2014).

Many of these strategies have been employed in Toronto as well – accounts of which emerged through my interviews. The senior planner I interviewed noted he rarely encountered such devoted turnouts as hosts made to an executive committee meeting on short-term rental regulations, which saw many hosts turn out to share their positive experiences with the platform:

> To come across very positively, they quite deliberately ... they stacked the consultation program we had with hosts who were, to some degree, had pre-scripted things to say. It was rather clear and obvious what was going on. That didn't necessarily take away from the quality of Airbnb's contributions. We just, you know, we had to be aware we weren't using rose-tinted glasses to look at the things they provided. And you've probably seen it with, and heard it with all of their advertising right now. They're making a concerted effort to make sure the ultimate decision makers, i.e., city council, think they're great people, and that they provide a great service. One of the things that was interesting about this particular exercise was the amount of groups that saw a need to counterbalance the PR work by Airbnb.

The organization has employed similar strategies in land use meetings in San Francisco, where Atkin boasts "we totally overwhelmed them, filled the hall, had queues of people waiting to testify down the halls of city hall, demonstrations, etc ... [W]e basically drenched lawmakers with our community" (CMX Summit 2017). However, the planner noted how deputations by hosts, many of whom are ostensibly engaged in modest forms of home-sharing and would not be significantly affected by proposed regulations, amounts to little more than praising the organization without advancing specific policy proposals or critiques.

According to former councillor John Campbell, Airbnb representatives approached him with opinion polls in a bid to influence his position, noting that ultimately he had little use for them. Petitions and opinion polls are a popular strategy for the organization, with a petition resisting New York legislation in 2014 gathering over 200,000 signatures (CMX Summit 2014). However, critics argue these exercises are more a numbers game than an expression of informed public opinion. As Mosendz and Smith IV (2014) of the *New York Observer* note, Airbnb's petition strategy deploys paid canvassers to comb the city for signatures pledging general support for Airbnb's legalization. They recount one canvasser's exchange as emblematic of this ambiguous appeal to support: "'Would you like to sign a petition saying you support Airbnb in New York City?' she asked, going one by one. 'Support what, exactly?' asked the first person she approached. 'Oh, you know, like the service Airbnb provides, and just what we're doing'" (para. 2).

These petitions have also circulated through Airbnb's own website and websites like Change.org, and Peers.org (now defunct). Peers.org was founded by Douglas Atkin as a for-profit consultancy, before becoming a non-profit advocacy organization for the broader sharing economy. Slee (2015) notes that of Peer's seventy partners, sixty were for-profit companies, with 85 per cent of Peer funding going to California companies based in Silicon Valley. Funded by tech-associated philanthropy organizations, the site's major backer was the Omidyar Network, a "philanthropic investment firm" run by the founder of eBay. Omidyar Network has been criticized "for co-opting and commercializing sharing innovations," receiving backlash for things like "relaunching CouchSurfing, the original lodging-sharing community, as a for-profit company, and promoting for-profit rather than non-profit models of microfinance lending" (Kamenetz 2013, 4). As such, Peers.org's grassroots corporatism branded the sharing economy's lobbying as a sort of crowdfunded social movement, a tactic known as "astroturfing" (Chittum 2013).

Airbnb has also signalled progressive contributions to civil society through programs like its Open Homes initiative, a program touted to make it easy for hosts to provide free accommodations for refugees and those displaced by persecution or natural disasters. While this is a positive use of the platform, the planner noted it was "abundantly clear to us it's all a PR exercise." The program is boosted through large advertising campaigns, has received substantial attention through the press, and because there is no money exchanged – hosts receive displaced guests for free – the marketing function of this program cannot be discounted.

Meetups, another website in which Atkin is involved, has been an important hub for "superhosts" – Airbnb's most successful and active hosts – to network, share knowledge, and strategize. At the time of writing, Toronto's largest superhost meet-up group was called Toronto Airbnb Hosts, carrying the tagline "Building your wealth one house at a time." The group, now defunct or potentially reorganized under a new guise, comprised 161 superhosts, holding regular meetings to "chat and mingle with Airbnb Hosts and local real estate investors and business professionals" (Grisdale 2018). At this critical time, when short-term rental regulations were still in development, this kind of mission statement raised questions about Airbnb's commitment to addressing Toronto's housing crisis. Indeed, it highlighted how many hosts were taking to Airbnb with the intention of professionalizing and commercializing their short-term rental operations in the city. The group's mission statement goes further: "Toronto is a growing city with increased tourism and business travel. Investors have realized this and have taken advantage of the opportunity by renting their properties on a daily basis instead of the traditional 1 year lease model. The purpose of this group is for hosts to come together and discuss ways that they can improve their daily rental businesses, earn more money, keep vacancy rates low, handle the struggles such as arranging key collection and cleaners and reduce the risks associated with this model" (Toronto Airbnb Hosts 2017).

The leader of Toronto Airbnb Hosts, Maria Rekrut, is a local superhost who exemplifies how the snowflake model is put to work to empower local entrepreneurs to organize independently. Leading the organization and planning of host meet-ups, she also hosted a "how-to" series of YouTube videos and podcasts providing advice for people to professionalize their short-term rentals. For example, in one YouTube video, previously accessible through the group's website, Rekrut and a local housing investor tout the benefits of short-term rentals, including greater earnings and freedom from tenancy law (Smart Home Choice 2017).

Just as Ananya Roy (2010) has been critical of how complex words such as "democracy" are deployed to promote the expansion of the microfinance industry in places like Bangladesh and Egypt, the grassroots ambitions of the "community-driven megabrand" deploys a similar narrative concerned with "democratization." In Airbnb's case, their Policy Tool Chest 2.0 (2017) explicitly claims their organization works to "democratize capitalism" by giving homeowners an accessible tool enabling them to become an entrepreneur with the click of a button. However, for critical scholars, this discourse must be interrogated, as it seeks to conflate "capitalist exchange [with] altruistic social values," and the empowerment of "micro-entrepreneurs" against corporate structures (Cockayne 2016, 73). From this perspective, insofar as Airbnb operates as a hybrid platform facilitating homesharing alongside commercial hotel operations, the positive campaign approach associated with the "consumer-driven megabrand" should be met with skepticism and commitments to hold the platform accountable. Analysis of interviews and statements made at city council deputations concerned with short-term rental regulation suggests that most stakeholders see regulation as inevitable and necessary, but that they should "reflect the casual and occasional nature of home sharing for the thousands of hosts here in Toronto" (City of Toronto 2017b).

Ambiguities are also apparent in Airbnb's public acceptance of its own regulation. For instance, one Airbnb employee argued the platform is committed to "true" home-sharing, claiming commercial hosts would have little future in the organization. Conversely, a senior planner at the City of Toronto I interviewed was skeptical of the company's positive reception to regulation, especially considering the significant profits that would inevitably disappear with the loss of its elite, commercialized enterprises. One superhost who operates multiple properties also admitted that home-sharing is becoming a less significant aspect of the platform's business model: "There are a lot of people who are professional property managers that list on Airbnb – more than I think even Airbnb knew. I think Airbnb also discovered that what their original business model was, and what it actually became – a lot of the travellers don't want to share accommodation, they don't want to be staying in someone else's house. They want to stay in a self-contained residential condominium or home or something like that."

In an interview, a policy officer with the city's Municipal Licensing and Standards Division noted the key reason the city stood back as long as it did was to ensure against regulating a fad, which would pass, and become a waste of time for city staff. However, considering the platform's global success, the real question is whether regulating commercial short-term rental operations across the world might make it such a fad. As such, the City Planning Department sought to create regulations by embracing a long-term view informed by an extensive global jurisdictional scan[6] of different regulatory frameworks and tools to achieve a "made-in-Toronto" approach. One Airbnb employee noted that the lack of an annual bookings cap, which affordability advocates still push for, is the result of this jurisdictional scan, where many cities that have such a cap see hosts get around it by switching platforms.[7] The interesting implication here is how Airbnb might also benefit from a lack of a cap, which, though restrictive, may also reinforce its monopoly in the sector. While some are critical of the drawn-out consultation that defines Toronto's development of short-term rental regulations, it has also been an important means to prevent the use of "fast policy" (Peck and Theodore 2015), which might fail to address macroeconomic implications of the platform. Thinking of the big picture was also identified as important to Municipal Licensing and Standards, with their policy officer noting, "We try when we regulate to kind of have ... this longer vision for the future, because we don't want to be writing rules that are out of date in a day or are really specific to one company, like Airbnb, or to Uber."

This remains a concern for one Airbnb employee who sees the possibility for "policy me-too-ism" of cities in Ontario facing different housing affordability dynamics. For instance, she noted that Hamilton, London, and Kingston were thinking of replicating Toronto's approach to Airbnb regulation, even though they faced different impacts from the platform. This was also emphasized by a policy advisor with the province's Sharing Economy Advisory Committee:

> I think there is a jurisdictional component to learning any topic, and government always does that ... It doesn't necessarily mean that you're going to mimic anything ... and Ontario is very focused on having its made-in-Ontario approaches, so it's not as simple as saying, "Oh, yeah we're going to do what they did in San Francisco or do what they did in Melbourne, Australia." It will never be as simple as that. Because I want to make the point that we have a principle-based approach. So if we're saying that our principles are to protect consumers, workers, and

communities, and fostering business and innovation, and, you know, these are the sorts of principles that we have as an organization.

However, in light of many cities taking a more gradual approach to regulation of new technologies, a second pillar to Airbnb's lobbying approach is a heavy investment in policy experts to lobby the government. One of the first things an Airbnb employee assured me was that just as Google "does" public policy, the same goes for Airbnb. Analyzing Uber's public policy approach, Sadowsky and Gregory (2015) argue that their ambition is not to become a transportation utility assuming responsibility for capital, infrastructure, and labour, but "a more apt understanding of Uber's ambitions is that the company wants to be involved in city governance – fashioning the new administrative capacities of urban environments. Rather than follow government rules, like any other utility, Uber wants a visible hand in creating urban policy, determining how cities develop and grow, eventually making the city itself a platform for the proliferation of 'smart,' data-based systems" (para. 7).

Airbnb appears to indicate this shift, positioning itself as an expert policy intermediator, offering insider knowledge on integrating these socio-technical practices into the urban economy. Of course, this policy narrative positions Airbnb as representing home-sharing more broadly. Insofar as the company controls the narrative on its own inevitable regulation, it will be well placed to maintain a relative monopoly and thereby maximize its extraction of profits in the short-term rental sector. According to one employee, Airbnb is best positioned among different policy actors to mediate and inform its own regulation because of the significant work it has put into doing jurisdictional scans. This appeal to expertise is deployed through Airbnb's "Policy Tool Chests" (2016, 2017) and other boosterist reports, curating compilations of regulation frameworks applied to short-term rentals around the world. Thus, the aim of its policy approach is to dominate and limit the discourse on regulation by assembling and promoting transferrable sets of policies and regulatory approaches most amenable to their interests. In practice, however, a policy mobilities approach reminds us that mobilization of their public relations and policy advocacy will likely become as multidirectional, hybrid, and geographically specific as the political responses to their business model.

CONCLUSION

Airbnb policy construction is characterized by a global campaign for legitimacy that uses two tactics. First, there is a grassroots "community-driven megabrand" initiative attempting to build a culture of trans-nationalism for everyday people, which aims to politicize its local hosts against established interests in the hotel and rental industries. Second, there is a public policy initiative mobilized through policy experts and lobbying organizations to construct and command expertise on regulatory best practices of the industry. This approach seeks to establish the normalization and monopoly of Airbnb by compiling and documenting regulatory examples that work to its benefit before pushing for its adoption in other cities.

A few theoretical implications might be gleaned from these provisional observations. First, if the "community-driven megabrand" represents the modus operandi of other platforms "disrupting" brick-and-mortar institutions (like Uber in the taxi industry), this can often be understood as a process leveraging the atomization experienced by everyday people under austerity and financialized capitalism. This is explicitly acknowledged by Atkin, who owes the success of his strategy to its capacity to tap into people's experiences of alienation under precarity and their desire to participate in strong communities and social institutions. However, the for-profit sharing economy that Airbnb represents should be challenged on its claims to community building and sustainability. By rethreading capitalist and entrepreneurial values through narratives of community, sustainability, and technological progress, this "platform capitalism" (Srnicek 2017) risks feigning communitarian values while reinforcing very neoliberal approaches to governance and policy (Cockayne, 2016; Martin, 2016). Indeed, this narrative leaves out perspectives advocating forms of "platform cooperativism" that aim to deploy technology towards communitarian ends (Scholz 2015). By reifying platforms like Airbnb and Uber as the only possible models for these emerging peer-to-peer economies, we risk ignoring the broader possibilities of platforms for organizing more democratic and locally embedded alternative economies.

Second, expanding on Srnicek's (2017) description of the "lean platform" as a "hyper-outsourced model, whereby workers are outsourced, fixed capital is outsourced, maintenance costs are outsourced, and training is outsourced" (76), it should also be noted how Atkin's "community-driven megabrand" outsources its public relations and lobbying to the grassroots by mobilizing hosts to take political action on behalf of the platform in their spare time. Although it empowers many individuals to make extra money from their assets, the ability of the platform to extract significant revenues from cities around the world to its tax havens in the British Isles depends on devolving risk and responsibility to those same communities. However, as Schor (2014) notes, the hyper-disconnection between administrative apparatus and workers, indicative of the platform economy, fosters potential for those workers to begin organizing themselves. Specifically, she notes how Airbnb's efforts to organize and politicize its hosts opens the possibility for them to push back against the platform or split completely to form municipally governed or cooperatively owned short-term rental platforms.

Addtionally, Airbnb strives to be an active maker of its own regulation in cities across the world. This is visible through its teams of lobbyists and public policy experts who engage local councils with curated jurisdictional scans of short-term rental regulations around the world. Due to the place-based nature of these platforms, the Airbnb strategy is premised on building a global community that stresses points of connection and regulatory precedents between cities, rather than encouraging cities to compete for their presence. Indeed, this contrasts with a company such as Amazon that is only investing in bricks-and-mortar bookstores now that it has established dominance in the industry through e-commerce. In this case, Amazon is now a powerful force driving competitive urbanism, recently pitting cities across North America, including Toronto, to vie for the location of their second headquarters. However, as long as Airbnb maintains its lean platform model, municipal governments are positioned to deploy significant control over the future of the industry (Davidson and Infranca 2016). Indeed, this was frequently echoed in the interviews herein, with many participants emphasizing the municipality as the most appropriate level for regulation. Nonetheless, as the impacts of short-term rentals are still being revealed, this chapter only scratches the surface of how a policy mobilities approach can facilitate greater understanding of the digital platform's emergence as a significant presence in contemporary cities.

NOTES

1 The Ontario Municipal Board (OMB) was dissolved on 3 April 2018,
   to be replaced by a Local Planning Appeal Tribunal (LPAT). The OMB
   was an independent administrative tribunal that heard any local planning
   appeals advanced across Ontario.
2 Other popular booking platforms include Vacation Rentals by Owner
   (VRBO), Flipkey, and HomeAway, as well as online classifieds like Kijiji
   and Craigslist.
3 Capital flight reflects a competitive environment of uneven development
   in which localities are disciplined with the threat of removal to ensure
   a conducive business environment for firms (Harvey 1989). Conversely,
   the business model of the short-term rental platform aims to touch down
   in every locality to the greatest extent it can.
4 This "fourth level" of governance is unofficial in that many urban services
   we understand to be provided to neighbourhoods through the municipality
   (via the municipal tax base) have in the condominium become the jurisdiction of a given building's private strata council, which is funded through
   condominium fees.
5 For instance, French President Emmanuel Macron announced he
   wanted France to be a country "that thinks and moves like a startup,"
   when announcing a new visa program to attract tech industry talent
   (Agnew, 2017).
6 Jurisdictional scans review regulatory frameworks in different jurisdictions
   to inform policy creation and legislation.
7 Toronto's short-term rental regulations have since added a night cap
   of 180 days for entire home units.

REFERENCES

Airbnb. 2016. *Airbnb Policy Tool Chest*. https://www.airbnbcitizen.com/
   wp-content/uploads/2016/12/National_PublicPolicyTool-ChestReport-
   v3.pdf.
– 2017. *Airbnb Policy Tool Chest 2.0*. https://press.airbnb.com/wp-content/
   uploads/sites/4/2019/08/Airbnb-Policy-Tool-Chest-2.0.pdf.
Atkin, D. 2005. *The Culting of Brands: Turn Your Customers into True
   Believers*. New York: Portfolio.
Beattie, S. 2018. "Appeal Stalls Toronto's Short-Term Rental Rules for
   at Least a Year." *Toronto Star*, 5 September 2018. https://www.thestar.

com/news/gta/2018/09/05/appeal-stalls-torontos-short-term-rental-rules-for-at-least-a-year.html.

Botsman, R., and R. Rogers. 2010. *What's Mine Is Yours: The Rise of Collaborative Consumption.* New York: Harpers Business.

Chhabra, S. 2019. "Toronto City Council Adopts Motion Requiring Short-Term Rentals 'Play by the Rules.'" Mobilesyrup, 1 February. https://mobilesyrup.com/2019/02/01/toronto-city-council-adopts-short-term-rental-motion/.

Chittum, R. 2013. "*Fortune* Flacks for the 'Sharing Economy.'" *Columbia Journalism Review*, 10 December. http://archives.cjr.org/the_audit/fortune_flacks_for_the_sharing.php.

City of Toronto. Executive Committee. 2016. *Developing an Approach to Regulating Short-Term Rentals.* http://www.toronto.ca/legdocs/mmis/2016/ex/bgrd/backgroundfile-97235.pdf.

City of Toronto. 2017a. "Lobbyist Registrar." https://www.toronto.ca/city-government/accountability-operations-customer-service/accountability-officers/lobbyist-registrar/.

– 2017b. "Proposed Regulations for Short-Term Rentals for Consultation." http://app.toronto.ca/tmmis/viewAgendaItemHistory.do?item=2017.EX26.3.

CMX Summit. 2014. "Douglas Atkin – Global Head of Community @ Airbnb – CMX Summit 2014." Video file. https://www.youtube.com/watch?v=X-PN5WWytgo.

Cockayne, D.G. 2016. "Sharing and Neoliberal Discourse: The Economic Function of Sharing in the Digital On-Demand Economy." *Geoforum* 77: 73–82.

Cocola-Gant, A., and A. Gago. 2019. "Airbnb, Buy-to-Let Investment and Tourism-Driven Displacement: A Case Study in Lisbon." *Environment and Planning A: Economy and Space.* https://doi.org/10.1177/0308518X19869012.

Combs, J., D. Kerrigan, and D. Wachsmuth. 2020. "Short-Term Rentals in Canada: Uneven Growth, Uneven Impacts." *Canadian Journal of Urban Research* 29, no. 1: 119–34.

Crommelin, L., L. Troy, C. Martin, and S. Parkinson. 2018. *Technological Disruption in Private Housing Markets: The Case of Airbnb.* AHURI Final Report 305. Melbourne: Australian Housing and Urban Research Institute Limited. https://doi.org/10.18408/ahuri-7115201.

Davidson, N.M., and J.J. Infranca. 2016. "The Sharing Economy as an Urban Phenomenon." *Yale Law & Policy Review* 34, no. 2: 215–79.

Ferreri, M., and R. Sanyal. 2018. "Platform Economies and Urban Planning: Airbnb and Regulated Deregulation in London." *Urban Studies* 55, no. 15: 3,353–68.

Finck, M., and S. Ranchordás. 2016. "Sharing and the City." *Vanderbilt Journal of Transnational Law* 49: 1–70.

Gray, J. 2016. "Condo Concierges Face Off against Tourists, Partiers in Airbnb War." *Globe and Mail*, 4 November. https://www.theglobeandmail. com/news/toronto/condo-concierges-face-off-against-tourists-partiers-in-airbnb-war/article32683576/.

– 2017. "Toronto Passes Strict Airbnb Rules Aimed at Preserving Long-Term Rental." *Globe and Mail*, 7 December. https://www. theglobeandmail.com/news/toronto/toronto-passes-strict-airbnb-rules-aimed-at-preserving-long-term-rental-supply/article37265435/.

Grisdale, S. 2018. "Displacement by Disruption: Platform Capitalism, Short-Term Rentals and Urban Transformation in Toronto." MA thesis, University of Toronto.

– 2019. "Displacement by Disruption: Short-Term Rentals and the Political Economy of 'Belonging Anywhere' in Toronto." *Urban Geography*. https://doi.org/10.1080/02723638.2019.1642714.

Gurran, N., and P. Phibbs. 2017. "When Tourists Move In: How Should Urban Planners Respond to Airbnb?" *Journal of the American Planning Association* 83, no. 1: 80–92.

Harvey, D. 1989. "From Managerialism to Entrepreneurialism: The Transformation of Urban Governance in Late Capitalism." *Geografiska Annaler. Series B, Human Geography* 71, no. 1: 3–17.

Joy, M., J. Shields, and S.M. Cheng. 2019. "Social Innovation Labs: A Neoliberal Austerity Driven Process or Democratic Intervention?" *Alternate Routes: A Journal of Critical Social Research* 30, no. 2: 35–54. http://www.alternateroutes.ca/index.php/ar/article/view/22487/18286.

Kamenetz, A. 2013. "Is Peers the Sharing Economy's Future or Just a Great Silicon Valley PR Stunt?" *Fast Company*, 13 September. https:// www.fastcompany.com/3022974/is-peers-the-sharing-economys-future-or-just-a-great-silicon-valley-pr-stunt.

Keil, R. 2017. "Toronto Alles Uber: Being Progressive in the Age of Progressive Conservative Urbanism." *Alternate Routes: A Journal of Critical Social Research* 28: 189–218.

Langley, P., and A. Leyshon. 2016. "Platform Capitalism: The Intermediation and Capitalisation of Digital Economic Circulation." *Finance and Society*, EarlyView, 1–21. http://financeandsociety.ed.ac.uk/ ojs-images/financeandsociety/FS_EarlyView_LangleyLeyshon.pdf.

Lee, D. 2016. "How Airbnb Short-Term Rentals Exacerbate Los Angeles's Affordable Housing Crisis: Analysis and Policy Recommendations." *Harvard Law and Policy Review* 10, no. 1: 229–53.

Lippert, R.K., and R. Steckle. 2016. "Conquering Condos from Within: Condo-Isation as Urban Governance and Knowledge." *Urban Studies* 53, no. 1: 132–48.

MaRS. 2017. "Mission." https://www.marsdd.com/systems-change/mars-solutions-lab/solutions-lab-mission/.

Martin, C.J. 2016. "The Sharing Economy: A Pathway to Sustainability or a Nightmarish Form of Neoliberal Capitalism?" *Ecological Economics* 121: 149–59.

Martin, C.J., P. Upham, and L. Budd. 2015. "Commercial Orientation in Grassroots Social Innovation: Insights from the Sharing Economy." *Ecological Economics* 118: 240–51.

McCann, E. 2011. "Urban Policy Mobilities and Global Circuits of Knowledge: Toward a Research Agenda." *Annals of the Association of American Geographers* 101, no. 1: 107–30.

McCann, E., and K. Ward, eds. 2011. *Mobile Urbanism: Cities and Policymaking in the Global Age.* Minneapolis: University of Minnesota Press.

McNeill, D. 2016. "Governing a City of Unicorns: Technology Capital and the Urban Politics of San Francisco." *Urban Geography* 37, no. 4: 494–513.

Molotch, H. 1976. "The City as a Growth Machine: Toward a Political Economy of Place." *American Journal of Sociology* 82, no. 2: 309–32.

Morozov, E. 2013. *To Save Everything, Click Here: The Folly of Technological Solutionism.* New York: PublicAffairs.

Mosendz, P., and J. Smith IV. 2014. "Hiding in Plain Sight: What Airbnb Doesn't Want You to Know about Their New Lobbyists." *Observer,* 23 July. http://observer.com/2014/07/hiding-in-plain-sight-what-airbnb-doesnt-want-you-to-know-about-their-new-lobbying-firm/.

Pasquale, F., and S. Vaidhyanathan. 2015. "Uber and the Lawlessness of 'Sharing Economy' Corporates." Guardian, 28 July. https://www.theguardian.com/technology/2015/jul/28/uber-lawlessness-sharing-economy-corporates-airbnb-google.

Paulauskaite, D., R. Powell, and J.A. Coca-Stefaniak. 2017. "Living like a Local: Authentic Tourism Experiences and the Sharing Economy." *International Journal of Tourism Research* 19, no. 6: 619–28.

PBS. 2004. Interview Douglas Atkin. *Frontline,* 9 November. http://www.pbs.org/wgbh/pages/frontline/shows/persuaders/interviews/atkin.html.

Peck, J. 2011. "Geographies of Policy: From Transfer-Diffusion to Mobility-Mutation." *Progress in Human Geography* 35, no. 6: 773–97.

Peck, J., and N. Theodore. 2010. "Mobilizing Policy: Models, Methods, and Mutations." *Geoforum* 41: 169–74.

– 2015. *Fast Policy*. Minneapolis: University of Minnesota Press.

Pofeldt, E. 2017. "A Booming Start-up Center North of the Border Is Rivaling Silicon Valley." CNBC, 6 March. http://www.cnbc.com/2017/03/06/booming-start-up-center-north-of-the-border-is-rivaling-silicon-valley.html.

Prince, R. 2012. "Policy Transfer, Consultants, and the Geographies of Governance." *Progress in Human Geography* 36, no. 2: 188–203.

Public Policy Forum. 2013. *Change Labs and Government in Canada: Summary Report*. https://ppforum.ca/wp-content/uploads/2018/03/Change-Labs-and-Government-in-Canada.pdf.

Richardson, L. 2015. "Performing the Sharing Economy." *Geoforum* 67: 121–9.

Roy, A. 2010. *Poverty Capital: Microfinance and the Making of Development*. New York: Routledge.

Sadowski, J., and K. Gregory. 2015. "Is Uber's Ultimate Goal the Privatisation of City Governance?" *Guardian*, 15 September. https://www.theguardian.com/technology/2015/sep/15/is-ubers-ultimate-goal-the-privatisation-of-city-governance.

Schäfer, P., and N. Braun. 2016. "Misuse through Short-Term Rentals on the Berlin Housing Market." *International Journal of Housing Markets and Analysis* 9, no. 2: 287–311.

Scholz, T. 2016. *Platform Cooperativism: Challenging the Corporate Sharing Economy*. New York: Rosa Luxembourg Stiftung. http://www.rosalux-nyc.org/wp-content/files_mf/scholz_platformcoop_5.9.2016.pdf.

Schor, J. 2014. "Debating the Sharing Economy." Great Transition Initiative. http://www.greattransition.org/publication/debating-the-sharing-economy.

Slee, T. 2015. *What's Yours Is Mine: Against the Sharing Economy*. New York: OR Books.

Smart Home Choice. 2017. "Successfully Investing in Short Term Rentals with Maria Rekrut." YouTube. https://www.youtube.com/watch?v=930KdGmnora.

Srnicek, N. 2017. *Platform Capitalism*. Cambridge: Polity.

Steenhoven, J.V.D., I. Burale, V. Toye, and C. Bure. 2016. "Shifting Perspectives: Redesigning Regulation for the Sharing Economy." MaRS Solutions Lab, 31 March. https://www.marsdd.com/research-and-

insights/shifting-perspectives-redesigning-regulation-
for-the-sharing-economy/.

Thiel, P. 2014. "Competition Is for Losers." *Wall Street Journal*,
    12 September. https://www.wsj.com/articles/peter-thiel-competition-
    is-for-losers-1410535536.

Toronto Life. 2017. "The Incredible Rise of Tech." https://torontolife.com/
    tech/the-incredible-unstoppable-rise-of-tech/.

Wachsmuth, D., D. Kerrigan, and D. Chaney. 2017. "Short-Term Cities:
    Airbnb's Impact on Canadian Rental Markets." Urban Politics and
    Governance Research Group, McGill School of Urban Planning,
    10 August. http://upgo.lab.mcgill.ca/airbnb/Short-term%20Cities%20
    2017-08-10.pdf

Wachsmuth, D., and A. Weisler. 2018. "Airbnb and the Rent Gap:
    Gentrification through the Sharing Economy." *Environment and
    Planning A: Economy and Space* 50, no. 6: 1,147–70.

Ward, K. 2018. "Policy Mobilities, Politics and Place: The Making
    of Financial Urban Futures." *European Urban and Regional Studies* 25,
    no. 3: 266–83.

Wiig, A. 2015. "IBM's Smart City as Techno-Utopian Policy Mobility."
    City 19, nos. 2–3: 258–73.

Wiig, A., and E. Wyly. 2016. "Thinking through the Politics of the Smart
    City." *Urban Geography* 37, no. 4: 485–93.

3

Who's the Boss?
The Impact of Digitally Mediated
Employment on Labour Markets
and the Nature of Work

Andrew Wolf

- The rise of platform-based employment generates important
  labour and employment issues that cities and urban planners must
  consider. Allowing companies to enter cities without regulation
  and to classify their workers as independent contractors further
  privatizes essential services such as transportation.
- While the size of platform employment remains small, its impacts
  can be large and concentrated in cities: taxi-app companies
  represent 30 per cent of New York City's traffic and employs
  84,000 drivers. Additionally, benefits and costs of the platform
  are being felt disparately, reproducing historical inequalities of
  race, gender, and class on these platforms.
- Platform economy companies in service industries are using
  innovative technologies and "algorithmic management" to
  transform the labour process, or the organization of work,
  from a world of managers and workers to one of algorithms
  and workers. Algorithmic management is combined with
  "gamification," which makes work additive, and ideological
  appeals to workers' notions of freedom to make them consent
  to the employment arrangement. Nevertheless, platform workers
  around the world are increasingly speaking up and forming
  labour unions.

INTRODUCTION

The rise of the gig economy in the last decade has caused a flurry of public interest and debate over what it means for the future of work. The gig economy is a subset of the larger platform economy in which employment in traditional service industries has become digitally mediated by the introduction of an electronic marketplace. A central feature of the gig economy is that companies operating in it claim they have no employees and that those who use their app to work are not company employees but are instead independent contractors (Dubal 2017). Disavowal of an employment relationship not only challenges urban labour markets but also questions our urban regulatory regimes. The fact that our cities allow these gig companies to define their own employment relationships and declare which legal regulations apply to them represents an ideological shift in the responsibility that cities have historically taken to maintain their urban infrastructure – physical and social. This further privatizes a city's socio-political economy. This chapter explores this debate in the context of the wider urban sphere.

To this end, this chapter evaluates the labour and employment issues raised by the gig economy for urban centres in the Global North and tracks how cities have responded. First, the size and scope of the gig economy is evaluated in relation to the global growth in precarious and informal work. Second, the impacts of the gig economy are evaluated to investigate how the historical inequalities of race, gender, and class are being reproduced on these platforms. Third, the labour market and the legal implications of gig companies that attempt to shed employment responsibility are explored. Fourth, this chapter investigates how gig employment is changing the nature of work, evaluating how the replacement of supervisors with algorithms affects workers and labour. Fifth, the response of urban, state, and provincial governments in the United States and Canada to the illegal entry of transportation network companies (TNCs) like Uber and Lyft is evaluated. Finally, this chapter discusses how workers and labour unions have responded to the entry of gig companies into their industries. Overall, this chapter finds that the entry of the gig economy to the urban sphere as well as the municipal response to it is chaotic and uneven. Yet the challenges raised by gig companies for workers and the urban infrastructure remain, leaving cities increasingly compelled to address them.

SIZE AND SCOPE OF THE GIG ECONOMY

The gig economy has been growing rapidly since its advent. The number of Uber drivers in the United States doubled every six months from 2012 to 2015, at a pace that if it were to continue would mean every American worker would have become an Uber driver within five years (Hall and Krueger 2017). While this growth has been massive, calculating just how large the gig economy is has proven particularly difficult. Survey data have often suffered from respondents failing to report gig work or failing to understand gig-related questions. In a prominent example of this problem, the US Department of Labor's attempt to survey digital platforms returned a large number of false positives, forcing the government to manually remove these cases from their results (BLS 2017). Similarly, studies using administrative data from gig companies to measure the scope of the gig economy tend to under-count the number of hours worked, because employees often work on several platforms at the same time. Conversely, when these data are aggregated across companies, this same phenomenon counts workers too many times, making it difficult to understand exactly how many workers there are.

Despite these limitations, evaluating efforts to account for the size of the gig economy does provide us with useful insights. A US Bureau of Labor Statistics study of electronically mediated work (table 3.1) found that gig work accounted for about 1 per cent of the US workforce and 1.6 per cent of part-time workers. The data also highlight disparities in access to gig employment. White employees are more likely to work higher-paying online gig jobs, compared to Black workers, who are far more likely to work in-person gig jobs. Interestingly, gig workers are also more highly educated than the overall workforce.

To evaluate the gig economy and larger platform economy from the perspective of those generating personal income, the JPMorgan Chase Institute (Farrell et al. 2018) took a sample of 39 million US Chase checking accounts in the twenty-three states Chase operates commercial banks, and tracked payments families received from 128 online platforms. They found 2.3 million account holders participated in the online platform economy from October 2012 to March 2018. The study looked at labour platforms (split into transportation and all other work apps) and capital platforms (split into selling and leasing). Over the course of study, the proportion of the sample generating any

Table 3.1
US Department of Labor survey of electronically mediated employment in the US,
May 2017

Characteristic	Total employed	Electronically mediated workers*			Electronic % of total employed		
		Total	In person	Online	Total	In person	Online
Total, 16 years and over (in thousands)	153,331	1,609	990	701	1.0	0.6	0.5
Men (%)	53.2	54.1	53.9	52.7	1.1	0.7	0.5
Women (%)	46.8	45.9	46.1	47.3	1.0	0.6	0.5
Age (%)							
16–24	12.4	10.3	7.4	15.6	0.9	0.4	0.6
25–54	64.4	71.2	72.6	69.5	1.2	0.7	0.5
55 and over	23.1	18.4	20.1	14.9	0.8	0.6	0.3
Race (%)**							
White	78.7	74.6	69.9	84.0	1.0	0.6	0.5
Black or African American	12.1	17.1	23.0	6.9	1.5	1.2	0.3
Asian	5.9	5.8	4.6	7.0	1.0	0.5	0.5
Hispanic or Latino ethnicity	16.6	16.4	18.5	13.4	1.0	0.7	0.4
Full-time (35+ hours) and part-time status (%)							
Full-time workers	81.7	72.4	69.4	78.1	0.9	0.5	0.4
Part-time workers	18.3	27.6	30.6	21.9	1.6	1.1	0.5
Educational attainment (%)							
Less than a high school diploma	7.1	4.5	5.7	2.0	0.7	0.6	0.1
High school graduates, no college	25.0	19.7	25.1	9.8	0.8	0.7	0.2
Some college or associate degree	26.9	26.0	28.9	21.3	1.0	0.7	0.3
Bachelor's degree only	25.1	27.9	21.4	38.7	1.2	0.6	0.7
Advanced degree	15.8	22.0	18.9	28.3	1.5	0.8	0.8

* Electronically meditated work might not add up to 100 per cent because some workers worked in person and online.
** Race does not add up to 100 per cent because Hispanic or Latino could be in any race group, nor do BLS figures include all races.

income from platforms rose from 0.3 per cent in October 2012 to 1.6 per cent in March 2018. As of March 2018, 4.5 per cent of the sample had earned income from a platform in the previous year.

While the gig economy represents only a small proportion of the US workforce, its geographic distribution is not uniform. Labour service gig companies such as Uber are highly concentrated in major metro areas. In 2014, just twenty market areas contained 85 per cent of Uber's drivers (Hall and Krueger 2017). Similarly, JPMorgan Chase found uneven concentration of gig employment (figure 3.1). They found the gig economy represents almost 3 per cent of Nevada and San Francisco's workforces. In Chase's sample, four states and eight cities (including three in California) had over 2 per cent of gig employment, or double the national average.

A report by McKinsey & Company (Manyika et al. 2016) situates the gig economy within the broader context of independent contractor work globally. Looking at the United States and five EU countries (France, the United Kingdom, Germany, Sweden, and Spain), they found that of these six countries in 2015 there were 162 million independent contractor workers, of which 15 per cent, or 24 million, were digital platform workers. More importantly, they found that those whose income was generated from selling goods or leasing assets were more likely to use digital platforms than those who provided labour, indicating the growth potential for labour service gig-jobs.

In Canada, the gig economy remains a comparatively small but growing segment of the workforce. Statistics Canada (2017) found that 9.5 per cent of people eighteen and over living in Canada participated in the platform economy (including peer-to-peer services like Uber and private accommodation services, such as Airbnb), as users or as workers, between November 2015 and October 2016. A study of the Greater Toronto Area found that 9 per cent of residents were working on gig platforms, and 38 per cent had worked on gig platforms. Of those working gig-economy jobs, 90 per cent had attended college or university, and 48 per cent had been working these jobs for over a year (Block and Hennessy 2017). The growth of gig work in Canada follows trends in the growth of precarious work in the country. The number of workers in the Toronto Census Municipal Area who described their jobs as "temporary" grew over 40 per cent, from 8.9 per cent in 1997 to 12.6 per cent in 2011 (PEPSO 2013). Overall, 2.18 million Canadians were categorized as temporary workers in September 2017, and one-quarter surveyed reported working part-time or contract work because they could not find permanent full-time work (Statistics Canada 2017).

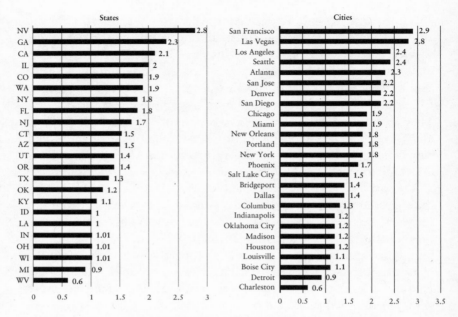

Figure 3.1 Percentage of Chase customers generating income from platforms, October 2017.

Within the world of the gig economy, Uber and ride-sharing loom large. It is estimated that two-thirds of platform-based labour market activity occurs on Uber, founded in 2009 (Harris and Krueger 2015). In Rosenblat's (2018) reporting of Uber's internal statistics, through mid-2017 Uber operated in 630 cities worldwide and provided 5 billion rides. By 2018 Uber had 3 million active drivers globally. Of these, Uber had 900,000 drivers in the United States and 50,000 in Canada (Rosenblat 2018). Their closest competitor, Lyft, had 700,000 active drivers in the United States. While these employment figures are large, most drivers do not rely on gig employment full-time. In 2015 Hall and Krueger, analyzing internal Uber data, found that 52 per cent of drivers worked full time at another job, and 32 per cent indicated they were working for Uber while looking for another job. Much evidence finds gig work is often used to smooth fluctuation in individual employment and earnings (e.g., Farrell et al. 2018). Similarly, Rosenblat (2018) found 78 per cent of Lyft drivers worked one to fifteen hours a week in 2015, and 60 per cent of Uber drivers work fewer than ten hours a week. Despite these findings, Rosenblat argues these results ignore the fact that most drivers work for more than one app. In fact, a 2016 investigation by the mayor of New York City found that 75 per cent of app drivers worked full-time but over multiple apps. These factors – temporary, part-time, and supplemental – make shaping policy on gig employment particularly difficult.

Beyond counting the reach of the gig economy, scholars have had trouble defining it. The gig economy grew out of the sharing economy movement, which served a particularly important function in helping individuals weather the Great Recession in 2008 (Schor 2020; Bajwa et al. 2018). The sharing economy promoted a more open-source and egalitarian version of mutual aid, through platforms such as Craigslist and couch surfing, and later found itself professionalized and commodified by the gig economy. The gig economy can be categorized into two forms: "crowd-work" and "work-on-demand via apps" (De Stefano 2016). The archetypical crowd-work platform is Amazon's Mechanical Turk, which allows people to hire workers to provide a variety of tasks that computers cannot reliably perform, including entering data and filling out social science surveys. Work-on-demand apps claim to simply create an electronic market. They are managed by firms that also provide quality standards, minimal monitoring, and selection screenings such as background checks (Aloisi 2016). The archetypical and largest work-on-demand app is Uber.

Adopting the continuum approach offered by Ticona et al. (2018) is useful to understanding the differences in degree of workers control in gig work, as summarized in figure 3.2. They advocate viewing platform work as a continuum composed of three main categories: marketplace platforms, on-demand platforms, and hybrids composing the middle. Unlike approaches that define gig work on the basis of whether it is performed in person or not – the crowd-work vs. on-demand distinction (e.g., Heeks 2017), the approach of Ticona et al. is based on the nature of worker autonomy, not the nature of the work itself. As shown in figure 3.2, both online crowd-work and in-person on-demand work can fall on both sides of Ticona et al.'s worker autonomy continuum. Market platforms generate digitally mediated employment that is primarily affecting the hiring process, by helping to match workers and clients. These market platforms aim to reduce overall transaction costs by providing service seekers and workers with information about each other that is sorted and ranked. These platforms, such as Care.com, are typically based on subscriptions, not percentage fees, and as such provide workers with greater autonomy.

Marketplace platforms, e.g., Care.com (in-person) and Gigster.com (on-line)	*Hybrid platforms*, e.g., Handy (in-person)	*Work-on-demand platforms*, e.g., Uber (in-person) & Amazon MTurk (on-line crowdwork)
• Greater worker autonomy • Subscription business model • Gig company, primary impact on the labour market via matching	• Attempts to limit worker autonomy by limiting worker-client communication • Attempts to impose fee-per-gig business model • Gig company primary impact on the labour market via matching but incorporates some algorithmic management	• Less worker autonomy • Fee-per-gig business model • Gig company primary impact on the labour market via algorithmic management

Figure 3.2 Continuum of gig-work platform types by worker autonomy.

In contrast, on-demand platforms indirectly manage the entire labour process. These platforms, such as Uber, typically make their profit through fees applied to each "gig" that workers perform. Beyond the hiring process – in which Uber recruits drivers, typically through advertisements, and provides minimal screening through a company background check – Uber also monitors and directs all actions of its workers through "algorithmic management" (Lee et al. 2015; Rosenblat and Stark 2016). In the middle are hybrids, which incorporate features of both. For example, Handy, an app that provides on-demand cleaning services, functions largely as a marketplace but operates on a fee structure and prevents workers and clients from communicating outside the constraints of the app. As Ticona and her co-authors explain, marketplace and on-demand platforms shift risk and rewards for workers in different ways. Marketplace platforms create an incentive for self-branding, rewarding those who are digitally fluent. On-demand platforms tend to outsource costs directly onto workers, rewarding workers who have the most financial independence and thus the least financial dependency on the apps.

WHO BENEFITS FROM THE GIG ECONOMY?

The difference between marketplace and on-demand platforms outlines the disparate impact that different forms of digital work have on workers. Those who benefit the most from the gig economy also benefit from the traditional economy: those who have greater assets

ble 3.2
Morgan Chase study on gig-income generation in the US, 2013–17

	Transportation	Non-transport work	Selling	Leasing
rnings 2013–17				
Average monthly platform earnings 2013	$1,469	$727	$556	$1,030
Average monthly platform earnings 2017	$783	$741	$608	$1,736
Change in earnings, 2013–17	-53%	1.9%	9.4%	69%
ansaction volume and platform use				
Transaction volume Q1 2018	56%	3.6%	18.9%	21.5%
Ratio earning income on multiple platforms	20.4%	1.9%	4.8%	1.9%
Earning frequency				
Families with platform income 1–3 months	58.3%	68.1%	70.7%	68.3%
Families with platform income 10–12 months	12.5%	9.1%	7.3%	9.8%
rning concentration and dependence				
Platform earnings going to top 10 per cent of earners, Q1 2018	56.9%	49.2%	80.5%	50.6%
Ratio of earnings to total observed take-home income	58.2%	50.1%	54.2%	42.8%
Fraction earnings exceeding 90 per cent of take-home income	43.8%	31.4%	38%	33.5%

and higher levels of education, are male, and are white. In making this claim, it is important to consider that the gig economy is not just about "Uberization." Beyond Uber there are marketplace platforms as well as capital platforms for selling goods and leasing assets such as houses or cars. Capital platforms unsurprisingly result in the highest compensation.

The compensation gap between capital and labour platforms has only become more pronounced over time. JPMorgan Chase's study (Farrell et al. 2018) of checking account holders' platform-based income showed that from 2013 to 2017 those whose income came from transportation gig jobs saw their average monthly earnings decrease 53 per cent, while asset-leasing earners (such as those using Airbnb) saw their earnings increase 69 per cent (table 3.2). This disparity exists even though the transaction volume was far greater for labour platforms. This furthers economic inequality, because transportation gig jobs are more accessible to those with lower incomes,

Table 3.3
BMO survey of Canadian gig workers' motivations and issues, 2018 (%)

	Boomers	Gen-Xers	Millennials	All respondents
Reason working gig jobs				
Making extra money on the side	35	44	53	49
Only way to make an income	35	27	28	27
Earning while seeking a better job	23	20	30	27
Issues				
No benefits	87	72	67	69
Insufficient income	57	36	43	41
Accumulating debt	7	34	29	29

while asset leasing benefits richer individuals, who can afford to own the capital. Additionally, the study found that those working on labour platforms were far more likely to be financially dependent on these apps, with 43.8 per cent of drivers making 90 per cent of their earnings from gig work, compared to only 33.5 per cent of leasers making 90 per cent of their earnings from their gig work. Furthermore, their findings show transportation gig workers were more likely to work more months of the year for gig companies. In short, individuals with less capital and more marginal standing were in the worst position to take advantage of the gig economy. In fact, marginal workers often needed to make up this capital difference to even access gig jobs. For example, a BMO study (2018) of Canadian gig workers found that younger workers were far more likely to take on debt to work gig jobs, likely in order to gain assets such as a nice enough car to meet Uber's or Lyft's minimal requirements (table 3.3).

Even within labour-based platforms, traditional inequalities are reproduced. Two of the largest and most politically active labour platforms are Uber and Handy. They represent the dominant employers in two industries – driving and housekeeping – which have been historically excluded from US labour law. These industries – housekeeping in particular – were excluded in the 1930s when Southern Democrats agreed to pass President Roosevelt's New Deal employment regulations. They demanded that traditionally Black industries be excluded from the new protections (Katznelson 2013; Perea 2011). As a result, workers in these industries were classified as independent contractors and did not receive fundamental worker rights, such as collective bargaining and unemployment insurance. The fact that gig-employment models have been concentrated in industries that have historically marginalized workers of colour exacerbates these historical inequalities and limits the ability of minorities to fully benefit from the rise of Silicon Valley.

The damage to these historically marginalized groups is not always obvious. Moving traditionally marginalized jobs to a digitally mediated context can have unforeseen impacts. For example, the advent of marketplace platforms apps such as Care.com take traditionally minority and immigrant occupations – in this case, home care – and arbitrarily imposes a digital barrier of entry that has no impact on a worker's actual ability to perform the work (Ticona et al. 2018). This rewards workers who have more digital fluency and puts those who do not at a disadvantage (Papacharissi and Easton 2013). In the home-care industry, this often means younger and whiter workers receive the highest-paying gigs. In the United States the majority of domestic workers are women of colour, but 64 per cent of white women hold the higher-paying nanny jobs (Ticona et al. 2018). This problem will only grow as domestic work becomes increasingly platform based. Amazon recently launched its home-cleaning company Amazon Homes Services, and the retail giant IKEA recently acquired TaskRabbit. These mergers are forming in care industries, which are projected to be among the fastest-growing industries in the United States.

Beyond historical inequalities, the gig economy has disparate impacts on workers, depending on employment status and age. Evaluating the employment status of gig drivers, Rosenblat (2018) notes that there are three kinds of Uber drivers: hobbyists, part-timers, and full-timers. Given the huge turnover at companies like Uber, which was found to have a 50 per cent turnover rate after a year and 66 per cent after two years (Hall and Krueger 2017), the company is extremely dependent on a constant churn of hobbyists and part-timers to fill its ranks. The transportation platforms make it extremely easy for those in school and/or between jobs to fill this role. A BMO study (2018) of Canadian gig workers found this phenomenon may also be attributed to generational differences (table 3.3). Millennials are more likely to work gig jobs as side jobs or to earn extra money, while boomers are more likely to turn to gig jobs out of necessity or desperation. With decreases in the manufacturing sector in the United States and Canada, the gig economy provides an easy entry into the service economy. Similarly, gig-dependent boomers are more likely to take issue with the gig economy's lack of traditional benefits or income level after experiencing the traditional economy's unionized workforce. Meanwhile, Gen-Xers and Millennials are more likely to need to accumulate debt, such as purchasing a car, to access gig jobs. These issues demonstrate that the benefits and costs of the gig economy are not felt uniformly and often tend to reproduce traditional economy inequalities.

LABOUR MARKET IMPACTS AND LEGAL ISSUES

The gig economy is a technological twist on decades-long trends in employment relations in the Global North that have resulted from the transition from a production economy to a service economy. In this sense one can see the gig economy as a continuation of the elimination of social protections at work through employment casualization, informalization, deskilling, and de-unionization. The gig economy is unique in how thoroughly firms utilize new technologies to reshape labour markets and the boundaries of the firm, which allow them to subvert the regulatory state. It is an extreme example and logical conclusion of what David Weil (2014) calls the fissured workplace. Weil uses the metaphor of fissuring rock to describe the dominant trends in US employment. When a tiny crack forms in a rock, that crack becomes a growing fissure that eventually completely undermines the stability of the surrounding bedrock. Weil argues that a similar process has happened to employment standards in America since the 1970s. The key to fissuring employment standards is the introduction of new technologies that have enabled employers to engage in greater outsourcing and subcontracting to avoid direct responsibility for employment law. The gig economy takes this a step further by attempting to eliminate employment altogether and subcontracting to each individual worker.

In the early twentieth century, for businesses to grow their profits, they had to grow in size. The key question for a firm was how big to grow and which tasks to rely on the marketplace to provide. For example, when making cars, Ford had to decide if it should produce all the parts itself or buy them from a supplier. While neo-classical economics seemed to indicate a company should aim to rely on the marketplace as much as possible, Williamson (1981), working in the tradition of Coase, argued that bureaucracy sometimes represented a cheaper alternative to relying on constant market transactions, because transactions themselves have costs. This bureaucratic logic dominated corporate strategies in the Global North in the postwar years until the financial crisis of 1975.

Following this crisis, Weil shows that in the 1980s and 1990s this trend reversed, as companies – facing increased quarterly profit demands from Wall Street – began to shed business activities and focus on their "core competencies" at the behest of Wall Street. Core competency became defined as brand development and managerial services. All other employment related to production or service provision was outsourced. Employment, which tends to be the largest cost for firms, became a particularly important target of shedding. As Weil argues, this resulted in companies recasting wage decisions as contracting decisions. In the old internal labour market environment (Doeringer and Piore 1971), the choice of market or bureaucracy was based on transaction costs. Now, because of technology, the decision between market and bureaucracy is driven by concerns of brand management and quality. For workers, this has resulted in a separation of employment from the locus of company value creation, rendering their power diminished (Weil 2014, 14).

The gig economy is an extreme form of economical fissuring. The core competency of gig companies is programming a digital platform. Aside from employing programmers at their headquarters, gig companies argue they have no other employees. By utilizing smart phone technologies they can contract out customer services to each individual driver. Meanwhile they can maintain the brand and provide quality control without managerial control by outsourcing employee coercion and management to algorithms and customers.

Companies have broken their social contract in large part because governments have let them do so. While firms and capital investors drive this extreme fissuring in the gig economy, it is predicated on government failure to enforce labour laws and pass new reforms, leaving workers and their advocates to turn to the courts in desperation. The bulk of the legal debate around these companies is about the status of their employees. Workers have filed lawsuits in the United States, Canada, and the United Kingdom claiming they have been "misclassified" as independent contractors and should instead be considered employees by the law.

In the United States three significant cases filed against Uber could determine the employment status of gig workers. The earliest class action case, *O'Connor v. Uber*, was filed in 2013 in Federal District

Court of Northern California. Another was filed in New York Federal
Court in 2016, *New York Taxi Workers Alliance v. Uber*. Finally, *Meyer
v. Kalanick* is an anti-trust action filed against Uber's co-founder Travis
Kalanick by a rider claiming the app amounts to a price-fixing con-
spiracy. The case argues that Uber's algorithm coordinates a uniform
price among supposedly independent contractors, which could be
considered price-fixing. Ultimately, the standing of the plaintiffs in all
three cases was undermined by the recent US Supreme Court ruling
in *Epic Systems Corp. v. Lewis*, which bolstered the supremacy of
corporate arbitration agreements in preventing class action lawsuits.
Ironically, these gig companies might regret the decision to force arbitration. The gig food-delivery company DoorDash was forced by a
US District Court to comply with its own mandatory arbitration clause
after the company tried to settle its claims all at once after facing a
$12 million arbitration bill (Cheng 2020).

As the Supreme Court ruling in Epic Systems seems to have stalled
federal response on the employment status question, there has been
movement at the state level. In New York the Unemployment Insurance
Appeal Board ruled that three Uber drivers and others who are "similarly situated" are employees according to the state's unemployment
insurance law and are therefore entitled to unemployment benefits.
Ultimately, in early 2019 Uber withdrew its appeal and accepted the
decision (Flamm 2019). This represented the first time Uber and Lyft
agreed to consider their drivers employees under any US law.

The case with greatest impact on the employment status of US gig
workers came in the California Supreme Court ruling in *Dynamex
Operations West, Inc. v. Superior Court of Los Angeles*. The decision
ruled that workers at Dynamex a courier company had been misclassified as independent contractor under California state law. In the decision the court laid out its "ABC test" for determining independent
contractor status as: "(A) that the worker is free from the control and
direction of the hirer in connection with the performance of the work,
both under the contract for the performance of such work and in fact;
(B) that the worker performs work that is outside the usual course of
the hiring entity's business; and (C) that the worker is customarily
engaged in an independently established trade, occupation, or business
of the same nature as the work performed for the hiring entity." This
decision sets an extremely high bar for corporations to overcome to
prove they only employ independent contractors. As a result of this
decision as well as two large strikes by Uber and Lyft drivers in Los

Angeles, there was a flurry of activity at the state legislature. The State of California passed the "AB 5" bill in 2019. which codifies the ABC test into law, making gig workers employees under state law. In response Uber, Lyft, DoorDash, and other gig companies spent $189 million funding Prop 22, a ballot initiative to overturn this law in the November 2020 election. Ultimately, this effort, which became the most expensive ballot measure in state history, was successful in getting voters the repeal the law. The labour movement, which opposed this initiative, argued that the companies' campaign was misleading, citing a study that found that 40 per cent of voters who voted in favour of the company proposition thought they were voting to support a living wage for gig-workers (Siddiqui and Tiku 2020). Seemingly confirming the fears of Prop 22's opponents, the supermarket giant Albertson announced in early 2021 that they would eliminate hundreds of their in-house union food-delivery workers and replace them with gig workers, who would be considered independent contractors (Hiltzik 2021). Other states are currently considering laws similar to AB 5 or Prop 22 in the coming year, assuring this debate will not be settled soon.

In Canada, the courts have similarly run into issues of how to address contractor status in light of Uber's arbitration agreement. In an early 2019 ruling on the largest gig-economy employment status case in Canada, the Ontario Court of Appeals invalidated a lower court decision in *Heller v. Uber Technologies Inc.* (2019). The court ruled that Uber's arbitration clause is unenforceable because it illegally sets aside provisions of the 2000 Ontario Employment Standards Act. If the court had upheld the lower court's 2018 ruling, it would have meant employees in Canada had to take their claims to arbitration in Amsterdam before the International Chamber of Commerce. Since the court ruled that Uber's arbitration agreement violated labour law, but Heller had not alleged violations of this labour law, this ruling does not ultimately determine drivers' employment status under Ontario law. Instead the ruling establishes only the illegality of Uber's arbitration agreement (McKenzie 2019). While the ruling does not ultimately determine the employment status of gig employees, in certainly opens the door to future litigation and sets a favourable precedent for gig workers in the province. In January 2020, the United Food and Commercial Workers Canada (UFCW Canada) filled complaint in both Vancouver and Toronto with the respective Labour Boards requesting Uber drivers be classified as employees. The Toronto petition also included an application for unionization (UFCW Canada 2020; Eagland 2020). Likely helping this case was a ruling in February 2020 from the Ontario Labour Relations Board that ruled that Foodora food-delivery workers were "dependent contractors" and therefore entitled to union rights. Foodora workers had formed Foodsters United and were organizing with the Canadian Union of Postal Workers in the Toronto area (Darrah 2020). Months after the ruling, the company filed for bankruptcy and left Canada. The relative success of workers' legal claims in Canada compared to the United States suggests Canada is unlikely to follow the Prop 22 route.

Gig workers' claims to employment status and employment protections made serious legal inroads in the United Kingdom. In 2018, a UK court ruled that a gig worker was not an "employee" but rather fell into a middle ground status of "worker" under the law in the *Pimlico Plumbers Ltd and Another v. Smith* (2018) decision. In this case a Kent plumber argued he was entitled to employment protections such as holiday pay and disability accommodations for which he was denied. He had attempted to work less in order to recover from a heart attack he had suffered. Similarly, in December 2018 a majority of the UK Court of Appeal ruled in *Uber BV v. Aslam* that Uber should treat its drivers as workers, not independent contractors. Uber was granted permission to lodge an appeal with the Supreme Court. The case was brought by the Independent Workers Union of Great Britain on behalf of drivers Farrar and Aslam, who were founders of the union. At the time of writing, the Supreme Court had heard the case in the summer of 2020 but had yet to issue a ruling. While the employment status of gig workers in the United Kingdom is far from settled, these cases set an early indication that the courts are inclined to extend employment protections to gig-workers.

While cases determining the employment status of workers continue to weave their way through the courts some, legal scholars and legislators have instead advocated for a middle ground. In Europe, Todolí Signes (2017) argues the online platform "profession" is fundamentally different enough to require a "special labour law" that would provide a middle path between employee and independent contractor. Similarly, in the United States, Harris and Kreuger (2015) claim gig workers also need a hybrid status, called "independent workers," which would provide them some employment protections such as collective bargaining rights but not the minimum wage, given the contract nature of the work. Advocates of these approaches are attempting to find a middle ground that acknowledges the temporary nature of the work without eliminating gig workers from the social contract.

This legal middle ground already exists in some parts of the world. In Canada, certain jurisdictions already have the status of "dependent contractor," which could, in theory, provide alternative protections such as collective bargaining. No court has ruled gig workers are covered by these statutes. There has been a push in the United Kingdom to create a "dependent contractor" status following the recommendations made by the Taylor Review convened by the government to evaluate gig work. Many have argued the UK Supreme Court's *Pimlico* ruling was influenced by the findings of the Taylor Review. A potential problem with this middle ground approach is that it still provides incentives to corporations to design work so that all work is middle-ground work and therefore would still undermine traditional employment protections.

Beyond the misclassification issue, Uber and other gig companies have faced lawsuits for violating union rights, operating illegal equipment leasing programs, underpaying, and violating gender and racial discrimination laws. In a recent example, Italian courts ruled that the very design of Deliveroo's algorithms was "discriminatory" and violated labour rights (Lomas 2021). All of these issues stem from a business model based on an extremely fissured workplace. While firms and investors on Wall Street prefer this employment model, it will be up to governments, regulators, and society if they will allow it to continue. If gig companies are permitted to shed all responsibility for employment, this trend will reverberate throughout the traditional economy as well. Employment fissuring is not unique to the gig economy.

IMPLICATIONS FOR THE NATURE OF WORK

Beyond the impact of the legal and economic issues of the gig economy upon workers, gig companies also threaten traditional companies in the industries they are moving into. For example, transportation systems in New York City, and the taxi industry specifically, have been greatly harmed by the growing presence of Uber cars on the road, as evidenced by suicides among taxi drivers who found their earnings diminished by the surge of Ubers in the market (Fitzsimmons 2018). The massive influx of Uber drivers in urban markets created what Marx called a reserve army of labour ([1867] 1906). Hall and Kreuger's (2017) evaluation of Uber's data found that 11 per cent of drivers drop

out after the first month, half by the first year, and two-thirds after
two years. As Rosenblat (2018) noted, this likely happens because Uber
depends on a constant churn of hobbyist, part-time, and temporary
workers who drive down the standards of full-timers and traditional
cab drivers.

Gig companies have also radically changed the nature of work by
eliminating interpersonal contact between employee and employer.
This is particularly noticeable in gig companies' use of algorithms that
replace traditional managerial roles. As Weil argues, technological
innovations allow this fissuring. In the case of gig companies, advances
in smartphone and GPS technologies have allowed them to take fissuring to an extreme and outsource all employment to each individual
worker. Having no employees gives way to a series of problems for
gig companies: they must provide customers with a uniform product
in an appropriate quantity. To maintain their legal claims that drivers
are independent contractors rather than employees, gig companies
cannot directly dictate when, where, or how workers work. Instead,
they must send indirect cues through algorithmic management (Lee
et al. 2015; Rosenblat and Stark 2016). Far from being truly independent, gig workers find their actions monitored through their cell phones.
Uber tracks how fast drivers drive, how hard they brake, and whether
or not they are taking the most efficient route. While they do not tell
drivers to follow explicit protocols, workers are given metrics they
must meet in order to continue to work for the company. Further, Uber
relies on psychological manipulation to maintain supply and compliance (Scheiber 2017). Uber's access to vast amounts of data, such as
workers' log-off times, enables them to send push notifications with
enticing psychological signals about surging demand that encourage
drivers to keep working.

Uber is particularly adept at employing algorithmic management
to direct its workers. For Uber drivers, the app works much like a slot
machine. While it does vary with geography and time, for the most
part, gig acceptance on the Uber app is blind, meaning drivers are told
only that a ride is available for them to claim. They are given no information about the length of the ride, where the ride will take them, or
how much they will make. Drivers have only fifteen seconds to take
the ride with hopes it will be profitable (Rosenblat 2018). Furthermore,
Uber employs dynamic pricing, which depends on market conditions.
Therefore, pay for the same route or ride can vary greatly, depending
on the pricing algorithm. In this way, like playing a slot machine,

sometimes drivers hit the jackpot, but more often they make minimum. It is a classic example of "gamification" of work (Walz and Deterding 2015), but the game is more like gambling and less like Tetris. Uber combines dynamic pricing and blind acceptance with strict requirements on the number of rides drivers can cancel (5 per cent) and the number they must accept (80–90 per cent, depending on the market) to continue to use the app (Rosenblat 2018). Additionally, gamification principles, such as weekly metric-based incentive bonus and surge pricing, keep drivers constantly hunting or "playing" for the highest-paying rides.

Beyond algorithmic management, gig companies also attempt to obscure their control over their workers by suggesting that they are providing a path to independent entrepreneurship. They employ popular rhetorical notions such as tech futurism, freedom, and entrepreneurship to claim their workers are not coerced (Griffith 2015; Irani 2015). The use of algorithms, given their inherent uncertainty and authority, helps gig companies project an air of neutrality over the systems, despite the fact that algorithms and the rules are ultimately written by management (Gillespie 2014). In fact, the algorithms provide a constricted "choice architecture" (Sunstein 2014), which guides workers to make the "choice" the company would have asked them to make if employing direct management. Similarly, gig companies' use of in-app ratings systems further outsources management to passengers. Uber drivers can be kicked off the app if they do not maintain a certain rating. Since passengers determine this rating, drivers must modify their behaviour to provide a standardized service (Bruder 2015). The company sends drivers algorithmically generated performance summaries and suggestions about how to standardize their behaviour to equal the performance of higher-rated drivers. This rating system amplifies the amount of "emotional labour" (Hochschild 1983) drivers must perform, in which they suppress their emotions to placate customers' demands, to a greater degree than in traditional service occupations.

The gig economy has implications for worker power, which typically takes two forms: structural and associational (Wright 2000). This power is not exogenously given but interacts with how employers structure work and employment tasks – what sociologists call the structure of the labour process. Employers can attempt to manipulate workers' structural power by making their task less integral to the success of the firm. Historically, this has been accomplished through capital investment but, as the gig employers highlight, this can be accomplished through regulatory and legal apparatuses as well. Employers can also attempt to manipulate workers' associational power through either atomization or consent (Burawoy 1979). Gig employers rely heavily on both forms of consent by situating each employee as an independent entrepreneurial contractor and by manipulating this atomization through ideological appeals to it.

For Marx ([1894] 1993) the labour process in capitalist production was characterized by the use of coercion to secure surplus value (or uncompensated work time) from the capitalist's employees. Burawoy (1979) turned the labour process argument on its head, noting that workers often seem more than happy to participate in their own exploitation. For Burawoy, the labour process is defined by both coercion and consent. When asked where their employer's profit comes from, most workers in his study failed to identify their own labour power as the source and instead claimed, "Profit is some form of earned reward for past sacrifices or for the risk of capital investment. Others argued that profit is generated in the market" (1979, 29). For Burawoy, a worker's surplus value is not just secured but is also obscured. He notes workers often participate in their own exploitation by turning work into a game to reduce the monotony of their industrial tasks, pushing themselves to work harder and provide their employer with more surplus value.

It appears that gig companies utilize new technologies in an attempt to construct the labour process through consent alone. For Marx, coercion was constructed on the shop floor and resulted in the formation of class consciousness. In the gig economy there is no employer and employee interaction at all, a source of constant frustration for gig workers facing payment problems. Coercion is informal, purely algorithmic, and psychological. Gig companies are in fact legally prevented from making demands like a standard employer if they want to maintain the illusion that they are purely technology companies (Rosenblat and Stark 2016; Dubal et al. 2018). Coercion is further outsourced to customers, who maintain the company's brand and quality by rating drivers. In constructing consent, employers offer ideological appeals to workers, suggesting that they are not workers but in fact mini-capitalists. Additionally, almost as if they read Burawoy as an employment guide, employers often design the app like a game, employing the principles of a slot machine to hook workers into working longer and harder (Rosenblat and Stark 2016). In the gig economy, capitalists erase the worker and extract surplus value by recasting profit as a service fee for the use of the app.

It is easy to find evidence that the ideological appeals of these companies is being internalized by workers and thereby securing their consent. For example, Hall and Kreuger (2017) found Uber drivers had deeply bought into the entrepreneurship narrative: 87 per cent of drivers surveyed cited joining Uber "to be my own boss and set my own schedule." The gamification design of the Uber app further shows how these apps gain workers' consent to work harder for these companies. Malin and Chandler (2016) interviewed one driver, Cheryl, who said, "I would kind of play this game with myself, where once I took a passenger and dropped him off I would just keep my app on and kind of head back home. And then if I got something, or if it looked like there was a surge somewhere I'd head over there, but mostly I would just kind of make my way around and if I had stuff to do then I had stuff to do, if I came home, then I came home." When Cheryl was ready to head home and end her shift she could not help playing the "game" of continuing to work. The addictive nature of working for Uber made Cheryl fully complicit in her own exploitation without ever actually interacting with a boss or human representative from her employer.

GOVERNMENT RESPONSE TO GIG EMPLOYMENT

Debate on the impact of the gig economy is often focused on the gig companies and gig workers. Gig companies "disrupt" not only those who use the app but also the economic sectors and the regulatory regimes in which they operate (Dubal et al. 2018). Their actions have spillover effects in the economy, as other sectors attempt to copy their employee-free business model. Furthermore, the companies are attempting to rewrite employment laws around the world. The National Employment Law Project estimates Uber spent $1.4–2.3 million a year, and Lyft spent $336,000–886,000 a year on lobbying in just five states between 2016 and June 2017, and employed 370 lobbyists – more than twice as many as Microsoft and Walmart and over three times as many as Amazon (Borkholder et al. 2018). Gig companies such as Uber use their structural power as large companies in combination with insider and outsider strategies to utilize their instrumental power (Dubal et al. 2018). They have even attempted to neutralize the opponents of labour through partnerships with activist allies such as

Mothers against Drunk Driving and the NAACP. Gig companies have used the app itself to mobilize drivers and consumers to engage in "clicktivism" on their behalf. In New York, when users logged on to the Uber app, they were prompted to click and express their displeasure with the mayor for attempting to cap Uber's growth in the city. Uber also used computer programs to manipulate a New York City survey by creating a program to fill in results for drivers in a manner favourable to the company (Isaac 2017). Despite these efforts, the practices of gig companies continue to raise employment, consumer, and public concerns, which governments have increasingly felt compelled to address.

When giving thought to the political economy of a city in relation to gig companies, especially in the transportation sector, it is important to consider the function of gig companies. Malin and Chandler (2016) describe Uber drivers as experiencing splintering precarity, because the benefits and costs of the gig economies' technological innovation depend on legacies of economic and racial inequality. The impact of the gig economy on different groups depends on their status and their exposure to insecurity and instability. As discussed above, those who stand to benefit from the gig economy have greater resources and greater social capital, and are from dominant social, racial, and gender groups. The gig economy provides differential access to the benefits of the gig economy. Malin and Chandler developed this idea from Graham and Marvin's (2001) notion of splintered urbanism, which noted that the privatization of telecommunications, transportation, and other city services splinter cities along economic, political, and racial lines, generating imbalances in how different groups interact with the urban infrastructure. As such, I argue that we should view the rise of Uber, or care companies such as Care.com or Handy, as a result of government failure to provide public social protection and as a privatization of public services. Uber was born, after all, in San Francisco, a city notorious for poor public transit breadth and a weak taxi infrastructure. In New York City, Uber billed itself to the public as a necessity given the city's failure to invest in its crumbling subway system (Kim 2019).

While cities in North America have largely opted for privately operated taxi systems, they are ultimately public utilities and have historically been regulated as such (Dubal 2017; Mathew 2005). As a public utility, taxi service plays an important function in a city's transportation infrastructure, particularly for those in distant corners of the city, the elderly, and the disabled. Traditionally, in the United States, cities have regulated taxi cabs (Dempsey 1996). The primary concern and justification of city regulation has been safety (both for consumers and drivers), consumer and driver protection, fair industry competition, labour protections for drivers, and public good issues such as congestion and pollution. Over time the regulation and permitting of taxis became a significant source of income for cities. The advent of transportation gig companies, commonly called transportation network companies (TNCs), eliminated some traditional justification for regulation by solving some problems with technology, such as minimizing safety concerns by implementing the rating system and eliminating cash transactions (Lobel 2016). Additionally, most cab companies have been regional TNCs that benefit from the network effect of operating in many cities (Rogers 2015). These technologically driven innovations have generated substantial confusion for regulators and weakened companies' position in maintaining their advantage.

Evaluating the entry of TNCs into major American cities illustrates their impact on regulatory regimes. The TNCs, embracing the Silicon Valley ethos of disruption, entered the taxi cab industry illegally, operating without licences and often in defiance of city regulators. Uber and Lyft covered all costs and expenses associated with fines that drivers received while operating illegally. They hoped, and have been largely proven correct, that if they could survive long enough, consumers and drivers would begin to depend on them and help fight for their legalization. When US cities have attempted to regulate the TNCs, they have responded by attempting to go to state legislatures and have them pre-empt the city action. As Dubal et al. (2018) noted, there are numerous motivations for a city to regulate TNCs, from safety to congestion control to ensuring competition. They found cities have focused mostly on consumer protection and safety instead of tackling the more contentious labour issues. TNCs have largely accepted these laws, as they increase consumer confidence at little cost.

Further complicating matters, taxi regulations in the United States have varied wildly. Broadly, Tzur (2017) argues for categorizing the pre-TNC regulatory environments into three categories: licence cities, restricted cities, and medallion cities. Licence cities simply required that taxi companies obtain a business licence. Restricted cities limited the number of licences issued in the city. Medallion cities also limited the number of licences available, but allowed licence holders to sell this licence on a secondary market. Tzur (2017) evaluated how

Table 3.4
US municipal response to entry of transportation network companies

City	State	Population (Metropolitan Statistical Area)	Pre-Uber environment	Regulatory response	State TNC law	State marketplace platform law	State pre-emption	State regulatory response	State law restricts employment status
New York	NY	8,622,698	Medallion	Strong	Yes	No	Partial (allows bans in cities of 100K and excludes NYC)	Legalized statewide, local regulation	No
Los Angeles	CA	3,999,759	Medallion	Weak	Yes	No	Yes	Regulated	No
Chicago	IL	2,716,450	Medallion	Strong	Yes	No	Yes	Legalized statewide, regulated	Yes
Houston	TX	2,312,717	Restricted	Strong	Yes	No	Yes and overturned	Regulated	Yes
Philadelphia	PA	1,580,863	Medallion	Strong	Yes	No	Partial (excludes Philadelphia)	Legalized statewide, regulated	No
San Antonio	TX	1,511,946	Restricted	Strong	Yes	No	Yes and overturned	Regulated	Yes
San Diego	CA	1,419,516	Restricted	Weak	Yes	No	Yes	Regulated	No
Dallas	TX	1,341,075	Restricted	Medium	Yes	No	Yes and overturned	Regulated	Yes
San Jose	CA	1,035,317	Restricted	Weak	Yes	No	Yes	Regulated	No
Austin	TX	950,715	Restricted	Strong	Yes	No	Yes and overturned	Regulated	Yes
Jacksonville	FL	892,062	Medallion	Weak	Yes	Yes	Yes and overturned	Regulated	Yes
San Francisco	CA	884,363	Medallion	Medium	Yes	No	Yes	Regulated	No
Columbus	OH	879,170	Restricted	Strong	Yes	No	Yes	Legalized statewide, regulated	Yes

City	State	Population							
Fort Worth	TX	874,168	Permit	Weak	Yes	No	Yes and overturned	Regulated	Yes
Indianapolis	IN	863,002	Permit	Weak	Yes	Yes	Yes	Legalized statewide, regulated	Yes
Charlotte	NC	859,035	Permit	Weak	Yes	No	Yes	Regulated	Yes
Seattle	WA	724,745	Restricted	Strong	No	No	No	Insurance only	No
Denver	CO	704,621	Restricted	Weak	Yes	No	Yes	Legalized statewide, regulated	Yes
Washington DC	DC	693,972	Permit	Weak	NA	NA	NA	NA	NA
Boston	MA	685,094	Medallion	Strong	Yes	No	Yes	Legalized statewide, regulated	No
El Paso	TX	683,577	Restricted	Weak	Yes	No	Yes and overturned	Regulated	Yes
Detroit	MI	673,104	Permit	Weak	Yes	No	Yes	Regulated	Yes
Nashville	TN	667,560	Restricted	Medium	Yes	Yes	Yes (excludes airports)	Legalized statewide, regulated	Yes
Memphis	TN	652,236	Restricted	Weak	Yes	Yes	Yes (excludes airports)	Legalized statewide, regulated	Yes
Portland	OR	647,805	Restricted	Strong	No	No	No	None	No

Sources: Tzur (2017), Racabi (2018), Moran (2017), NELP (2018), and US Census (2017).

forty US cities responded to TNCs illegally entering the market. Thirty-one formally legalized them, six informally let them exist through failure to enforce, and only three issued cease-and-desist orders. It was in medallion cities with concentrated taxi-business interests that TNCs were most thoroughly regulated

Building on Tzur's research, I looked at how all US cities with over 200,000 residents responded to the introduction of TNCs. Of the initial sample of 118 cities spanning thirty-seven states, only eighty of these cities had an opportunity to regulate TNCs, meaning TNCs entered their markets before states had pre-empted local authority to regulate TNCs (Wolf 2021, under review). Table 3.4 presents the findings for the twenty-five largest cities. I present data on how cities responded to the advent of TNCs as well as how the states in which these cities are embedded have responded to TNCs and marketplace platform companies such as Handy and Care.com. This allows us to evaluate municipal response and the issues of state pre-emption and how states chose to address the employment status of gig workers. The state response data were compiled largely from Racabi (2018) and Moran (2017).

Only three of the largest cities in the United States are in states that have taken no action to regulate TNCs. Nearly all states pre-empt local ordinances, although there are sometimes legal carve-outs for individual cities. For example, New York's law excluded the state's largest cities from coverage. State laws give cities leeway in enacting some regulations, especially consumer protection regulations. In Texas and Florida, liberal cities have attempted to regulate TNCs, only to have their regulations overturned by their conservative state governments. In all other cases, states passed a law pre-empting a city's ability to pass local laws before any city in the state had enacted municipal regulations of TNCs. Only seven states have passed marketplace platform laws, which have been written by the industry and a conservative legal think tank, the American Legislative Exchange Council. Handy, the home-cleaning gig company, has been particularly involved in such efforts to set their own terms and ensure their employees are considered independent contractors according to state law. In four states, laws were proposed to regulate marketplace platforms in a way that would define employees as independent contractors, but these laws were not passed, in large part because of the efforts of the National Domestic Workers United (NDWU). NDWU is the largest union in the United States that represents domestic workers and is organizing gig workers in domestic service industries. Most, but not all, state TNC laws restrict employment status, ensuring that TNC drivers are considered independent contractors, not employees. Cross tabulations of regulatory response are provided in figure 3.3. Cities with a traditionally more regulated taxi industry were more likely to respond strongly to the advent of TNCs than historically licensed-based cities. The largest cities, which also tended to have the most entrenched interests, were also highly likely to respond with strong regulatory action. Surprisingly, the smallest of these metro areas were also likely to respond with strong regulatory action. Some of cities in the smaller two size groups did still take strong regulatory response. These cities were often liberal bubbles in conservative southern or rural states. The smallest size group present here, which tended to be southern cities or cities in tech-friendly California, were more likely to take weak actions or no action in response to TNCs. Overall, of the twenty-five largest cities in the United States, about half took weak or no action in response to the entry of TNCs to their cities.

In the United States, cities tend to be more liberal than their surrounding rural area. In the case of the gig economy these same cities have largely accepted these companies' demands with barely any contention. It is unclear if US cities will continue this approach to the gig economy. Notably, some cities and states that originally made no attempt to regulate Uber, such as New York City, Seattle, and California, have since mounted stronger regulatory responses. Seattle, in response to the Teamsters Local 117's organizing of Uber drivers, passed an innovative collective bargaining law for TNC drivers, but it was ultimately held up in court. In August 2018, New York City, under pressure from the New York Taxi Workers Alliance, and in light of a rash of driver suicides, passed sweeping TNC regulation that capped the number of TNC drivers who could be on the road, similar to traditional medallion regulations, and forced TNC companies to ensure their drivers are paid a living wage after expenses. These laws were made permanent in 2019, and NYC added "cruising limits" on TNCs requiring that by August 2020 drivers can be on the app driving or cruising with no passenger only 31 per cent of the time. This rule was implemented after the city determined TNCs now represented 30 per cent of traffic during rush hour, creating a lot of congestion (NYC TLC & DOL 2019). In a radical reversal of direction following two large driver strikes in Los Angeles and the California Supreme Court's

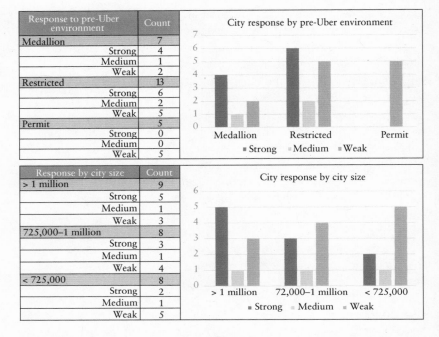

Response to pre-Uber environment		Count
Medallion		7
	Strong	4
	Medium	1
	Weak	2
Restricted		13
	Strong	6
	Medium	2
	Weak	5
Permit		5
	Strong	0
	Medium	0
	Weak	5

Response by city size		Count
> 1 million		9
	Strong	5
	Medium	1
	Weak	3
725,000–1 million		8
	Strong	3
	Medium	1
	Weak	4
< 725,000		8
	Strong	2
	Medium	1
	Weak	5

Figure 3.3 Municipal response to transportation network companies by regulatory environment and city population.

landmark *Dynamex* ruling (discussed above), the state has now codi-fied the ruling in state law and applied it to all gig-economy workers (Said 2019). It remains to be seen if this trend towards regulation will continue or if TNCs will be successful in using state pre-emption to prevent municipal action.

In Canada, Uber has operated far less aggressively than in the United States. Nonetheless TNCs still entered numerous markets illegally. While Uber drivers in Canada had their legal expenses, such as tickets and fines, covered by the company, they also found themselves facing direct pressure from traditional cab drivers while on the road, par-ticularly in Montreal (Rosenblat 2018). Unlike in the United States, Uber attempted to strike agreements with some municipal and prov-incial governments in Canada. Uber reached an agreement with the province of Quebec on 9 September 2016 legalizing Uber operations in the entire province. The agreement covered public safety, public good, and employment issues. It legalized Uber but forced the company to comply with traditional cab rules, requiring drivers to obtain a cab licence and follow the province's minimum tariff structure. Importantly, the agreement with Quebec included provisions that Uber had fought vigorously in the United States. In Toronto, the city and Uber had been engaged in legal battles until the city council voted on 4 May 2016 to legalize Uber in exchange for Uber following the minimum base fare consistent with what was already enforced on taxis. To ensure fair competition, Toronto also allowed traditional taxis to start implementing surge pricing.

In a particularly open embrace of Uber, the Town of Innisfil, Ontario, outsourced part of its public transit system to Uber under the expectation that it would save the town $8 million a year (Canadian Press 2018). Residents attempting to book trips to "key destinations" within the town are guaranteed a flat fee of three to five dollars. Despite initial enthusiasm, the privatization scheme has run into ballooning costs, forcing the city and Uber to impose monthly ride caps. As one resident lamented, "I would never get on a bus in Toronto and hear the driver say, 'Sorry, but you've hit your cap.' Uber was supposed to be our bus" (Bliss 2019). Uber is now legal in many of the largest municipalities in Ontario, Alberta, and Manitoba. British Columbia was the lone TNC holdout for years faced with taxi industry and labour backlash, but finally TNCs became legal in January 2020. Vancouver had been the largest North American city to not legalize TNCs.

WORKER RESPONSE TO THE GIG ECONOMY

Gig workers are not uniform, and workers' experience with the gig economy tends to be mediated by their economic opportunities and life situation. While it works for some, the costs of the gig economy are concentrated on individuals who are most dependent on these industries, and they have not always endured their plight quietly. Gig workers are a relatively tech-savvy group who often turned to online driver forums on sites such as Reddit and Facebook to find collective solutions and emotional support for the workplace issues they face (Rosenblat 2018; Kessler 2018). These forums have even been used to coordinate protests and circulate petitions, often having an impact on company policies. While these sites have produced some collective responses, they have tended to be small and temporary, as workers have largely failed to move the organizing beyond the online platforms. Although the union in Los Angeles has found innovative ways to use these online platforms (Dolber 2019). Still, workers' geographic isolation from each other has made collective responses to their problems challenging.

While their isolation makes organizing difficult, it does not make it impossible, and there have been some notable attempts. In Seattle, TNC drivers have been organizing a union with the Teamsters Local 117. The drivers are demanding a say in the companies' rates, as well as medical coverage and retirement benefits. The union pushed city council to pass legislation giving them a right to unionize, the first such law in the country. Also in Seattle, the worker centre Working Washington has been organizing food delivery and grocery-shopper workers at Instacart, Uber Eats, and DoorDash, where they have won changes to company policies and are pursuing legal reforms in the state and city. The workers centre Working Partnership USA has also begun organizing gig workers in Silicon Valley under the name Gig Workers Rising, inspired by the unionization of cafeteria workers, security guards, and bus drivers at leading Valley firms such as Google and Apple by UNITE HERE, the Service Employees International Union (SEIU), and the Teamsters. Workers centres such as Working Partnership USA and Working Washington are different from traditional unions in that they do not have official legal recognition to represent the workers they fight for. Instead workers voluntarily join these organizations to push for improvements at work without seeking formal recognition. They are particularly prominent in the United States in industries that are hard to organize, such as immigrant-dominated industries with large numbers of undocumented workers (Fine 2006). Deliveroo and Uber Eats couriers as well as Uber drivers have long been organizing and protesting for higher pay and benefits in the United Kingdom under two branches of the Independent Workers of Great Britain. In the United States the National Domestic Workers United has been organizing domestic workers working for marketplace and hybrid apps, such as Care.com and Handy. These efforts helped prevent five states from passing Handy's marketplace platform bill in 2018. These laws would have defined all workers working on apps in the marketplace platform sector of the gig economy as independent contractors, ensuring fundamental benefits would be denied to home-care workers, including cleaners and elder-care workers. In Canada, food-delivery workers for Foodora in the Greater Toronto Area organized the union Foodsters United. Following their legal victory with the OLRB, which ruled the drivers were "dependent workers," the delivery people voted overwhelmingly (88.8 per cent) in favour of the union. This was the first victory of its kind in Canada. Unfortunately, it was a pyrrhic victory, as the vote came months after Foodora had filed for bankruptcy and left Canada. Foodsters United continues to organize delivery workers in the Greater Toronto Area and is looking to form a worker-owned cooperative (Darrah 2020). Uber drivers in Canada have been organizing with the UFCW Canada, and in Toronto the union has filed an application to represent 300 drivers with the Ontario Labour Board (UFCW Canada 2020). The Independent Workers' Union of Great Britain recently organized the first international conference of app-worker unions, forming the International Alliance of App-Based Transport Workers. This new international federation includes drivers from all over the world and aims to coordinate their campaigns against Uber and other app companies (Varghese 2020). The meeting generated core principles, strategies, and a network for future organizing.

Some labour groups have attempted to partner with gig companies to improve conditions, a move often criticized by others in the labour movement as aiding corporate white-washing efforts. Uber hired the Freelancers Union in 2016 to create a portable benefits plan. Portable benefits plans have been explored in US cities as a method to provide benefits that are traditionally tied to employment in the United States – such as health care and pensions – to workers who tend to face short-term employment. Similarly, Uber has attempted to partner with SEIU, which was already working to design a portable benefit program. A strategy increasingly employed by gig companies is to dress up their independent contractor legislation with popular progressive initiatives to garner votes. For example, the marketplace platform laws pushed by Handy in more progressive states included provisions to begin establishing portable benefits for workers (NELP 2018). Ironically, defining the workers as independent contractors, the bills preclude them from receiving traditional benefits such as social security and unemployment insurance. In New York City, in response to the organizing efforts of the New York Taxi Workers Alliance (NYTWA), Uber reached an agreement with a Machinists Union Local to form the Independent Driver Guild (IDG). The contents of this agreement remain undisclosed but are believed to prevent striking or unionization in exchange for Uber providing the IDG with funding. The IDG's purpose is instead to meet with workers and report problems to the company. The NYTWA maintains that the IDG is an illegal company union prohibited under the National Labor Relations Act, while the IDG maintains it provides a valuable service.

One of the more robust organizing efforts of gig workers has been undertaken by the NYTWA in New York City. An American Federation of Labor and Congress of Industrial Organizations affiliate, it represents 19,000 drivers, half of whom are TNC drivers. The NYTWA is unique because it represents workers who technically do not have collective bargaining rights under the law, unlike most unions in the United States, which operate under a principle of exclusive representation established through elections requiring a showing of majority representation. The NYTWA operates more like unions do in European countries such as France, without the principle of exclusive representation and engaging in tripartite bargaining with the city and the companies. Any driver can become a NYTWA member simply by signing up. The NYTWA is in this sense more like the non-profit worker centres, which have proliferated in marginalized and informal immigrant industries in the United States, where the possibility of unionization is unlikely. Yet NYTWA is adamant it is a union, even if the law will not formally recognize it as such. Since its founding in the late 1990s, the NYTWA has utilized its unique minority unionism approach to become the dominant voice for drivers in the city, launching two successful strikes, which helped establish de facto bargaining through the city's Taxi and Limousine Commission (TLC) (Mathew 2005). By opening its doors to TNC drivers, instead of maintaining its base in traditional yellow cabs, the NYTWA not only survived the threat of the TNCs, in August 2018 it forced the city to make it subject to the same rules, caps, and wage rates as the TLC requires of other taxi companies. The NYTWA has forced the city to take responsibility for the taxi and TNC industry, and recognizes it as an important component of the city's overall transportation system.

Building on the success of the NYTWA, gig drivers across the United States have begun organizing in other cities as well. A new union based in Los Angeles and inspired by the NYTWA, Rideshare Drivers United (RDU), has grown to represent 4,300 drivers in the last few years. RDU built the union off an innovative "online to off-line" model in which the union recruited drivers in the sprawling city of Los Angeles primarily through online forums and online ads. Importantly, it worked to translate online contacts into off-line traditional labour organizing (Dolber 2019). Rideshare Drivers United has held two high-profile strikes against Lyft and Uber in advance of each company's initial public offering on the New York Stock Exchange. Its second strike ahead of Uber's stock listing turned into a worldwide event (Wolf 2019). The union contends the two strikes have been instrumental in spurring the state legislature to reverse course and begin moving on a bill to define gig-workers as employees and not independent contractors under state law. While the most prominent worker organizing has happened in New York City, Los Angeles, San Francisco, London, and Seattle, there have been worker protests against gig-taxi companies in a majority of major US Cities (Wolf 2021). The workers' victories and government response in New York City and Los Angeles show the way forward in addressing the challenges of gig work.

CONCLUSION

Paradoxically, the rise of gig employment in major Western cities is simultaneously nothing new and a radical change. As another form of informal, casual, and precarious work, gig employment is a continuation of a decades-long trends in the United States and Canada since the 1970s. Yet technological innovations have allowed these companies to upend the labour process and provided an ideological justification to refuse to adhere to urban regulatory regimes. This chapter argues that cities should be particularly attuned to these two innovations. Beyond the legal debate over employment status, cities must decide how they fit technologically mediated work into the regulatory aims of public safety, consumer protection, economic inequality, and global climate change, amongst others. Employment fissuring is not caused solely by companies that enact it but also by governments that allow it to happen. Cities cannot buy into the myth that algorithms and technology are inherently neutral constructs providing purely altruistic benefits for society. Technology, algorithms, and the gig economy are very much a human and social creation of profit-driven corporations, which are foremost beholden to Wall Street investors and not the urban communities they operate in. Allowing them to operate as they wish – carte blanche – represents a particularly pernicious form of splintered urbanism. Unlike previous urban privatization schemes, the current trend of gig privatization of cities makes it difficult for us even to realize that we are also privatizing our social services.

REFERENCES

Aloisi, A. 2016. "Commoditized Workers: Case Study Research on Labor
Law Issues Arising from a Set of 'On-Demand/Gig Economy Platforms.'"
Comparative Labor Law & Policy Journal 37, no. 3: 620–53.
Bajwa, U., L. Knorr, and E. Di Ruggiero. 2018. Towards an Understanding
of Workers' Experiences in the Global Gig Economy. Toronto:
University of Toronto. https://www.glomhi.org/uploads/7/4/4/8/
74483301/workers_in_the_global_gig_economy.pdf.
Bliss, L. 2019. "'Uber Was Supposed to Be Our Public Transit.'" CityLab,
29 April. https://www.bloomberg.com/news/articles/2019-04-29/
when-a-town-takes-uber-instead-of-public-transit.
Block, S., and T. Hennessy. 2017. "'Sharing Economy' or On Demand
Service Economy in the Greater Toronto Area." Toronto: Canadian
Centre for Policy Alternatives Ontario Office.
BMO Wealth Management. 2018. *The Gig Economy: Achieving Financial
Wellness with Confidence*. Montreal: BMO Wealth Management.
Borkholder, J., M. Montgomery, M. Chen, and R. Smith. 2018. *Uber State
Interference: How Transportation Network Companies Buy, Bully,
and Bamboozle Their Way to Deregulation*. New York: National
Employment Law Project. https://s27147.pcdn.co/wp-content/uploads/
Uber-State-Interference-How-Transportation-Network-Companies-
Buy-Bully-Bamboozle-Their-Way-to-Deregulation.pdf.
Bruder, J. 2015. "These Workers Have a New Demand: Stop Watching Us."
Nation, 27 May. http://www.thenation.com/article/these-workers-have-
new-demand-stop-watching-us/.
Burawoy, M. 1982. *Manufacturing Consent: Changes in the Labor Process
under Monopoly Capitalism*. Chicago: University of Chicago Press.
Bureau of Labor Statistics (BLS), US Department of Labor. 2017. *Labor
Force Statistics from the Current Population Survey: Contingent Worker
Survey*. Washington, DC: Bureau of Labor Statistics.
Campbell, A.F. 2019. "Uber and Lyft Have Launched a Campaign
to Avoid Government Regulation in California." Vox, 29 October.
https://www.vox.com/identities/2019/10/29/20938109/ab5-uber-
lyft-ballot-initiative-referendum.
Canadian Press. 2018. "Uber Transit Partnership Saving Innisfil, Ont.,
$8M per Year," 15 March. https://globalnews.ca/news/4084807/
uber-innisfil-transit-savings/.
Cheng, M. 2020. "DoorDash Is Learning Just How Binding Arbitration Is."
Quartz at Work, 12 February. https://qz.com/work/1801652/doordash-
is-learning-just-how-binding-arbitration-is/.

Darrah, D. 2020. "How Foodsters United Is Organizing Canada's Gig Economy." *Jacobin*, 9 November. https://jacobinmag.com/2020/11/foodsters-united-canada-gig-economy-foodora.

Dempsey, P.S. 1996. "Taxi Industry Regulation, Deregulation & Reregulation: The Paradox of Market Failure." *Transportation Law Journal* 24, no. 1: 73–120.

De Stefano, V. 2016. "The Rise of the 'Just-in-Time Workforce': On Demand Work, Crowdwork, and Labor Protection in the 'Gig Economy.'" *Comparative Labor Law and Policy Journal* 37, no. 3: 461–71.

Doeringer, P.B., and M.J. Piore. 1971. *Internal Labor Markets and Manpower Analysis*. Lexington, MA: Heath.

Dolber, B. 2019. "From Independent Contractors to an Independent Union." Media Inequality Change Center, University of Pennsylvania's Annenberg School and Rutgers University's School of Communication and Information.

Dubal, V.B. 2017. "The Drive to Precarity: A Political History of Work, Regulation, & Labor Advocacy in San Francisco's Taxi & Uber Economies." *Berkeley Journal of Employment & Labor Law* 38, no. 1: 73–135.

Dubal, V.B., R.B. Collier, and C. Cater. 2018. "Disrupting Regulation, Regulating Disruption: The Politics of Uber in the United States." *Perspectives on Politics* 16, no. 4: 919–37.

Eagland, N. 2020. "Uber and Lyft Still Face Employment Rights Challenge in B.C." *Vancouver Sun*, 24 January. https://vancouversun.com/news/local-news/uber-and-lyft-still-face-employment-rights-challenge-in-b-c.

Farrell, D., F. Greig., and A. Hamoudi. 2018. "The Online Platform Economy in 2018." JPMorgan Chase & Company Institute. https://www.jpmorganchase.com/content/dam/jpmc/jpmorgan-chase-and-co/institute/pdf/institute-ope-2018.pdf.

Fine, J. 2006. *Worker Centers: Organizing Communities at the Edge of the Dream*. Ithaca, NY: Cornell University Press.

Fitzsimmons, E.G. 2018. "Why Are Taxi Drivers in New York Killing Themselves?" *New York Times*, 2 December. https://www.nytimes.com/2018/12/02/nyregion/taxi-drivers-suicide-nyc.html.

Flamm, M. 2019. "Uber Gives Up Fight over Unemployment Insurance Decision." Crain's New York Business, 4 May. https://www.crainsnewyork.com/transportation/uber-gives-fight-over-unemployment-insurance-decision.

Gillespie, T. 2014. "The Relevance of Algorithms." In *Media Technologies: Essays on Communication, Materiality, and Society*, edited by

T. Gillespie, P. Boczkowski, and K. Foot, 167–94. Cambridge, MA: MIT Press.

Graham, S., and S. Marvin. 2001. *Splintering Urbanism: Networked Infrastructures, Technological Motilities and the Urban Condition.* New York: Routledge.

Griffith, E. 2015. "The Problem with 'Uber for X.'" *Fortune*, 11 August. http://fortune.com/2015/08/11/uber-profitable-business-model/.

Hall, J.V., and A.B. Krueger. 2017. "An Analysis of the Labor Market for Uber's Driver-Partners in the United States." *ILR Review* 71, no. 3: 705–32.

Harris, S.D., and A.B. Krueger. 2015. "A Proposal for Modernizing Labor Laws for Twenty-First-Century Work: The 'Independent Worker.'" Hamilton Project Discussion Papers.

Heeks, R. 2017. "Decent Work and the Digital Gig Economy." Development Informatics, paper no. 71 http://hummedia.manchester.ac.uk/institutes/gdi/publications/workingpapers/di/di_wp71.pdf.

Hiltzik, M. 2021. "In Wake of Prop. 22, Albertsons Is Converting Its Home Delivery to Gig Work." *Los Angeles Times,* 5 January. https://www.latimes.com/business/story/2021-01-05/prop-22-albertsons-home-delivery.

Hochschild, A.R. 1983. *The Managed Heart: Commercialization of Human Feeling.* Los Angeles: University of California Press.

Irani, L. 2015. "Difference and Dependence among Digital Workers: The Case of Amazon Mechanical Turk." *South Atlantic Quarterly* 114, no. 1: 225–34. https://read.dukeupress.edu/south-atlantic-quarterly/article/114/1/225/3763/Difference-and-Dependence-among-Digital-Workers.

Isaac, M. 2017. "Uber's C.E.O. Plays with Fire." *New York Times,* 23 April. https://www.nytimes.com/2017/04/23/technology/travis-kalanick-pushes-uber-and-himself-to-the-precipice.html.

Katznelson, I. 2013. *Fear Itself: The New Deal and the Origins of Our Time.* New York: W. W. Norton.

Kessler, S. 2018. *Giggged: The End of the Job and the Future of Work.* New York: St. Martin's.

Kim, T.E. 2019. "How Uber Hopes to Profit from Public Transit." *New York Times,* 2 June. https://www.nytimes.com/2019/05/30/opinion/uber-stock.html.

Lee, M.K., D. Kusbit, and E. Metsky. 2015. "Working with Machines: The Impact of Algorithmic and Data-Driven Management on Human Workers." Proceedings of the ACM CHI'15 Conference on Human Factors in Computing Systems.

Lobel, O. 2016. "The Law of the Platform." *Minnesota Law Review* 101: 87–108.

Lomas, N. 2021. "Italian Court Rules against 'Discriminatory' Deliveroo Rider-Ranking Algorithm." *Tech Crunch*, 4 January. https://techcrunch. com/2021/01/04/italian-court-rules-against-discriminatory-deliveroo-rider-ranking-algorithm/.

Malin, B.J., and C. Chandler. 2016. "Free to Work Anxiously: Splintering Precarity among Drivers for Uber and Lyft." *Communication, Culture and Critique* 10: 382–400.

Manyika, J., S. Lund, J. Bughin, K. Robinson, J. Mischkey, and D. Mahajan. 2016. "Independent Work: Choice, Necessity, and the Gig Economy." McKinsey Global Institute, October. https://www.mckinsey.com/featured-insights/employment-and-growth/independent-work-choice-necessity-and-the-gig-economy.

Marx, K. (1867) 1906. *Capital: A Critique of Political Economy: The Process of Capitalist Production.* New York: Modern Library.

– (1894) 1993. *Capital: A Critique of Political Economy*, vol 3. London, UK: Penguin Classics.

Mathew, B. 2005. *Taxi!: Cabs and Capitalism in New York City.* Ithaca, NY: Cornell University Press.

McKenzie, B. 2019. "Ontario Court of Appeals Invalidates Arbitration Clause Requiring Arbitration in Foreign Jurisdiction." Lexology, 8 January. https://www.lexology.com/library/detail.aspx?g=f4390e6d-d5c1-4316-9e30-2791d00cd073.

Moran, M. 2017. "Motor Carrier Code Review: Considerations for the Legislation of Transportation Network Companies." Texas A&M Transportation Institute. https://policy.tti.tamu.edu/technology/motor-carrier-code-review-considerations-for-tnc-legislation/.

National Employment Law Project. 2018. "'Marketplace Platforms' and 'Employers' under State Law: Why We Should Reject Corporate Solutions and Support Worker-Led Innovation." NELP, Policy Brief. https://www.nelp.org/publication/marketplace-platforms-employers-state-law-reject-corporate-solutions-support-worker-led-innovation/.

NYC Taxi & Limousine Commission & Department of Transportation. 2019. "Improving Efficiency and Managing Growth in New York's for-Hire Vehicle Sector."

Papacharissi, Z., and E. Easton. 2013. "In the Habitus of the New." In *A Companion to New Media Dynamics*, edited by J. Hartley, A. Bruns, and J. Burgess, 167–84. West Sussex, UK: John Wiley & Sons.

PEPSO. 2013. "It's More Than Poverty: Employment Precarity and Household Well-being: Poverty and Employment Precarity in Southern Ontario." PEPSO, McMaster University, and United Way Toronto.

Perea, J.F. 2011. "The Echoes of Slavery: Recognizing the Racist Origins of the Agricultural and Domestic Workers Exclusion from the National Labor Relations Act." *Ohio State Law Journal* 72, no. 1: 95–138.

Racabi, G. 2018. "State TNC and MC Legislation: Preemption and Employment Status of Drivers." *On Labor*, 19 October. https://onlabor.org/state-tnc-and-mc-legislation-preemption-and-employment-status-of-drivers/.

Rogers, B. 2015. "The Social Costs of Uber." *University of Chicago Law Review Dialogue* 82, no. 1: 85–102.

Rosenblat, A. 2018. *Uberland: How Algorithms Are Rewriting the Rules of Work*. Berkeley: University of California Press.

Rosenblat, A., and L. Stark. 2016. "Algorithmic Labor and Information Asymmetries: A Case Study of Uber's Drivers." *International Journal of Communication* 10: 3,758–84.

Said, C. 2019. "California Assembly Passes Gig Work Bill, Limiting Contractor Status." *San Francisco Chronicle*, 29 May. https://www.sfchronicle.com/business/article/California-Assembly-passes-gig-work-bill-13904777.php.

Scheiber, N. 2017. "How Uber Uses Psychological Tricks to Push Its Drivers' Buttons." *New York Times*, 2 April. https://www.nytimes.com/interactive/2017/04/02/technology/uber-drivers-psychological-tricks.html.

Schor, J. 2020. *After the Gig: How the Sharing Economy Got Hijacked and How to Win It Back*. Oakland, CA: University of California Press.

Siddigui, F., and N. Tiku. 2020. "Uber and Lyft Used Sneaky Tactics to Avoid Making Drivers Employees in California, Voters Say. Now, They're Going National." *Washington Post,* 17 November. https://www.washingtonpost.com/technology/2020/11/17/uber-lyft-prop22-misinformation/.

Statistics Canada. 2017. "Use of Peer-to-Peer Ride Services Highest among Younger Canadians." Daily, 18 February. https://www150.statcan.gc.ca/n1/daily-quotidien/170228/dq170228b-eng.htm.

Sunstein, C.R. 2014. "Nudging: A Very Short Guide." *Journal of Consumer Policy* 37, no. 4: 583–8.

Ticona, J., A. Mateescu, and A. Rosenblat. 2018. *Beyond Disruption: How Tech Shapes Labor across Domestic Work & Ridehailing*. New York: Data & Society.

Todolí-Signes, A. 2017. "The 'Gig Economy': Employee, Self-Employed or the Need for a Special Employment Regulation?" *Transfer: European Review of Labour and Research* 23, no. 2: 193–205.

Tzur, A. 2017. "Uber Über Regulation? Regulatory Change Following the Emergence of New Technologies in the Taxi Market." *Regulation & Governance*, 21 September.

United Food & Commercial Workers Canada. 2020. "Toronto Uber Drivers First to Apply for Unionization in Canada." News release, 13 January. https://www.globenewswire.com/news-release/2020/01/13/1969307/0/en/Toronto-Uber-drivers-first-to-apply-for-unionization-in-Canada.html.

US Census Bureau. 2011. "Metropolitan and Micropolitan Statistical Area Population and Estimated Components of Change: April 1, 2010 to July 1, 2017." https://www.census.gov/data/tables/2017/demo/popest/total-metro-and-micro-statistical-areas.html.

Varghese, S. 2020. "Gig Economy Workers Have a New Weapon in the Fight against Uber." *Wired*, 17 February. https://www.wired.co.uk/article/gig-economy-uber-unions.

Walz, S. and S. Deterding. 2015. *The Gameful World: Approaches, Issues, Applications.* Cambridge, MA: MIT Press.

Weil, D. 2014. *The Gameful World: Approaches, Issues, Applications. The Fissured Workplace: Why Work Became So Bad for So Many and What Can Be Done to Improve It.* Cambridge, MA: Harvard University Press.

Williamson, O.E. 1981. "The Economics of Organization: The Transaction Cost Approach." *American Journal of Sociology* 87, no. 3: 548–77.

Wolf, A. 2019. "The City Is Ours, Not Uber's." *Jacobin Magazine*, 8 May. https://jacobinmag.com/2019/05/ubers-ipo-strike-lyft-cities-governance.

– 2021. Under review. "City Power in the Age of Silicon Valley: Evaluating Municipal Regulatory Response to the Entry of Uber to the American City."

Wright, E.O. 2000. "Working-Class Power, Capitalist-Class Interests, and Class Compromise." *American Journal of Sociology* 105, no. 4: 957–1,002.

4

Ride-Hailing Platforms Are Shaping the Future of Mobility, but for Whom?

Mischa Young and Steven Farber

- This chapter establishes who is likely to benefit from ride hailing and, more importantly, who is most at risk of being excluded from it.
- We consider seven potentially neglected population segments and postulate the potential benefits and barriers of ride-hailing services for them.
- These equity concerns shape our discussion and inform our recommendations for an agenda to research equity concerns about ride hailing.

INTRODUCTION

That ride-hailing (RH) companies have disrupted the transportation sector is an understatement. The ability and vision of companies such as Uber and Lyft to harness smartphones' GPS technologies, provide real-time information about wait times, and facilitate cashless transactions has enabled them to effectively compete with the taxi industry and potentially capture a sizeable share of the ridership of other modes as well. RH companies have also enabled drivers to use their own vehicles and encouraged them to make their own schedules based on their availabilities. Through their alluring low costs and great convenience, many people living in major US metropolitan regions are now reconsidering the value of private vehicle ownership and instead prioritize accessibility to diverse mobility tools in order to fulfill their daily needs (Clewlow and Mishra 2017). There is no group for which this trend is more apparent than for millennials – those aged twenty to thirty-five years old – among whom a striking decline in car owner-ship has been observed in the United States and elsewhere (McDonald 2015; Delbosc 2016; Blumenberg et al. 2012). For an increasing number of urban dwellers, RH services provide the same level of mobility as automobile ownership but without the associated costs (e.g., maintenance, insurance, licence, parking, etc.). RH services are now increasingly accepted within cities and have rapidly positioned themselves among the most valuable companies in the transportation sector. Although it is a relatively new field of research, studies have focused mostly on its impacts on the transportation sector and on the regulatory and policy frameworks that should be implemented to encourage or deter its usage. Little work has been done on who ben-efits from RH and the equity concerns that it may engender, notwith-standing research by Brown (2018) and Ge et al. (2016). In this chapter, we explore these largely unaddressed concerns by situating RH within the well-established transport equity literature that has long focused on disparities in access and mobility between different social, economic, and demographic groups. This allows us to elaborate on the potentially restrictive nature of RH for many segments of the population. Once unveiled, these equity concerns will shape our dis-cussion and inform our recommendations for an agenda to research equity concerns in RH.

EQUITY IN TRANSPORTATION

Transportation is intrinsically linked to almost every aspect of our lives. It shapes human interactions, contributes to economic prosperity, and influences the quality of life of individuals and communities at large. Inversely, the lack of – or inability to use –transportation services is a catalyst to poverty, unemployment, and other socioeconomic disparities as it impedes access to these very same vital opportunities (Lucas et al. 2008; Currie et al. 2007; Paez et al. 2009). Recognizing the synergies between transportation access and socioeconomic out-comes, transportation planners have long sought to maximize the fair and just distribution of transportation services. The problem, however, is that by their spatial nature, cities and transportation infrastructures produce inequalities. Meyer and Miller (2001) show that transporta-tion investments typically reflect the concerns and issues of their time and often shape investment choices made in the future. Planning in the 1950s, for instance, was focused mainly on highway network expansion, the results of which – automobile dependency – can still be felt today. By orienting our cities around cars, we provided those capable of affording vehicles with more flexibility and the ability to access a broader range of opportunities. Unfortunately, even in the most motorized societies, many cannot afford to own an automobile and must instead rely on alternative modes of travel, such as walking and transit, which have increasingly been rendered inefficient by the unbundling of work, home, and leisure activities to accommodate car travels. Government policies and planning aimed at improving car travels have made owning an automobile indispensable, even if this comes at a disproportionate cost for those in poverty (Badoe and Miller 2000; Sheller and Urry 2000; Urry 2004). Those without cars are consequently at a transport disadvantage and at a much higher risk of socio-economic disadvantage. This chain of events descends into a negative feedback loop, as the socio-economic disadvantages resulting from a lack of opportunities, such as a higher propensity for unemployment, compound the transport disadvantages, such as not being able to afford a vehicle, and intensify the overall level of exclusion (Lucas 2012).

Faced with this discrepancy, many have argued in favour of subsidizing automobile ownership as a way to overcome the barriers preventing people from reaching employment, health, and other socio-economic opportunities in the near term (Mercado et al. 2012; Blumenberg 2017). Despite mounting evidence to support how the absence of automobile access will only exacerbate socio-economic disparities, policy-makers have been reluctant to implement automobile subsidy programs, as they correctly assume that this will increase automobile use and will inevitably worsen congestion, pollution, and sprawl. Furthermore, it would continue to exacerbate the inequalities between those with vehicles and those who will remain carless or unable to drive, even under a hypothetical ownership subsidy.

RH services are seen as a potential solution to this problem, as they enable carless individuals to access a wider range of socio-economic opportunities, at a cheaper cost than traditional taxi and car-share services. While still up for debate, some argue that RH may actually reduce automobile usage, as it discourages vehicle ownership and eliminates much of the wasteful driving associated with the search for parking (Anderson 2014). Moreover, by stressing its gap-filling potential, others believe that RH complements more than it substitutes transit use and may increase accessibility for carless individuals in areas with poor transit supply (Feigon and Murphy 2016; Komanduri et al. 2018).

RH critics, however, have painted a much more cynical picture of what is to come, pointing out the ways in which RH may further exacerbate socio-economic inequalities. Despite being cheaper than taxis, RH services remain considerably more expensive than transit and can therefore provide mobility only to those who can afford to use them. Additionally, these services rely on smartphone technologies and necessitate electronic forms of payment, which impose financial constraints and limit its uptake in certain socio-economic strata.

While RH services exhibit undeniable potential for increasing individual mobility, they also come with a substantial share of concerns, and there is no consensus on whether those suffering from transport poverty actually benefit from the mobility gains that RH proposes (Palm et al. 2020). In order to pick this apart, we will now consider different potentially neglected groups – socio-economically and spatially – and postulate the potential benefits and barriers of RH services for them.

CONSIDERING THE SOCIO-ECONOMIC COMPOSITION OF RIDE HAILING

The opening sentence of Uber's mission statement reads, "Good things happen when people can move, whether across town or towards their dreams. Opportunities appear, open up, become reality" (Uber 2018a). Clearly, this company understands the synergy between transportation accessibility and socio-economic outcomes and is deliberately portraying itself as the solution to increase access to a broader range of opportunities. Lacking from this statement, however, is a caveat explaining how such accessibility benefits, as with those provided by any transportation service, may be inequitably distributed among the population. Unfortunately, in large part as a result of their novelty, RH services have not yet been subjected to the same scrutiny as other, more traditional modes of travel, and the factors preventing people from using RH services have still not been fully established. Factors preventing access to RH may take various forms, some more visible than others and to different degrees. Socio-economic factors such as income, age, gender, race, and disabilities are often responsible for transport inequalities, and on the basis of available research we will now explore how different socio-economic groups may be excluded from benefiting from RH services.

Income

In its current form, RH cannot be considered a broadly affordable mode of transportation. Income is consistently shown to correlate positively with RH use (Young and Farber 2019; Rayle et al. 2016), so we categorize this travel mode as a luxury service. The cost of RH in comparison to public transit, and its use of smartphones and electronic payment methods, further attribute to this categorization.

While its use of smartphone technologies is perceived as convenient for most, it also restricts the use of RH services among low-income populations, as many are unable to afford the devices and phone plans required to fully take advantage of these services. For example, in 2018 in the United States only 67 per cent of those making less than $30,000 per year owned a smartphone capable of ordering RH trips (Pew Research Center 2018). While smartphone ownership is on the rise, many segments of the population continue to struggle to afford mobile devices and are inherently excluded from taking advantage of the benefits that RH services are said to provide.

For convenience and safety reasons, RH companies allow only cashless transactions in most markets. While applauded as an attractive feature for many users, this technological advancement also forces users to have a credit or debit card in order to request trips. Those without bank accounts, who typically comprise lower-income households, represent 5 per cent of the adult population in the United States as of 2017 (Federal Reserve Board 2018) and remain unable to use RH services, even if they have access to a mobile device (Shaheen and Cohen 2018).

Surge pricing is another potential barrier to RH use among low-income populations. Used as a way of meeting consumer demand and incentivising drivers, surge pricing involves raising the cost of rides during rush hour or other periods of the day when demand exceeds supply. While this is an effective business strategy, these real-time price adjustments render RH services even less affordable to low-income individuals. The inability to predict the occurrence and level of surges makes matters worse, as some, fearing the risk of a surge, will decide to use other, more predictable modes of transportation. In order to combat this problem, companies such as Uber and Lyft enable customers to schedule trips in advance, but acknowledge that knowing when one might need a ride is not always possible ahead of time. Combined, the expensive requirements and unpredictable pricing strategy of RH services impose substantial barriers to usage, and narrow the probability that low-income individuals will actually benefit from the added mobility that RH services aim to provide.

Fortunately, whether RH companies are grasping the magnitude of this problem or merely trying to attract an untapped source of new riders, they are now beginning to offer split fare features and carpooling options (e.g., UberPool and LyftLine) to facilitate cost sharing and enable passengers travelling in the same general direction to share rides. These features reposition RH well within the per-rider cost range of public transit, at least for shorter distance trips, and may enable previously excluded low-income travellers to benefit from the mobility advantages that RH services provide, assuming they can afford the other requirements. In Toronto, for instance, public transit costs $3.25 per person, which means that any RH trip below $12, would be cheaper if split four ways.

To summarize, as the result of cost, technological barriers, and banking and payment requirements of RH, many low-income individuals may be excluded from its use. Additional research is required to determine the extent of each of these barriers and to evaluate whether, and under which circumstances, low-income individuals are willing to pay for the increased convenience and comfort of a RH trip.

Age

RH is often characterized as a younger generation phenomenon. This is predominantly a consequence of the digital divide between younger and older generations, and of older people not owning or being unaccustomed to the smartphone technologies required to request trips. Estimates in the United States reveal that roughly four in ten adults, aged sixty-five and over, do not own a smartphone capable of ordering RH trips (Anderson and Perrin 2017), and Canada appears to display a similar divide, as only 2 per cent of RH users in Toronto are sixty and above (Young and Farber 2019).

Despite this digital divide, RH services do propose substantial advantages to seniors. This is especially true for those who are no longer able to drive, as it provides them with a car-based option to regain their independence at a significantly lower cost than traditional taxi services. An increasing yet concerning trend in North America is seniors' tendency to live in suburbs – areas incidentally in which public transit services are often infrequent and unreliable, and where distances are too great for walking (Golant 2015). Consequently, many depend heavily on friends and family for their travel needs (Rosenbloom 2009). By 2030, it is estimated that 72 million people in the United States will be aged sixty-five and over, and 11.5 million of them will be aged eighty-five and over (US Census Bureau 2008). Very few will be interested in moving or able to do so from their suburban homes and will see their mobility dissipate as driving and alternative modes of travel become increasingly difficult to use. In this scenario, RH appears to be a viable solution, as it presents an alternative to meet the growing challenge that carless seniors will face.

Mistrust and confusion surrounding RH also pose a problem for getting senior citizens to adopt these services. Shirgaokar (2017) reveals that seniors are often uncertain of the differences between taxis and RH services and that many are opposed to the notion of surge pricing. Moreover, the study finds that lack of trust is a key issue amongst old people, and reports that many fear using credit cards for online transactions. An additional matter, perhaps a combination of both these reactions, is the perception that RH remains too controversial to be used. Senior citizens raise several concerns about safety and the qualifications of RH drivers, and they question the ethics of RH companies operating while being unlicensed or unregulated. While these are legitimate concerns, it is likely that this mistrust and confusion will be resolved, and future cohorts of seniors – those in their fifties and sixties at the moment – will have had more time to familiarize themselves with the technologies required to request RH trips. In the meantime, companies such as Uber have recognized the opportunity that seniors present and have introduced new features to enable users to request trips for other people. This, it hopes, will help remove the technology barrier that prevents older people from using RH services, and gradually build more trust into the online platform.

At the other end of the age spectrum are children, another demographic group with travel demands that are unlikely to be serviced by RH technologies. Although some companies provide a child car seat upon request for accompanied children, few RH companies permit drivers to pick up unaccompanied minors. Seizing this opportunity, specialized RH companies such as Zūm and Sheprd cater to children and their parents. These services closely replicate the RH model but provide additional features to facilitate scheduling and ensure safety. Notably, children are given a code word to help find the right driver, and parents are provided the vehicle's location and speed in real time. These services also conduct more scrupulous background checks, provide more training for drivers than typical RH companies, and allow parents to schedule trips ahead of time for their children to reduce wait times. While still in their early phases, such companies have faced setbacks. Most notably, there is a lack of demand during school hours and a subsequent lack of supply during after-school periods, not to mention the ingrained fear of entering into a stranger's car that public safety norms have long advocated.

So where does this leave us with regards to children? RH services are still unable to pick up unaccompanied minors, and child-friendly alternatives continue to struggle to turn a profit, leaving children widely excluded from RH services. Parents report that safety is the primary reason for choosing to drive their children to school in the morning (McDonald and Aalborg 2009), but if safe RH trips become available, parents' perceptions may change. The availability of verified and trusted RH drivers may eventually help appease parents' safety concerns and lighten the burden of having to drive their children to school, but this will not increase active school commutes. Walking and cycling to school are an important source of children's physical activity (Faulkner et al. 2009) and are a priority for school boards across Canada and the United States. There is safety in numbers, and if children continue to be driven to school, regardless of whether by their parents or a RH driver, active school commutes will not increase, and safety will remain an issue.

Gender

Feminist geographers have laid the groundwork for research concerned with the differences between men's and women's travel behaviours. Research on gender and transportation has revealed the extent to which women's experiences with gender-based violence and sexual harassment have limited their access to mobility and consequently affected their ability to participate in activities (Law 1999; Dunckel Graglia 2016). We now explore whether RH offsets this gender exclusion by offering a safer travel alternative, or rather perpetuates fear and limits their mobility even further.

Studies have found that men use RH services more frequently than women (Rayle et al. 2016; De Souza et al. 2018). This may be because women do not want to embark on a trip with a stranger, or because RH companies face mounting harassment and discrimination charges; several women plaintiffs are involved in a class-action lawsuit against Uber over sexual harassment allegations and discriminatory pay practices (Wakabayashi 2018). These concerns are by no means abated by the fact that RH companies remain entirely revenue driven, and that eventually, when presented with an opportunity to sacrifice passenger safety for profits, the latter may likely prevail. Consider, for instance, the case in Delhi in 2014, where the medical files belonging to a woman claiming to have been assaulted by an Uber driver were mishandled by Uber's senior executives to cast doubt on her accounts and protect the company (Isaac 2017). While harassment and assault are rare in comparison to the total RH trips, they deter some people – especially women – from using them. These safety concerns may also dissuade women from becoming RH drivers and perhaps explain why women make up fewer than 15 per cent of all Uber drivers (Hall and Krueger 2017).

That being said, the literature on gender and transportation offers another perspective and reveals how, in some contexts, women may perceive RH as the safest travel alternative. Having access to a car enables women to travel safely during off-peak hours when transit services are often scarce or unreliable (Blumenberg 2004). Moreover, it provides safety when traveling at night, when women are most concerned for their personal safety (Schulz and Gilbert 1996; Law 1999). RH may provide women with a safer travel option than walking or using public transit at night or in unsafe neighbourhoods.

While flawed, the five-star rating system adopted by most RH companies offers additional safety, as it enables users to select drivers with whom they feel comfortable, on the basis of previous passenger recommendations. In turn, they are encouraged to rate their own RH experience in order to help others make safer travel decisions. Unfortunately, this rating system does not prevent all incidents of harassment and assault and has led some new companies to develop single-sex RH services. By-women/for-women services such as Safr and DriveHER, aim to provide a safer RH experience to customers and drivers but are in the midst of a legal battle, because refusing to employ men as drivers contravenes the American Civil Rights Act, which prohibits gender discrimination (Brown 2017). While women-only transportation may have little precedence in the United States, it has occurred elsewhere. Responding to mounting violence and harassment allegations against women travellers, Mexico City established a women-only public transportation service in the early 2000s. By designating specific subways cars to women during peak periods, Mexico City removed the immediate problem and significantly reduced the gender-based violence threatening women's mobility (Dunckel Graglia 2016). Regardless of whether such single-sex services become legal in the United States, safety has become a priority amongst major R H companies and has induced them to develop incident-prevention tools such as phone number anonymization, emergency assistance buttons, and more thorough criminal background screenings to ensure the safety of their passengers. Both Uber and Lyft now claim that safety is among their top priorities (Uber 2018d; Lyft 2018).

Race

Racial discrimination has been embedded in transportation decisions in America for decades. During the Jim Crow era, Black patrons were forced to ride at the back of the bus and to give up their seat when asked to do so by white passengers. More recently, during the development of the US national highway system, vulnerable low-income Black neighbourhoods were systematically targeted for demolition in order to accommodate inner-city highway expansions. Even now African Americans are three times more likely to live in a zero-vehicle household than Caucasians, limiting their mobility and significantly impeding their access to employment opportunities (Blumenberg 2017). In addition, public transit investments have disproportionately favoured wealthy Caucasian users; despite buses accounting for the bulk of all transit trips in America, suburban commuter rail expansion receives the majority of government subsidies. This is justified by rail's ability to attract discretionary riders and more effectively divert commuters away from driving. Yet given the racial and economic composition of bus and rail users, these subsidies also clearly favour wealthy Caucasian users (Blumenberg 2017; Grengs 2002). Given this long history of discrimination in transportation, it is reasonable to question whether the arrival and widespread usage of R H has helped to mitigate this disparity, or whether instead it has widened the divide.

Put simply, R H services are not immune to racial discrimination. For instance, a report found that drivers on average take longer to pick up African-American passengers than Caucasians (Ge et al. 2016). While concerning, this discrepancy in wait time is actually an improvement over the taxi industry, which, despite its regulatory framework, has systematically been shown to discriminate against visible minorities. In a recent comparative study in Los Angeles, African-American taxi riders were found to wait, on average, 52 per cent longer for their taxi than their Caucasian counterpart, equivalent to a wait time that was longer by six to fifteen minutes. African-American RH users, on the other hand, were found to wait only one to two minutes longer for their driver to arrive and were also less likely to experience cancelations than Caucasians RH users (Brown 2018). Similar patterns of discrimination were noted in Seattle and Boston (Ge et al. 2016). While speculative, the prejudice towards African-Americans may be attributed to the fact that nearly half of all Uber drivers in America identify as being Caucasian (48.6 per cent) and only 8.1 per cent identify as African-American (Statistica 2018). These studies illustrate how RH may be an improvement over taxis in wait times but do not address whether RH helps mitigate racial discrimination as a whole. To answer this broader question, more data on the intersectionality of race and other socio-economic characteristics will expose whether minorities are excluded from RH as the result of more profound societal problems.

Disabilities

Disabilities have long been recognized as a barrier to the access and use of transportation services (Evans and White 1998; Lucas 2004; Currie and Senbergs 2007). Every movement, even walking, requires a specific set of abilities and skills, and when lacking, may hinder a person's mobility. As with any other barrier to mobility, disability will affect the number of opportunities available and result in much broader socio-economic impacts. Considering this, we will now explore whether RH provides a solution to improve the mobility of those with disabilities, or whether it further excludes them by overlooking and omitting them completely.

Much like drivers of taxis, RH drivers will often help passengers who require assistance, and by offering this help at a lower fare cost than taxis, there is potential for RH to improve the mobility of those with disabilities. But RH services remain particularly exclusive. For example, their application interfaces are seldom adapted to visual impairments, and vehicles are not often modified to accommodate disabled passengers. This may be a result of drivers using their own vehicles, very few of which are equipped to handle wheelchairs or motorized scooters. Even the RH companies that do provide wheelchair-accessible vehicles do not provide enough of them to meet demand, and the ensuing wait time for such vehicles is estimated to be four times longer than for regular RH service, if available at all (NYLPI 2018). Another growing concern is that RH drivers may not receive the necessary training to assist disabled passengers. Taxi drivers are often compelled to take a disability awareness certification to properly assist such passengers, but this training is not required by RH companies and has led to instances of mistreatment and abuse (Weatherby 2018).

Fortunately, RH companies appear to be listening to these concerns and are committed to finding new ways to provide better services to individuals with disabilities. In Toronto for instance, RH companies have agreed to abide by a city-imposed average wait time requirement that aims to reduce transport inequalities by ensuring that all users – including those who require accessible transport services – experience similar wait times (Young and Farber 2020). Uber and Lyft are now involved in a pilot program in New York City to provide pooled wheelchair-accessible vehicles to their users, route them through a centralized dispatcher to facilitate, and ultimately accelerate matching. Despite these efforts, critics insist that in their current form, RH companies will never provide enough wheelchair-accessible vehicles to accommodate demand, and they argue that economic incentives must first be offered to encourage drivers to make their cars wheelchair-accessible (NYLPI 2018).

SPATIAL EQUITY

Recent research shows a suburbanization of poverty in the United States and Canada, and its authors are increasingly concerned by the implication it may have for transportation (Allen and Farber 2018; Deboosere and El-Geneidy 2018). Low-income households are even more disadvantaged in the suburbs, as their mobility depends heavily upon transit, which is rendered inefficient by the dispersion of home, work, and leisure activities that has become quintessential to suburban landscapes (El-Geneidy et al. 2015; Currie and Stanley 2007; Lucas 2012). Others have extended transportation disadvantage to encompass broader socio-economic outcomes, arguing that the absence of mobility may exacerbate socio-economic inequalities (Lucas et al. 2008). RH offers a potential solution because it can provide access to carless individuals, especially those living in areas with poor transit access. The question remains whether enough RH drivers choose to operate in low-density suburbs to ever render wait times acceptable. And will the cost of RH remain low enough to enable low-income suburbanites to use and benefit from the mobility advantages that RH services allegedly provide?

RH is primarily an inner-city phenomenon. In Toronto, over a quarter of all RH trips occur entirely within the city's central Planning District, which encompasses the central business district and the densest parts of the city. Three-quarters of all trips in Toronto either begin or end within this Planning District (TTS 2016). The prominence of trips downtown is largely due to demand and to drivers' ability to converge on this area in order to satisfy demand. Unfortunately, this preference and ability for drivers to operate in central areas creates an imbalance of supply in other areas and renders service inefficient in lower-density suburban neighbourhoods without sufficient RH demand. Drivers rightfully recognize that they can increase their revenues by commuting downtown and by picking up passengers in areas where demand is high and wait times between trips are low. Uber further encourages this behaviour by advertising areas where most requests occur, and by incentivising drivers to converge to these hotspots. In Toronto, for instance, Uber recommends drivers begin in the Financial District and other downtown shopping areas in order to maximize revenues (Uber 2018c). It therefore appears that a minimum demand threshold is required to persuade drivers to stay in a given location, especially when demand in adjacent areas is much higher. Some may notice that downtown neighbourhoods, where the bulk of RH trips occur, are also where individuals' need for mobility are already best met by public transportation. Adding RH services to these areas only marginally increases individuals' participation rates and likely replaces trips that elsewise would have been conducted by transit. So RH will only increase the mobility of those living in well-served transit areas and perpetuate the level of transport inequality between the inner and outer parts of the regions.

MODAL EQUITY

The fear that RH may be cannibalising a substantial portion of transit demand is widely expressed in literature (Hall et al. 2017; Clewlow and Mishra 2017; Zwick and Spicer 2018; Young et al. 2020). If accurate, the increase in RH demand at the expense of transit ridership may cause damage in the long run, as transit agencies, witnessing a decrease in demand, may have no choice but to reduce transit supply, harming travellers who depend upon transit and who are unable to shift to RH. Others, however, have drawn much more optimistic conclusions about the modal impacts of RH, suggesting that it will act as a complement to – rather than a substitute for – transit. Proponents of this view emphasize the potential of RH to serve as the first/last mile of transit trips, and its ability to provide access to carless individuals in areas with low transit supply (Feigon and Murphy 2016; Komanduri et al. 2018). As evidenced by this debate, much uncertainty remains about the effect of RH on transit ridership and whether these services will be able to coexist.

Car drivers may also be affected by the arrival and widespread usage of RH. If RH results in more vehicles on the road, there will be greater congestion. In San Francisco, RH vehicles accounted for approximately half the increase in traffic congestion between 2010 and 2016 (Erhardt et al. 2019), and similar trends appeared in New York City (Mangrum and Molnar 2017). Others are less convinced of its detrimental impact and believe that the arrival and widespread usage of RH may result in less congestion, because it removes the need to own a private vehicle (Rayle et al. 2016; Clewlow and Mishra 2017; Young 2018). To support this view, researchers point to the small, yet consequential portion of RH users who have given up their personal vehicle, or who plan to do so in response to the arrival of RH (Clewlow and Mishra 2017). Moreover, the reported late-night popularity of RH may also suggest that RH services are reducing the amount of dangerous vehicle kilometres travelled. Greenwood and Wattal (2015) found that the entry of UberX, Uber's most popular service, was associated with a decrease of up to 5.6 per cent in motor vehicle homicides in California between 2009 and 2013. This finding was corroborated by survey participants reporting, even when unprompted, that alcohol consumption was a major determinant in their decision to use RH services (Clewlow and Mishra 2017; Feigon and Murphy 2016). Thus while potentially increasing congestion within cities, RH may also reduce the rate of motor vehicle fatalities that result from drunk driving.

CONCLUSION AND THE FUTURE
OF RIDE-HAILING RESEARCH

What is most evident when examining groups that may be excluded from RH is the complexity and uncertainty that remain. Because it is novel and there is a related paucity of data, many of the effects of RH cannot be established with certainty, and many of its intersectionalities with transport inequalities remain largely unexplored. In the area of gender-related transportation exclusion, for instance, some women may perceive RH as a safer alternative than walking alone at night, whereas others may not want to embark on a RH trip with complete strangers under any circumstances – be they other passengers or the driver – and may see their mobility decrease as congestion increases and other modes of travel become slower or less feasible.

In light of this uncertainty, our recommendations are divided into two parts. The first considers what can and arguably should be done to minimize equity concerns and persuade RH companies to reduce exclusion. In this section we offer policy advice to ensure that the objectives of RH companies align with those of governments, and propose regulatory measures to penalize those that do not comply. Our policy recommendations will centre on minimizing exclusion from a rider's perspective, but drivers can also experience safety or equity concerns, and governments should also respond to their needs when framing policy. Recognizing that many unknowns remain with regards to RH, the second part of this section considers the issue from a research perspective and examines the updates and improvements that must occur in data collection. We do not have sufficient data to fully grasp the effects of RH, and this latter section will elucidate which additional sources of data and research approaches should be explored in order to properly inform policy decisions.

Policies to Minimize Exclusion

In an effort to make RH more affordable, governments should consider subsidizing pooled RH trips, especially in areas with low transit supply. Although this would not address the technology barriers or banking/payment requirements, which would be better resolved through a wealth distribution mechanism such as income taxes (Rietveld 2007), it would help make RH an affordable means of travel, while promoting sustainable behaviours. It would also alleviate congestion. Congestion remains a primary concern for RH, and despite having a much higher average occupancy rate than taxis, the majority of RH trips are still taken alone (Rayle et al. 2016). Other forms of trips that governments should consider subsidizing are those that begin or end at transit stations. Many believe that RH companies will play a crucial role in servicing the first/last mile of transit trips, and that in doing so they will render transit more appealing. RH companies know exactly where each passenger is picked up and dropped off, and by integrating this information with smart transit passes, governments could accurately determine whether RH were used for the first/last mile of a transit trip. A variance of this subsidy was launched in Philadelphia during the summer of 2016 when the Southeastern Pennsylvania Transportation Authority (SEPTA) partnered with Uber and offered a 40 per cent discount on all RH trips used as access or egress to suburban rail stations. Early results found this partnership to have been a success, and showed it had increased ridership at these rail stations while also alleviating their parking problems (Campbell 2016). Together these subsidies would reduce the cost of RH, while ensuring that it remains a complement to – rather than substitute for – transit. To finance these subsidies and further encourage such behaviours, governments could establish a feebate system in which they tax undesired RH trips and use the revenue from this tax to subsidize those they wish to encourage. Using the trip data collected by RH companies, governments could impose additional fees to users travelling alone, and to trips that could have been easily replaced by transit. These efforts could be supplemented by surge price restrictions, which would enable RH companies to apply surge pricing only to users travelling alone, and would further encourage pooled trips. No longer fearing the risk of a surge, low-income users would be more inclined to use RH as well.

To address racial and gender exclusion, governments should require RH companies to provide their drivers with thorough discrimination, harassment, and sensitivity training. Such training would be monitored and upheld by government agencies, and non-complying firms would be prevented from operating within their jurisdictions. Instead of reducing the training requirements for both taxi and RH drivers, in hopes of levelling the playing field, cities such as Toronto could seize this opportunity to revisit and update their training requirements.

Using data from the RH and taxi industry, governments could pinpoint ways in which passengers are being discriminated against, and could tailor their training programs accordingly. For instance, if observed in the data, racial prejudices and misogynistic behaviours could be emphasized during training sessions, and the effects of such training could be monitored using subsequent data on harassment incidents and on wait-time discrepancies between minorities and Caucasians.

Gender exclusion is also often associated with safety concerns, which governments could address by imposing stricter background checks and by requiring that they be conducted by government agencies rather than private firms. RH companies such as Uber have been reluctant to accept government-run background checks for their drivers, often claiming that they are burdensome for their business model (Zwick and Spicer 2018). This may all have to change, however, if governments want to address the causes of gender exclusion. In contrast to Uber's current self-run background checks, which are prone to error (Hill 2015), governments could prevent drivers from applying under a false name and require fingerprinting to screen and potentially remove those with criminal records.

To ensure RH improve the mobility of those with disabilities, cities could compel all RH drivers to complete a disability awareness certification. This requirement would ensure that all drivers receive the necessary training to properly assist disabled passengers and would likely incentivise more drivers to convert their cars into wheelchair-accessible vehicles. If, despite these efforts, the supply of wheelchair-accessible vehicles remains insufficient, governments could also impose minimal accessible vehicle requirements for RH companies in order to operate within their jurisdictions. These could range between 5 and 10 per cent of total RH vehicle fleets, depending on demand.

A final recommendation would be to limit the supply of RH permits. The impact of RH on congestion and on the ridership of other modes remains complex and largely unexplored, and to simply assume that the revenue-driven objectives of RH companies will produce an optimal level of supply is overly optimistic. Governments should instead take pre-emptive measures to ensure that the supply of RH vehicles aligns with societal objectives, and err on the side of caution in recognizing that there are still many uncertainties about RH; the supply of permits can always be increased as needed. In 2018 New York City became the first US city to cap the number of RH vehicles on the road, but this law has since been challenged by Uber and other RH proponents, who deem it an anti-competitive practice (Fitzsimmons 2018). If left unchecked, as it is in Toronto and in most cities, the supply of RH vehicles will likely continue to rise, and once entrenched as such, regulating the industry any further in hopes of scaling it back could be politically prohibitive.

Data Needs and Improvements to Data Collection

To ensure that RH companies behave in ways that limit rather that propagate transport inequalities, governments must also make an effort to fully understand the impacts of RH. This will include collecting new data from public and private sources, and will ultimately require an update and improvement in how they collect data.

Clearly there is a need for more frequent and exhaustive travel surveys, and to include RH as a travel mode within them. Associating users' characteristics with their travel behaviours will enable government officials to determine groups that are under-represented and at risk of being excluded from this mode. This, in turn, will inform them of areas that deserve to be emphasized during the discrimination, harassment, and sensitivity training sessions. Because of their low sampling rates, however, these travel surveys cannot accurately expose how RH will affect congestion or reveal how it will affect ridership in other modes of travel. For this, governments must rely on other sources of data, and updating their data collection process will therefore also involve partnering with RH companies to obtain data from them directly. While somewhat reluctant to share their data in the past, RH companies have warmed to the idea and are now beginning to grant governments with access to many of their datasets. This shift on sharing data has been most noticeable with Uber, which reversed its notoriously long-held confrontational stance with local governments to now offer a stand-alone data-sharing tool entitled *Uber Movement* in order to "provide anonymized data from over two billion trips to help urban planning around the world" (Uber 2018b). Despite these encouraging efforts, collaborations such as these remain in their early stages, and governments must continue to enact policies that compel RH companies to share their data in order to operate within their jurisdictions. RH companies possess disaggregated trip data, which includes the location, duration, cost, and type of vehicle for each trip. This information is crucial in order to properly assess the volume of traffic for which RH is responsible, and to determine whether this mode acts more as a complement to – or substitute for – transit. Using data on the location and duration of trips, cities could calculate how easily these trips would have been replaced by transit, and introduce policy measures accordingly. The cost of trips could also be used to evaluate whether, and under what circumstances, low-income individuals are willing to pay for RH. Obtaining data on the frequency and duration of surge pricing would further enrich this understanding and offer insight into the behavioural response of users to such pricing mechanisms. RH companies also have data on wait times that could be used to discern racial discrimination in the form of wait-time discrepancies and establish how much congestion is actually caused by travelling to the passenger's pick-up location in the first place. From this trip dataset, city officials could also determine the proportion of trips that are pooled and detect those that begin or end at transit stations. This would inform policymakers of the proportion of trips that should be subsidized and of the monetary value of these subsidies if they are to be effective.

Even if successful in obtaining these data from RH companies directly, governments will still face uncertainties about RH and will depend on researchers to further advance their understanding. Qualitative approaches are especially well suited to answer the issues raised in this chapter; interviewing elders, minorities, women, and members from other potentially neglected groups will elucidate the reasons for which they use or avoid RH, and will shed light on the policy that must be enacted to ensure they are not excluded.

REFERENCES

Allen, J., and S. Farber. 2018. "Sizing Up Transport Poverty: A National Scale Accounting of Low-Income Households Suffering from Inaccessibility in Canada, and What to Do about It." *Transport Policy* 74: 214–23.
Anderson, D.N. 2014. "'Not Just a Taxi'? For-Profit Ridesharing, Driver Strategies, and VMT." *Transportation* 41, no. 5: 1,099–117.
Anderson, M., and A. Perrin. 2017. "Tech Adoption Climbs among Older Adults." Pew Research Centre, 17 May. http://www.pewinternet.org/2017/05/17/technology-use-among-seniors/.
Badoe, A.D., and E. Miller. 2000. "Transportation-Land-Use Interaction: Empirical Findings in North America, and Their Implications for

Modeling." *Transportation Research Part D: Transport and Environment* 5, no. 4: 235–63.

Blumenberg, E. 2004. "En-Gendering Effective Planning: Spatial Mismatch, Low-Income Women, and Transportation Policy." *Journal of the American Planning Association* 70, no. 3: 269–81.

– 2017. "Social Equity and Urban Transportation." In *The Geography of Urban Transportation*, edited by S. Hanson and G. Giuliano, 4th ed., 232–58. New York: Guilford.

Blumenberg, E., B.D. Taylor, and M.J. Smart. 2012. "What's Youth Got to Do with It? Exploring the Travel Behavior of Teens and Young Adults." University of California Transportation Center, Berkeley, CA.

Brown, A. 2018. "Ridehail Revolution: Ridehail Travel and Equity in Los Angeles." University of California, Los Angeles (UCLA). https://escholarship.org/uc/item/4r22m57k.

Brown, E. 2017. "Fare Trade: Reconciling Public Safety and Gender Discrimination in Single-Sex Ridesharing." *Yale Law & Policy Review* 35: 367–406.

Campbell, H. 2016. "How Are Uber and Lyft Working with Public Transportation Authorities?" https://therideshareguy.com/how-are-uber-and-lyft-working-with-public-transportation-authorities/.

Clewlow, R., and G. Mishra. 2017. "Disruptive Transportation: The Adoption, Utilization, and Impacts of Ride-Hailing in the United States." Institute of Transportation Studies, University of California, Davis. https://escholarship.org/uc/item/82w2z91j.

Currie, G., and Z. Senbergs. 2007. "Identifying Spatial Gaps in Public Transport Provision for Socially Disadvantaged Australians: The Melbourne 'Needs Gap' Study." *Australasian Transport Research Forum in 2007*. Melbourne, Australia.

Currie, G., and J. Stanley. 2007. *No Way to Go: Transport and Social Disadvantage in Australian Communities*. Australia: Monash University ePress.

Deboosere, R., and A. El-Geneidy. 2018. "Evaluating Equity and Accessibility to Jobs by Public Transport across Canada." *Journal of Transport Geography* 73: 54–63.

Delbosc, A. 2016. "Delay or Forgo? A Closer Look at Youth Driver Licensing Trends in the United States and Australia." *Transportation* 44, no. 5: 919–26.

De Souza Silva, L.A., M.O. de Andrade, and M.L.A. Maia. 2018. "How Does the Ride-Hailing Systems Demand Affect Individual Transport Regulation?" *Research in Transportation Economics* 69: 600–6.

Dunckel Graglia, A. 2016. "Finding Mobility: Women Negotiating Fear and Violence in Mexico City's Public Transit System." *Gender, Place & Culture* 23, no. 5: 624–40.

El-Geneidy, A., R. Buliung, and E. Diab. 2015. "Non-Stop Equity: Assessing Daily Intersections between Transit Accessibility and Social Disparity across the Greater Toronto and Hamilton Area (GTHA)." *Environment and Planning B: Planning and Design* 43, no. 3: 540–60.

Erhardt, G.D., S. Roy, D. Cooper, B. Sana, M. Chen, and J. Castiglione. 2019. "Do Transportation Network Companies Decrease or Increase Congestion?" *Science Advances* 5, no. 5: eaau2670. https://doi.org/10.1126/sciadv.aau2670.

Evans, J., and M. White. 1998. "A Review of Transport Resources for People with Disabilities: A State-of-the-Art Review." Review Report 3. Vermont South, Victoria: ARRB Transport Research.

Faulkner, G.E., R.N. Buliung, and P.K. Flora. 2009. "Active School Transport, Physical Activity Levels and Body Weight of Children and Youth: A Systematic Review." *Preventive Medicine* 48, no. 1: 3–8.

Federal Reserve Board. 2018. *Report on the Economic Well-Being of U.S. Households in 2017.* Board of Governors of the Federal Reserve System. https://www.federalreserve.gov/publications/files/2017-report-economic-well-being-us-households-201805.pdf.

Feigon, S., and C. Murphy. 2016. "Shared Mobility and the Transformation of Public Transit." Report submitted by the Shared-Use Mobility Center for the American Public Transportation Association. No. Project J-11, Task 21.

Fitzsimmons, G.E. 2018. "Why a Cap on Uber in New York Would Be a Major Blow for the Ride-Hail Giant." *New York Times*, 18 August. https://www.nytimes.com/2018/08/08/nyregion/nyc-uber-cap-regulations.html.

Ge, Y., R.C. Knittel, and D. MacKenzie. 2016. "Racial and Gender Discrimination in Transportation Network Companies." NBER working paper no. 22776.

Golant, S.M. 2015. *Aging in the Right Place.* Baltimore, MD: Health Professions.

Greenwood, B., and S. Wattal. 2015. "Show Me the Way to Go Home: An Empirical Investigation of Ride Sharing and Alcohol Related Motor Vehicle Homicide." Fox School of Business research paper no. 15-054.

Grengs, J. 2002. "Community-Based Planning as a Source of Political Change: The Transit Equity Movement of Los Angeles' Bus Rider Union." *Journal of the American Planning Association* 68, no. 2: 165–78.

Hall, J.D., C. Palsson, and J. Price. 2017. "Is Uber a Substitute or Complement for Public Transit?" *Journal of Urban Economics* 108: 36–50.

Hall, J.V., and A.B. Krueger. 2017. "An Analysis of the Labor Market for Uber's Driver-Partners in the United States." *ILR Review* 71, no. 3: 705–32.

Hill, S. 2015. "The Ticking Time Bomb of Uber." *Truthout*, 22 December. https://truthout.org/articles/the-ticking-time-bomb-of-uber/.

Isaac, M. 2017. "Uber Is Sued by Woman Who Was Raped by One of Its Drivers in India." *New York Times*, 15 June. https://www.nytimes.com/2017/06/15/technology/uber-india-rape-lawsuit.html.

Komanduri, A., Z. Wafa, and K. Proussaloglou. 2018. "Assessing the Impact of App-Based Ride Share Systems in an Urban Context: Findings from Austin." *Transportation Research Record* 2,672, no. 7: 34–6.

Law, R. 1999. "Beyond Women and Transport: Towards New Geographies of Gender and Daily Mobility." *Progress in Human Geography* 23, no. 4: 567–88.

Lucas, K. 2004. "Transport and Social Exclusion." In *Running on Empty: Transport, Social Exclusion and Environmental Justice*, edited by K. Lucas, 39–53. Bristol, UK: Policy.

– 2012. "Transport and Social Exclusion: Where Are We Now?" *Transport Policy* 20: 105–13.

Lucas, K., S. Tyler, and G. Christodoulou. 2008. *The Value of New Transport in Deprived Areas: Who Benefits, How and Why?* York, UK: Joseph Rowntree Foundation.

Lyft. 2018. "Safety Policies." https://help.lyft.com/hc/en-ca/articles/115012923127-Safety-policies.

Mangrum, D., and A. Molnar. 2017. "The Marginal Congestion of a Taxi in New York City." Working paper, Vanderbilt University.

McDonald, N. 2015. "Are Millennials Really the 'Go-Nowhere' Generation?" *Journal of the American Planning Association* 81, no. 2: 90–103.

McDonald, N.C., and A.E. Aalborg. 2009. "Why Parents Drive Children to School: Implications for Safe Routes to School Programs." *Journal of the American Planning Association* 75, no. 3: 331–42.

Mercado, R.G., A. Paez, and S. Farber. 2012. "Explaining Transportation Mode Use of Low-Income Persons for Journey to Work in Urban Areas: A Case Study of Ontario and Quebec." *Transportmetrica* 8, no. 3: 157–79.

Meyer, D.M., and J.E. Miller. 2001. *Urban Transportation Planning*. 2nd ed. New York: McGraw-Hill.

NYLPI. 2018. "Left Behind: New York's for-Hire Vehicle Industry Continues to Exclude People with Disabilities," 18 August. http://www. nylpi.org/wp-content/uploads/2018/05/Left-Behind-Report.pdf.

Paez, A., R.G. Mercado, and S. Farber. 2009. *Mobility and Social Exclusion in Canadian Communities: An Empirical Investigation of Opportunity Access and Deprivation from the Perspective of Vulnerable Groups.* Toronto: Policy Research Directorate Strategic Policy and Research.

Palm, M., S. Farber, A. Shalaby, and M. Young. 2020. "Equity Analysis and New Mobility Technologies: Towards Meaningful Interventions." *Journal of Planning Literature.* https://doi.org/10.1177/0885412220955197.

Pew Research Center. 2018. "Mobile Fact Sheet." Pew Research Center. http://www.pewinternet.org/fact-sheet/mobile/.

Rayle, L., D. Dai, and N. Chan. 2016. "Just a Better Taxi? A Survey-Based Comparison of Taxis, Transit, and Ridesourcing Services in San Francisco." *Transport Policy* 45: 168–78.

Rietveld, P. 2007. "Urban Transport Policies: The Dutch Struggle with Market Failures and Policy Failures." In *A Companion to Urban Economics*, edited by J. Arnott and P.D. McMillen, 292–305. Hoboken, NJ: Wiley-Blackwell.

Rosenbloom, S. 2009. "Meeting Transportation Needs in an Aging-Friendly Community." *Generations* 33, no. 2: 33–43.

Schulz, D., and S. Gilbert. 1996. "Women and Transit Security: A New Look at an Old Issue/Women's Travel Issues." Proceedings from the second national conference, FHWA-PL-97-024, October. Office of Highway Information Management, HPM-40, Federal Highway Administration. Washington, DC: US Department of Transportation.

Shaheen, S., and A. Cohen. 2018. "Equity and Shared Mobility." *ITS Berkeley Policy Briefs.* https://doi.org/10.7922/G2MC8X6K.

Sheller, M., and J. Urry. 2000. "The City and the Car." *International Journal of Urban and Regional Research* 24, no. 4: 737–57.

Shirgaokar, M. 2017. "Which Barriers Prevent Seniors from Accessing Transportation Network Company (TNC) Services? Identifying Ways Forward for a Gendered Policy Approach." Paper presented at the 96th Annual Meeting of the Transportation Research Board, Washington, DC, 2017. https://trid.trb.org/view/1438905.

Statistica. 2018. "Distribution of Uber's Employees in the United States in 2017 and 2018, by Ethnicity." https://www.statista.com/statistics/693838/uber-employee-ethnicity-us/.

Transportation Tomorrow Survey. 2016. "TTS 2016 Data Guide." http://
dmg.utoronto.ca/pdf/tts/2016/2016TTS_DataGuide.pdf.

Uber. 2018a. "About Us: We Ignite Opportunity by Setting the World
in Motion," 18 August. https://www.uber.com/en-CA/about/.

– 2018b. "Uber Movement," 18 August. https://movement.uber.com/.

– 2018c. "Where to Drive: Toronto," 18 August. https://www.uber.com/
en-CA/drive/toronto/where-to-drive/.

– 2018d. "Your Safety Is Our Priority," 18 August. https://www.uber.com/
en-CA/blog/safety-features/.

Urry, J. 2004. "The 'System' of Automobility." *Theory, Culture & Society*
21, nos. 4–5: 25–39.

US Census Bureau. 2008. "Projections of the Population by Selected Age
Groups and Sex for the United States: 2010–2050." Population
Division. Table 2. Washington, DC. https://www2.census.gov/programs-
surveys/popproj/tables/2008/2008-summary-tables/np2008-t2.xls

Wakabayashi, B. 2018. "Former Uber Engineer's Lawsuit Claims Sexual
Harassment." *New York Times*, 18 August. https://www.nytimes.
com/2018/05/21/technology/uber-sexual-harassment-lawsuit.html.

Weatherby, B. 2018. "Disabled Bristol Man Left 'Embarrassed' and
'Mortified' after Uber Drivers Refuse to Pick Him Up." BristolLive,
26 January. https://www.bristolpost.co.uk/news/bristol-news/
disabled-bristol-man-left-embarrassed-1124216.

Young, M. 2018. "Ride-Hailing's Impact on Canadian Cities: Now Let's
Consider the Long Game." *Canadian Geographer* 63, no. 1: 171–5.

Young, M., J. Allen, and S. Farber. 2020. "Measuring When Uber Behaves
as a Substitute or Supplement to Transit: An Examination of Travel-
Time Differences in Toronto." *Journal of Transport Geography* 82,
article 102629.

Young, M., and S. Farber. 2019. "The Who, Why, When of Uber and
Other Ride-Hailing Trips: An Examination of a Large Sample
Household Travel Survey." *Transportation Research Part A: Policy
and Practice* 119: 383–92.

– 2020. "Using Wait-time Thresholds to Improve Mobility: The Case
of UberWAV in Toronto." *Transport Findings*, 1–7.

Zwick, A., and Z. Spicer. 2018. "Good or Bad? Ridesharing's Impact
on Canadian Cities." *Canadian Geographer* 62, no. 4: 430–6.

5

Disrupting Stuff:
Material Flows in the Platform City

Clarence Woudsma

- Urban freight transport is central to city vitality, while also generating significant and often negative impacts on land use and transportation systems.
- As a key part of urban freight flows, last-mile delivery of consumer goods is increasing dramatically in the platform city, with added complexities in labour, environment, and built form developments.
- The diversity and complexity of actors, business models, and evolving flows in the platform city need a policy response and present new opportunities to move beyond traditional regulations.

INTRODUCTION

Think about all your stuff: your personal property comprising materials, supplies, and goods, all sharing the key characteristic that they are movable. Now try to imagine the transportation effort invested in all of your stuff – from the more enduring household items of furniture, electronics, and clothing, to the shorter-term stuff in your kitchen and refrigerator. Each item has had its own journey to end up in your possession – the "last mile" of delivery to you (or your door), not to mention the journeys of the inputs into the creation of that item. Böge (1995) provided a pioneering look into a simple product – a single-use plastic pot of strawberry yogourt – that revealed a web of transportation activity related to the production of that seemingly simple piece of "stuff." The object's range of inputs results in a complex mapping of input flows, and an extensive impact on energy and emissions. However, what she did not include in that analysis was the last-mile transportation from the store to the home – the consumption side of that exchange. In 1995, the consumer would have travelled to the store, purchased that single pot along with other items, and carried it, using some mode of transport back home – a final addition of energy and emissions to an already complex flow in the life cycle of the humble yogourt pot.

Fast forward to today and the transportation dimensions of the production and consumption of our "stuff" has undergone a seemingly unending radical transformation. A major driver of that transformation most recently is the rise of the platform economy. As a result of this transformation, the way last-mile delivery occurs has evolved. You can now order the simple yogourt pot from your smartphone and have it delivered to your door by cargo bike, car, van, drone, or sidewalk robot, or picked up with your order at your local store, or maybe even delivered to you by your neighbour. This chapter will introduce the flows of materials – urban freight – in our cities, frame the transformations underway, explore the changing markets, and discuss what it all means for the digital city.

"FREIGHT" IN THE CITY: FOUNDATIONS

It is important to establish a base understanding of the nature of material flows and their multi-faceted relationship with the city. Further, there is a need to recognize prior transformations in this arena that are stepping stones on the path explored here.

The material flows in our cities are categorized in several ways. We use general terms like "goods" to indicate materials in a market exchange sense, contrasted with "waste materials," which are also an important part of physical material flows. "Freight" denotes goods transported for remuneration, typically between businesses, typically in larger lots and volumes, and usually associated with rail, truck, and marine modes of transport. A further distinction is the spatial character of material flows, with many trips involving circulation within the urban area (intra-urban) while other trips are interurban, involving import or export between cities. Lastly, we can distinguish between flows of raw materials or commodities, intermediate goods, and final goods.

These flows are associated with key spatial structures in the city. It is estimated (with significant variation in city size and function) that

10–15 per cent of all vehicle travel is related to the movement of goods, and 3–5 per cent of urban land is devoted to freight transportation and warehousing (Dablanc and Rodrigue 2017). In general, most urban areas devoted to transportation and warehousing include traditional land-use zones where we see a focus of freight activity – terminals such as ports, airports, railyards, and intermodal yards generate significant freight-related trips (Metrolinx 2016). Logistics zones with concentrations of warehousing, distribution centres, or fulfillment centres can be identified with more traditional manufacturing zones and associated high levels of heavy truck activity in truckload movements. Finally, commercial zones as agglomerations of office, retail, and institutions can generate significant freight traffic in the traditional central business district or suburban sub-centres. Typically these flows involve midsize or smaller trucks (vans) and less-than-truckload or smaller lots of shipments. When the flows are to a final point of consumption, they are typically referred to as "last mile delivery."

Most aspects of urban form and life are affected in some way by freight activity. The infrastructures of transportation are largely shared between passenger and freight activity. The economic vitality and competitiveness of cities is tied to the efficiency of those systems. In contrast, the relatively low proportions of freight activity (in the overall stream of traffic) belies the significance of their negative effects. Freight activity is a major source of air pollutants, greenhouse gas (GHG) emissions, and noise and vibration pollution. It contributes to system congestion. And it can degrade livability through accidents, visual intrusion, and traffic dissonance (Cui et al. 2015).

The central tension in urban freight is between efficiency and externalities, between the "goods" and the "bads." This tension is the focus of planning, policy, and regulation and of the interplay between the private and public realms. In one example, the private sector is profit driven and seeks efficiency while the public realm is safety driven with policies that enhance safety but perhaps harm profit. Ogden (1992) provides a seminal text in which the planning objectives for urban freight are grouped into descriptive categories: economy (focused on supporting the broader economy and trade), efficiency (reduce congestion and costs broadly), safety (road design, traffic management), environment, infrastructure design, and management, and urban structure (land use and transportation interaction). Despite clear expression of the objectives, planning for urban freight has seldom been a priority in many cities, often completed ad hoc (Woudsma 2001).

The motivation of regulation has been to control and restrict freight activity, rather than accommodate and understand. A classic example is the establishment of truck routes by municipalities in an effort to reduce conflicts with passenger traffic and optimize the investment in engineering infrastructure to accommodate heavy trucks. We plan extensively to accommodate passenger mobility throughout the urban landscape but have attempted to confine freight to specific routes.

In a fashion similar to the lack of planning for freight, the emphasis in academic research and policy creation is placed heavily on passenger transportation, which is a reality easily grasped by those in the academic and public policy realms – but also results in a world view that ignores the complexities of freight transport (Giuliano et al. 2013). In terms of volume of traffic, the emphasis on passenger activity may be warranted but it belies the critical importance of urban freight in the broader economic and social context.

REVOLUTIONS IN TRANSPORTATION

The previous section provides the general context for understanding freight flows in the city from a traditional perspective. Many of the concepts transcend eras and are still applicable – the critical importance and impacts of urban freight, the tension between efficiency and externalities, and the spatial structures of the core, industrial zones, and centres of commercial activity. However, key elements have changed dramatically, responding to internal and external disruptions in urban freight.

Tuttle and Wykle (2003) offer an interesting argument about previous revolutions in transportation and their impacts on the broader economy. They describe how each revolution in transportation took place alongside a revolution in communications. The first, in the 1800s, was the introduction of the railway, which took place alongside the arrival of the telegraph. The combination of accelerated movement caused by the train and of communication enabled by the telegraph had a massive impact on the urban economy. The second revolution occurred as broad adoption of the automobile/truck and expansion of the US highway network took place alongside the rise of the telephone. Again, this resulted in tremendous impacts on the speed, scope, and geography of urban/regional economics.

The policy and regulatory aspects of these first two revolutions are important to appreciate when exploring the platform economy and its impact in our cities. Railways, with their high fixed costs related to establishing their networks, result in monopoly markets that led to governmental economic regulation on market entry, exit, price, and conditions of service or an "obligation to serve." In contrast, trucking had relatively low entry costs and, with many entrants in key markets, there were concerns about the opposite – "destructive competition." Ease of entry led to many firms competing for traffic, which led to small profit margins and decline in operating standards. Firms cut necessary costs, such as vehicle maintenance and training, while ignoring regulations. Hence while railways were regulated to prevent the abuse of monopoly power, trucking was regulated (including regulation of entry, price, exit, and service) in the name of public interest. Trucking regulations ensure a level of safety and protect industry incumbents from destructive competition, similar to the regulation of the taxi industry in many cities.

The third revolution is where things get interesting! The information and communications foundation of the platform city – the internet, or the "World Wide Web" – emerged in the 1980s and early 1990s and is the newest manifestation of the communication side of the transportation/communication interplay of the previous two revolutions. However, there is no clear new mode of transportation to emerge alongside it – no "rail" or "road." Tuttle and Wykle (2003) argued that the transportation revolution should be a massive investment in infrastructure in the name of national economy competitiveness. Although it is not a new mode per se, Rodrigue (2017) identifies the rise of containerization as part of the emergence of global production networks in the post-Fordist era – a key part of globalization and arguably an essential part of a third revolution. Indeed the combination of internet-driven commerce and container shipping has given rise to the emergence of the concept of "the physical internet." Conceptually, goods encapsulated in modular containers (boxes) affixed with a digital header of information (think bar code) can be routed through our cities, aspiring to the efficiency of packets of digital information moving through the internet (Buldeo Rai et al. 2017). The container and its role in establishing modern global supply chains could be the "mode" of the third revolution, while the internet could be the concomitant "communication" revolution.

Another significant part of timing of the third revolution is that it coincides with the era of privatization and deregulation in many transportation markets around the globe (Banister and Button 2016).

Trucking and rail in the United States were effectively deregulated, and governments sold off state-run enterprises and infrastructure assets (airports and ports, for example) as part of the onset of neo-liberalism and the emphasis on competitive market forces. As part of the public debate on trucking deregulation, common arguments were that regulatory control on entry had introduced x-inefficiency – poor management and a lack of innovation without the focus provided by intense competition. A second major argument was that labour unions had extracted excess wages. The topics of competitive efficiency, innovation, and labour costs are still central to understanding the challenges we face today in moving freight in the digital city.

REVOLUTIONS IN THE PLATFORM CITY

The discussion of previous revolutions in transportation and the inability, so far, to declare one for our current era, set up the remaining exploration of modern freight-moving systems. We accept that (1) railroads transformed national economies and have resurged as part of the modern intermodal movement of containers, (2) roads and trucking are an integral part of the twentieth-century auto-centric North American city, and (3) containerization and the internet are the foundation of global commerce. Supporting the revolutions have been the key neo-liberal shifts represented by privatization of national transportation assets and deregulation of transportation markets (namely in road and rail). The third revolution's anchor of the communication transformation of the internet spurred the development and widespread adoption of supply chain management and logistics as core business elements. Supply chain management involves directing the parts of the distribution system (supply chains), including production scheduling and inventory control, transportation, warehousing, wholesaling, retailing, and brokerage. Logistics is a key part of supply chain management and is the process of planning, implementing, and controlling the flow and storage of goods (and services and related information) from the point of origin to the point of consumption.

A prime example of supply chain and logistics in action is "just in time" manufacturing in automobile production, where suppliers are required to provide inputs to production locations as they are needed rather than on-site storage. A second example is "quick response" retailing where information flows are as important as the physical flows of rapidly designed and distributed fashion. There is broad characterization of moving from "stock" models – keeping goods on hand in inventory – to "flow" models, where delivery timing is critical. The results? In recent decades, growth in freight flows has outstripped economic growth, dominated inventory, expanded in geographic scope, concentrated in key locations, and is carried increasingly by road, intermodal, and air (Hesse and Rodrigue 2004; Woudsma 2012). Not surprisingly, freight-related GHG emissions have doubled since 1990 levels in many Western economies, while passenger-related transport GHG emissions have declined. While supply chain efficiencies drive business profitability, their logistics activities are associated with increasingly negative effects on congestion, safety, and the environment in our cities (Savelsbergh and Van Woensel 2016).

A recent article presents yet another variation on the "third revolution" in transportation, suggesting boldly that "ridesharing is just the first phase of the movement to end car ownership and reclaim our cities" (Zimmer 2016). Written by the co-founder of transportation network company Lyft, this more recent perspective moves beyond "the internet," alluding to the disruptive rise of mobility as a service, predicated on the key role of the now ubiquitous smartphone. Forget "revolution," we are now talking about a full-on digital disruption in transportation! The internet changed retail and production supply chains and logistics in the 1990s, but the widespread adoption of smartphones in the 2010s and the emergence of the platform economy and retailing e-commerce has turned the realm of material flows in the platform city on its head (Qi et al. 2017).

E-commerce is generally characterized by online shopping by most people of the platform age. Its annual double-digit growth in many markets has disrupted traditional retail markets. As online shopping has grown, shopping at brick-and-mortar retail has declined precipitously. As consumers, we now have the power to purchase what we want, when we want, and at the best price, through whatever device we have connected to the internet (phone, tablet, car, etc.). Now, rather going to a brick-and-mortar store to pick up our purchases, a transportation service provider completes the transaction through last-mile delivery to our door. The impact on emissions is complex; consolidating deliveries in a single vehicle rather than having multiple customers driving to a store offers opportunities to reduce overall per unit emissions. However, scouting trips to review products before purchase, returns of online purchases, and failed deliveries erode the efficiencies. As online shopping has grown, there has been a parallel rise in demand for last-mile delivery of all those parcels. In addition, the character and form of our cities is changing as retailing land uses evolve and new physical additions like parcel lockers and pickup/drop-off centres emerge. Retailing is undergoing the latest in a long history of disruptions that include the shopping mall of the 1960s, the rise of big box retailing in the 1980s, and the persistent challenge to Main Street (High Street) vitality in many cities. The role of the automobile and the revolutions in transportation described here are an integral part of how these disruptions have affected the city.

Last-mile delivery is not new. It has a long history in business-to-business (B2B) document and parcel delivery and is associated with the major global logistics providers such as UPS, FedEx, and DHL. In the city, these flows have been geographically focused on industry and business concentrations like the city centre or business parks. But online shopping has resulted in a significant increase in business-to-consumer (B2C) parcel last-mile delivery and the emergence of new markets like B2C prepared food (think Uber Eats) and the re-emergence of B2C grocery. Last-mile delivery is a central part of the urban freight landscape and as such touches on the key objectives of urban freight planning – economic vitality, congestion mitigation, infrastructure design and operations, safety, and environmental concerns.

The B2C grocery is a fascinating market and home to one of the largest failures of the dot.com era – Webvan circa 2000. The Webvan model was to offer the price and product of traditional grocery stores delivered to your door, and their Achilles heel was a massive miscalculation of the complexity and costs of providing last-mile delivery. Creating a website version of a grocery store and stocking a distribution centre with the needed items was relatively straightforward – the delivery part not so. Webvan went public in 1999, rose quickly in valuation to $6 billion, with revenues of only $5 million and each delivery costing twenty-seven dollars. They were bankrupt by 2001 (Simpson 2010). Last-mile delivery is the most costly part of the supply chain, with estimates of it being five to twenty times more expensive for retailers than in-store purchasing (Allen et al. 2018). Fast forward nearly twenty years and there are new efforts underway to tackle online shopping and groceries, exemplified in Amazon's purchase of Whole Foods in 2017. Key lessons learned from the Webvan experience includes using brick-and-mortar stores as the source of orders rather a purpose-designed (and expensive) warehouse, and the use of platform economy labour – picker and delivery person in one.

This is but one example of the myriad developments influencing the movement of materials in the platform city. The most recent revolution has spawned new actors, new business models, and new pressures to tackle the underlying tensions between our time-sensitive desire to consume and the costs of that consumption in the platform city. Cities still have areas where freight movement is concentrated – airports and warehouses, for example – but more than ever, it seems that every location in a city has become a potential destination point, as the demand for last-mile delivery increases significantly. And, as delivery moves beyond the traditional actors and markets involved in moving stuff, in some cases the people who demand increasingly dispersed delivery also become the people who are *literally* driving it around.

MOVING STUFF AND THE CROWD

"Turning ordinary citizens into couriers" (McKinnon 2016) – neighbours receiving parcels for neighbours, or you picking up your friend's parcel at a retail pickup location and bringing it home to her – all fall into the spectrum of "the crowd" participating in the new logistics of moving stuff in the platform city, particularly when it involves the last mile. Digital disruption occurring via platforms is beginning throughout the goods-movement industry – there is "Uber Freight," which is an app that matches traditional truck drivers with shippers and carriers, and "Flexe," an on-demand start-up analogous to Airbnb, except the space being "shared" is warehousing. On the food delivery side, most are familiar with SkipTheDishes, or Uber Eats apps, where the delivery workers share the platform ecosystem with those ordering and producing their food.

While these examples are interesting, the focus of this chapter is on the most dynamic segment in the platform city: last -mile logistics. Within this field, venture capital and start-ups are churning in a highly fragmented urban delivery market (Netzer et al. 2017). The intuitive concept of "last-mile delivery" has been replaced by a more nuanced definition: "Last-mile logistics is the last stretch of a business-to-consumer (B2C) parcel delivery service. It takes place from the order penetration point to the final consignee's preferred destination point" (Frederick et al. 2018, 310). Order penetration points include warehouses, stores, fulfillment centres, or even factories – it's where your product starts after your order is placed. Your preferred destination point could be your home, office, a reception box (locker), pickup point, or collection/delivery point.

There are distinct markets in last-mile delivery, differentiated by product, geography (spatially), and time. The major product segments include prepared food delivery from restaurants, with firms in the segment including SkiptheDishes, Uber Eats, Postmates, and DoorDash in North America. In the grocery space, Instacart, Shipt, and Amazon are the major players in the North American market. E-commerce retail parcels make up the final and largest product space. Within e-commerce, the big three traditional courier delivery firms (UPS, FedEx, and the US Postal Service) account for 85 per cent of the estimated $35 billion spent for services in this market. Of that 85 per cent, UPS occupies 52 per cent, FedEx 23 per cent, and the US Postal Service 12 per cent. Regional couriers occupy 12 per cent of the remaining 15 per cent overall market share, and crowdsourcing only amounts to 1 per cent of e-commerce delivery (Monahan and Hu 2017).

Geographically, last-mile delivery markets differ not only in the geography of the delivery but the geographic scope of the firms providing the service. UPS and FedEx are global in their coverage, whereas many incumbent courier firms in the B2B and B2C space have a regional scope, while emerging urban delivery services like Instacart and Delivery Hero operate within the densest metropolitan regions. They cannot provide delivery to the far-flung reaches of the globe, but they can deliver the goods from point to point via e-commerce transactions within a city. Temporally, estimates from a global consumer survey suggest that about 70 per cent of online shoppers are more concerned with price than time, preferring the cheapest option (Joerss et al. 2016), regardless of time. However, a growing preference trend is for same-day delivery (23 per cent of consumers) or instant delivery (within a two-hour window at 2 per cent). The desire for timeliness is a huge influence on how stuff moves around a city and the subsequent impacts that delivery methods have on the city.

An excellent example of how this plays out is the rise of Amazon as a market-segment-blurring giant, especially its efforts to place products in fulfillment centres close to where the demand occurs. A traditional warehouse implies storage of products; a distribution centre involves shorter-term storage and redistribution of products to businesses and consumers, while a fulfillment centre is typically operated to satisfy e-commerce orders. Between 2010 and 2016, Amazon spent

$13 billion building fulfillment centres in fifty of the largest urban markets in the United States, in order to be able to provide timely delivery for their most popular items (Monahan and Hu 2017). Rather than having centralized supply and using a dense hub-and-spoke network for delivery only (like UPS or FedEx), the Amazon model decentralizes order penetration points and relies on a more diverse set of options for the last-mile delivery. Thus, with the diversification and decentralization of delivery, the adaptation and innovation in last-mile logistics increases.

BUSINESS MODELS

The crowd is a role-player in the disrupted last-mile delivery segment of the platform city. There is a range of business models at play, from traditional corporate delivery firms to the amateur and ad hoc nature of delivery via crowdsourcing. Pure "crowdshipping" is less about the platform economy and more about sharing – it is a web-enabled transaction in which ordinary citizens (private drivers) make deliveries during trips they would already be making anyway. Roadie, as an example, bills itself as the "on the way delivery network," as it originated as a service to connect people that needed stuff moved with those already traveling to that location. Movers are compensated, but the terms are more variable and negotiated through the app/web environment. I may be driving from Toronto to Ottawa and have room in my vehicle, and you need to get your bike to Ottawa for a term at school. You post the need on their platform, I offer to take your bike, and we establish the terms of the shipment. This type of activity is definitely more niche and outside the realm of typical business activity.

The broader term popularized to describe the platform economy and last-mile delivery is "crowd logistics." This is defined as "an information connectivity enabled marketplace concept that matches supply and demand for logistics services with an undefined and external crowd that has free capacity with regards to time and/or space, participates on a voluntary basis and is compensated accordingly" (Buldeo Rai et al. 2017, 38). Collaborative platforms and mobile apps connect individuals (a mass of actors) and firms to peers, with the distinction from traditional services being that mostly amateur individuals are performing logistics services on an ad hoc basis. For example, if you have a vehicle and look to make extra money, you can apply to participate as a delivery person – once qualified, sign in to the company app and start providing services making parcel deliveries. You are part of the "crowd" providing labour, but you are not considered an employee. Rather, you are an independent contractor of sorts. This determination of "employee" is at the heart of contentious labour relations in the gig economy. Recent efforts to organize crowdshipping individuals into unions have been met with pushback from some firms they provide services to (Canadian Press 2019).

Indeed, McKinnon (2016) stresses the importance of the distinctions between "crowdshipping" and "crowd logistics" through three types of crowds: the casual crowdshipper, subcontractors, and professional drivers. In common, they have no specific shipper training, provide the physical vehicle asset, and connect through technology. For the true casual crowdshipper (peer-to-peer), the motivations are often linked to community and environment – helping a neighbour in need of delivery and helping the environment because the trip was being made anyway. For others in the crowd, it is yet another example of gig-economy employment where the lure of making extra money or freedom of self-employment drives their involvement in dedicated delivery trips. The growth in e-commerce purchasing has driven the increase in last-mile material flows and spurred the rise of crowd logistics. As an example of the growth in this sector, Dablanc et al. (2017) report that in France there were 13,500 self-employed jobs in the parcel and courier sector in 2016, compared to 3,900 in 2015, and only 2,000 in 2014.

The incumbent major parcel delivery firms (UPS, FedEx) and retailers like Amazon and WalMart have all ventured into this crowd logistics space. DHL tested a partnership with crowd logistics start-up bring. BUDDY, UPS has collaborated with Deliv, and Amazon has introduced Amazon Flex – its version of gig employment, which complements its own logistics business of Amazon Prime. Walmart has established and then terminated relationships with Deliv, Skipcart, and Uber over the years, as these delivery firms have all struggled to be profitable in the grocery delivery arena, citing a lack of delivery-point density in suburban areas as a key driver. DoorDash, which exemplifies the new business model disrupting this space – the on-demand urban delivery provider –employs demand aggregation via its own mobile platforms and dedicated in-house operations that usually enable (almost) instant delivery (Netzer et al. 2017).

The operational differences between traditional business-logistics-oriented major parcel-delivery firms or national post office carriers and crowd logistics urban-delivery providers are critically important to understand. The business logistics firms leverage their ability to consolidate demand because they are so large and serve that demand systematically with standardized fleets of vehicles and employees (contract or otherwise) that uphold service levels. Their hub-and-spoke networks allow delivery routes to be maximally fuel efficient with many stops and high drop-density. In contrast, the crowd logistics firms that rely on the platform to generate demand lead to more point-to-point delivery with higher costs, delivery service variability (with other services like personal shopping added on), and risk of unreliability in capacity. Ultimately, crowd logistics needs to grow. The number of participants on the service and customer sides must expand in order for delivery to expand. More shops and drivers mean more choice for consumers, and more consumers mean greater potential for earnings – a cycle of positive feedback with significant growth potential (Netzer et al. 2017). Their advantage is the software they have created that guides their resource crowd and uses "the city is a warehouse" as they draw from a diverse and fragmented pool instead of a single fulfillment centre.

IMPACTS AND IMPLICATIONS

The significant growth in last-mile deliveries is being driven by forces like the double-digit growth in e-commerce across a range of market segments from prepared food, to grocery, to retail items and beyond. The impacts of this increase in activity are also significant, and not limited to the last-mile delivery itself. It's not just about vehicles on the roads making deliveries, but also the "preferred destination point," which could be your house, a parcel locker, or a pickup point at a retail store. You can have a vehicle drive around your neighbourhood stopping at each home to drop a parcel, or you can have a neighbourhood parcel locker visited once by a truck, leaving the last-mile activity up to you. Both options affect the transportation system, the built form, and labour in our cities, with important implications for policy and regulation: more vehicles contributing to congestion, increased GHG emissions, poor air quality, parked delivery vehicles in cycling lanes, delivery lockers appearing on the urban landscape, parcel theft (porch pirates), and evolving design requirements.

The volume of vehicles involved in last-mile deliveries is increasing as is their trip-making activity, but overall traffic levels on our streets are not necessarily increasing in conjunction as last-mile parcel delivery substitutes for passenger shopping trips (Visser et al. 2014). However, direct substitution is not always realized, as people make trips to review potential purchases before ordering online, over-purchase online knowing they can make free returns (leading to reverse logistics activity or "returns"), or failed deliveries occur, which further last-mile delivery travel.

The central tension in urban freight between efficiency and externality remains even more relevant today. Last-mile delivery vehicles – from the iconic five-tonne brown UPS truck to your neighbour's non-descript SUV – spend a great deal of time on their delivery tours parked, as employees make the last leg of the delivery on foot. Parking carries its own host of issues, from contributing to congestion – illegal or double-parking reducing lane capacity – to conflicts with active transport when bike lanes become delivery stop lanes. There may be efforts to create dedicated delivery zones, or increase ticketing of illegal parking, but when the crowd is involved, stop locations ubiquitous, the battles for curb space become intense. Similarly, active transport infrastructure and public transit can feel the increasing pressure of delivery activity, as they are also utilized by foot/bike/transit-based delivery workers.

Built form impacts are occurring at a slower temporal scale than traffic impacts, as businesses and developers adjust to the changing urban freight landscape. Amazon's blanketing of North American cities with huge fulfillment centres over the past decade has added to the traditional urban industrial landscape. However, increasing demands for next-day, same-day, or instant deliveries is driving a new development of smaller footprint logistics spaces in the inner city and urban core to ensure the ability to meet ever-shortening delivery timelines – from next-day, to same-day, to instant. Placing products close to markets is the objective in this race, and traditional retailers are leveraging the geographic advantage of their bricks-and-mortar locations, adding functionality to serve the "click-and-collect" shoppers or urban delivery services (driven by crowd logistics). New built forms – parcel lockers or pickup points – are becoming more common, especially in dense urban areas with traditional high drop density, and challenging traffic circulation. However, consumer uptake remains limited, with the overwhelming preference for actual home delivery (Joerss et al. 2016). Finally, the design of new buildings, such as condominiums, now incorporates last-mile logistics activities with specific spaces designed to hold parcels (instead of stacked in the lobby) and even hot and cold locker storage built in the lobby for food deliveries.

Last-mile delivery is costly on a number of fronts, with labour costs a major competitive factor. The incumbent major parcel-delivery firms use a combination of employees and contractors, and franchise models have been employed in the past. In the franchise model, local delivery operators own and operate a franchise of a parent firm that provides the inter-regional transportation services connecting franchise locations in different cities. In the platform-economy-driven crowd logistics environment, self-employed workers or "lifestyle couriers" are prominent with performance-based pay a reality (Bates et al. 2018). The labour spectrum runs from "casual crowdshipper" and "lifestyle courier" to "contractor" or "delivery service partner." As decreases in the price of delivery occur, coupled with shorter delivery time frames, the opportunities to consolidate and become efficient decrease. Add into the mix the competition among delivery services that overlap in activity spaces, and the prospects for reliable delivery incomes become less assured and the questions on what is fair and just work in last-mile logistics more pronounced. These questions are relevant across the spectrum of delivery workers and firms. Amazon is no stranger to labour unrest, and recent allegations of misconduct under the Employment Standards Act in Ontario include pressure tactics for performance and alleged firings of contractors trying to organize a union presence (Canadian Press 2019).

DELIVERING STUFF: THE FUTURE

The growth in urban freight activity, and specifically the last-mile delivery market, is broadly characterized by high costs – for both business and the urban environment, in addition to consumers who are not willing to pay for it. Even if a consumer pays for membership to a retail service, like Amazon Prime, which covers some of the business costs, no one is paying for the externalities – congestion, safety, pollution. Of the current sustainability-friendly developments – from pure crowdshipping and parcel lockers to unlocking the underutilized capacity in all of our current auto trips – none is popular, gaining ground, or expected to have a major impact. There is the potential to push electrification of vehicles to reduce local pollution (but not impact traffic) and some speculation that in the next decade, automated vehicles will provide the efficiencies we seek. Automated ground vehicles with parcel lockers are projected to handle 80 per cent of the current delivery market in the decade ahead, as only one example of many potential technological developments (Joerss et al. 2016).

The new business models of the platform economy are disrupting urban freight, and urban governance needs to seriously consider how planning and regulation need to adapt as well (Dablanc et al. 2017). The prior regimes of regulation in transportation were driven by a desire to control monopoly power (hello Amazon) or destructive competition (to ensure road safety, fair labour, quality of services) in the name of the public interest (how many delivery firms do we need in one city?). Reintroducing regulation to control firm entry into the delivery market or size of firms may be an option, and regulated/incentivized use of shared facilities and delivery capacity has occurred in European markets (urban consolidation centres, or micro-hubs). In today's digital environment, transparency and reputation would arguably be more effective than rigid regulations (Borsenburger 2017). Given the pace and character of change underway in the platform city, the future of urban freight is becoming less sustainable unless governments can find a more effective way to engage the crowd and the firms they serve.

REFERENCES

Allen, J., M. Piecyk, and M. Piotrowska. 2018. "Understanding the Impact of E-commerce on Last-Mile Light Goods Vehicle Activity in Ur-Ban Areas: The Case of London." *Transportation Research,* Part D: Transport and Environment, 61, Part B: 325–38.

Banister, D., and K. Button. 2016. *Transport in a Free Market Economy.* London: Palgrave Macmillan.

Bates, O., A. Friday, J. Allen, T. Cherrett, F. McLeod, T. Bektas, T. Nguyen, M. Piecyk, M. Piotrowska, S. Wise, and N. Davies. 2018. "Transforming Last-Mile Logistics: Opportunities for More Sustainable Deliveries." In *Proceedings of the 2018 CHI Conference on Human Factors in Computing Systems,* Paper 526, 1–14. https://doi.org/10.1145/3173574.3174100.

Böge, S. 1995. "The Well-Travelled Yogurt Pot: Lessons for New Freight Transport Policies and Regional Production." *World Transport Policy & Practice* 1, no. 1: 7–11.

Borsenberger, C. 2017. "The Sharing Economy and the 'Uberization' Phenomenon: What Impacts on the Economy in General and for the Delivery Operators in Particular?" In *The Changing Postal and Delivery Sector: Towards a Renaissance*, edited by M. Crew, P.L. Parcu, and T. Brennan, 191–203. Cham, Switzerland: Springer.

Buldeo Rai, H., S. Verlinde, and J. Merckx. 2017. "Crowd Logistics: An Opportunity for More Sustainable Urban Freight Transport?" *European Transport Research Review* 9, article 39, 1–13.

Canadian Press. 2019. "Labour Complaint against Amazon Canada Alleges Workers Who Tried to Unionize Were Fired." CBC News, 30 January. https://www.cbc.ca/news/business/amazon-canada-labour-complaint-1.4998744.

Cui, J., J. Dodson, and P.V. Hall. 2015. "Planning for Urban Freight Transport: An Overview." *Transport Reviews* 35, no. 5: 583–98.

Dablanc, L., E. Morganti, N. Arvidsson, J. Woxenius, M. Browne, and N. Saidi. 2017. "The Rise of On-Demand 'Instant Deliveries' in European Cities." *Supply Chain Forum: An International Journal* 18, no. 4: 203–17. https://doi.org/10.1080/16258312.2017.1375375.

Dablanc, L., and, J.P. Rodrigue. 2017. "The Geography of Urban Freight." In *The Geography of Urban Transportation*, edited by G. Giuliano and S. Hanson, 4th ed., 34–58. New York: Guilford.

Frederick, S., W.T. Lim, X. Jin, and J. Singh Srai. 2018. "Consumer-Driven e-Commerce: A Literature Review, Design Framework, and Research Agenda on Last-Mile Logistics Models." *International Journal of Physical Distribution & Logistics Management* 48, no. 3: 308–32.

Giuliano, G., T. O'Brien, L. Dablanc, and K. Holliday. 2013. *NCFRP Report 23: Synthesis of Freight Research in Urban Transportation Planning*. Washington, DC: Transportation Research Board of the National Academies.

Hesse, M., and J.P. Rodrigue. 2004. "The Transport Geography of Logistics and Freight Distribution." *Journal of Transport Geography* 12: 171–84.

Joerss, M., J. Schröder, and F. Neuhaus. 2016. "How Customer Demands Are Reshaping Last-Mile Delivery." McKinsey & Company. https://www.mckinsey.com/industries/travel-transport-and-logistics/our-insights/how-customer-demands-are-reshaping-last-mile-delivery.

McKinnon, A.C. 2016. "Crowdshipping: A Communal Approach to Reducing Urban Traffic Levels?" Working paper. https://doi.org/10.13140/RG.2.2.20271.53925.

Metrolinx. 2016. "Urban Goods Movement: Technical Paper 5 to Support the Discussion Paper for the Next Regional Transportation Plan." Toronto: Province of Ontario.

Monahan, S., and M. Hu. 2017. "US E-Commerce Trends and the Impact on Logistics." Kearney. http://www.atkearney.ca/transportation/featured-article/-/asset_publisher/S5UkOozyovnu/content/us-e-commerce-trends-and-the-impact-on-logistics/10192.

Netzer, T., J. Krause, and L. Hausmann. 2017. "The Urban Delivery Bet: USD 5 Billion in Venture Capital at Risk?" McKinsey & Company. https://www.mckinsey.it/sites/default/files/the-urban-delivery-bet-usd-5-billion-in-venture-capital-at-risk.pdf.

Ogden, K.W. 1992. *Urban Goods Movement: A Guide to Policy and Planning*. London: Ashgate Publishing.

Qi, W., L. Li, and S. Liu. 2017. "Shared Mobility for Last-Mile Delivery: Design, Operational Prescriptions and Environ-Mental Impact." SSRN. https://ssrn.com/abstract=2859018.

Rodrigue, J.P. 2017. *The Geography of Transport Systems*. New York: Routledge.

Savelsbergh, M., and T. Van Woensel. 2016. "50th Anniversary Invited Article – City Logistics: Challenges and Opportunities." *Transportation Science* 50, no. 2: 579–90.

Simpson, S. 2010. "Webvan and Other IPO Epic Failures." *Forbes Magazine*, 13 December. https://www.forbes.com/sites/greatspeculations/2010/12/13/the-biggest-ipo-flops/#82775286391f.

Tuttle, W., and K. Wykle. 2003. "The Third Transportation Revolution." *Transportation Quarterly* 57, no. 1: 47–58.

Visser, J., T. Nemoto, and M. Browne. 2014. "Home Delivery and the Impacts on Urban Freight Transport: A Review." *Procedia: Social and Behavioral Sciences* 125: 5–27.

Woudsma, C. 2001. "Understanding the Movement of Goods, Not People: Issues, Evidence and Potential." *Urban Studies* 38: 2,439–55.

– 2012. "Freight, Land and Local Economic Development." In *Cities, Regions and Flows*, edited by P. Hall and M. Hesse, 226–45. New York: Routledge.

Zimmer, J. 2016. "The Third Transportation Revolution: Lyft's Vision for the Next Ten Years and Beyond." *Medium*, 18 September. https://medium.com/@johnzimmer/the-third-transportation-revolution-27860f05fa91.

SECTION TWO

Governing Platforms

6

Ride Hailing in Canadian Cities

by Shauna Brail

- Ride hailing is a relatively new and disruptive form of local ground transportation, made possible through the convergence of wireless networks, GPS technology, and software applications, combined with the widespread adoption of smartphones.
- Despite its disruptive nature, ride hailing is now a regulated activity in most large Canadian cities.
- Ride hailing presents a challenge to municipal government regulators, and their responses will have wide-ranging policy implications.

INTRODUCTION

Digital ride hailing is the practice of connecting drivers of private vehicles to prospective passengers through a platform-economy firm acting as an intermediary or connector. The process is arranged through the use of a smartphone, the cost to the rider is confirmed in advance, the payment is electronic, and the transaction is facilitated by a digital intermediary.

The convergence of technological innovations drove the establishment of ride hailing as an industry. Ride hailing became possible as a direct result of the convergence of wireless networks, GPS technology, and software applications (or apps) in combination with the widespread adoption of smartphones. Ride hailing as we know it is an example of a highly disruptive, transformative, and scalable activity made possible through the emergence of the digital platform economy.

A common measure of the impact of a new technology is the length of time it takes for it to be used by 50 per cent of households in a given area. A market is considered to have reached saturation once adoption rates reach 80 per cent of households. Smartphones are one of the fastest growing consumer technologies in history. Whereas more than fifty years passed before telephones were present in 50 per cent of US households, and just under twenty years until computers were adopted by half of all US households, smartphones were adopted by 50 per cent of US households in less than ten years. By 2012, smartphone adoption rates reached the 50 per cent threshold (Dediu 2012). By 2016, US households were saturated (Lella 2017).

It is no coincidence that ride-hailing firms also began to disrupt local ground-transportation services in 2012 – the same year that smartphone adoption rates reached the 50 per cent threshold. Ride-hailing firms leveraged the digital trifecta of wireless, GPS, and smartphone saturation to develop new, scalable business models that frequently circumvented regulations and constraints. Since 2012, ride hailing has expanded and scaled quickly. Ride hailing's rapid ascent is credited to aggressive start-up firm business practices; consumer and producer benefits linked to cost savings, efficiency, and customer service improvements associated with digital ride hailing; and the rewriting of municipal regulations to enable ride-hailing firms to legally operate as part of a municipality's ground transportation system (Brail 2017).

Since its entrance, ride hailing's presence as a form of local ground transportation has grown rapidly. When ride hailing first launched, platform economy firms utilized technology and smartphones to connect licensed limousine and taxi drivers with prospective passengers. It was not until 2012 that ride-hailing firms, led in the United States by Lyft, began to launch services that recruited and connected unlicensed drivers in privately owned vehicles with passengers. Ride hailing began to grow and raise alarm amongst regulators at the same time (Rayle and Flores 2016; Lashinsky 2017). Within six years of launching, ride-hailing operations became firmly global. Uber, the largest ride-hailing firm, operates in sixty-five countries and nearly 700 cities around the world. Ride hailing operates in more than 2,600 cities around the world (Brail and Donald 2018).

Beyond offering new ways of connecting drivers with riders, ride hailing is also recognized as being disruptive. Ride hailing is strongly criticized for harming local ground transportation, especially taxi operations and public transit (Graehler et al. 2018); adding congestion and vehicle miles travelled to city streets (Schaller 2017); and creating a workforce of precarious, underpaid drivers (Reader 2018).

The remainder of this chapter introduces ride hailing's emergence, traces the rollout of ride hailing in Canada's thirty largest cities from 2012 to 2019, and addresses controversies and contributions that have resulted from it. The chapter then reviews changes in regulatory approaches that characterize three periods of activity: Launch, Regulation 1.0, and Regulation 2.0. It concludes by addressing the prospects for ride hailing and its connection to a much broader emphasis on transformations in urban mobility.

RIDE HAILING: GROWTH, MEASUREMENT, CONTROVERSY, AND CONTRIBUTIONS

Ride hailing entered Canada in 2012, with the launch of Uber's luxury car and taxi service in Toronto. In September 2014, UberX, a service that connects private drivers holding a standard (i.e., non-commercial) driver's licence with passengers, launched in Toronto. Within a year it was estimated that 17,000 riders were using the service in Toronto each day (Cook 2015). As of December 2019, ride-hailing services operate across the country and are regulated in twenty-six of Canada's thirty largest municipalities by population (see table 6.1).

Statistics Canada (2017) found that between November 2015 and October 2016, 7 per cent of Canadians over the age of eighteen used app-based ride-hailing services, and spending on these services totalled $241 million. Consistent with other research (Hathaway and Muro 2016), the use of ride hailing was shown to be concentrated in cities. Ottawa-Gatineau led ride-hailing usage, with over 17 per cent of people aged eighteen and over reporting they had used a ride-hailing service, followed by Toronto (14.8 per cent) and then Edmonton (9.8 per cent).

It is clear from US data comparing ride hailing and public transit that in the approximately five years since the emergence of ride hailing, it has gained significant ground relative to public transit use. A study based on the 2017 US National Household Travel Survey found that 10 per cent of Americans used ride hailing in the month prior to the survey (Conway et al. 2018). By comparison, just under 17 per cent of respondents used public transit at least once in the month leading up to the survey (Conway et al. 2018). Although ride hailing has scaled up and expanded rapidly, Conway et al. (2018) found that the total number of trips taken via ride hailing represent a mere 0.5 per cent of all trips. This statistic helps to place the significance of ride hailing as a mode of total trips into context.

Table 6.1
Status of ride-hailing regulation in Canada's thirty largest municipalities,
as of December 2019

Municipality	Province	Regulations (Y/N)	Municipality	Province	Regulations (Y/N)
Brampton	ON	Y	Montreal	QC	Y
Burlington	ON	N	Oakville	ON	Y
Burnaby	BC	Y	Ottawa	ON	Y
Calgary	AB	Y	Quebec City	QC	Y
Edmonton	AB	Y	Regina	SK	Y
Gatineau	QC	Y	Richmond	BC	Y
Greater Sudbury	ON	Y	Richmond Hill	ON	N
			Saskatoon	SK	Y
Halifax	NS	N	Sherbrooke	QC	Y
Hamilton	ON	Y	Surrey*	BC	Y
Kitchener	ON	Y	Toronto	ON	Y
Laval	QC	Y	Vancouver	BC	Y
London	ON	Y	Vaughan	ON	Y
Longueuil	QC	Y	Windsor	ON	Y
Markham	ON	N	Winnipeg	MB	Y
Mississauga	ON	Y			

* There are regulations governing ride-hailing, but Surrey has refused to develop a business licence for ride-hailing firms.

Ride hailing is often credited with expanding and improving transportation options and opportunities for individuals and transit agencies. Some municipalities have entered into partnerships with ride-hailing firms, finding it more cost-effective to provide customers with vouchers for ride-hailing services than operating inefficient publicly funded bus routes on low density routes. For instance, the municipality of Innisfil, Ontario, located approximately ninety kilometres north of Toronto, entered into a partnership with Uber in 2017. Instead of investing in the creation of two public routes, the municipality partnered with Uber to provide subsidized, flat fare rides to residents. After analysis of the first year of operation, the municipality estimated that the Uber partnership saved the municipality $8 million over what it would have cost to operate public transit (Canadian Press 2018). The subsidy per passenger in 2017 was $5.62, which was higher than originally estimated but lower than the $33 per passenger subsidy required to operate the same level of service via a traditional bus route (Canadian

Press 2018). However, the example of Innisfil also highlights the challenges of privately run transportation systems as a substitute for public transit. The program was a success in terms of ridership, which ultimately meant that the city had exceeded the budget allocated to offsetting the cost of rides for residents. In the spring of 2019, Innisfil changed the terms of transportation services and discounts offered to residents. Per-trip discounts were reduced from $5 to $4, and total rides per month capped at thirty (Bliss 2019). The example of Innisfil highlights both the opportunity for municipalities to experiment with alternatives to public transit and at the same time raises the challenge of subsidizing a service for which the price increases along with the number of users.

The City of Belleville provides another example of how municipalities are adapting their public transit offerings on the basis of the advent of ride hailing. In Belleville, the local transportation agency is reporting success, with a pilot program being referred to as "bus-hailing." Rather than subsidizing residents to use private ride-hailing services, Belleville Transit has changed the technology that they use to run their bus routes. Through this initiative, Belleville Transit is working with a Toronto-based firm that developed and supports a mobile application that enables riders to schedule a bus ride, using an algorithm to adjust bus routes according to demand, in real time (Dunne 2018).

CONTROVERSY AND CONTRIBUTIONS

The narrative associated with ride hailing is complicated. On one hand, ride hailing is seen as decimating the taxi sector, and this narrative continues to permeate conversations about the regulation of ride hailing. In 2015, the number of Uber vehicles in operation outnumbered operating taxis in New York City, Los Angeles, and San Francisco (Ahsan and Hensley 2015). By 2016, business travellers were choosing to use ride-hailing service in place of car rentals (Associated Press 2016). And in 2017, it was notably less expensive to commute via UberPool than in a private vehicle in four of the five largest cities in the United States: New York City, Chicago, Washington, DC, and Los Angeles (Meeker 2018). An October 2018 headline in the *Globe and Mail* reads "Do Canada's Taxi Drivers Have a Place in Transportation's Changing Future?" While Canadian cities continue to have both taxi and ride-hailing services being offered, it remains to be seen whether digital ride hailing will replace traditional taxi services entirely.

The promise of ride hailing creates opportunities for travellers. Given the right set of policy and regulatory tools, ride hailing can help reduce congestion and environmental degradation (Sperling et al. 2018), expand services to populations and geographic locations that are typically underserved (Brown 2018), and strengthen connections to public transit by providing services from transit stations located in dense areas to nearby, lower-density residential areas that may not be well served by transit (Sperling et al. 2018). Furthermore, ride hailing can be appealing to consumers who find it easy to use, less expensive than taxi services, and more convenient than public transit services.

These prospective benefits come at a cost to individuals and society. One of the most frequently cited concerns surrounding the use of ride hailing is its negative impact on drivers' income and employment prospects (Rosenblat 2018), and the unequal regulatory systems that govern the seemingly similar activities of taxis and ride hailing (Ranchordas 2015). In addition, there is some evidence that ride hailing contributes to congestion and vehicle kilometres travelled (VKT) (Schaller 2017; Clewlow and Mishra 2017) in cities such as New York and San Francisco. There are, however, important nuances in understanding the impact of ride hailing on VKT. For example, a study of six US cities in which Uber and Lyft operate found that while ride hailing contributed a small proportion of VKT when measured at the metropolitan level, ride hailing's contributions to VKT ranged from 2 to 13 per cent in the core and central city of each metropolitan area (Fehr & Peers 2019).

Critics of ride hailing point out that, on its own, ride hailing does not address congestion and may not have a significant impact on reducing the total number of vehicles on city streets (Zwick and Spicer 2018). A car carrying only one passenger is far less efficient in terms of street space utilization than a bus or streetcar and does little to address the desire to shift urban travel to more active modes of transportation such as walking, cycling, or scootering. As such, "traditional" ride hailing cannot be the sole solution to reducing congestion. However, pooled (or shared) ride-hailing services, particularly in larger-capacity vehicles, can begin to ameliorate some of the challenges associated with urban congestion while simultaneously providing the convenience of door-to-door service for passengers. Collectively, these findings imply that while further study is warranted, there is cause for concern.

Thus the prospects for ride hailing are decidedly mixed. Zwick and Spicer (2018) aptly summarize the pros and cons of ride hailing. It produces efficiency gains that are appreciated by consumers and provides the benefits of job creation and corrections to the taxi market. Yet they maintain that it is impossible to ignore its social costs, such as compromises to vehicle and passenger safety, contributions to precarious labour, and added congestion.

RIDE HAILING: ROLLOUT AND REGULATION ACROSS CANADA

In Canada, local ground transportation services such as taxis, limousines, and ride hailing are regulated by either the province or municipality. In British Columbia and Quebec, the provincial government has the authority to regulate ground transportation, thus determining the regulations that cities in each province must abide by. In most provinces, however, local ground transportation is a municipal responsibility. Therefore while Toronto and Mississauga City Councils can each develop its own regulations, Quebec City and Montreal must follow provincial regulations for local ground transportation. In Saskatoon, the provincial legislation allows ride-hailing firms to operate in the province, but municipalities are responsible for developing regulations that set the terms for allocating licences, setting fares, and establishing vehicle standards (Davis 2018). Although provincial-level discussion on the introduction of ride-hailing regulation had begun at least in the spring of 2016 (Zussman 2016), the first set of regulations on ride hailing in BC, were approved in November 2018 (Nair 2020). Furthermore, municipalities continued to establish and manage business licensing. As a result, and as shall be discussed later in this chapter, several large BC municipalities leveraged their powers to delay the introduction of ride hailing. Following unanticipated delays, ride-hailing firms were in a position to operate legally in BC in January 2020 (Nair 2020).

Adding further complexity, even when municipal governments set ride-hailing regulations, the development and approval of insurance products takes place at the provincial level. Therefore, when Edmonton legalized ride hailing in March 2016, ride-hailing firms in the city had to cease operations until July, as it took additional time for the provincial introduction of the required insurance products.

Phases of Ride-Hailing Regulation

Government regulations protect the public good. They include enforcement of rules developed and approved by government. Generally, they are designed in consultation with stakeholders, including industry groups and public representatives. Regulations are intended to ensure the safe and suitable operation of services, and to protect producers, consumers, and society more broadly.

Ride hailing poses a challenge to regulators. First, although the industry may have initially looked a lot like taxis, courts in Ontario determined that there was a distinction between taxi services and ride hailing. As a result, in order to enact regulations governing ride hailing, governing bodies needed to develop distinct rules. Second, because ride hailing continues to undergo rapid change, it is difficult to ensure that regulations are designed to respond to current needs (Brail 2018). Within these circumstances, efforts to regulate ride hailing can best be understood as taking place within three distinct phases: Launch, Ride Hailing 1.0, and Ride Hailing 2.0.

Launch: Legal Grey Zone

UberX, the version of Uber's ride-hailing service that matches private drivers to private riders, launched in Canada's largest city – Toronto – in September 2014 (Owram 2014). At the time, the key concerns expressed by the city about this renegade "taxi" service included risks to personal safety for drivers and passengers, vehicle safety amid a lack of safety standards, and lack of insurance.

During the launch phase, which lasted from approximately 2012 to 2016, Uber tested municipal regulations and responses with what was often seen as an aggressive, illegal approach. Uber launched its UberX service in most large Canadian cities in 2014 and 2015. Three notable exceptions were Vancouver, Halifax, and Calgary. Uber was barred from operating in Vancouver shortly after launching in 2012 and was shut down by the provincial Passenger Transportation Board (Bailey 2016; Xu 2017). Although Uber attempted to launch in Halifax in June 2014, the company was restricted by regulations that permitted services to be offered only through existing limousine and taxi companies. Halifax is one of only a few large Canadian cities in which Uber does not operate. In Alberta, the two largest cities – Calgary and Edmonton – initially took different approaches to Uber. Whereas Calgary effectively banned the service by setting a minimum limousine fare of $78, Uber continued to operate in Edmonton, despite a lack of regulation (Ahsan and Hensley 2015).

In response to concerns, the City of Toronto attempted at first to rein in Uber's activities by requiring it to follow regulations applied to the taxi industry. However, in July 2015, the Ontario Supreme Court ruled that Uber was not required to abide by the city's taxi regulations (Szychta et al. 2015).

While the 2015 Ontario Supreme Court decision preceded ride-hailing regulation in Canada, it did not precede ride-hailing operations. Between May 2012 and November 2015, Uber launched operations in twenty-two of Canada's thirty largest municipalities, including Toronto, Montreal Vancouver, Calgary, Ottawa, and Edmonton, and continued to operate and launch in other cities, insisting that since it was a technology company and not a transportation firm, taxi regulations did not apply to it. While some municipalities levied fines against drivers for operating without taxi licences, this approach ultimately proved ineffective and unenforceable (Ahsan and Hensley 2015).

Regulation 1.0

Edmonton City Council was the first Canadian city to pass regulations for ride-hailing operations in January 2016. The regulations required a minimum fare, set by the city at $3.25, and stipulated that all drivers required commercial insurance. Regulations making ride hailing legal came into effect in Edmonton in March 2016, but the required provincially regulated insurance products were not available until the following July. As a result, Uber withdrew services from Edmonton between March and July and returned once the required driver insurance was available.

Following on the heels of Edmonton's decision to permit Uber to operate in compliance with dedicated regulations, several Ontario municipalities also passed ride-hailing regulations in 2016: Toronto, Kitchener, Brampton, Oakville, and Sudbury. In Quebec, where local ground transportation is a provincial responsibility, in September 2016 the provincial government implemented a pilot program to allow ride hailing. This meant that ride hailing was regulated in many of Quebec's largest municipalities, including Quebec City, Gatineau, Montreal, Laval, and Longueuil. By 2017, an additional five Ontario municipalities passed ride-hailing regulations or developed ride-hailing pilot programs: Mississauga, Hamilton, London, Windsor, and Vaughan.

Early ride-hailing regulations typically incorporated basic safety measures for passengers, drivers, and vehicles. They include driver screening and licensing, the maximum age of a vehicle, and requirement for winter tires as well as a minimum level of insurance. Unlike taxi regulations that limit the number of vehicles operating, the first set of ride-hailing regulations in Canadian cities did not attempt to manage vehicle numbers.

In Toronto, ride-hailing regulations were introduced at the same time as revisions to taxi regulations, in an effort to distinguish the two types of service and create a more balanced playing field by reducing regulations for taxis. This included the removal of traditional taxi driver training. At the launch of regulations, municipalities also established a fee structure to recoup the costs of regulating ride hailing. Edmonton instituted an annual fee paid by each licensed driver, a fee paid by the transportation network company, and a per trip fee (City of Edmonton 2017). In Quebec, ride hailing has operated under a pilot program introduced by the Ministry of Transportation in September 2016. The pilot regulations required a criminal background check, vehicle inspection, Class 4C licence (essentially a taxi licence), and per trip fee (Grillo 2016). Quebec was one of the first places in Canada to tighten regulations on ride hailing after the first year of their pilot project. The shift to stricter regulation can be seen through the introduction of Regulation 2.0.

Regulation 2.0

Regulation 2.0 is characterized by regulatory reviews and modifications, and the introduction of ride-hailing legislation in some of the large Canadian cities that had not initially permitted ride hailing. This phase of regulation underscores the dynamic character of ride hailing and the need for regulatory flexibility.

The latest round of regulatory activity can be subdivided into two categories. First were municipalities in which ride-hailing regulations were developed early and matured to a second phase that includes review and revision of original regulations. Second were municipalities developing their first ride-hailing regulations, benefitting from insight and knowledge gained through observation and discussion with peer municipalities that had already regulated the sector.

Regulatory Review and Modification

The early days of regulation in ride hailing did not last long. Some government bodies that first developed and implemented ride-hailing legislation showed foresight in building reviews into regulations, or implemented pilot programs rather than permanent legislation to govern ride hailing.

As mentioned earlier in this chapter, Quebec was one of the first governments to implement ride-hailing regulations through a pilot program introduced in September 2016. Quebec is also an early example of how efforts have unfolded to revise regulations after a relatively short period of implementation and observation. In October 2017, the provincial regulator announced changes to minimum training requirements for drivers – raising the number of training hours from twenty to thirty-five and adding a requirement for criminal background checks on drivers to be confirmed by police. At the time, Uber was also reprimanded for not obeying regulations in Quebec, particularly on background checks, age of vehicles, and accepting rides through street hailing rather than through the digital hail system associated with using an app (Reuters 2017). Although Uber threatened to leave Quebec in response to the newly revised regulations, claiming that the regulations would not work with its business model, the firm remained. Quebec relied on a pilot program to govern ride hailing between 2016 and 2019. In October 2019, just prior to the expiration of the pilot program, the province passed legislation enabling ride hailing to operate permanently.

In Toronto, initial regulations for ride hailing included the stipulation that a review be conducted one year after the program began. However, the review was delayed, and instead of taking place in July 2017 as planned, it was initiated in the fall of 2018. The review included city-led consultations and studies of the impact of ride hailing on the city. A commissioned report suggested that there was insufficient evidence to conclude that ride hailing had increased congestion in downtown Toronto. However, data did indicate that ride hailing affects public transit and taxi ridership (City of Toronto 2019). Toronto continues to be criticized for weak driver-training requirements, especially when compared to previous taxi regulations, which required completion of an in-person training program. The city's updated ride-hailing regulations took effect in early 2020 and included tightening of some rules and introduction of others, such as driver training, an accessible-vehicle fee, and digital and physical requirements to signal to passengers the need to check for cyclists.

Canadian cities and provinces are not alone in their efforts to revise ride-hailing regulations. In August 2018, New York City voted to place a moratorium on issuing new licences to ride-hailing vehicles for one year out of concern about rising congestion. In December 2018, New York City established a minimum wage for ride-hailing drivers in an effort to address criticisms and challenges regarding low pay for platform economy employees, particularly rampant in ride hailing (Campbell 2018). In US cities, key items being revisited under Ride Hailing 2.0 include questions about guaranteeing minimum driver wages, legal queries about whether drivers are self-employed or employees of ride-hailing firms, efforts to reduce congestion, and negative impacts on public transit.

The evolution of ride-hailing regulations show that from a policy perspective, and over a relatively short period of time, Canadian city governments have responded to the pressures of the shifting digital economy with dynamic policy approaches.

Ride Hailing Abstainers

A relatively small number of Canada's largest cities and provinces chose to disallow ride hailing. For the most part, these places chose to enter the legislative arena only after a period of observation and learning, and ride hailing had matured. Most notable amongst ride-hailing abstainers was the province of British Columbia and the municipality of Halifax, collectively representing five out of thirty of the country's largest municipalities.

After a period of prohibiting ride hailing outright, British Columbia introduced and passed the first portion of its long-awaited ride-hailing legislation in the fall of 2018. Before ride-hailing services could legally operate in the province, however, additional regulations and insurance products needed to be developed. One important feature of BC's provincial regulations is the division of the province into four geographic zones in which ride-hailing firms can operate. These zones include multiple municipal boundaries. Following passage of the final set of provincial regulations in the fall of 2019, municipalities were tasked with the creation of business licences for ride-hailing firms. In Greater Vancouver, municipalities and industry lobby groups pushed back against provincial regulations and took several months to approve business licences for ride-hailing vehicles. Vancouver was the first municipality to offer a ride-hailing business licence in late January 2020. Surrey refused to issue a business licence to ride-hailing vehicles, and in Richmond, the cost of a business licence in January 2020 was set at $510 – the same as for a taxi licence (Boynton 2020). In early 2020, efforts were underway to develop an inter-municipal licence for ride-hailing vehicles, which would circumvent the need for ride-hailing firms to obtain multiple licenses from individual municipalities within the same region.

Revised regulations in Toronto and across Quebec, and the approach to ride hailing developed in British Columbia, represent a shift in platform economy governance. Edmonton, Toronto, and Montreal enforced the first set regulations, which appeared mainly to appease the requests of ride-hailing firms for light regulation and in many respects effectively deregulated ground transportation services. In Ride Hailing 1.0, regulations were typically characterized by low costs to drivers, reduced safety measures for taxi services, no caps on the number of vehicles, low per-trip fees, and dynamic pricing. In BC, where the provincial government emphasized the need for slower, careful policy development, regulators eschewed vehicle caps but required drivers to hold commercial licences, which require an additional level of testing and are thought to provide more protection with regard to driver safety (Province of British Columbia 2019). Despite the province's best intentions of developing a thoughtful made-in-BC solution to ride hailing, BC's experience demonstrates that the decision to hold off on policy development and then attempt to develop an ideal policy solution, is an imperfect approach that leads to uncertain outcomes. Overall, these policy shifts embody ride-hailing regulation version 2.0 and signal the move to a regulatory environment in which the regulator reinforces the role of policy and indicates a stronger role for government-led management of ride hailing.

Furthermore, Ride Hailing 2.0 does not represent the end state of ride-hailing regulation and activity across Canada. Rather, it demonstrates the dynamic nature of cities, policy, and regulation. It can be reasonably expected that as the industry changes, matures, and adapts, municipal and provincial regulation will continue to shift as well.

Ride Hailing in Canada: State of the Nation

It is a testament to the speed with which provincial and municipal government can operate that by the end of 2019, ride-hailing regulations were established in twenty-six of the thirty largest cities in the country.

In 2019, discussion about the introduction of regulations permitting ride hailing in Markham, Ontario, continued, although no legislation was introduced. Other large cities in Ontario that had not passed ride-hailing regulations as of December 2019 included Richmond Hill and Burlington. Nevertheless, ride hailing operates in each of these three cities as de facto extensions of ride hailing in the adjacent municipalities of Toronto and Hamilton.

With the regulation of ride hailing in British Columbia, Halifax became the largest city in Canada that does not permit ride hailing and disallows any activity outside of the city's taxi and limousine regulations.

CONCLUSION

This chapter traced the entry of ride hailing as a new type of local ground transportation across Canada's thirty largest cities. The emergence of ride hailing and the use of digital technologies to facilitate a matching of private drivers with riders represents a disruptive mobility innovation. Over a relatively short period of time, ride hailing has become an important option for transportation that is relied upon in most of Canada's largest cities.

Ride hailing has demonstrated the potential to shift the ways in which people move around in cities, for better and for worse. On the one hand, ride hailing can create new opportunities for accessibility and can lower the costs of automobile travel and acquisition for people who choose ride hailing over vehicle ownership. At the same time, studies have pointed to increases in downtown congestion and vehicle miles travelled, and to decreases in public transit use. These shifts have been tied directly to the growth of ride hailing.

As such, ride hailing presents a series of challenges to governments, particularly on their role in managing and protecting the public interest. Municipal and provincial governments have shown an ability to regulate ride hailing as a component of the digital platform economy. By tracing the short history of ride-hailing regulation in Canada, the chapter presents an overview of the ways in which the impacts of a dynamic sector undergoing rapid and regular change can be managed through an evolving regulatory process and through intentional policy direction. The digital technologies underlying ride hailing initially offered the promise of a reduced need for regulation, in light of the opportunity for safety and trust to be managed through ratings systems integrated into ride-hailing apps. Perhaps the irony of governing a digital economy is that while regulation may look different from how it has been seen in the past, regulatory efforts appear to require greater – and not less – government attention.

REFERENCES

Ahsan, S., and L. Hensley. 2015. "Summer of Uber: Everything You Need to Know about the Upstart Ride-Sharing Service." *National Post*, 21 August. https://nationalpost.com/news/canada/summer-of-uber-everything-you-need-to-know-about-the-upstart-ride-sharing-service.

Associated Press. 2016. "Uber Will Let Drivers Ask for Tips and Pay up to $100 million to Settle Lawsuit in California and Massachusetts." *Daily Mail Online*, 22 April. https://www.dailymail.co.uk/news/article-3553230/Uber-pay-100-MILLION-settle-lawsuits-firm-drivers-contractors-2-states.html.

Bailey, I. 2016. "BC Rejects Uber Request to Revise Licensing Regulations." *Globe and Mail*, 21 January. https://www.theglobeandmail.com/news/british-columbia/bc-rejects-uber-request-to-revise-licensing-regulations/article28332937/.

Bliss, L. 2019. "'Uber Was Supposed to Be Our Public Transit.'" CityLab, 29 April. https://www.citylab.com/transportation/2019/04/innisfil-transit-ride-hailing-bus-public-transportation-uber/588154/.

Boynton, S. 2020. "Burnaby Urges Uber to Pick Up Business Licences or It Could Start Issuing Fines, Too." Global News, 30 January. https://globalnews.ca/news/6481980/burnaby-uber-business-licence-fines/.

Brail, S. 2017. "Promoting Innovation Locally: Municipal Regulation as Barrier or Boost?" *Geography Compass*. https://doi.org/10.1111/gec3.12349.

– 2018. "From Renegade to Regulated: The Digital Platform Economy, Ride-Hailing and the Case of Toronto." *Canadian Journal of Urban Research* 27, no. 2: 51–63.

Brail, S., and B. Donald. 2018. "Canada Left Behind as Ride-Hailing Services Go Global." Conversation. https://theconversation.com/canada-left-behind-as-ride-hailing-services-go-global-102625.

Brown, A.E. 2018. "Ridehail Revolution: Ridehail Travel and Equity in Los Angeles." UCLA. https://escholarship.org/uc/item/4r22m57k.

Campbell, A.F. 2018. "New York City Passes Nation's First Minimum Pay Rate for Uber and Lyft Drivers." Vox, 5 December. https://www.vox.com/2018/12/5/18127208/new-york-uber-lyft-minimum-wage.

Canadian Press. 2018. "Innisfil, Ont., Estimates It Saves $8M Yearly Using Uber as Alternative to Public Transit." CBC News, 15 March. https://www.cbc.ca/news/canada/toronto/innisfil-uber-public-transit-1.4577331.

City of Edmonton. 2017. "Bylaw 17400 Vehicle for Hire." https://www.edmonton.ca/documents/Bylaws/C17400.pdf.

City of Toronto. 2019. "The Transportation Impacts of Vehicle for Hire in Toronto, Executive Summary." Prepared by City of Toronto Transportation Services Big Data Innovation Team. https://www.toronto.ca/legdocs/mmis/2019/gl/bgrd/backgroundfile-135307.pdf.

Clewlow, R.R., and G.S. Mishra. 2017. *Disruptive Transportation: The Adoption, Utilization, and Impacts of Ride-Hailing in the United States.* Research Report UCD-ITS-RR-17-07. Institute of Transportation Studies, University of California, Davis.

Conway, M.W., D. Salon, and D.A. King. 2018. "Trends in Taxi Use and the Advent of Ridehailing, 1995–2017: Evidence from the US National Household Travel Survey." *Urban Science* 2, no. 3: 79. https://doi.org/10.3390/urbansci2030079.

Cook, T. 2015. *Staff Report: 2015 Ground Transportation Review: Taxis, Limos and Uber.* City of Toronto. https://www.toronto.ca/legdocs/mmis/2015/ls/bgrd/backgroundfile-83268.pdf.

Davis, A.M. 2018. "Lyft Joins Chamber of Commerce; Could Operate in Regina before 2020." *Regina Leader-Post,* 31 August. https://leaderpost.com/news/local-news/lyft-joins-chamber-of-commerce-could-operate-in-regina-before-end-of-2019.

Dediu, H. 2012. "When Will Smartphones Reach Saturation in the US?" ASYMCO, 11 April. http://www.asymco.com/2012/04/11/when-will-smartphones-reach-saturation-in-the-us/.

Dunne, J. 2018. "Uber for Buses? How Some Canadian Cities Are Using Technology to Tackle Transit Troubles." CBC News, 19 October. https://www.cbc.ca/news/business/uber-lyft-ride-hailing-on-demand-public-transit-1.4842699.

Fehr & Peers. 2019. "Estimated TNC Share of VMT in Six US
    Metropolitan Regions (Revision 1)." 6 August. https://www.
    fehrandpeers.com/what-are-tncs-share-of-vmt/.
Graehler, M., R. Mucci, and G.D. Erhardt. 2018. "Understanding the
    Recent Transit Ridership Decline in Major US Cities: Service Cuts
    or Emerging Modes?" *98th Annual Meeting of the Transportation
    Research Board*, 19.
Grillo, M. 2016. "Uber Presents Details of One-Year Pilot Project
    in Quebec." Global News, 21 October. https://globalnews.ca/
    news/3035151/uber-to-present-details-of-one-year-pilot-project/.
Hathaway, I., and M. Muro. 2016. "Tracking the Gig Economy: New
    Numbers." Brookings, 13 October. https://www.brookings.edu/research/
    tracking-the-gig-economy-new-numbers/.
Lashinsky, A. 2017. *Wild Ride: Inside Uber's Quest for World
    Domination*. London: Penguin Publishing Group.
Lella, A. 2017. "U .S. Smartphone Penetration Surpassed 80 Percent in
    2016." Comscore, 3 February. https://www.comscore.com/Insights/Blog/
    US-Smartphone-Penetration-Surpassed-80-Percent-in-2016.
Meeker, M. 2018. "Internet Trends 2018." Kleiner Perkins, 30 May.
    https://www.kleinerperkins.com/perspectives/internet-trends-report-
    2018/.
Nair, R. 2020. "Vancouver's Long and Winding Road to Ride-Hailing."
    CBC News, 25 January. https://www.cbc.ca/news/canada/british-
    columbia/timeline-uber-vancouver-1.5439522.
Province of British Columbia. 2019. "Province Announces Regulation
    and Insurance for Ride-Hailing Services," 8 July. https://news.gov.bc.ca/
    releases/2019TRAN0121-001409.
Ranchordas, S. 2015. "Does Sharing Mean Caring: Regulating Innovation
    in the Sharing Economy." *Minnesota Journal of Law, Science and
    Technology* 16: 413–76.
Rayle, L., and O. Flores. 2016. "How Lyft Taught Uber to Break the
    Rules." Medium, 7 March. https://medium.com/@lisa_one/how-lyft-
    taught-uber-to-break-the-rules-dfcccd044384#.pq6sv7dbv.
Reader, R. 2018. "For Ride-Hail Drivers, the Future Is Paved with Low
    Wages and More Gig Work." Fast Company, 16 May. https://www.
    fastcompany.com/40563508/for-ride-hail-drivers-the-future-is-paved-
    with-low-wages-and-more-gig-work.
Reuters. 2017. "Uber Says It Will Pull Out of Canada's Quebec Province."
    CNBC News, 27 September. https://www.cnbc.com/2017/09/26/uber-
    says-it-will-pull-out-of-canadas-quebec-province.html.

Rosenblat, A. 2018. *Uberland: How Algorithms Are Rewriting the Rules of Work*. Oakland: University of California Press.

Schaller, B. 2017. "Unsustainable? The Growth of App-Based Ride Services and Traffic, Travel and the Future of New York City." Schaller Consulting, 27 February. http://schallerconsult.com/rideservices/unsustainable.pdf.

Sperling, D. 2018. *Three Revolutions: Steering Automated, Shared, and Electric Vehicles to a Better Future*. Washington, DC: Island.

Sperling, D., A. Brown, and M. D'Agostino. 2018. "Can Ride-Hailing Improve Public Transportation Instead of Undercutting It? The Conversation." *Scientific American*, 5 July. https://www.scientificamerican.com/article/can-ride-hailing-improve-public-transportation-instead-of-undercutting-it/.

Statistics Canada. 2017. "The Sharing Economy in Canada," 28 February. http://www.statcan.gc.ca/daily-quotidien/170228/dq170228b-eng.pdf.

Szychta, B., C. Bisbee, and C.G. Carter. 2015. "Regulating Uber: What This Means for Municipalities." *Municipal Liability Risk Management* 16, no. 6: 45–9. https://www.frankcowan.com/site/pdf/news/Regulating_Uber_what_this_means_for_Municipalities.pdf

Xu, X. 2017. "Ride-Sharing Companies Slip through Cracks as Uber Faces Pressure from Regulators." *Globe and Mail*, 3 July. https://www.theglobeandmail.com/news/british-columbia/ride-sharing-companies-slip-through-cracks-as-uber-faces-pressure-from-regulators/article35538333/.

Zussman, R. 2016. "B.C. Green Party Introduces 'Rideshare Enabling' Legislation." CBC News, 25 April. https://www.cbc.ca/news/canada/british-columbia/b-c-green-party-introduces-rideshare-enabling-legislation-1.3552769.

Zwick, A., and Z. Spicer. 2018. "Good or Bad? Ridesharing's Impact on Canadian Cities." *Canadian Geographer/Le Géographe Canadien* 62, no. 4: 430–6. https://doi.org/10.1111/cag.12481.

7

Taking Kingston for a Regulatory Ride? Uber's Entrance into Kingston, Ontario

Betsy Donald and Morgan Sage, with Anna Moroz

- Ride-hailing companies have forced municipalities across Canada to rewrite regulations. Local context and history have played a central role in determining regulatory responses and outcomes to ride hailing.
- Kingston, Ontario, offers a unique case study that emphasizes the impact of place and local governance structure on policy outcomes. Unlike the majority of municipalities in Ontario, Kingston's taxi industry is not regulated by the city or enforced by the local police force, but rather by a separate governing body, the Kingston Area Taxi Commission (KATC).
- After concerns that ride-hailing companies would side-step regulation and disrupt the local taxi industry, the KATC rewrote policy to regulate ride-hailing companies. However, their jurisdictional limitations have caused ride-hailing companies in Kingston to remain unregulated.

INTRODUCTION

Over the last few years, a growing literature has emerged on the impact of ride-hailing corporations on municipal laws and regulations. Canada is particularly interesting, given that each province and municipality has a different regulatory structure for managing taxis and ride hailing in their respective localities, creating a variegated geography of regulation and activity across the country. In examining the making of these regulations, we see how local history and the social dynamics of place play out when global actors come to town.

While Canadian municipalities are gradually accepting and regulating Uber and other transportation networking companies (TNCS), questions about regulatory matters, due in part to the asymmetries of information and power, create an uneven playing field between global firms and local actors. We see this reality playing out in Uber's entrance into Kingston, Ontario, and the ensuing debates around Uber and the regulation of other TNCS alongside the taxi industry.

DIGITAL RIDE HAILING: A BRIEF HISTORY IN CANADA

Digital ride hailing is part of the platform economy. The platform economy comprises a distinct, new set of economic relations that depend on the internet, computation, and big data. The platform economy is an ecosystem with its own source of value that sets terms by which users can participate (Kenney and Zysman 2016). Ride hailing uses the widespread adoption of smartphone technology, GPS, and wireless internet service to enable a digital match between a driver operating a private vehicle and a passenger.

Digital ride hailing first entered Canada in 2012, with the launch of Uber in Toronto. In the same year Uber briefly offered its black car service in Vancouver, though it was shut down by the provincial Passenger Transportation Board shortly after launching (Bailey 2016; Saltman 2017; Xu 2017). In January 2016, Edmonton became the first Canadian municipality to develop distinct regulations governing ride hailing. As of July 2018, ride hailing is regulated in twenty-one of Canada's thirty largest cities. Extrapolating from current plans, twenty-eight of Canada's thirty largest cities will have ride-hailing regulations in place by the end of 2019 (Brail 2018; Brail and Donald 2020).

LITERATURE REVIEW

Ride hailing is the subject of great controversy in popular and scholarly discourse. The growing literature on digital ride hailing covers a range of themes and debates, including the economic costs and benefits, labour geographies, technological innovation, urban mobility, and the geographies of regulation and policy. In this chapter, we will focus on the regulatory and policy aspects and how they play out in a smaller city with a patchwork of regulatory approaches.

The legal and regulatory response to digital ride hailing in jurisdictions around the world is a growing theme in the digital ride-hailing literature (Ranchordas 2015; Anttiroiko 2016; Barglind 2016; Elliott 2016). Brail (2017) shows how initial legal concerns in Canada about technology and insurance faded as the ride-hailing industry was gradually accepted and regulated across Canadian municipalities (see also Shields 2016). However, there are still debates and questions about regulatory matters, especially given the uneven playing field between global firms and local actors (Calo and Rosenblat n.d.). On the one hand, multinational platform firms like Uber have exclusive access to a host of useful data. In contrast, municipalities without access to good data or expertise are grappling with how best to regulate and assess the impacts to society of new ride-hailing entries.

Researchers have begun to examine costs and benefits systematically. Spicer (2018) found that the City of Toronto's approach to regulating Uber will be revenue neutral for the municipality. However, this is the only study on the impact of digital ride hailing on municipal revenue in Canada, and there are still many unanswered questions, including whether actual revenues and costs of regulating will mirror projected revenues. In Toronto, the regulations were supposed to undergo review one year after implementation began. The one-year review was intended to result in adjustments to the regulations if there was a revenue shortfall. Two years passed with review, in part the result delayed pressure on the city to develop regulations for other emerging sectors, such as short-term house renting. As stated above, Canada is particularly interesting because ride-hailing approaches and regulations differ across the country. Documenting the distinct ways in which Canadian jurisdictions are responding to ride hailing is a useful exercise for highlighting the varying power dynamics between global firms and local actors. Moreover, local stories underscore the realities of place- and time-specific regulations while also highlighting the interactions between local and global firms and the populations they serve.

THE KINGSTON CASE STUDY

Kingston, Ontario, is a small, public sector city (population 161,000[1]) located in eastern Ontario, situated on the Highway 401 corridor within the Toronto, Montreal, and Ottawa triangle. It is best known for its higher education institutions, including Queen's University,

St. Lawrence College, and the Royal Military College. Every fall, the city comes alive with thousands of students moving in, taking up residence downtown and patronizing the downtown restaurants and bars. When the majority of students leave for the summer holidays, the city is noticeably quieter before the tourist season begins. The taxi and ride-hailing industry depends heavily on the student presence and their nightlife. But another geography of Kingston serves as a large customer base for taxis: the elderly. Kingston's elderly, working class, and people with disabilities rely on taxi and ride-hailing services to get around for grocery shopping, doctor's appointments, and other daily activities. This unique social geography is due in part to the heavy presence of major public-sector institutions, including the university, the military, correctional services, and health-care services. "This heavy reliance on the public sector affects the city in many profound ways and has implications for how private-sector innovation works, how labour markets operate, and how governance is shaped and plays out in the local economy. Moreover, the particular labour market – with its steady, well-paying public-sector jobs, and weaker, more precarious service-oriented ones – contributes to a spatially, socially, and politically polarized urban environment" (Donald and Hall 2016, 311–12).

We see this polarization play out in many contexts, and the debates about the regulation of the global ride-hailing firms is no exception. In many ways, the social geography of Kingston mirrors the social geography of the platform economy: a growing social-spatial and digital divide between those with access to credit cards, access to smartphone technology, and the knowledge to use platform apps, and those without. In the past, students and the local working-class populations worked closely together, but, in this case, we see a clear social and generational divide between the young, knowledge-intensive students "from away," and the older, more localized working-class populations of Kingston.

The results from this case study of Kingston are based on two years of research and observation on Uber's entrance into the Kingston area. We reviewed writings on the social dynamics of economic performance in the city, the history of the Kingston Area Taxi Commission, the introduction of Uber in Kingston in 2016, and the regulatory response, including the making of regulations and their withdrawal. In researching this case study, we spent time attending local events related to the development of the Uber regulations and interviewing important actors in the taxi and ride-hailing industry, including members of the Kingston Area Taxi Commission, taxi owners and drivers, and consumer stakeholders. What follows is a description of the regulatory-making process in Kingston.

In particular, we found a municipality grappling with how best to regulate and assess the impacts on society of new ride-hailing entries. We also witnessed how an asymmetry of power between a global firm and local place maps onto a unique social geography of a transient, yet powerful digitally savvy student population and a more locally rooted population with different needs and access to services. What become clear in this narrative are the uneven power imbalances between a global player and the local context and the ways in which the local context shapes particular outcomes.

KINGSTON AND THE UBER CASE STUDY

The Kingston Area Taxi Commission

Kingston's taxi industry offers a unique perspective on the impact of ride-hailing corporations on municipal laws and regulation. The taxi industry in Kingston and the surrounding area is under the regulation of the Kingston and Area Taxi Commission (KATC). Unlike a vast majority of the municipalities in Ontario, Kingston's taxi industry is not regulated by the city or enforced by the local police force; rather, it is regulated and enforced by the katc (see figure 7.1), created by the province.[2] After years of inconsistencies and conflict between the City of Kingston and the surrounding municipalities, a single body was allowed to regulate the entire taxi industry in the region (Bennett 1993).

The province directed the commission to be separate from the City of Kingston. It is categorized as a "stand-alone committee," the only one of its kind in Kingston, the only committee that does not answer to city council (City of Kingston 2018). It is also a legislated committee, meaning the commission can pass by-laws for licensing, regulating, and governing the owners and drivers of taxicabs, giving the commission independence to regulate the taxi industry (Bennett 1993; City of Kingston 2018). The KATC itself is a board of equals composed of two local government representatives – one city councillor from Kingston and one official from Loyalist Township – and five volunteer

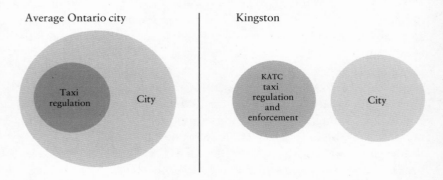

Figure 7.1 Taxi regulation, KATC, and the city.

citizens (see figure 7.2).[3] To sit on the KATC, volunteer citizens must undergo an application process to determine skill sets and ensure no conflicts of interest. However, commissioners often have some vested interest in the taxi industry.

The commission's history is an under-researched topic in Kingston.[4] Bennett (1993) discussed the evolution of the commission from its formation in 1981 as a regulating body for the area's taxis, its amalgamation with the surrounding townships in 1983, and the complications in regulating across different political jurisdictions. It was in the public's interest to create a uniform taxi industry (Bennett 1993). In 1989, a private member's bill was submitted so that Kingston and the surrounding area could have a taxi licensing body across municipalities, which required special legislation (*City of Kingston and townships of Kingston, Pittsburgh and Ernestown Act* 1989). The bill gave the regulating body the power to create by-laws for licensing, regulating, and governing the owners, drivers, and brokers of taxicabs (*City of Kingston and townships of Kingston, Pittsburgh and Ernestown Act* 1990).

The commission heavily regulates the taxi industry in Kingston. Unlike other municipalities, the Taxi Commission owns the plates and leases them out.[5] Kingston drivers get 39 per cent of the gross revenue and tips, and the company pays all the expenses of the vehicle, such as a yearly brokerage fee, in addition to other high costs including insurance, operating costs, safety certification, gas, and maintenance.[6] The commission itself is paid for by fees from the taxi industry (Bennett 1993).

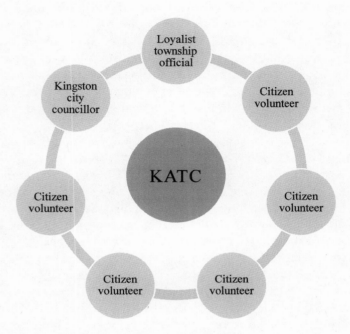

Figure 7.2 Kingston Area Taxi Commission composition.

THE INTRODUCTION OF UBER IN KINGSTON
AND ITS SUBSEQUENT REGULATION

The Taxi Industry

Kingston's taxi industry expressed several concerns after Uber's entrance into the local market. While the local taxi industry has acknowledged that Uber has raised the bar for some companies in service and innovation,[7] like the development of mobile applications by Kingston's taxi companies, Amey's Taxi and Modern City Taxi, concerns with Uber's market domination remain.[8]

Despite the Ontario Superior Court ruling in 2015 that stated that ride-hailing companies are not taxi brokers (Loriggio 2015), the Kingston taxi industry believes that moving a passenger from point A to point B for monetary compensation is the definition of a "taxi."[9] It sees the taxi industry as being forced to play by strict rules, but when companies such as Uber enter that provide similar services, they are permitted to operate with little to no regulations.[10] The taxi industry argues that laws are being modified to accommodate ride-hailing companies, and that companies such as Uber should be required to follow the same rules as taxis.[11] The Kingston taxi industry has argued that ride-hailing companies are sidestepping every regulation, destroying small taxi businesses, and harming taxi and Uber drivers alike.[12] Some in Kingston's taxi industry believe that Ottawa and Toronto were not strict enough with Uber, and that Uber should be treated like taxis because of the strong similarities it shares with taxi services.[13]

At times people in the Kingston taxi industry speak about Uber with skepticism, particularly about the lack of Uber's taxation, and the marketing Uber has done within the city.[14] There is also concern that Uber and other ride-hailing corporations will undercut and eventually eliminate the taxi industry.[15] The taxi industry in Kingston also claims to offer better employment for drivers compared to Uber.[16] However, some taxi brokers say it is already difficult to make a living as a taxi driver, but it is hard to demonstrate that Uber is a direct cause.[17]

The Kingston taxi industry has also noted safety issues with ride-hailing companies. It argues that its cabs are safer than Uber's because of its regular criminal record checks, in-car cameras, and car safety checks.[18] The only "'protection'" Uber has to offer its passengers and drivers is online reviews.

In addition, the Kingston taxi industry boasts one of the lowest taxi rates in Ontario and notes that it is often less expensive than Uber, while always keeping a set price when Uber has surge pricing.[19] Industry representatives say they are more inclusive because, unlike Uber, they have accessible vehicles, and passengers are not required to have a smartphone, a data plan, and a credit card to use their services.[20] Overall, the Kingston taxi industry is concerned primarily with public safety, legality, and fairness. It has emphasized it does not necessarily want Uber pushed out of Kingston, rather it advocates for "an evening out of the playing field."

The Taxi Commission and Rewriting Regulation

The Kingston Area Taxi Commission refers to ride-hailing companies such as Uber and Lyft as transportation networking companies (TNCS). In By-Law 4 (KATC 2018), TNCS are defined as "any person or company that accepts calls or otherwise facilitates prearranged transportation services for compensation using any software or application or telecommunications platform or digital network to connect passengers with TNC Drivers."

THE TASK FORCE

According to a commissioner on the KATC,[21] in 2016 the commission created a task force to examine the issue of Uber in Kingston and to make recommendations to the commission. The task force meetings were public discussions where representatives from both the taxi industry and Uber were present. The task force recommended that TNCs should not require top signs, should not need taxi meters because they have their own way of measuring and determining fees, should not be allowed to pick up street hails, should not need a radio licence because they communicate through apps, and the number of TNCs should be capped at 150 drivers, with only fifty cars operating at any given time. The restriction on the number of TNC vehicles operating at any given time was viewed as "only fair" because the commission already controls the supply of taxis, so therefore they should control the supply of TNCs.

The task force raised issues that Uber found contentious, such as the requirement for a Canadian Police Information Centre (CPIC) background check. Taxi drivers are required to complete regular vulnerable sector police checks, which include a record check for sexual offences, intended to be completed by people working with those in the vulnerable sector such as children, older adults, people with disabilities, etc. (RCMP 2018). The task force recommended that Uber and other TNC drivers be required to complete a vulnerable sector police check too. However, Uber wanted to do their own check through a police department in the United States. Despite Uber's complaints, the KATC drafted policy, By-Law 4, outlined that TNC drivers were required to undergo a CPIC check.

DRAFTING OF BY-LAW 4

In an attempt to regulate TNCs, the Kingston Area Taxi Commission drafted By-Law 4 using the recommendations from the task force and the existing By-Law 2, which regulated the taxi industry only.[22] They did not revise or update By-Law 2 in the process. In the first drafts of By-Law 4, the KATC applied a majority of the By-Law 2 regulations to TNCs. For example, taxi brokers in Kingston are required to have a storefront, primarily to act as a location for passengers to complain. Originally, the KATC was going to require that TNCs have a storefront.

Uber opposed this suggested regulation, arguing that it was unnecessary to have a storefront because they have developed their own online method of managing complaints.

During the drafting, the commission examined regulations in the municipalities of Hamilton and Ottawa, and also held public meetings within the city about By-Law 4. At the meetings, stakeholders – including individuals from the taxi industry, Uber drivers, representatives from TNCs, and students at Queen's University – voiced their opinions. During the proceedings members of the taxi industry expressed numerous concerns, including the lack of safety regulations. The by-law did not require Uber vehicles to have in-car cameras, a protective shield between the driver and passengers, or a 911 light on the backs of vehicles. On the other hand, students who spoke at the task force meetings, represented primarily by the undergraduate society at Queen's University, argued that Uber is the most convenient way to get home safely after a night downtown.

PASSING BY-LAW 4

On 27 June 2018, the KATC passed By-Law 4, which contained regulations to ensure the safety of the passengers using TNC services. Under the by-law, TNC drivers must undergo a criminal record check, have a photo ID licence issued by the KATC that they renew annually, perform annual safety checks on their vehicles, operate vehicles that are no more than eight years old, and be restricted to driving only twelve of every twenty-four hours (KATC 2018). Drivers are required to pay an initial $600 for their photo ID licence, then $300 every year after that for renewal, pay for their criminal record check, and pay for any safety inspections or upgrades their car may need every year (KATC 2018). By-Law 4 also restricts drivers from accepting street hails, outlines a dress code, requires drivers to establish the price prior to the trip, and requires them to charge a minimum of $3.20 per trip (KATC 2018). The commission also requires that Uber and other TNCs pay $40,000 to operate, then another $35,000 annually following their start-up year (CBC News 2018; Krause 2018). Finally, a restriction on the number of TNC vehicles on and off the road total 150, with only 50 operating at any given time, was established (KATC 2018).

REACTIONS TO BY-LAW 4

After three years of research and work with a wide range of interested parties (Snowdon 2018c), By-Law 4 was set to go into effect on

15 September 2018. Kingston's taxi industry saw By-Law 4 as an adequate attempt to level the playing field for their industry and Uber (Mazur 2018). However, between 27 June and 15 September there was an uproar among Queen's University undergraduate students and Uber drivers across Kingston. Uber drivers in Kingston accused the commission of trying to push Uber out of Kingston (Mazur 2018; Ferguson 2018).

Under the by-law, Uber drivers, who had not been required to pay fees to operate in Kingston, would now be required to pay licensing fees. Councillor Liz Schell, an elected official on the KATC at the time of passing By-Law 4, said the fees were meant to cover the costs incurred in regulating more vehicles, such as hiring another taxi inspector (Mazur 2018). After the initial entry fee, Uber was expected to pay $35,000 per year, and their drivers were to pay $300 each in addition to undergo regular criminal record checks and vehicle tests (CBC News 2018; KATC 2018). Kingston's approach to have drivers pay $300 is different from other cities in Ontario that put the cost of regulating onto Uber, not the drivers. For example, Toronto requires TNCs to pay $20,000 initially, $15 per driver per year, and $0.30 per trip; and Hamilton requires TNCs to pay $50,000 and $0.06 per trip (Craggs 2017; Spicer 2018).

Uber drivers are not the only party disgruntled about the implications of By-Law 4. Students at Queen's University have been the driving force behind Uber's operation in Kingston.[23] In September 2018, the *Queen's Journal* Editorial Board (2018) reiterated some of the irritation that the Queen's student body has voiced before. They said that the restrictions placed on Uber, in order to protect an outdated taxi industry, would prevent them from providing optimal services. They argued that in turn this would risk student safety and innovation in the city. Key safety features that Uber offered included GPS trackers and the ability for students to find a safe ride home with the click of a button. Students at Queen's started a petition to keep the ride-hailing company operating in Kingston (Sherriff-Scott 2018). By November 2018, there were over 725 signatures on the petition (Williams 2018).

This is not the first time Queen's students have petitioned against regulations on Uber. In 2016, the Alma Mater Society (AMS) launched a petition to prevent Uber from being forced out of Kingston through strict regulations that the KATC initially introduced, including security cameras, and minimum fares (O'Reilly 2016). The AMS sent out the petition in a mass e-mail to students with an emphasis on student convenience and safety, especially after a night of drinking (O'Reilly 2016). Then in 2017 the AMS took an official stance against what the commission was proposing with By-Law 4 (Sherriff-Scott 2018).

Uber drivers and students alike have argued that the by-law will ultimately push Uber out of Kingston (Snowdon 2018a). However, Liz Schell assures that it was not the intention. Rather, the by-law was an attempt to level the playing field for Uber and the taxi industry in Kingston because the ride-hailing company was operating with no rules while the taxi industry "have quite a list of rules they have to follow under our bylaw" (CBC News 2018). However, the Competition Bureau of Canada recommends altering restrictions on local taxi industries while generating appropriate regulations for TNCs (Competition Bureau Canada 2015).

BY-LAW 4 ON HOLD

Amidst the controversy over By-Law 4, the regulation was put on hold. The Ontario Superior Court ruled in 2015 that Uber is not a taxi broker (Loriggio 2015), leaving the Kingston and Area Taxi Commission in a difficult position because under law they have purview over taxi brokers only, and not ride-hailing companies like Uber (Snowdon 2018b). All along, the Uber spokesperson in Kingston, Chris Schafer, has said that the KATC does not have the jurisdiction to regulate TNCs (Ferguson 2017). By-Law 4 is up for legal review, has been put on permanent hold, and is to be discussed further during KATC meetings (Snowdon 2018a, 2018b). The Competition Bureau was also alerted to the by-law and is investigating a claim made against the Kingston Area Taxi Commission (Snowdon 2018a). The commission has since removed By-Law 4 from its website and states, "Following additional legal consultations, it has been determined that the bylaw merits further review before implementation" (KATC 2018). Despite the setback, the commission is still dedicated to its original goal of regulating TNCs and levelling the playing field (Snowdon 2018b). Since the fall of 2018, there has been little news on ride-hailing companies and By-Law 4. The KATC's meeting minutes show that there has been no real discussion of By-Law 4 since January 2019 when they were continuing to "work towards resolutions for TNC Bylaw issues." The city has remained out of the ride-hailing conversation, preferring to let the market dictate the balance between taxis and technology companies, rather than getting involved in the politics of idiosyncratic governance structures. In the meantime, Uber will continue to operate without regulation in Kingston.

CONCLUSION

This case study of ride-hailing companies in Kingston highlights how local context and history matter in shaping outcomes. At the time of this writing, the by-law to regulate Uber and other global TNCs in the Kingston area is on hold, meaning that these firms continue to operate without local regulation in Kingston and surrounding area. This contrasts with the local taxi industry, which operates within a set of local regulations. Because of the unique historical and regulatory context of Kingston – its taxi industry is not regulated by the city nor under the jurisdiction of the local police force – the City of Kingston has been immune to the heated local politics around the regulation of global TNCs.

This contrasts with many other local municipalities that have faced feverish public political battles between the taxi industry, on the one hand, and Uber and other global TNCs in the making of their local regulations, on the other. On the upside, this entire episode may have allowed the local industry in Kingston to move faster with quality innovations to keep pace with new service demands of customers rather than become mired in a public media battle that could have resulted in the loss of customers. On the downside, this has meant that Kingston missed an opportunity for a locally informed democratic debate on the costs and benefits of digital ride-hailing firms in their communities. Many people in Kingston are unaware that Uber and other TNCs are not regulated in the same way as in cities such as Toronto, Ottawa, or Hamilton. Moreover, few people think about the economic loss when Uber pays no local fees or money that used to circulate in the local economy now leaves the country as Uber takes a profit. Additionally, few consider the lack of an even playing field for the practices of Uber and other TNCs and the local taxi industry.

As Uber and other TNCs continue to operate in Kingston, time will tell whether the social, generational, and digital divide between student needs and those of the local population will accelerate. Time will also tell whether we will continue to see the asymmetries of information and power between global firms and local actors as increasing numbers of platform firms and services enter local markets and disrupt services in the process. A further question is whether Kingston and other Canadian municipalities will continue to be consumers of new global platform products or use the regulatory process to enact and encourage local service innovation in ride hailing and other new platform services.

NOTES

1 The Census Metropolitan Area population is 161,000, while the city proper is about 124,000.

2 *City of Kingston and townships of Kingston, Pittsburgh and Ernestown Act*, 1989; taxi broker #1, personal communication, 2 February 2017; taxi broker #2, personal communication, 1 August 2018; and taxi driver #1, personal communication, 2 February 2017.

3 Commissioner #1, personal communication, 13 August 2018.

4 Bennett (1993) is one of the few sources that examines the history of the KATC, and as a result, we rely heavily on his comprehensive 1993 paper for this historical context.

5 Taxi broker #1, personal communication, 2 February 2017; and taxi driver #1, personal communication, 2 February 2017.

6 Taxi broker #1, personal communication, 2 February 2017.

7 Ibid.

8 Ibid.; and taxi broker #2, personal communication, 1 August 2018.

9 Taxi broker #2, personal communication, 1 August 2018.

10 Taxi broker #1, personal communication, 2 February 2017; taxi broker #2, personal communication, 1 August 2018; and taxi driver #1, personal communication, 2 February 2017.

11 Snowdon (2018a); taxi broker #1, personal communication, 2 February 2017; taxi broker #2, personal communication, 1 August 2018; and taxi driver #1, personal communication, 2 February 2017.

12 Taxi broker #1, personal communication, 2 February 2017; and taxi broker #2, personal communication, 1 August 2018.

13 Taxi broker #2, personal communication, 1 August 2018; and taxi driver #1, personal communication, 2 February 2017.

14 Taxi broker #2, personal communication, 1 August 2018; and taxi driver #1, personal communication, 2 February 2017.

15 Taxi broker #2, personal communication, 1 August 2018.

16 Taxi broker #1, personal communication, 2 February 2017; and taxi broker #2, personal communication, 1 August 2018.

17 Taxi broker #2, personal communication, 1 August 2018.

18 Taxi broker #1, personal communication, 2 February 2017; and taxi broker #2, personal communication, 1 August 2018.

19 Taxi broker #1, personal communication, 2 February 2017; and taxi broker #2, personal communication, 1 August 2018.

20 Taxi broker #1, personal communication, 2 February 2017; and taxi broker #2, personal communication, 1 August 2018.

21 Commissioner #1, personal communication, 13 August 2018.
22 Ibid.
23 Taxi broker #1, personal communication, 2 February 2018; and Queen's
   University Student Government representative #1, personal communication,
   27 January 2017.

REFERENCES

Anttiroiko, A. 2016. "City-as-a-Platform: The Rise of Participatory
   Innovation Platforms in Finnish Cities." *Sustainability* 8, no. 9: 2–31.
Bailey, I. 2016. "Ride-Sharing Services 'Inevitable' in B.C., Transportation
   Minister Says." *Globe and Mail*, 20 January. https://www.
   theglobeandmail.com/news/british-columbia/uber-in-bc-is-inevitable-
   transportation-minister-says/article28277819/.
Barglind, K. 2016. "Innovation, Technology and Transportation: The Need
   to Address On-Demand Ridesharing and Modernize Outdated Taxi
   Regulations in the US." *Wisconsin International Law Journal* 33, no. 3:
   701–27.
Bennett, G. 1993. *The Metro Taxi Licensing Commission: Evolution
   of a Private Monopoly.* Queen's University.
Brail, S. 2017. "Promoting Innovation Locally: Municipal Regulation
   as Barrier or Boost?" *Geography Compass* 11, no. 12. https://doi.org/
   10.1111/gec3.12349.
– 2018. "How Partnerships Can Help Cities Cope with Technological
   Disruption." *Policy Options*, 3 July. http://policyoptions.irpp.org/
   magazines/july-2018/how- partnerships-can-help-cities-cope-with-
   technological-disruption/.
Brail, S., and B. Donald. 2018. "Canada Left Behind as Ride-Hailing
   Services Go Global." The Conversation, 10 September. https://
   theconversation.com/canada-left- behind-as-ride-hailing-services-
   go-global-102625.
– 2020. "Digital Cities: Contemporary Issues in Urban Policy and
   Planning." In *Canadian Cities in Transition*, sixth edition, edited by
   M. Moos, T. Vinodrai, and R. Walker, 70–86. Toronto: Oxford
   University Press.
Calo, R., and A. Rosenblat. n.d. "The Taking Economy: Uber, Information,
   and Power." *Columbia Law Review* 117, no. 6. http://columbialawreview.
   org/content/the-taking-economy-uber-information-and-power/.
CBC News. 2018. "Kingston Set to Rein in Uber," 8 August. https://www.
   cbc.ca/news/canada/ottawa/kingston-set-to-regulate-uber-1.4776408.

City of Kingston, by-law no. 2010–205, a by-law to define the mandate
and meeting procedures for committees established by the corporation
of the city of Kingston, 26 June 2018, s C-3.

*City of Kingston and townships of Kingston, Pittsburgh and Ernestown
Act, 1989,* SO 1989, c Pr29. https://digitalcommons.osgoode.yorku.ca/
cgi/viewcontent.cgi?article=1871&context=ontario_statutes.

*City of Kingston and townships of Kingston, Pittsburgh and Ernestown
Act, 1990,* SO 1990, c Pr35. https://digitalcommons.osgoode.yorku.ca/
cgi/viewcontent.cgi?article=1963&context=ontario_statutes.

Competition Bureau Canada. 2015. *Modernizing Regulation in the
Canadian Taxi Industry.* Ottawa: Government of Canada. http://www.
competitionbureau.gc.ca/eic/site/cb-bc.nsf/eng/04007.html.

Craggs, S. 2017. "If You Can't Beat Them, Licence Them: Hamilton
Set to Regulate Uber." CBC News, 13 January. https://www.cbc.ca/
news/canada/hamilton/uber-bylaw-1.3933333.

Donald, B., and H. Hall. 2016. "The Innovation Challenge of a Public
Sector City." In *The Economic Performance of Canadian City-Regions,*
edited by Meric Gertler and David Wolfe, 311–33. Toronto: University
of Toronto Press.

Elliott, R.E. 2016. "Sharing App or Regulation Hack(ney)? Defining Uber
Technologies, Inc." *Journal of Corporation Law* 41, no. 3: 727–56.

Ferguson, E. 2017. "Critics Give Uber a Rough Ride." *Kingston Whig
Standard,* 18 September. https://www.thewhig.com/2017/09/18/
critics-give-uber-a-rough-ride/wcm/2d2e267a-0024-7a79-a354-
391b59e3a230.

– 2018. "New Bylaw Designed to Drive Uber Out of Kingston, Driver
Says." *Kingston Whig Standard,* 17 August. https://www.thewhig.com/
news/local-news/new-bylaw-designed-to-drive-uber-out-of-kingston-
driver-says.

Kenney, M., and J. Zysman. 2016. "The Rise of the Platform Economy."
Issues in Science and Technology 32, no. 3: 61–9.

Kingston Area Taxi Commission. 2018. By-Law No 4. http://www.katc.ca/
index.php/by-laws.

Krause, K. 2018. "Uber Faces Saturday Deadline to Stay in Kingston."
Global News, 10 September. https://globalnews.ca/news/4439105/
deadline-uber-kingston/.

Loriggio, P. 2015. "Ontario Court Sides with Uber in Legal Battle with
City of Toronto." Global News, 3 July. https://globalnews.ca/news/
2091546/ontario-court-sides-with-uber-in-legal-battle-with-city-
of-toronto/.

Mazur, A. 2018. "Kingston Taxi Commission Passes Bylaw to Limit Uber, Lyft." Global News, 2 August. https://globalnews.ca/news/4367939/ kingston-taxi-commission-passes-bylaw-to-limit-uber-lyft/.

O'Reilly, M. 2016. "AMS Launches Petition to Prevent Uber from Being Forced out of Kingston." Queen's University Journal, 6 October. https://www.queensjournal.ca/story/2016-10-06/news/ ams-launches-petition-to-prevent-uber-from-being-forced-out-of-kingston/.

Ranchordas, Sofia. 2015. "Does Sharing Mean Caring? Regulation Innovation in the Sharing Economy." Minnesota Journal of Law, Science and Technology 16, no. 1: 413–75.

RCMP. 2018. "Types of Criminal Background Checks," 29 March. http://www.rcmp-grc.gc.ca/en/types-criminal-background-checks.

Saltman, J. 2017. "Ride-Hailing Still Coming to B.C., but NDP, Greens Offer Few Details." Vancouver Sun, 1 June. https://vancouversun.com/ news/local-news/ride-hailing-still-coming-to-b-c-but-ndp-greens-offer-few-details.

Sherriff-Scott, I. 2018. "Uber Regulations to Come into Effect Mid-September." Queen's University Journal, 7 September. https://www. queensjournal.ca/story/2018-09-07/news/uber-regulations-to-come-into-effect-mid-september/.

Shields, L. 2016. "Driving Decision Making: An Analysis of Policy Diffusion and Its Role in the Development and Implementation of Ridesharing Regulations in Four Canadian Municipalities." University of Western Ontario, Local Government Program. https://ir.lib.uwo.ca/ cgi/viewcontent.cgi?article=1149&context=lgp-mrps.

Snowdon, F. 2018a. "Canadian Competition Bureau Gets Involved in Kingston Uber Dispute, Uber Driver Says." Global News, 17 September. https://globalnews.ca/news/4452176/canadian-competition-bureau-kingston-uber-dispute/.

– 2018b. "Kingston's Uber Bylaw Suspended after Legal Review." Global News, 20 September. https://globalnews.ca/news/4470099/kingstons-uber-bylaw-suspended-after-legal-review/.

– 2018c. "Kingston Taxi Broker Speaks Out after Ride-Sharing Bylaw Put on Hold." Global News, 18 September. https://globalnews.ca/ news/4463575/kingston-taxi-driver-ride-sharing-bylaw-on-hold/.

Spicer, Z. 2018. The Platform Economy and Regulatory Disruption: Estimating the Impact on Municipal Revenue in Toronto. Toronto: Institute on Municipal Finance & Governance, University of Toronto. https://tspace.library.utoronto.ca/bitstream/1807/88262/1/

imfgpaper_no4o_platformeconomyregulatorydisruption_zacharyspicer_
june_5_2018.pdf.
Spicer, Z., and A. Zwick. 2019. "Good or Bad? Ridesharing's Impact
on Canadian Cities." *Canadian Geographer* 62, no. 4: 430–6.
Williams, A. 2018. "Save Uber in Kingston [Online petition]." August.
https://www.change.org/p/bryan-paterson-save-uber-in-kingston.
Xu, X. 2017. "B.C. Ride-Sharing Companies Slip through Cracks as Uber
Faces Pressure from Provincial Regulators." *Globe and Mail*, 3 July.
https://www.theglobeandmail.com/news/british-columbia/ride-sharing-
companies-slip-through-cracks-as-uber-faces-pressure-from-regulators/
article35538333/.

8

A New Public-Private Partnership for the Platform Age? Uber as Public Transit

Zachary Spicer

- A growing number of municipalities are exploring use of ride-hailing firms to complement transit options or replace new transit plans. Many are low-density, suburban communities.
- Partnerships with ride-hailing firms are effectively forms of public-private partnerships (PPPs), but, unlike other PPPs, these relationships do not transfer risk to the private sector. Instead, operational and policy risk are carried by the municipality and those recruited to drive by the ride-hailing firm.
- Such partnerships will likely increase in the future, given the small capital costs needed to engage Uber as a "transit provider" on a limited basis.

INTRODUCTION

Ride-hailing services, such as Uber, generally court controversy in every market they enter. To overcome challenges from hostile taxi companies and drivers and often equally hostile local politicians and regulators, ride-hailing companies have typically resorted to aggressive tactics to secure a place in local transportation-for-hire markets. Firms such as Uber have been blamed for safety violations (Saner 2017; Kerr 2014; Feeney 2015), increased congestion on roadways (Leblanc 2018; Bliss 2017), environmental degradation (Galbraith 2016; Hawkins 2015), consumer protection violations (Calo and Rosenblat 2018; Cleveland 2014; Koopman et al. 2015), and labour market precarity, amongst other issues (Rogers 2015; Malin and Chandler 2016; Younglai 2015). Some municipalities, however, have overlooked the poor reputation of many of these firms and are beginning to see ride hailing in a very different light. To many, Uber is no longer a rogue transportation outlaw, but rather a partner and potential solution to transit challenges.

How did ride-hailing firms become a partner for local governments? How do these partnerships come about? To answer these questions, this chapter examines four jurisdictions that have pursued partnerships with Uber: Innisfil (Ontario), Almonte Springs (Florida), Pinellas County (Florida), and Edmonton (Alberta). Overall, we find that ride hailing is seen largely as a solution to the "last-mile" problem in regional transit networks in several of these markets. However, the municipalities examined are partnering with ride-hailing firms to reach a scattered array of policy ends with little consistency. We conclude that such partnerships will likely increase, given the small capital investment required to engage Uber as a transit partner on a limited basis. However, we also find that these relationships depart from a typical public-private partnership model, as they do not spread risk among private sector actors.

This chapter proceeds in four sections. First, we examine the growth of Uber and detail some of its initial struggles to find legitimacy in several markets. We then explore the literature on public-private partnerships and present ways of understanding the attraction to partner with ride-hailing firms for public transit. In the following section, we examine four case studies, exploring the dynamics in each community that eventually brought about a cooperative relationship (or in one case led to an aborted partnership) with Uber. The final section concludes the chapter.

FROM OUTLAW TO PARTNER: UBER AND RIDESHARING IN NORTH AMERICAN CITIES

Ride-hailing firms like Uber and Lyft are known commodities in most North American cities. Uber, which operates in over seventy countries and 500 cities around the world, is the market leader and is likely the best known of the multitude of ride-hailing companies operating throughout North America. The digital ride-hailing service, which effectively sidesteps taxi regulations by directly connecting passengers and drivers through mobile devices, has proven extremely popular with consumers; Uber claims to have provided over two billion rides since 2009 (Alba 2016). But such phenomenal growth – as well as that of similar ridesharing services – has ignited protests and demonstrations from the traditional taxi industry that argue Uber has unfairly entered their marketplaces and disregards established vehicle-for-hire regulations. Regulators have responded to these calls, often setting up a particularly unstable and occasionally hostile relationship with Uber.

Uber launched in San Francisco in July 2010 under the name "UberCab." At the time, the service was conceived as an app-based taxi-hailing system, where consumers could request a car in San Francisco by sending a text. Just three months after its launch, UberCab closed a $1.25 million angel financing round, injecting much-needed cash to grow the company's operations while setting it up as an emerging star in the Silicon Valley technology ecosystem (Chokkattu and Crook 2014). In that same month, however, both the San Francisco Metro Transit Authority and the California Public Utilities Commission issued cease-and-desist orders, claiming UberCab was operating illegally (Ha 2012). The company responded by changing its name from UberCab to simply Uber, in order to appear that it was not operating a traditional taxi service.

In May 2011, Uber launched in New York City, its second US market, as a dispatch service for licensed private car services (town cars, black cars, limousines, and livery cabs), generating revenue by taking a percentage of the regulated fare. The company faced minimal political resistance until July 2012, when it launched UberTAXI for standard (yellow) taxicabs. The city's Taxi and Limousine Commission initially signalled support for the service (Chen 2012), but soon warned that taxi drivers or owners found using electronic devices could face fines or the suspension or revocation of their licences (NYCTLC 2012). When the company ignored these warnings, the commission sought a legal injunction, forcing UberTAXI to temporarily suspend operations in October 2012 (Uber Newsroom 2012).[1]

Uber encountered similar resistance from institutional regulators in Chicago and Boston when it launched in both cities during the fall of 2011. Chicago initially licensed Uber as a dispatch service, but soon fined the company for violating city ordinances, including charging riders a mandatory 20 per cent gratuity (Dizikes and Dardick 2012). After it established operations in Boston, Uber received a state-wide ban; officials in the Massachusetts Division of Standards argued that the GPS technology used in Uber's smartphone application was untested and, therefore, unable to reasonably measure taxi fares (Farrell 2012).

In February 2012, Uber launched in Los Angeles and introduced its UberX service, which allowed users to hail a ride from drivers operating personal vehicles. The city's transportation department responded quickly, issuing cease-and-desist letters to Uber, as well as market rivals Lyft and Sidecar, citing concerns about public safety (Tuttle 2013). Uber encountered a similar reaction in Atlanta, after its launch in August 2012, and Toronto, in September 2012, where the company was immediately charged with twenty-five municipal licensing offences, including operating an unlicensed taxi brokerage and unlicensed limo service (Winsa 2012). Uber was received similarly in Miami when it expanded operations there in June 2014. Uber drivers were treated as unlicensed taxis and targeted by Miami-Dade county police, who issued seventy-seven citations to UberX (as well as Lyft) drivers, including nine vehicle seizures (Mazzei 2014).[2]

Uber was seen as an outlaw, callously shrugging off municipal licensing and taxicab standards while flagrantly disregarding all legal means of halting its operations (Spicer et al. 2019). Once Uber arrived in a given city, it quickly built a network of drivers and attracted consumers by offering a fare structure far below that charged by traditional taxicab operators (Morozov 2016). This strategy generated a large base of loyal, motivated drivers and customers who could be mobilized via in-app alerts and electronic notices to apply pressure to local and state regulators to favour Uber's lobbying positions (Sottek 2014).[3] At the same time, Uber established relationships with key political actors, such as Mayor Ed Lee of San Francisco, Mayor Michael Bloomberg in New York City, and Mayor John Tory in Toronto, all of whom helped the company pave a political path to regulation (Lawler 2012). Understanding that it would be extremely difficult to stop Uber's operations entirely, municipalities began to slowly license and regulate Uber (and similar firms, such as Lyft) in separate transportation categories, thereby allowing them to operate alongside traditional cab companies (Biber et al. 2017).

Uber has evolved from an irritant in the eyes of local officials, to (in some cases) a necessary component of local transportation networks, even though little of the behaviour that once generated ire in regulators and the general public – poor labour relations, lax regulations on safety and security, and flagrant skirting of local regulations – has ended (see Hawkins 2017; O'Sullivan 2018).

Uber has also reached a point where its operations are diversifying beyond ride hailing and has recently explored other business lines, including food delivery. Included in this push is exploration of partnerships with public and private organizations. For instance, Uber recently partnered with the owners of a large real estate development company in San Francisco to allow developers to offer tenants a monthly $100 transportation stipend for purchasing a unit without a parking space (Hawkins 2016).[4] In exchange Uber provided tenants with an Uber Pool ride from their apartment complex to public transit hubs capped at five dollars (Hawkins 2016). Similarly, the City of Summit, NJ, initiated a six-month pilot program that allowed residents with pre-paid parking permits to secure free Uber rides to and from the Summit train station (Muoio 2016). Those without parking permits were able to get two-dollar rides each way, making a round-trip fare equal to the four-dollar daily parking pass rate (Muoio 2016). The arrangement, which was estimated to cost the city $167,000, was implemented in an effort to avoid building a new $10 million parking lot (Muoio 2016).

Such partnerships are not uncommon. Over the last year, Uber has pursued transit service agreements with local governments in San Francisco, Atlanta, Philadelphia, Dallas, Cincinnati, and Pittsburgh. Uber has even explored a partnership with Washington, DC, that would allow Uber vehicles to respond to select 911 calls in place of ambulances (Woodman 2016).

PUBLIC-PRIVATE PARTNERSHIPS

Uber's newfound relationships with municipal governments can best be conceived of as public-private partnerships (PPPs), which are designed to deliver public projects jointly between government and private sector actors (Siemiatycki 2015). Specifically, PPPs can be defined as "a long-term contractual arrangement between the public and private sectors where mutual benefits are sought and where ultimately (a) the private sector provides management and operating services and/or (b) puts private finance at risk" (Garvin and Bosso 2008, 163). Generally, these arrangements are used for infrastructure projects such as roads, public transportation, and hospitals (Tiesman and Klijin 2002). In most infrastructure arrangements, the PPP model calls upon a facility to remain publicly owned and regulated, but the private-sector partner is offered a long-term concession, such as user fee revenues, to undertake some combination of facility design, construction, financing, operations, and/or maintenance (Siemiatycki 2015).

Siemiatycki (2015) identifies four common rationales for delivering infrastructure through PPPs. The first is to bring in new money for infrastructure. Simply put, governments of all sizes often struggle to deliver high-quality infrastructure investments for residents with limited funds (Boardman and Vinning 2012). Allowing the private sector to invest in a project without the government taking on more debt is an attractive proposition. Second, PPPs enable what Siemiatycki (2015) refers to as "off balance sheet accounting" of infrastructure, meaning that governments do not have to include the project as a liability on their balance sheets, thereby freeing up capital for other projects (at least on paper). Third, Siemiatycki (2015) argues that PPPs allow government to restructure the provision of public services, moving decision-making away from elected officials onto independent arm's-length agencies (Cohn 2008; Newman 2013). Finally, PPPs are seen as a way to transfer construction and operations risk to the private sector (Grimsey and Lewis 2004).

While PPPs are used primarily to finance large infrastructure projects, they have also become increasingly popular for public transit. For instance, the Bus Rapid Transit (BRT) project of Cape Town, South Africa, involved transfers of buses from the government to private operations for specified contractual periods, during which the private sector was required to operate and maintain the BRT fleet (Goldwyn 2013). The private sector would, therefore, be responsible for the operational risk and costs for the service and collect fare revenue in exchange. In Cape Town, the fundamental purpose of the project remained the same as large infrastructure projects: the private sector absorbed the financial risk for the operation and maintenance of the fleet, while the public sector provided oversight and regulation of the service.

MODELS OF UBER-MUNICIPAL PARTNERSHIPS

Despite the inherent attractiveness of PPPs to local governments, Uber remains a peculiar partner for municipalities. As noted above, much of Uber's early history was spent battling municipalities in court and in the public sphere for acceptance in local transportation markets. Given its history, most municipalities should not view Uber or any other ride-hailing firm as a potential partner. As we shall see, however, many have rejected this concept and eagerly formed a relationship with the ride-hailing giant.

If they do not initially spur Uber's advances, municipal actors may view Uber's role in one of two ways when it comes to public transit provision: *complement* or *substitute*. Both depend upon their perception of Uber's impact on their public transit network. A municipality may view Uber as complementing its public transit system. In this, municipal actors do not view Uber as a fundamental pest or irritant. History may be informative in this instance. Instead, these communities believe Uber can help fill gaps in the transit system, allowing residents to better navigate the community. A municipality may also view it as a substitute, in that it is able to replace or fundamentally fill in absences or gaps in public transit.

If Uber or other ride-hailing firms are viewed favourably, there are options available to municipal decision-makers, depending on their appetite for contractual service provision. The first is partnership. In this case, growing cities may not be able to meet their public transit needs on their own (e.g., underfunded transit systems, uneven geography for transit use, inability to scale operations or provide twenty-four-hour service). The second is replacement. In this case, municipalities, mostly rural or highly suburban, never had a viable public transit system as a result of their small size, sprawl, or chronic underfunding. However, as their community matured, residents began to demand transit-oriented development. To fill the gap, these communities may view partnering with Uber to help fulfill service needs.

CASES: MUNICIPALITIES, RIDE SHARING, AND PUBLIC TRANSIT

We now examine the municipal partnerships with Uber in four local governments: Innisfil (Ontario), Almonte Springs (Florida), Pinellas County (Florida), and Edmonton (Alberta). Two are in Canada, while the other two are in the United States. Three of the partnerships formed with Uber are still in place, while the fourth – in Edmonton – was explored and abandoned. Two are relatively mid-sized, suburban communities, while two – Pinellas County and Edmonton – are large municipalities. Three were complementary to transit offerings, while the fourth – this time, Innisfil – was viewed as a replacement for a needed transit system. Table 1 provides a summary of the cases.

Table 8.1
Summary of cases

Case	Population (2016)	Design of partnership	Status
Pinellas County	960,730	Complement	Implemented, active
Altamonte Springs	43,492	Complement	Implemented, active
Innisfil	36,566	Complete replacement of transit system plan	Implemented, active
Edmonton	932,546	Complement	Proposed, cancelled

Pinellas County, Florida

Pinellas County was one of the first municipal governments to explore a partnership with Uber. In February 2016, the Pinellas Suncoast Transit Authority (PSTA), which serves the outskirts of Tampa Bay, Florida, began a partnership with Uber to provide subsidized rides to and from designated bus stations. Local taxi firm United Taxi was included in the arrangement. The pilot project, which ran from February to August 2016 in geographically limited areas of the county, expanded quickly after its implementation. First, the PSTA launched Transit Disadvantaged, a program that provided twenty-three free rides per month from Uber or local cab firm United Taxi to low-income riders between 9:00 p.m. and 6:00 a.m. – times in which the PSTA bus system does not operate – from any starting point to any destination. Those eligible for the program would also receive one free ride per month during daytime hours. According to the PSTA, in order to qualify for the program, a person must live in Pinellas County, not be able to get a ride from household members or others for life-sustaining or vital trips, and have a documented household income not exceeding 150 per cent of the federal poverty guideline (Bliss 2016).

In January 2017, the PSTA announced it would expand the original program to the entire county for approximately a dollar a ride (Johnston 2017). Under the plan, the county would be divided into eight zones, each of which would have a designated stop that was a transit hub for multiple routes. Trips had to be within the zone and start or end at the designated bus stop (Johnston 2017). After this second phase, the PSTA expanded the program once again to every stop across the network of the transit authority. The growth of the Uber partnership did not come as a surprise, given that the

PSTA reported the pilot program saved the transit agency more than $100,000 (Irwin 2017).

Altamonte Springs, Florida

Altamonte Springs, a suburb of Orlando in central Florida, soon followed the lead of Pinellas County and also explored a partnership with Uber. The pilot project between Altamonte Springs and Uber launched on 21 March 2016 and involved the municipality subsidizing 25 per cent of Uber fares to or from the city's commuter train stations on the SunRail line, which connects suburbs within the Orlando metropolitan area (Richardson 2016). The municipality also subsidized 20 per cent of the fare for using Uber on all trips that began and ended within Altamonte Springs, which municipal administrators viewed as a way of "easing traffic congestion." City Manager Frank Martz estimated the year-long pilot project would cost about $500,000. Altamonte Springs would be responsible for approximately $300,000 of that cost, with the remainder being paid by unnamed sponsors (Comas 2016).

The arrangement between Altamonte Springs and Uber was the culmination of nearly two decades of failed transit planning. Martz had been trying to overhaul the community's transit system for twenty years, proposing through this period a fleet of demand-responsive public busses, which he called FlexBus. As conceptualized, FlexBus would have used custom-designed software to optimize routes for vehicles that riders would order from kiosks or even desktop computers – a system thought ideal for a low-density municipality with a widely dispersed population that made traditional transit planning challenging. Despite Martz's leadership and the interest of municipal politicians, FlexBus never came to fruition. The project was dogged by delays and disagreements with the regional transit authority – which operated the Lynx regional bus system throughout the six-county area where Altamonte Springs is located. The idea was finally abandoned after the Federal Transit Administration withdrew millions in vital funding in October 2015 (Woodman 2016).

The partnership of Altamonte Springs with Uber caught the attention of its neighbours, who, much like Altamonte Springs, were also suburban enclaves of Orlando and faced similar challenges connecting their disparate populations. In July 2016, the program in Altamonte Springs was expanded to include Lake Mary, Maitland, Sanford, and Longwood, and resembled the original Altamonte Springs deal with

Uber. Each municipality involved would subsidize 20 per cent – up to $5.00 –, for the cost of an Uber trip into their cities from any of the other participating cities. Trips to and from the SunRail stations in each community would garner a 25 per cent discount for riders up to $6.25. When the partnership was announced, the stated intention was to reduce congestion on regional highways between each municipality, but individual partners soon acknowledged that there was also a strong desire to lure visitors to neighbouring communities. Sanford spokeswoman Lisa Holder conceded, "We hope our friends in these cities will come to Sanford to enjoy our downtown and its restaurants," making the partnership appear to be less of a transit-oriented solution and more of an economic development initiative. A report issued one year after the program's inception noted that Altamonte Springs paid Uber nearly $32,000 for discounts for travel within its city, while Sanford paid $25,132, Lake Mary paid $2,686, Longwood paid $1,791, and Maitland paid $1,192 (Comas 2017).

The collective, referred to as the Municipal Mobility Working Group (MMWG), described the pilot project as an "innovative public private partnership." Data from the first phase of the pilot showed a 74 per cent increase in Uber trips during the first year of the program in all participating municipalities. The report also stated that over fifty North American cities had contacted the MMWG with inquiries on the service, demonstrating interest in implementing a similar system in other communities. Interestingly enough, congestion was not mentioned as a policy goal in reporting from the first phase of the pilot, but the MMWG was enthusiastic about the ability of residents of their communities to utilize amenities in another: "This pilot allows Maitland residents to check out the nightlife in downtown Lake Mary; for an Altamonte Springs resident who wants to take an Uber to visit Sanford's vibrant, historic downtown; for a Longwood resident to shop at the Atlamonte Mall" (Altamonte Springs 2017).

Innisfil, Ontario

While Innisfil officially launched its ridesharing partnership with Uber in May 2017, decision-making began nearly two years earlier (Pelley 2017). Although Innisfil did not have a public transit system at the time, rapid growth within the community due to proximity to Barrie and Toronto caused a demand for public transit.[5] A transit feasibility study produced by MMM Group Limited included a survey of residents, which indicated that 77 per cent supported the introduction of a public transit system, with 60 per cent willing to pay an additional $25 per year in property taxes for transit service (MMM Group Limited iv). Innisfil's transit feasibility study produced two options for bus service: a single bus service and a two-bus service (MMM Group 2015, vii). The MMM Group estimated the initial costs for a single-bus route to be $561,000, with yearly operating costs of around $400,000 thereafter (vii). The two-bus route had an estimated cost of $980,000 in the first year, with yearly operating costs of around $650,000 (vii). Given the limited service a single- or two-bus system would provide, city council requested that staff explore other options, leading to a request for expressions of interest from private contractors to establish, operate, and maintain some type of public transit system (Town of Innisfil 2017).

While Innisfil received responses from several firms, Paul Pentikainen, a senior policy planner with the town, argued that "it wasn't what we were looking for." In response, Innisfil staff approached Uber to discuss a potential partnership (Chhabra 2017).[6] An arrangement was struck shortly after. The established partnership allows Innisfil residents to book subsidized trips through Uber's ridesharing platform. Key destinations deemed of community interest, such as the regional rail stations, town hall, and recreation complexes, have set rates of three to five dollars, while all rides booked through Uber in Innisfil to other destinations receive a five-dollar discount (Pelley 2017). Residents requiring an accessible vehicle can also book a trip through Barrie Taxi for the same rates (Town of Innisfil 2017).

At the conclusion of the initial project pilot (15 May to 30 September 2017), staff produced a report to council highlighting the results. During the initial pilot, 12,393 rides were taken through the town's partnership with Uber. There were not any wheelchair-accessible trips taken through Barrie Taxi. A total of 2,366 residents had taken at least one trip with the service. Uber had 930 different drivers service these passengers. The town's subsidy of these rides was $71,000, with an average of $5.73 per passenger – a stark contrast to the estimated $33.00 per passenger subsidy forecasted for a single bus route in the town's Transit Feasibility Study (Town of Innisfil 2017).

The report also included the results from a passenger satisfaction survey, which contained 195 responses. In total 62 per cent of respondents indicated there were either "satisfied" or "strongly satisfied" with the service. The availability of drivers (43 per cent), wait times (23 per cent), and cost (18 per cent) were identified as the largest concerns (Town of Innisfil 2017).[7] A CTV report identified similar concerns about the availability of drivers and high wait times amongst certain users. The report also noted a number of drivers recently left Uber after the company failed to deliver incentives such as bonuses and guaranteed income rates. Some residents also complained that promised kiosks that were to be installed around Innisfil to hail an Uber car intended to ensure those without smartphones could use the service had not been installed (Arsalides 2017).

Innisfil's experiment with Uber changed dramatically in April 2019. As of 1 April, flat fares for Uber booked through Innisfil's system rose by $1, while trip discounts dropped to $4, and a thirty-ride monthly cap was implemented. The rationale was that the service was just simply too popular and the town could no longer cover the costs of the program as designed. The decision angered some residents who argued that Uber was supposed to be their public transit and that a cap to ride the bus in any municipality would never be imposed. One city councillor argued that the cap was needed because the system was being "abused": "The system was being abused by those in the youth bracket who were using Uber at $3 to go to Starbucks (as an example), purchase a drink, then go back to school or meet their friends" (Bliss 2019).

Edmonton, Alberta

As part of the consultation for its new transit plan, Edmonton Transit explored partnering with Uber and other ridesharing firms to transport transit users to express bus stops. The plan was to help the city address its "last-mile" transit problem and allow it to re-allocate transit service funding to more frequently used routes (Stotle 2017).

Despite the projected benefits, Edmonton councillors rejected the proposal to incorporate ride-sharing services in a five-to-five vote.[8] Much of the dissent from the council involved the distaste for privatization of the city's transit services. "Transit is a service we provide ... that is essential for the well-being of our citizens and it is best handled within house," argued Councillor Tony Caterina during debate (Neufeld 2017). Mayor Don Iveson took an opposing position, arguing that "people use taxis today and if there's a way to make that more effective, particularly for people with mobility challenges say, it would have been good to look at that ... I think it was an unfortunately ideological position" (Neufeld 2017).

The city's past relationship with Uber also played into the decision. The City of Edmonton had a contentious debate about regulating Uber when it tried to enter their market just a few years earlier. Those interviewed for this project recognized that this affected the decision-making of some around the council table who simply did not want to enter into a working relationship with Uber after such a combative debate about regulation. Ultimately, the city opted to examine reviving a "dial-a-bus" service, where residents would hail a bus by phone (Neufeld 2017).

DISCUSSION AND CONCLUSION

Given Uber's early acrimony with municipal regulators and the firm's continued poor corporate behaviour, why have some municipalities now chosen to partner with it? The four cases in this chapter present a variety of rationales. Each project was proposed as a pilot. It is important to recognize that these were viewed as temporary arrangements. Given the nature of Uber's business model and the minor capital costs involved, a municipality (or Uber, as well) could conclude the pilot with little or no notice. In this, there is value in at least testing an Uber-type transit model, given that the perceived risk involved is low. Additionally, each of these cases is a low-density municipality – with the exception of Edmonton. Because the communities in question are sparsely populated, expanding transit routes and lines or creating new ones requires substantial investment – especially in a case like Innisfil, where there was no transit system at all.. It is no surprise, then, that these communities turned to Uber as a solution to problems with access to transit. How long they continue, however, remains to be seen.

A summary of the rationale to pursue cooperation with Uber is displayed in table 8.2.

While each community initiated a partnership with Uber for seemingly different reasons, all of the communities examined in this chapter shared a similar rationale in hoping to solve the "last-mile" challenge – which is a persistent challenge for transit planners from communities of all shapes and sizes. Each of these cases feeds into a regional transit system. Edmonton is the only municipality of the four that is really the centre of their transit system, but the remaining three communities all rest on the outskirts of their metropolitan region. As such, they have each struggled with how best to get transit users from their homes to regional transit stations – the "last mile" of a resident's commute.

Table 8.2
Rationale for partnership

Rationale	Innisfil	Altamonte Springs	Pinellas County	Edmonton
Save money	X			X
Solve "last mile" challenge	X	X	X	X
Ease congestion		X		
Economic development		X		
Fill gaps in transit service		X		X
Assist low-income riders			X	
Expand transit ridership hours			X	

Almost unanimously Uber was seen as a solution, largely because it offered a relatively quick and inexpensive answer to local transit woes, albeit largely a short-term one.

Edmonton and Innisfil both indicated that saving money in service delivery was a factor in their decision. In contrast, Altamonte Springs saw their partnership with Uber as a method to increase economic development, allowing residents to move around the region more easily, perhaps shopping or dining in another municipality in the area. In fact, there seemed to be minimal regard for how the local transit system fit into the equation. Pinellas County, on the other hand, designed their partnership to feed riders into the transit system and used Uber to make local mobility more equitable, assisting lower-income riders and expanding the hours in which transit was available.

Edmonton is the outlier in the cases examined, given that its partnership with Uber was explored but never implemented. For the most part, this revolved around concern for ensuring the public transit system remained in public hands. Involving Uber would mean a partial privatization, which the local transit union considered to be a creeping concern. Without this opposition on council, Edmonton might have implemented a small-scale trial, much like Pinellas County. These two larger population centres give us some indication of how cities view Uber in regards to their public transit network. For the most part, politicians in both municipalities viewed transit as a public good and even a redistributive mechanism throughout the community. While Edmonton decided that this public good was best kept in public hands, Pinellas County opted to expand their transit system by incorporating Uber on a limited scale as a way to increase transit equity.

Given the minimal capital costs involved, these types of partnerships are seen as relatively costless, making them a viable solution as a pilot project. Likely we will see more such pilots. What all of these communities have in common is that they embraced low-density development and, as a result, cannot find the appropriate scope for their transit needs. These are also relatively wealthy; their residents have expressed a desire for low taxes and comparably low service levels, making PPP-type relationships with Uber particularly attractive. Given these factors, it is likely that Uber and other ride-hailing firms will find willing partners in communities that share the same characteristics: low density and growing, with a neoliberal governance model that favours lower taxes.

Municipal partnerships with Uber also represent a modern take on the traditional PPP model. As Siemiatycki (2015) demonstrates, there are four main rationales traditionally given for pursuing a PPP: (1) bring in new money for infrastructure, (2) enable off-balance-sheet accounting, (3) restructure the provision of public services, and (4) drive value for money in public procurement. Using Uber to complement or replace transit systems accomplishes most of these goals. By partnering with Uber, Innisfil, Altamonte Springs, and Pinellas County were able to keep infrastructure costs off their balance sheet and restructure the provision of public services by placing more responsibility for service provision on a private actor. They were also able to keep their investments in their new transit models to a predictable level (i.e., the extent of the contract they signed with Uber).

However, questions remain about how much risk is actually transferred to the private sector. Traditional PPPs have been criticized on this front as well, with some arguing that government is the ultimate backstop for all risk during these relationships in case of poor contractor performance or default (Shaoul 2009). Others argue that some PPP concessions have been unstable, meaning that there is a need to frequently renegotiate contracts that were constructed to favour the contractor, slowly moving the risk back to the local municipalities (Cruz and Marques 2013).

The same criticism could be levelled at the ride-hailing partnerships in Innisfil, Altamonte Springs, and Pinellas County. Ultimately, these governments are responsible for deficiencies in local transportation services, placing the risk inherent in transit operations back onto the public sector, absolving firms like Uber of much responsibility. For instance, when Innisfil decided to place a cap on the number of rides each user could take per month, criticism was levelled at the municipality, not Uber. As a result, the responsibility to find a better solution has been laid at feet of public decision-makers, rather than the private firm that is providing the service in question.

Also, unlike the PPP for BRT in South Africa described earlier, responsibility for the operation and maintenance of the "fleet" is placed upon individual drivers. The ride-hailing business model relies upon private citizens using their own vehicles, effectively transferring operational risks to the drivers (Ticona et al. 2018), which, as Wolf demonstrates in this volume, effectively absolves the ride-hailing firm of paying for the operations and maintenance of vehicles, but also removes the risk naturally included with operating a motor vehicle and a small business. This model, when packaged as an extension or replacement for transit, effectively perpetuates this risk-avoidance scheme on a larger scale and allows ride-hailing firms to sidestep the risk involved in a PPP. Uber has done nothing more than accept a guaranteed concession for their services. They have invested nothing in capital in the community and do not take on any additional responsibility or risk throughout the duration of the partnership.

The other big question is whether partnerships with Uber and other ride-hailing firms provide value to the public. For the most part, transit administrators have responded favourably to agreements with ride-hailing companies, but these arrangements are not without criticism from the public. It can be argued that the presence of a transportation service that relies on smartphones and credit or debit cards inherently excludes those who have neither (Smith 2017). There are also concerns about potential lack of drivers, periods of service unavailability, and increased congestion at peak travel times (Smith 2017). As was evident by Innisfil's recent decision to place a cap on ride-hailing trips through their partnership, these relationships with Uber cannot scale in the same manner as traditional public transit, meaning that an influx of riders to a bus network increases profitability and sustains the system, but the same effect in a ride-hailing partnership stretches the arrangement to its limits and threatens the fiscal health of the system as a whole.

Such criticism has led some municipalities to adopt ride-hailing-like technology into exiting transit services. Belleville, Ontario, for instance, has created a smartphone application that allows riders to hail a public bus at their nearest bus stop, while an algorithm provides the optimal route to the driver based upon users' desired drop-off locations (Dunne 2018). Municipalities have options when trying to work their way out of the transit challenges created by low-density development and an aversion to creating a traditional bus network. Perhaps, then, ride-hailing technology is better seen as the innovation municipalities need in their transit systems, rather than ride-hailing firms. Time will tell, but the future of mobility will depend on municipalities and different transit services trying different models to find the best fit. As it stands, ride-hailing-firm partnerships appear to work at a limited scale in certain circumstances. The challenges incumbent with these relationships need to be seriously contemplated by any municipality hoping to develop innovative solutions for their transit problems.

NOTES

1 UberTAXI would eventually be rolled into Uber's main operations and thereafter be referred to only as "Uber."
2 Regulatory authority for taxicabs and other passenger vehicles in Miami falls to the county level, not the city, which is governed by a county mayor and members of the Miami-Dade Board of County Commissioners.
3 This strategy was described internally as "Travis's law" in reference to Uber founder Travis Kalanick. Lobbyist and venture capitalist Bradley Tusk details the strategy in his autobiography, *The Fixer*. In it, Tusk discusses the creation of an early lobbying strategy that argued that Uber is better off entering a market with or without permission, demonstrating the product to the public and building a consumer base that could turn riders into advocates and use grassroots political pressure to ensure Uber's continued existence in the market. For more information, see Tusk (2018).
4 At least $30 from the $100 stipend must be spent on Uber trips. For more information, see Hawkins (2016).
5 Innisfil had grown 17 per cent from 2006 to 2016, ballooning to 37,000 residents. See Bliss (2019).
6 Innisfil staff note they did not receive interest from local taxi firms. In an August 2017 interview Paul Pentikainen stated that "they did not respond to our expression of interest document" (Chhabra 2017).
7 Among respondents, 22 per cent of respondents indicated they had "no concerns" using the service (Town of Innisfil, 2017).
8 Three councillors were absent from the vote (Neufeld 2017).

REFERENCES

Alba, D. 2016. "Uber Hits 2 Billion Rides as Growth in China Soars –
For Now." *Wired*, 18 July. https://www.wired.com/2016/07/
uber-hits-2-billion-rides-growth-china-soars-now/.
Altamonte Springs. 2017. "Five Central Florida Cities Enhance Unique
Uber Pilot Introducing Discounted Inter-City Travel." Altamonte
Springs, FL: City of Altamonte Springs.
Arsalides, M. 2017. "Uber Public Transit a Huge Success According
to Innisfil." CTV News, 4 August. https://barrie.ctvnews.ca/uber-public-
transit-a-huge-success-according-to-innisfil-1.3533924.
Biber, E., S.E. Light, and J.B. Ruhl. 2017. "Regulating Business Innovation
as Policy Disruption: From the Model T to Airbnb." *Vanderbilt Law
Review* 70: 1,561–620.
Bliss, L. 2016. "A Florida Transit Agency Takes On the Digital Divide in
a Partnership with Uber." CityLab, 20 June. https://www.citylab.com/
transportation/2016/06/pinellas-county-uber-dial-a-ride/487568/.
– 2017. "The Ride-Hailing Effect: More Cars, More Trips, More Miles."
CityLab, 12 October. https://www.citylab.com/transportation/2017/10/
the-ride-hailing-effect-more-cars-more-trips-more-miles/542592/.
– 2019. "City Lab Daily: 'Uber Was Supposed to Be Our Public Transit.'"
CityLab, 29 April. https://www.citylab.com/newsletter-editions/2019/04/
citylab-daily-uber-was-supposed-be-our-public-transit/588376/.
Boardman, A.E., and A.R. Vining. 2012. "The Political Economy
of Public-Private Partnerships and Analysis of Their Social Value."
Annals of Public and Cooperative Economics 88, no. 2: 117–41.
Calo, R., and A. Rosenblat. 2018. "The Taking Economy: Uber,
Information and Power." *Columbia Law Review* 117, no. 6: 1,623–8.
Chen, B.X. 2012. "Uber, an App That Summons a Car, Plans a Cheaper
Service Using Hybrids." *New York Times,* 1 July. https://www.nytimes.
com/2012/07/02/technology/uber-a-car-service-smartphone-app-plans-
cheaper-service.html.
Chhabra, S. 2017. "Innisfil Saved $73,500 by Using Uber as a Public
Transportation Service." Mobilsyrup, 9 August. https://mobilesyrup.
com/2017/08/09/innisfil-saved-73500-by-using-uber-as-a-public-
transportation-service.
Chokkattu, J., and J. Crook. 2014. "A Brief History of Uber." TechCrunch,
14 August. https://techcrunch.com/gallery/a-brief-history-of-uber/
slide/27.

Cleveland, P. 2014. "Uber Ignores Consumer Protection." *Ottawa Citizen*, 9 October. https://ottawacitizen.com/news/local-news/cleveland-uber-ignores-consumer-protection.

Cohn, D. 2008. "British Columbia's Capital Asset Management Framework: Moving from Transactional to Transformative Leadership on Public-Private Partnerships or a 'Railroad Job'?" *Canadian Public Administration* 51, no. 1: 71–97.

Comas, M.E. 2016. "Need a Ride? Altamonte Springs Will Help Pay Your Uber Trip within Its City." *Orlando Sentinel*, 4 March. https://www.orlandosentinel.com/news/seminole-county/os-altamonte-springs-uber-transportation-20160304-story.html.

– 2017. "Need to Get Away? Five Central Florida Cities Soon Will Help You Pay for Uber Rides." *Orlando Sentinel*, 12 August. https://www.orlandosentinel.com/news/os-uber-discount-central-florida-cities-20170810-story.html.

Cruz, C.O., and R.C. Marques. 2013. "Endogenous Determinants for Renegotiating Concessions: Evidence from Local Infrastructure." *Local Government Studies* 39, no. 3: 352–74.

Dizikes, C., and H. Dardick. 2012. "Chicago Accuses Cab Dispatch Company of Violating City Ordinances." *Chicago Tribune*, 26 October. https://www.chicagotribune.com/news/ct-xpm-2012-10-26-ct-met-cab-company-citation-20121026-story.html.

Dunne, J. 2018. "Uber for Buses? How Some Canadian Cities Are Using Technology to Tackle Transit Trouble." CBC News, 29 September. https://www.cbc.ca/news/business/uber-lyft-ride-hailing-on-demand-public-transit-1.4842699.

Farrell, M.B. 2012. "State Reverses Ban on Uber Car Service Ordering App." *Boston Globe*, 16 August. https://www.bostonglobe.com/business/2012/08/15/state-reverses-ban-uber-car-service-ordering-app/yQTQNP9c1BQiEM3Mrri20O/story.html.

Feeney, M. 2015. "Is Ridesharing Safe?" *Policy Analysis*. Washington, DC: Cato Institute.

Gailbraith, K. 2016. "Are Uber and Lyft Helping or Hurting the Environment?" *Guardian*, 21 January. https://www.theguardian.com/environment/2016/jan/21/uber-lyft-helping-hurting-environment-climate-change.

Garvin, M., and D. Bosso. 2008. "Assessing the Effectiveness of Infrastructure Public-Private Partnership Programs and Projects." *Public Works Management and Policy* 13, no. 2: 162–78.

Goldwyn, E. 2013. "The limits of Bus Rapid Transit: A Cape Town Case Study." CityLab, 14 March. https://www.citylab.com/transportation/2013/03/limits-bus-rapid-transit-cape-town-case-study/4968/.

Grimsey, D., and M. Lewis, M. 2004. *Public Private Partnerships.* Cheltenham, UK: Edward Elgar.

Ha, A. 2012. "Uber Says San Francisco Class Action Lawsuit Is 'Baseless.'" TechCrunch, 14 November. https://techcrunch.com/2012/11/14/uber-class-action-lawsuit-response/.

Hawkins, A.J. 2015. "Uber and Lyft Will Be the Subjects of an Environmental Impact Study." *Verge,* 13 November.

– 2016. "Uber and a Bay Area Landlord Will Pay New Tenants $100 a Month to Go Car-Free." *Verge,* 18 May. https://www.theverge.com/2016/5/18/11691904/uber-parkmerced-maximus-real-estate-stipend-san-francisco.

– 2017. "Uber Is Leaving Quebec After Tough New Rules Passed." Verge, 26 September. https://www.theverge.com/2017/9/26/16368754/uber-app-canada-quebec-pulled-government-regulation.

Irwin, J. 2017. "PSTA Widens Its Reach with Taxi, Uber Partnership." *Tampa Bay Business Journal,* 19 January. https://www.bizjournals.com/tampabay/news/2017/01/19/psta-widens-its-reach-with-taxi-uber-partnership.html.

Johnston, C. 2017. "Pinellas Bus Riders Can Now Grab a $1 Uber or Taxi Ride from Their Bus Stops." *Tampa Bay Times,* 19 January. https://www.tampabay.com/news/transportation/pinellas-bus-riders-can-now-grab-a-1-uber-or-taxi-ride-from-their-bus-stops/2310233.

Kerr, D. 2014. "How Risky Is Your Uber Ride? Maybe More Than You Think." *CNET,* 8 October. https://www.cnet.com/news/how-risky-is-your-uber-ride-maybe-more-than-you-think/.

Koopman, C., M. Mitchell, and A. Thierer. 2015. "The Sharing Economy and Consumer Protection Regulation: The Case for Policy Change." *Journal of Business, Entrepreneurship & the Law* 8, no. 2: 530–40.

Lawler, R. 2012. "While the California PUC Cracks Down on Ride-Sharing, Sidecar and Lyft Commit to Staying on the Road." *TechCrunch,* 8 October. https://techcrunch.com/2012/10/08/cpuc-ride-sharing-c-and-d/.

Leblanc, S. 2018. "Uber and Lyft Ride-Hailing Services Are Increasing Traffic Congestion, Studies Show." *Toronto Star,* 26 February. https://www.thestar.com/business/2018/02/26/uber-and-lyft-ride-hailing-services-are-increasing-traffic-congestion-studies-show.html.

Malin, B.J., and C. Chandler. 2016. "Free to Work Anxiously: Splintering Precarity among Drivers for Uber and Lyft." *Communication, Culture & Critique* 10, no. 2: 382–400.

Mazzei, P. 2014. "Commissioner Proposes Way to Make Lyft, UberX Legal in Miami-Dade." *Miami Herald*, 14 July.

MMM Group Limited. 2015. *Town of Innisfil Transit Feasibility Study*. Toronto: MMM Group.

Morozov, E. 2016. "Cheap Cab Ride? You Must Have Missed Uber's True Cost." *Guardian*, 31 January. https://www.theguardian.com/commentisfree/2016/jan/31/cheap-cab-ride-uber-true-cost-google-wealth-taxation.

Muoio, D. 2016. "A New Jersey Town Is Giving Commuters Free Uber Rides Instead of a New Parking Lot." *Business Insider*, 3 October. https://www.businessinsider.com/free-uber-rides-for-summit-new-jersey-commuters-2016-10.

Neufeld, L. 2017. "Edmonton's New Transit Strategy Will Not Include Uber." CBC News, 11 July. https://www.cbc.ca/news/canada/edmonton/edmonton-transit-strategy-uber-bus-route-1.4200385.

Newman, J. 2013. "The Governance of Public-Private Partnerships: Success and Failure in the Transportation Sector." PhD diss., Simon Fraser University.

New York City Taxi and Limousine Commission (NYCTLC). 2012. Industry Notice #12-31. "Electronic Hailing and Payment," 6 September.

Pelley, L. 2017. "Innisfil, Ont., Partners with Uber to Create Substitute for Public Transit." CBC News, 15 May. https://www.cbc.ca/news/canada/toronto/innisfil-uber-partnership-launching-1.4114816.

O'Sullivan, F. 2018. "In London, Uber Faces Its Day of Reckoning." CityLab, 8 June. https://www.citylab.com/transportation/2018/06/in-london-uber-faces-its-day-of-reckoning/562322.

Richardson, M. 2016. "Altamonte Springs Launches Uber Partnership – and Here's How It's Going to Work." *Orlando Business Journal*, 21 March. https://www.bizjournals.com/orlando/news/2016/03/21/altamonte-springs-launches-uber-partnership-and.html.

Rogers, B. 2015. "The Social Costs of Uber." *University of Chicago Law Review Dialogue* 85: 85–102.

Saner, E. 2017. "Will the End of Uber in London Make Women More or Less Safe?" *Guardian*, 25 September. https://www.theguardian.com/lifeandstyle/2017/sep/25/will-the-end-of-uber-in-london-make-women-more-or-less-safe.

186

Shaoul, J. 2009. "Using the Private Sector to Finance Capital Expenditures: The Financial Realities." In *Policy, Management and Finance for Public-Private Partnerships*, edited by A. Akintoye and M. Beck, 27–46. Oxford: Wiley-Blackwell.

Siemiatycki, M. 2015. "Public-Private Partnerships in Canada: Reflections on Twenty Years of Practice." *Canadian Public Administration* 58, no. 3: 343–62.

Smith, C.S. 2017. "A Canadian Town Wanted a Transit System. It Hired Uber." *New York Times,* 16 May 16. https://www.nytimes.com/2017/05/16/world/canada/a-canadian-town-wanted-a-transit-system-it-hired-uber.html.

Sottek, T.C. 2014. "Uber Has an Army of at Least 161 Lobbyists and They're Crushing Regulators." Verge, 14 December. https://www.theverge.com/2014/12/14/7390395/uber-lobbying-steamroller.

Spicer, Z., G. Eidelman, and A. Zwick. 2019. "Patterns of Local Policy Disruption: Regulatory Responses to Uber in Ten North American Cities." *Review of Policy Research* 36, no. 2: 146–67.

Stolte, E. 2017. "Edmonton Transit Looks at Forming Partnership with Uber as It Scales Back on Community Bus Routes." *Edmonton Journal,* 2 April. https://edmontonjournal.com/business/local-business/edmonton-looks-at-uber-partnership-subsidies-as-it-scales-back-on-bus-routes.

Ticona, J., A. Mateescu, and A. Rosenblat. 2018. *Beyond Disruption: How Tech Shapes Labour Relations across Domestic Work and Ridehailing.* New York: Data and Society.

Tiesman, G., and E. Klijin. 2002. "Partnership Arrangements, Government Rhetoric or Governance Scheme?" *Public Administration Review* 62, no. 2: 197–205.

Town of Innisfil. 2017. *Staff Report DSR-171-17: Ridesharing Transit System: 4½ Month Update.* Innisfil: Town of Innisfil.

Tusk, B. 2018. *The Fixer: My Adventures Saving Startups from Death by Politics.* New York Penguin.

Tuttle, B. 2013. "Rideshare Battle Shifts to LA: City Tells Uber, Lyft, SideCar to Stop Picking Up Riders." *Time,* 27 June. http://business.time.com/2013/06/27/rideshare-battle-shifts-to-l-a-city-tells-uber-lyft-sidecar-to-stop-picking-up-riders.

Uber Newsroom. 2012. "UberTAXI in NYC Shutting Down for Now: No Changes to UberNYC Black Car Service." Uber Newsroom, 16 October.

Winsa, P. 2012. "Taxi App Company Uber Charged with Licensing Offences." *Toronto Star,* 5 December. https://www.thestar.com/news/

gta/2012/12/05/taxi_app_company_uber_charged_with_licensing_
offences.html.

Woodman, S. 2016. "Welcome to Uberville: Uber Wants to Take Over
Public Transit, One Small Town at a Time." *Verge.* https://www.theverge.
com/2016/9/1/12735666/uber-altamonte-springs-fl-public-transportation-
taxi-system.

Younglai, R. 2015. "Rise of 'Sharing' Services Uber, Airbnb Points to
a Precarious Labour Climate." *Globe and Mail,* 25 October. https://
www.theglobeandmail.com/report-on-business/economy/jobs/rise-of-
sharing-services-uber-airbnb-points-to-a-precarious-labour-climate/
article26968204.

9

Regulatory Paradigms for the Coming Age of Autonomous Vehicles

Austin Zwick and Eamonn Dundon

- Autonomous vehicles will fundamentally change private and public transportation over the next several decades, with far-reaching societal implications.
- This chapter reviews key concepts of autonomous vehicle technologies and their implementation, major players racing to the future, and predicted adoption timelines.
- Extrapolating from platform economy trends and contemporary governance constructs, three simplistic paradigms are developed – Smithville, Marxtown, and Keynesport – to contrast differences in autonomous vehicle regulatory approaches.

INTRODUCTION

As we stare into our smartphones, we look into the gateway of the future of mobility; autonomous vehicles (AVs) will arrive at our doorstep before we know it. Policy-makers can decide whether they want to shape the race, or play catch-up after the order has been set. By understanding how different governments view and regulate the platform economy, using the United States, China, and Canada to exemplify broader paradigms, we derive insights on how the coming age of automated mobility may be regulated. This chapter addresses key concepts, contemporary major players, and adoption timelines, and finally explores possible future paradigms for autonomous vehicle regulation.

When we have places to be, we open an app, and three options appear. On the right side of the screen there is a choice for Smithville

(United States), where individual ownership in the free market reigns; on the left is Marxtown (China), where the government maintains a public sector monopoly on mobility; and sitting in the centre is Keynesport (Canada), where an interventionist government plays a strong role in regulating private industry. While perhaps overly simplistic, this example indicates the policy choices that governments will be forced to make as autonomous technology continues to grow rapidly and shifts our society into one of these autonomous futures.

KEY CONCEPTS

As we move into this age of further competition and development of mobility through tech platforms, it is important to understand some of the terminology that defines the landscape. The most important concept is establishing what "autonomous" means for vehicles, which will lead us to an understanding of the technologies necessary to advance vehicles to full automation. A recent report by McKinsey notes that this transformation will result in a fundamental shift in the way automakers and transportation providers view their business models. No longer will making cars, supplying parts and software, and providing transportation services through apps be siloed businesses with little to no cooperation. Rather, these three business functions will combine to create the new future of mobility where these activities are carried out through partnerships and integrated services that make travel between and within cities a seamless experience for customers (Pizzuto et al. 2019).

Standards for the level of vehicle autonomy created by SAE International are widely understood to be the industry standard referenced by companies and governments around the world. The SAE *Six Levels of Automation* is a technological hierarchy that serves as an important guide for gauging the sophistication of an AV, as well as the market at large. At level zero we see the cars that we all know and have driven for decades, machines powered by combustion engines that ultimately rely on human intelligence to guide and operate them. At level zero, cars do nothing unless directed to do so by their drivers. Moving up the chain, levels one and two are the beginning stages of automation, with some tasks being performed automatically by the car, such as acceleration and braking, under the close supervision of a human driver who is ready to step in should the environment become too complex for the car to handle on its own. Level three represents the point at which the car can handle all aspects of driving but is limited to predictable environments without hazards or confusions. If these situations do occur, level three automation requires a driver to step in and take control. The more consequential jump is to level four, where automation can handle almost all driving conditions without the need for human intervention. Google's industry-leading Waymo is the first to reach level four, with their current programs in California and Arizona (Welch and Behrmann 2018). Level five remains an elusive goal for companies and involves improvements on the adaptability of AVs in all driving situations. These six levels help to frame discussion on the uptake of AVs and the associated implications (SAE International 2016).

The first step in facilitating AV technology into a veritable fleet of functional public transportation is the hard infrastructure necessary to accommodate these highly complex machines. As we think of them today, the technology in cars is largely self-contained, with the driver making most, if not all, of the intelligent decisions by reacting in real time to situations around them (think parked cars, curbs, road construction, pedestrians, etc.). To successfully transfer the decision-making process from a human to a computer driver not only requires the car to have technology that captures video and sensor readings, but also requires roads to have technology capabilities that offer cues for vehicles to better understand the dynamic landscape.

The main component of the infrastructure network needed to facilitate AV navigation is *vehicle-to everything* (V2X) connections. This term is defined by Wang et al. (2017) as the ability for vehicles to connect to their surroundings using cellular technology to better guide vehicles and alert them to obstacles. These connections include vehicle-to-vehicle (V2V), vehicle-to-pedestrian (V2P), vehicle-to-network (V2N), and vehicle-to-infrastructure (V2I). Using cellular connections to these various objects, vehicles can sense their local environments and predict the best course to move around. For instance, in a vehicle-to-pedestrian connection, the vehicle will recognize the cellular phone of a pedestrian and note her movement to avoid hitting her. The SAE level of automation in a vehicle will increase as more V2X connections are realized, reducing or removing the need for human supervision and correction.

V2I is the first intermediary step in attaining full V2X connectivity. In a V2I scenario, vehicles receive direction and information from sensors in fixed locations that can provide information on traffic flow and road structure, which the vehicle uses to modify its pace and movements. In an example from IEEE Control Systems Society, a sensor on a light post might connect to a vehicle to inform it of traffic flow, which the vehicle then uses to regulate its speed for safety and optimal fuel economy (Glielmo 2011). The more difficult step in v2x connectivity is v2v connections, which require collaboration between sensors on cars from various manufacturers and AV parts suppliers. In a v2v connection, cars talk to each other in local networks that allow for cars to indicate to one another when they are turning or shifting lanes, reducing the chance of collisions and making the movement of traffic more efficient (Glielmo 2011).

Once the connective v2x infrastructure is established, it is important to think of AV adoption in terms of accessibility. How do users connect with a car that is no longer sitting in their driveway waiting for them to put the key in the ignition and press the gas, but rather roaming around the city picking up and dropping off drivers in a variety of locations?

The platform economy has expanded into an increasing variety of established industries, but none has been more disrupted than transportation. Apps like Uber and Lyft, alongside bikeshare providers like Citi Bike in New York and Mobi in China, are upending the way we commute to our destinations and how we pay for transportation. These fleets of shared vehicles constitute what is known as *shared mobility services*. As defined by the US Department of Transportation, shared mobility services are "an innovative transportation strategy that enables users to gain short-term access to transportation modes on an as-needed basis" (United States Department of Transportation 2016). They go on to note that these services have led to a decrease in vehicle ownership and vehicle miles travelled by increasing the use of public transportation and car-pooling. Cities like Sydney estimate that the use of one shared car can replace twelve privately owned cars, dramatically improving the efficiency of urban car use (Waller 2016).

Shared mobility services are often an important bridge for people who struggle to solve the *first/last-mile problem,* the issue created by public transportation where many people live outside of walking distance from a transit stop and therefore must find another form of transportation to begin or end their journey, thus making them significantly less likely to utilize public transportation at all. For instance, a daily commuter who lives one kilometre from the closet commuter rail station might use a ride-sharing service like Lyft to get from his house to higher-order transit (e.g., a subway or commuter rail station), then once he arrives in the city centre he might use a bike-sharing service to navigate the remaining distance from the train station to his office. The way governments are partnering with ridesharing services is discussed more in chapter 8.

The solution in the example above also illustrates *multi-modal mobility*, which involves travellers combining multiple forms of transportation into a single trip. In a dynamic modern city this could include transportation options as diverse as autonomous trains, buses, and cars, human-operated ferries, and smaller vehicles such as bikes and motorized scooters. The key here is that all these options are combined into a single service that enables users to seamlessly plan a trip across all platforms. Multi-modal mobility services are the foundation for *Mobility as a Service* (MaaS), which consolidates all modes of public and private transportation into a single platform that allows for door-to-door trip planning, booking, and payment. In an example from Goodall et al. (2017), Helsinki-based MaaS-provider Whim allows users to replicate the ease of door-to-door single-car transportation with the seamless integration of private rideshare companies with public transportation providers. They note that MaaS platforms represent the natural evolution of transportation planning around the world, as cities continue to look for ways to reduce congestion in manners that complement, but do not supplant, traditional public transportation providers such as buses and trains.

Jittrapirom et al. (2017) believe this delivery method of transportation marks a shift from an "ownership-based transport system toward an access-based one," fundamentally changing what vehicle use looks like in cities. The common definition of MaaS includes some form of payment model within the platform that allows users to either pay as they go in a one-stop location or buy monthly subscriptions for transportation, similar to the way we purchase monthly transit passes today. Waller points out that MaaS platforms are extremely efficient, as transportation providers can better collect large amounts of data on customers to make point-to-point journeys more seamless and thus more appealing (Waller 2016).

Today, most of these shared mobility services likely operate on traditional buses, trains, cars, and bikes with human drivers behind the wheel. However, they are expected to become operated by autonomous vehicles. As we have seen, Uber, Lyft, and Google are just a few examples of the companies that have significant projects underway to test autonomous vehicle fleets in cities. These are called *autonomous mobility services*, which represent the future of connected transportation environments in urban transportation.

As cities attempt to bring these ever-growing transportation technologies together, the focus must remain on the user. *User-centric mobility services* are essential in encouraging consumers to embrace public transportation and shared mobility services rather than single car ownership. Maghraoui et al. (2017) note that in most current transportation-planning environments, each component of urban transportation systems is designed in isolation, whereas to facilitate adoption of shared mobility fleets on a large scale; cities must engage in holistic, integrated transportation planning from the viewpoint of the use. If a regional transportation system is fractured among several transportation providers, it becomes difficult for users to navigate the transportation landscape, making them more likely to revert to car ownership and abandon multi-modal mobility services altogether.

MAJOR PLAYERS

As we imagine this newly automated transportation system, we must first examine the major players that are defining the landscape, shaping adoption trajectories, and travelling habits of travellers around the world. Traditional automakers are perhaps the most obvious players to create autonomous vehicle technologies. After all, they already have the production capabilities, auto engineering know-how, and distribution networks to lead the transition from human-controlled cars to ones operated by advanced computing. General Motors Co. seems to have an early head start amongst the traditional heavyweights. Their autonomous unit, Cruise LLC, has a fleet of autonomous vehicles on the road in San Francisco that operate at speeds of 25 mph (Welch and Behrmann 2018). These types of partnerships in the previously secretive and competitive automaking industry are the new norm, part of what is dubbed the "data value chain," with GM recently announcing a $2.5 billion investment from Honda, through which the automakers will combine forces in an attempt to be first to market with fully autonomous vehicle fleets (i.e., SAE level five automation) that operate without the pedals and steering wheels found in cars today (Boudette 2018). It is now a necessity for the titans of yore to partner with small technology firms to unlock the technological promise of AV fleets for deployment in cities around the world (McGee 2019).

Daimler and BMW have also announced a broad multi-modal partnership that will include services for ridesharing, carsharing, an electric vehicle charging network, and a route-management service that will use MaaS services to develop a seamless journey from point A to point B (Eisenstein 2018).

Ridesharing companies such as Uber and Lyft see AVs as the future for their platforms, as implementation will eliminate their dependence on drivers and provide a more efficient experience for riders. Uber's Advanced Technologies Group is responsible for these developments, although it has also been saddled with profitability issues, losing $100–$200 million a quarter, along with a high-profile accident involving the death of a pedestrian in Tempe, Arizona, in 2018 (Booth 2018). Nevertheless, company leaders still view autonomous vehicles as an essential part of their strategy to disrupt urban transportation and are exploring lower-cost methods such as outsourcing AV production through automaker partnerships rather than doing so in-house (Isaac et al. 2018). Lyft has taken a slightly different approach to AV investment by viewing the partnerships, like those that Uber is just beginning to consider, as an essential component of their strategy from the get-go, aggressively courting AV part suppliers and expanding their partnerships to include traditional automakers in their quest to establish a fully functioning fleet of AVs. They are partnering with AV developer Aptiv and launched their first fleet of AVs in August 2018 in Las Vegas, albeit with two human safety monitors behind the wheel (Somerville 2018).

While Lyft and Uber continue to pursue AV expansion, Google remains the leader (McGee 2019). Their subsidiary, Waymo, has been at the forefront of AV development for years. The most expansive program in their portfolio involves the purchase of a fleet of tens of thousands of minivans and SUVs from Chrysler and Jaguar that are now part of a pilot program in Arizona where they operate without human safety monitors behind the wheel. This program has been impressively successful, with low accident rates (Welch and Behrmann 2018). In California, Waymo's cars enjoy the highest levels of miles travelled before requiring human intervention (an important metric in establishing the technological sophistication of an AV), averaging around 10,000 kilometres – much higher than their closest rival, GM, which clocks in at around 2,000 kilometres. Google is in the early stages of testing these fleets on real customers. Other partnerships underway include one with the Phoenix Transportation Authority, which will allow self-driving cars to shuttle passengers to the closest bus stops (Randall and Bergen 2018), developing one of the first application cases of AV user-centric mobility.

Growth within the AV sector has sparked furious competition. Perhaps the most notorious example is a recent fight between Uber and Google, in which a former Google executive allegedly downloaded thousands of proprietary files relating to Google's AV technology as he considered moving to Uber's AV business unit. With such high stakes, the dispute devolved into an explosive lawsuit in which Uber offered over $500 million to settle the case. More importantly, Uber had to agree to abstain from using Google's technology acquired through the illegal theft of their proprietary technology which Google saw as necessary to solidify Waymo's technological lead (Wakabayashi and Conger 2018).

Despite these cases of competitive animosity, the autonomous vehicle landscape is defined largely by cooperation in many forms, including co-investors, collaborations, partnerships, affiliations, acquisitions, mergers, and joint start-ups between manufacturers, component creators, software companies, digital mapping firms, fleet managers, customer suppliers, and more. It would be a gross oversimplification to think of the above three categories – traditional automakers, ridesharing firms, and software companies – working in isolation. Rather, firms are collaborating to offer tandem pieces of autonomous vehicle production (traditional automakers), software deployment (software firms), and shared mobility services (ridesharing companies) accordingly: It's not Silicon Valley vs. Detroit; It's Silicon Valley *and* Detroit (Eichenberg 2019).

ADOPTION TIMELINES

Mobility as a Service, V2X, and other important concepts are the technological goals, but what are the timelines to achieve them, and what are the biggest roadblocks to creating cities where autonomous ride-sharing fleets are easily accessed on your mobile device? While providing definitive timelines for AVs are a fool's errand in this fast-changing landscape, Woudsma and Braun (2017) predict AV adoption to be at 25–60 per cent by 2050. This is generally in line with consensus estimates that AVs will become a majority of vehicles in about 2050. Further, Woudsma and Braun (2017) note that the average timeline of AV market penetration will depend upon three key factors: technology, policy, and economy. Each factor holds decision power that will determine AV's market growth.

On the technology side, consistently demonstrating safe AV operations will mark the starting point of disruption. Other influences include advancements in artificial intelligence, adopting connected technology, and electric powering systems. Different driving environments are more favourable for AV adoption, as they pose minimal driving obstacles and hazards. Litman (2020) examines the susceptibility of different sub-markets to automation. His research predicts that freight trucking will be strongly affected by automation because of high labour costs and limited routes, mostly on grade-separated highways. He also foresees that long-distance suburban and rural trips may be affected by automation, though this will be likely be through privately owned AVs (i.e., household ownership). Additionally, local urban and transit trips are likely to utilize AV technology to reduce traffic through shared AV mobility services. As driving environments become denser and more complicated, the time horizon for widespread AV adoption lengthens to accommodate the development of technologies that can navigate more complex situations. The technological gap between teaching an eighteen-wheeler truck to drive in a straight line on a highway for 500 kilometres and teaching a passenger car to navigate city streets crowded with pedestrians is wide. Thus, we need to consider AV adoption in the context of multiple environments, rather than one.

Most literature concurs that while AV technology development will pose challenges, policy and regulation, including vehicle testing standards, liability, and privacy laws are roadblocks that are more difficult to address. With the connections to infrastructure and personal technology devices necessary for AV adoption, Lim and Taeihagh (2018) argue that data privacy concerns are one of the biggest threats to widespread implementation of AVs. They note that these connections are essential to make AVs function, but are also prone to abuse by private corporations and government bodies if personal data are recorded, accessed, and disseminated in ways that exceed their intended purpose. In other words, this can be a barrier for AV market penetration if consumers feel they are a means for private or public entities to collect personal data. With consumer data harvesting at the forefront of debates on social media and the internet, AV providers must be cognizant of the degree to which people seek trust in those who hold their private data.

Considering economical and societal factors, consumer demand will be determined by the relative pricing, convenience, and perceived safety of AVs. Bosch et al. (2018) conducted a detailed cost estimate of current and future transport modes, with special consideration of AVs. The study found that while fleets of shared autonomous vehicles (SAVs) will be cheaper than traditional modes, the difference will be small, especially when considering commonly ignored cost factors such as SAV cleaning and upkeep. Thus, there will still be competition from other modes and by private car ownership, which may well persist after widespread adoption of automated vehicle technologies. Grush et al. (2016) also examine the costs associated with transitioning from non-automated to semi- and fully automated vehicles. They claim that the cognitive transition costs, such as the disruption of established transportation habits, in addition to the capital costs associated with purchasing new vehicles (regardless of the level of automation) will delay the switch to the shared-vehicle world that many predict.

THREE REGULATORY PARADIGMS

So what does this all mean for government policy-making, and what can we expect the future of AVs to look like? Cities will continue to grapple with these questions, and it is likely that no two cities will have an identical AV environment. We already know that government, culture, and economics will all be deciding dynamics in the adoption and implementation of AVs. That same variability applies to the different policy paradigms that will unfold around the world.

Smithville

Adam Smith, the mid-eighteenth-century moral philosopher commonly referred to as "the father of economics" believed that the role of government ought to be limited to the protection and maintenance of free markets. He believed that the "invisible hand" of the free market unintentionally optimizes social good through competition of private producers.

Smithville represents the autonomous future most aligned with the goals of private industries, with Uber, Google, and others competing for dominance in a largely unregulated market. The United States is already getting a preview of this future as the largely devolved federalized policy-making structure of the country lends itself to a patchwork of state and local policies aimed at attracting private investment in AVs, causing what some industry experts dub a regulatory "race to the bottom" by state and local governments. This is largely a result of historic policy roles that drive regulations in the United State. The federal government has long overseen regulation for vehicle production and safety but has left driver regulation – now including automated drivers – to state and local governments. Mukherjee (2018) suggests that industry and government must step back from this competitive climate in these early days of AV implementation and collaborate on a shared set of standards from which to operate.

Nevada was the first state in America to pass a comprehensive AV regulation, in 2011, with twenty-six other states (including DC) following since then, meaning that twenty-four states and all other US territories lack any form of AV regulation (National Conference of State Legislatures 2019). This has led to a regulatory environment with varying laws from state to state, where states are competing against each other to attract companies that are making investments in this technology with favourable regulations. Arizona is perhaps the best example of the path many states have taken with AVs: little to no regulation that allows companies to set many of the rules. Governor Doug Ducey swept into power on a mandate that opened Arizona up to innovation and gave private companies full power in the testing and piloting of new technologies. While many AV companies were based in California, the state's burdensome regulations, which include public disclosure of vehicle travel duration before a safety driver intervention is needed, led Governor Ducey to believe he could pull technology companies away from California by offering less stringent regulations. Arizona held back on issuing any rules for AV companies beyond the requirement of a licensed driver being present in the vehicle. This permissive environment led to a flood of companies moving their AV testing operations to Arizona, including Waymo and Uber. The response from safety and consumer advocates has been swift, however, with many calling the approach reckless and harmful to the safety of Arizona citizens (Kang 2017). In response, California has tried to regain the interest of companies by scrapping their regulation requiring that a safety driver be present in the vehicle (Wakabayashi 2018).

These state regulations (or lack thereof) have contributed to an environment where automakers seek more regulation from the federal government that would provide unified standards and a nationwide blueprint for AV development. The US Department of Transportation has begun outlining safety guidelines and operation standards for AVs through broad policy structures, but these guidelines lack the enforcement mechanisms inherent in formal regulation or law. Transportation Secretary Elaine Chao has stated that the key to unlocking the promised safety and efficiency benefits of AVs is a permissive regulatory environment that relies on states to do most of the work required to test and permit these vehicles (Preston 2018). The belief is that by allowing more and more AVs on the road, safety will inherently improve, because companies will have more time to learn how to operate safely in real-life environments (Holder 2017). With this mixed outlook, it is likely that fragmentation and private industry will continue to be the key players informing AV policy development in the foreseeable future.

Based on these observed patterns of "permissionless innovation" (Thierer 2014), a Smithville paradigm for autonomous vehicles would result in a largely privately owned system of autonomous vehicles that are not imminently conducive to MaaS applications. Ridesharing services will continue to operate much as they do today, separate from other transit options. However, the vehicle that picks you up will no longer have a person behind the steering wheel. In this paradigm, a network of vehicles with little to no regulatory links offers minimal opportunities for regional and municipal governments to create comprehensive policy frameworks that enable AV transportation for wide-scale public transportation applications.

Marxtown

Karl Marx, the mid-nineteenth-century social philosopher who founded the social theory that bears his name, believed that all profit was derived from the exploitation of human labour. He believed the proper role of government was to create a classless society by possessing the means of production. Social good would be achieved through government optimization of production.

If Smithtown offers an AV framework with little to no government intervention and unfettered access for private companies, Marxtown does the exact opposite: it provides a tightly controlled environment with government ownership and management of shared autonomous mobility services and infrastructure whose goal is optimal efficiency.

In this paradigm, the government not only builds the underlying infrastructure and vehicle regulations, but also directly owns the fleet and manages its operations. Where the Smithville model raised questions about corporate control and public safety, in Marxtown the chief concerns are data privacy and government efficiency.

China exemplifies Marxtown. However, this paradigm is most likely to emerge in other autocratic policy environments (e.g., Singapore, Saudi Arabia, Russia) that do not protect individual liberty. In a world where free market economics has come to define all indicators of global wealth, prestige, and geopolitical influence, Chinese leaders realized that they had to exploit global markets in a manner that ensured an outward-looking system of liberal markets coupled with the maintenance of the strict authoritarian regimes that have always been key to the power of the Communist Party of China (Xing 1996). Since the 1990s, China has evolved from a complete communist state-ownership model and into a more tightly government-controlled mixed economy known as state capitalism. Here the government ostensibly has bestowed private ownership onto select firms but still tightly retains oversight and regulation. This showcases the birth of the modern system of state-owned enterprises (SOEs), a highly networked system that blurs the lines between government and business (Schweinberger 2014). This scheme consists of more than a hundred state-owned enterprises (with many thousands of subordinate component firms) that answer to the upper levels of powerful ministries in Beijing.

Even for non-SOE companies, integration with the government's philosophy and control power has enormous implications for the way business is conducted in the country, especially for how the deployment of AV technology will play out. In China's recent policy guidelines for AV safety and testing, the chief requirement for testing permit holders is being registered in China as a legal entity – a hurdle the government often employs to maintain control over firms' data and technology (Feifei 2018). For instance, the first set of AV licence plates issued in Beijing went to internet conglomerate Baidu, a company with close ties to the Chinese government (Xinhua 2018). In Shanghai, that honour went to SAIC Motor Corp., one of China's "big-four" state-owned car manufacturers. The southern city of Shenzhen has been a key leader in the testing of autonomous shuttle busses. Starting in 2017, Shanghai was among the first cities in the world to test autonomous busses, which are all owned and operated by their local transport authority, Shenzhen Bus Group (*China Daily* 2017). Didi Chuxing, China's version of Uber, is seeking to be a homegrown champion of this technology through data-sharing partnerships with local governments built upon data points from 550 million users who take over 30 million rides a day in 400 Chinese cities. These governmental authorities then use the data to better plan transportation needs throughout a city or province (Choudhury 2018).

All this activity is buffeted by a government that exacts strict control and influence in the technology sector. As part of the government's "Made in China 2025" plan, local companies are racing to cement China's lead in the industries of the future, including artificial intelligence and autonomous vehicles. To meet these goals, the government is relying heavily on state-owned firms and their private counterparts to cede data and control to government oversight and management. This has led to an environment where Chinese firms are soon expected to control 80 per cent of the domestic vehicle module-marker and 100 per cent of the domestic market for satellite navigation technology (Sweden Trade and Invest Council 2016). McKinsey notes that while this intense government control may be a boon to the development of Chinese AV technology in the short term, in the long term, companies might struggle against international counterparts, as they will be less able to implement technologies created in other countries with such strict government oversight and market control (Pizzuto et al. 2019).

One necessary component to provide safe operation of AVs, particularly in urban environments, is highly detailed maps that offer precise navigation boundaries to computers. In China, access to the massive amounts of information needed to create these maps is tightly controlled by the government, which has issued just fourteen licences for this type of data collection to a handful of state-owned and state-allied firms. This requires foreign-owned firms to partner with local ones to access this critical information. While this system has worked to the advantage of some companies, such as Ford, who have acquiesced to government demands for control over data, competitors such as Waymo have been locked out because they refused to comply with this level of government involvement (Zhang et al. 2018).

Chinese internet conglomerate WeChat provides a preview of what is to come in this burgeoning economy, home to over a billion people with sixty-five highly populated cities. Started as a messaging platform akin to Facebook or iMessage in 2001, WeChat has evolved into the everything app for over 930 million Chinese consumers, allowing them to message friends, order food, hail a car, complete peer-to-peer money transfers, and much more, all with just a few taps on their platform (Mittal 2019). The next frontier for Tencent Holdings, the parent company behind WeChat, appears to be autonomous vehicles. Along with other Chinese internet conglomerates such as Alibaba and Baidu, Tencent is aggressively partnering with automakers to gain a foothold in this space and connect its users with a fleet of AVs to ferry them around China's cities (Moss and Lin 2018). These partnerships, such as one with Visteon on "intelligent cockpit solutions," are built upon the formidable expertise of Tencent in artificial intelligence and cloud computing (Visteon 2019). Liu and Liu (2020) argue that this centralization of online activities has empowered authoritarianism by the Chinese government as it has access to countless data on their citizens. In one example, WeChat can share real-time location data with the government, giving the government views into people's mobility patterns. Thus, with the movement of these "super-app" companies into the AV world, it is easy to imagine a future where the government holds the ability to peer into the millions of trips Chinese citizens are taking every day. While the Chinese government sees this data sharing as essential to maintaining control and public safety, such control exhibits the dangerous potential for government overreach and privacy issues that cloud the breakneck pace of China's AV technological innovations.

Because a Marxtown paradigm would be embodied by government ownership and operation of an AV fleet akin to treating transit as a public utility, the AV fleet would be fully integrated into *user-centric mobility services* platform applications, allowing smartphone users to instantly comparison shop all transportation options and their associated costs. The role of local and state government would be determined in accordance with which level of government is the owner-operator of the fleet.

Keynesport

John Maynard Keynes, the twentieth-century economist who launched a branch of economic thought that bears his name, believed the government needs to play an active role in the management of the economy to create macroeconomic stability and to promote the public good. Social good would be achieved through public and private investment in a regulated market.

In a Keynesport-type society we need to imagine the policy structures of Smithville and Marxtown meeting somewhere in the middle, with a clear role for both government regulation and oversight, as well as the presence of free-market competition by private firms. Finding this middle ground would most likely occur in the majority of European countries. It might be helpful to imagine this model in the context of the many private activities where the government plays an important supporting or guiding role. For example, think of the world's financial markets, which are highly regulated by governments to the benefit of all private corporations, who generally play by the rules and behave fairly and safely within the system. The Keynesport model of AV policy similarly entails the efforts and activities of the government dovetailing with those of private corporations to further the shared goal of widespread adoption of AVs.

The cities of Vancouver and Surrey (2018) presents a suitable case study for this model that understands the power of cities to set expansive regulatory frameworks while constructing advanced municipal infrastructure, with the idea that private companies will lead the way in the ownership and management of the actual AV fleets. Suffering from high levels of traffic congestion and vehicle-related accidents, Vancouver and its neighbouring city of Surrey set out to engineer the transportation corridors of the future: fully integrated with AV technology to speed the potential for widespread AV sharing and delineate a clear government role in designing and maintaining AV infrastructure and regulations.

The first layer to this smart corridor project is construction of the connected underlying infrastructure to make widespread adoption of AVs technologically feasible. The cities of Vancouver and Surrey have proposed technological improvements including the addition of sensors to traffic lights to manage traffic flow, connected streetlights that measure activity on the streets and adjust lighting appropriately, parking sensors that alert vehicles to parking availability and assist AVs in parking, connected pedestrian crossings that adjust light timings, and retractable bollards that allow for real-time control of traffic flow and street closures for public events. By building roads from the ground up with the type of v2x connections needed for passenger AVs in a dense urban environment, these cities are using the government's ability to fund and regulate infrastructure construction to set a clear vision of what private AV adoption will entail.

In addition to the "hard" infrastructure elements of the smart corridor project, Surrey and Vancouver also set out frameworks for advanced data and analytics. As we saw in the Smithville and Marxtown examples, the data collection of AV users is massive and requires thoughtful deliberation on appropriate collection methods and uses. In this model, the city envisions some role for the big data collected in issuing real-time safety and traffic reports for the public, as well as ensuring the ability for municipal officials to use the data to update to congestion flows and transportation plans. They are clear, however, that the data must be collected and stored in a manner that is accessible to the public, as well as private vendors who will partner with the city on AV technology.

The final component of the smart corridor project is the multi-modal transport options designed to work in harmony with the connected infrastructure components of the project. The principal method of transportation envisioned by the proposal is a network of autonomous shuttles, with the goal to reduce congestion and eliminate the human error that leads to vehicle accidents. These shuttles would work seamlessly with the V2X connections made possible by the underlying infrastructure upgrades. Notably, the planning documents state that these shuttles would not be managed by government entities, but instead be operated by private vendors under a regulatory framework and set of standards issued by the government. Additional components of the multi-modal mobility system planned for these corridors include AV charging stations, new wayfinding applications, bike-share infrastructure, a MaaS navigation application, and connected road signs. These all promote use of the municipal connected resources and frameworks by private companies in a relationship in which the government's efforts complement those of private industry, and vice versa.

The Vancouver case exemplifies the Keynesport paradigm, as the role of the local and state government is regulation of privately owned fleets. MaaS would be achieved by mandating the integration of *autonomous mobility services* – which would continue to compete for customers and public transportation into mobile applications that present mobility options for the user.

CONCLUSION

Although SAE stage five autonomous vehicles are several years to several decades away, the seeds of regulatory paradigms are already being sown. This chapter laid out three potential paradigms of AV regulation – Smithville, Marxtown, and Keynesport – and their implications for transportation governance based on how platform and autonomous vehicles are being regulated now and in the future. Rather than have their future decided for them through inaction, state and local governments ought to proactively plan how they would like to integrate autonomous vehicles into the array of mobility service options. They need to critically weigh multidimensional trade-offs between rights of personal ownership, efficiency of transportation, privacy of the consumer, financial costs and benefits, and more.

While we have applied the paradigms in this chapter to the topic of AVs, they are also helpful when thinking about the greater themes in the introduction of new technologies to our urban landscape. In a Smithville-esque example, innovators enjoy light regulation, or none at all, to explore the bounds of technological progress, but that can come at a cost to safety, equity, and efficiency. However, after going too far in the other direction, one is saddled with the regulatory burdens and potential state ownership that is often associated with stagnation, bureaucracy, and prioritization of societal needs over individual rights. Somewhere in the middle lies the Keynesport approach, similar to the efforts to manage the Sidewalk Labs project (as discussed further in chapter 12), which may serve as an example for other cities of the implications of policy decisions.

Policy-makers at all levels of government are waking up to these increasingly relevant topics of debate, and cities around the globe are grappling with the issues that our hypothetical towns of Smithville, Marxtown, and Keynesport illustrate. Policy is often contemplated on a structural level, abstracted from the political context in which decisions are made. Just "becoming smart" will not happen overnight, the transition from completely manual cars to fully autonomous fleets will not either. In reality, these policy frameworks are an oversimplification of a slow aggregation of countless incremental changes over decades. This chapter has attempted to define the contours of these complex policy discussions to illuminate the direction that cities such as Shanghai, Toronto, and San Francisco may take in the implementation of AVs, along with the subsequent planning around MaaS and public transportation writ large that will transform the way billions of people around the world commute, recreate, and ultimately interact with the built environment around them.

REFERENCES

Al Maghraoui, O., F. Vallet, and J. Puchinger. 2017. "Framing Key Concepts to Design a Human Centered Mobility System." *Proceedings of the 21st Conference on Engineering Design* (ICED 17), Vancouver, 91–100. https://hal.archives-ouvertes.fr/hal-01526780v2/document.

Booth, J. 2018. "Fatal Crash May Slow Uber's Autonomous Vehicle Program But It Won't Stop Self-Driving Cars." *Chicago Tribune*, 27 March. https://www.chicagotribune.com/business/blue-sky/sns-tns-uber-self-driving-cars-crash-20180327-story.html.

Bosch, P.M., F. Becker, and H. Becker. 2018. "Cost-Based Analysis of Autonomous Mobility Services." *Transport Policy* 64: 76–9. https://doi.org/10.1016/j.tranpol.2017.09.005.

Boudette, N. 2018. "Honda Putting $2.75 Billion into G.M.'s Self-Driving Venture." *New York Times*, 3 October. https://www.nytimes.com/2018/10/03/business/honda-gm-cruise-autonomous.html.

China Daily. 2017. "Four Self-Driving Buses Tested in Shenzhen," 4 December. http://english.gov.cn/news/top_news/2017/12/04/content_281475964408678.htm.

Choudhury, S.R. 2018. "Driverless Cars Will Need Cities Covered in Sensors, China's Didi Chuxing Says." CNBC, 27 November. https://www.cnbc.com/2018/11/27/east-tech-west-chinas-didi-chuxing-on-future-of-self-driving-cars.html.

City of Vancouver and City of Surrey. 2018. "Smart Cities Challenge Application," 20 April. https://www.smartertogether.ca/wp-content/uploads/2019/03/smart-cities-challenge-smarter-together-finalist-proposal.pdf

Eichenberg, P. 2019. "It's Silicon Valley and Detroit, not Silicon Valley vs Detroit (Pt. II)." QAD Blog. https://www.qad.com/blog/2019/06/its-silicon-valley-and-detroit-not-silicon-valley-vs-detroit-pt2.

Eisenstein, P.A. 2018. "Frenemies BMW, Daimler Team Up on Ridesharing, Mobility as Partnerships Become the Norm." CNBC, 22 February. https://www.cnbc.com/2019/02/22/bmw-daimler-team-up-on-ride-sharing-other-mobility-services.html.

Feifei, F. 2018. "Guidelines to Ensure Safe Self-Driving Vehicle Tests." *China Daily*, 13 April. http://english.gov.cn/state_council/ministries/2018/04/13/content_281476110368454.htm.

Glielmo, L. 2011. "Vehicle-to-Vehicle/Vehicle-to-Infrastructure Control." In *The Impact of Control Technology*, edited by T. Samad, and A.M.

Annaswamy. http://ieeecss.org/sites/ieeecss.org/files/documents/IoCT-Part4-13VehicleToVehicle-HR.pdf.

Goodall, W., T.D. Fishman, and J. Bornstein. 2017. "The Rise of Mobility as a Service." *Deloitte Review* 20. https://www2.deloitte.com/content/dam/Deloitte/nl/Documents/consumer-business/deloitte-nl-cb-ths-rise-of-mobility-as-a-service.pdf.

Grush, B., J. Niles, and E. Baum. 2016. "Ontario Must Prepare for Vehicle Automation." Residential and Civil Construction Alliance of Ontario. http://www.rccao.com/research/files/RCCAO_Vehicle-Automation_Part-2_OCT2017_WEB.pdf.

Holder, S. 2017. "Feds to Self-Driving Car Makers: Regulate Yourself." CityLab, 15 September. https://www.citylab.com/transportation/2017/09/feds-to-self-driving-car-makers-regulate-yourself/539829/.

Isaac, M., D. Wakabayashi, and K. Conger. 2018. "Uber's Vision of Self-Driving Cars Begins to Blur." *New York Times*, 19 August. https://www.nytimes.com/2018/08/19/technology/uber-self-driving-cars.html.

Jittrapriom, P., V. Caiati, A.M. Feneri, S. Ebrahimigharehbaghi, M.J.A. González, and J. Narayan. 2017. "Mobility as a Service: A Critical Review of Definitions, Assessments of Schemes, and Key Challenges." *Urban Planning* 2, no. 2: 13–24. https://doi.org/10.17645/up.v2i2.931.

Kang, C. 2017. "Where Self-Driving Cars Go to Learn." *New York Times*, 11 November. https://www.nytimes.com/2017/11/11/technology/arizona-tech-industry-favorite-self-driving-hub.html.

Lim, H.S.M., and A. Taeihagh. 2018. "Autonomous Vehicles for Smart and Sustainable Cities: An In-Depth Exploration of Privacy and Cybersecurity Implications." *Energies* 11, no. 5: 1,062. https://doi.org/10.3390/en11051062.

Litman, T. 2020. "Autonomous Vehicle Implementation Predictions." Victoria Transport Policy Institute, 5 June. https://www.vtpi.org/avip.pdf.

Liu, P., and M. Liu. (2020). "Digital Authoritarianism in the People's Republic of China." In *Democracy in Crisis around the World*, edited by S. Sarsar and R. Datta, 176–84. Lanham, MD: Lexington Books.

Maghraoui, O.A., F. Vallet, and J. Puchinger. 2017. "Framing Key Concepts to Design a Human Centered Urban Mobility System." 21st International Conference on Engineering Design (ICED 17), Vancouver, 91–100.

McGee, P. 2019. "Robotaxis: Can Automakers Catch Up with Google in Driverless Cars?" *Financial Times*, 31 January. https://www.ft.com/content/dc111194-2313-11e9-b329-c7e6ceb5ffdf.

Mittal, M. 2019. "WeChat: The One App That Rules Them All." Digital Initiative, 4 March. https://digital.hbs.edu/innovation-disruption/ wechat%E2%80%8A-%E2%80%8Athe-one-app-rules/.

Moss, T., and L. Lin. 2018. "Don't Call It a Car: China's Internet Giants Want to Sell You 'Mobile Living Spaces.'" *Wall Street Journal*, 18 March. https://www.wsj.com/articles/now-chinas-internet-giants-are-shaking-up-the-car-industry-1521374401.

Mukherjee, P. 2018. "Autonomous Vehicle Regulation: What the Future Holds." Smart Cities Dive, 30 April. https://www.smartcitiesdive.com/ news/autonomous-vehicle-regulation-what-the-future-holds/522361/.

National Conference of State Legislatures. 2019. "Autonomous Vehicles | Self-Driving Vehicles Enacted Legislation." http://www.ncsl.org/research/ transportation/autonomous-vehicles-self-driving-vehicles-enacted-legislation.aspx.

Pizzuto, L., C. Thomas, and T. Wu. 2019. "How China Will Help Fuel the Revolution in Autonomous Vehicles." McKinsey & Company. https:// www.mckinsey.com/industries/automotive-and-assembly/our-insights/ how-china-will-help-fuel-the-revolution-in-autonomous-vehicles.

Preston, B. 2018. "Elaine Chao Says Deregulation Should Smooth the Way for Autonomous Vehicles." Drive, 31 January. http://www.thedrive. com/tech/18123/elaine-chao-says-deregulation-should-smooth-the-way-for-autonomous-vehicles.

Randall, T., and M. Bergen. 2018. "Waymo's Self-Driving Cars Are Near: Meet the Teen Who Rides One Every Day." Bloomberg, 31 July. https:// www.bloomberg.com/news/features/2018-07-31/inside-the-life-of-waymo-s-driverless-test-family.

SAE International. 2016. "U.S. DoT Chooses SAE J3016 for Vehicle-Autonomy Policy Guidance." SAE International, 20 September. http:// articles.sae.org/15021/.

Schweinberger, A. 2014. "State Capitalism, Entrepreneurship, and Networks: China's Rise to a Superpower." *Journal of Economic Issues* 48, no. 1: 169–80.

Somerville, H. 2018. "Lyft Surpasses 5,000 Self-Driving Rides with Aptiv Fleet." Reuters, 21 August. https://www.reuters.com/article/us-lyft-selfdriving/lyft-surpasses-5000-self-driving-rides-with-aptiv-fleet-idUSKCN1L61AX.

Sweden Trade and Invest Council. 2016. "Autonomous Driving and the Next Generation of Transport in China." https://www.business-sweden.se/contentassets/dfd94f9060af4d499f98de5237bae251/ autonomous-driving-industry-insight-161213.pdf.

Thierer, A. 2014. "Permissionless Innovation: The Continuing Case for Comprehensive Technological Freedom." Mercatus Center at George Mason University.

United States Department of Transportation, Federal Highway Administration. 2016. *Shared Mobility: Current Practices and Guiding Principles* (FHWA-HOP-16-022). https://ops.fhwa.dot.gov/publications/fhwahop16022/fhwahop16022.pdf.

Visteon. 2019. "Visteon to Cooperate with Tencent on Autonomous Driving and Intelligent Cockpit Solutions for Guangzhou Automobile Group R&D." *GlobeNewsWire,* 8 January. Retrieved 21 August 2019. https://www.globenewswire.com/news-release/2019/01/09/1682524/0/en/Visteon-to-Cooperate-with-Tencent-on-Autonomous-Driving-and-Intelligent-Cockpit-Solutions-for-Guangzhou-Automobile-Group-R-D.html.

Wakabayashi, D. 2018. California Scraps Safety Driver Rules for Self-Driving Cars." *New York Times,* 26 February. https://www.nytimes.com/2018/02/26/technology/driverless-cars-california-rules.html.

Wakabayashi, D., and K. Conger. 2018. "Uber's Self-Driving Cars Are Set to Return in a Downsized Test." *New York Times,* 5 December. https://www.nytimes.com/2018/12/05/technology/uber-self-driving-cars.html.

Waller, S.A. 2016. "Disruption Ahead: Personal Mobility Is Breaking Down Old Transport Divides." Conversation, 20 December. https://theconversation.com/disruption-ahead-personal-mobility-is-breaking-down-old-transport-divides-70338.

Wang, X., S. Mao, and M.X. Gong. 2017. "An Overview of 3GPP Cellular Vehicle-to-Everything Standards." *GetMobile* 21, no. 3: 29–4. https://doi.org/10.1145/3161587.3161593.

Welch, D., and E. Behrmann. 2018. "Who's Winning the Self-Driving Car Race?" Bloomberg, 7 May. https://www.bloomberg.com/news/features/2018-05-07/who-s-winning-the-self-driving-car-race.

Woudsma, C., and L. Braun. 2017. "Tomorrow Has Arrived: Cities and Autonomous Vehicles." Pragma Council Discussion Paper. https://uwaterloo.ca/planning/sites/ca.planning/files/uploads/files/tomorrow_has_arrived_-_cities_and_autonomous_vehicles_pragma2017_cw_report1_opt.pdf.

Xing, L. 1996. "Democracy and Human Rights: China and the West," *Monthly Review* 48, no. 7: 29–41.

Xinhua. 2018. "Beijing Releases Licenses for Self-Driving Car Road Testing," 23 March. http://english.gov.cn/news/video/2018/03/23/content_281476087216526.htm.

Zhang, Y., D. Ramli, and L. Chen. 2018. "Wanted in China: Detailed Maps for 30 million Self-Driving Cars." *Bloomberg*, 22 August. https:// www.bloomberg.com/news/articles/2018-08-22/wanted-in-china-detailed-maps-for-30-million-self-driving-cars.

SECTION THREE

Cities as Platforms

The Promise and the Peril
of the Smart City

Maxwell Hartt, Austin Zwick, and Brian Webb

- This chapter discusses the conceptual and practical history of the concept of "smart cities," then defines the term in manner that encapsulates its inherent nebulousness.
- We detail three common critiques of smart city developments: technological solution-ism, profits-driven urbanism, and panoptic surveillance.
- These themes are derived from a multitude of international smart city examples and experiences from academics and policy-makers alike.

Smart cities are exciting, they are unnerving, and talk of them is everywhere. From India's 100 Smart City Mission to Sidewalk Labs in Toronto, technological advances are disrupting and reshaping our cities and societies. In some ways, smart cities are nothing new; we are used to red-light cameras at intersections and navigating using Google Maps on our smartphones. From building materials to automobiles, emergent technologies have always influenced urban development – ultimately the urban form of cities makes way for the emergent industries that arise from these technologies. And as Kitchin (2016, 1) notes, "For as long as data have been generated about cities various kinds of data-informed urbanism have been occurring." However, the transition from data-informed to data-driven urbanism has ushered in an era of networked, integrated, knowable, and controllable city functions. The fundamental overhaul of urban operational governance is resulting in increasingly responsive, directed, and even predictive city services. In short, data are influencing and controlling how urban systems respond and perform. In this chapter, we first examine the conceptual and practical history of smart cities in order to unpack and define the concept. Then we identify and expound upon three common strands of smart city criticism: technological solution-ism, profits-driven urbanism, and panoptic surveillance.

WHAT IS A SMART CITY?

The idea of smart cities evolved from the "smart growth" movement in the 1990s (Levinson 2016). Smart growth advocates for traditional new urbanism ideas – dense mixed-use, transit-oriented development with complete streets to be deployed strategically instead of universally. These ideas were first formalized by the American Planning Association (2002). As technological advances began to reshape every sector of society, technology-based urban development was integrated with notions of smart growth under the banner of smart cities. The private sector quickly realized that many of the goals of the smart city (e.g., cost-effective delivery of services) could be achieved through paid-for technological solutions. IBM first championed the concept of smart cities in the early 2000s, and now IBM's Smarter Cities Challenge is one of many private sector grants to municipalities to ferment public-private partnerships – partly to showcase the firm's capabilities and partly to attract a new customer base. IBM's work, along with that of other multinationals (e.g., Cisco, Nokia), contributed significantly to the concept's popularization – along with improving the bottom line of these companies.

There is no universally accepted definition of what exactly smart cities are. Galdon-Clavell (2013) notes that although there is an abundance of definitions, they are all very ambiguous. One example is Hall et al. (2000, 1), who see the goal of smart cities to be efficiently transactional, as "all structures – whether for power, water, transportation, etc. – are designed, constructed and maintained making use of advanced, integrated materials, sensors, electronics, and networks which are interfaced with computerized systems comprised of databases, tracking, and decision-making algorithms." Caragliu et al. (2009, 6), offering another definition, consider "a city 'smart' when investments in human and social capital and traditional (transportation) and modern (informatin and communication technology-based) infrastructure fuel sustainable economic growth and a high quality of life, with a wise management of natural resources, through participatory government." Part of this vagueness stems from differing opinions on what makes a city smart. Is it merely the integration of technology into infrastructure? Or is it the strategic use of technology to achieve certain outcomes?

Yet despite this nebulousness – or perhaps because of it, allowing its easy use as a buzzword – the term "smart city" has been widely embraced by policy-makers and other urban stakeholders throughout the world and "has displaced the 'sustainable city' and 'digital city' as the word of choice to denote ICT-led urban innovation, and new modes of governance and urban citizenship" (Moir et al. 2014, 4). Other commonly used terms that capture the same essence include "platform city," "information city," and "future city" – all capturing a slightly different essence of the same idea. There is no consensus on what a smart city is; projects and competitions under the label are diverse in nature and form.

However, there are emerging smart city narratives, national challenges, and broader public sector innovations that constantly reshape our idea of what smart cities can be. Infrastructure Canada's Smart City Challenge – a competitive grant that awards funds to winning municipalities to incorporate technology into their urban plans, – is not unique on the international stage, as discussed in chapter 11. Smart city competitions have been held in the European Union, the United Kingdom, the United States, China, India, and many other countries. However, emphasis in the Canadian model on community engagement, along with its open-ended focus area of specialization, makes it distinctive. It exemplifies how the many ways that technology can improve the liveability of cities, presenting a path forward to apply digital engineering and information systems to a host of policy challenges (see chapter 11).

Because of the term's widespread use, the smart cities literature has rapidly grown in the past few years, now extending across disciplines including business, engineering, political science, urban planning, information studies, and more. Books have explained the rise of smart city technologies (Townsend 2013), highlighted corporate smart city case studies (Herzberg 2017), questioned policy-making on smart city technology (Green 2019), offered critical reviews of smart city practices (Datta and Odendaal 2019), and more. The proliferation of smart city publications demonstrates that practitioners and researchers have spent considerable time and energy trying to understand the potential benefits and costs of these new technologies.

Unlike the platform economy literature discussed in this book, it is worth noting that much of the smart city literature discusses future possibilities instead of substantiated problems and solutions in the present (Lim et al. 2018). As a result, the literature speaks to foreseen future problems and predicted solutions rather than measurable impacts and concrete implementation plans – akin to how good science fiction is a commentary on the present. However, as long as the scope of what is included in the term "smart cities" is broad, it is certain that "smart city technologies, the data they generate, and the analytics applied to them [already] have significant direct and indirect impact on people's everyday lives" (Kitchin 2016, 10).

Bringing together numerous interpretations and social objectives, the authors of this chapter and the editors of this volume define smart cities as the inclusion of telecommunications, digitalization, and automation, leading to a data-driven transformation of urban policy, planning, and governance. This definition allows the widest inclusion of technologies, implementation methods, and public-sector objectives – with the consistent underlying theme that cities are becoming more savvy and systematic about how they produce and collect data, paving the way for more dynamic policy and governance (Kitchin 2016; Bibri 2019). The benefit of this definition is that it captures the nebulousness of the term while also excluding traditional municipal governance methods; cities are not "smart" because they engage in more planning and incorporating greater expertise as they continue business as usual, but rather only when they include technology that changes *how* government functions. After all, cities are going to become smart in ways uniquely responsive to their needs and objectives. Every city has a unique local history and context-specific social dynamics that will greatly influence its own regulatory outcomes – exactly the same as regulation of the platform economy, as discussed in chapter 7.

The spread and subsequent regulation of the platform economy was just the first phase of a much longer process of technology transforming urban life. Yet many of the promises and perils of smart cities derive their path dependencies from current regulatory frameworks developed for the platform economy. We identify three common strands of criticism of smart cities: technological solution-ism, profits-driven urbanism, and panoptic surveillance.

TECHNOLOGICAL SOLUTION-ISM

Silicon Valley is what comes to mind when using the word "smart," as it is the centre of American innovation through a dense network of institutions, businesses, and talent. Set out to change the world – and make a hefty profit in doing so – the prevailing philosophy among Silicon Valley futurists is techno-optimism. This is defined as the belief that the current problems of the world will continue to intensify – at an increasingly worrisome rate – unless technological innovation intervenes. Technology is seen as not one possible answer, but the only answer, the criticism being, "When you only have a hammer, every problem looks like a nail." This discourse emphasizes "a disruptive (seen as positive) change of society: references to outmoded twentieth-century governance models, the need for fundamental transformation, even a whole new way of thinking etc., together make clear the smart city's ambition to reach profoundly into the social realm" (Joss et al. 2019, 23). This world view recasts all wicked problems "as neatly defined problems with definite computable solutions ... that can be easily optimized if only the right algorithms are in place!" (Mozorov 2013, 5). Following this thinking, smart cities can be governed only through the use of sensors, data, and software in real time.

Such an approach, however, risks a narrow view of governance where "hard facts trump other kinds of knowing, and undermine and displace other scientific forms of urban knowledge that are less systematic and continuous, such as policy analysis, interviews, focus groups, surveys, etc." (Kitchin et al. 2015, 19). The danger, then, is that such data-driven decision-making can lead to an over-reliance on real-time data, focusing on what can be measured instead of what matters. This may result in the city being governed in a form of "stasis," as day-to-day real-time monitoring and management lead to a focus on the present while neglecting to plan, imagine, and aspire towards the future city as its residents might wish it to be (Vanolo 2013).

In some instances, regulators may be overwhelmed by the pace of change of technology and therefore wait to act until interest groups coalesce to present an alternative. In other instances, elected officials find themselves concerned that their city would be viewed as "backward" or "Luddite-like" if they do not pave the way for technological solutions – as conveyed by mayors who legalized ride hailing (Spicer et al. 2019). Elected officials and policy-makers alike fear the implication that if you are not seen to be a "smart city," then you must be a "dumb city." And in others still, elected officials adopt the techno-optimist mindset themselves. Such was the power of the techno-centric narrative that early adopters became beholden to corporate interests and marketing (McNeil 2015; Paroutis et al. 2014; Söderström et al. 2014). This led to smart cities being "understood as marketplaces for technology products and services" (Viitanen and Kingston 2014, 803–4). As Viitanen and Kingston (2014) argue, many cities were poorly prepared to assess and utilize the ICT that was being sold to them, as most municipal IT staff were either contracted out to the very same corporations trying to sell them their services or were ill-trained to critically evaluate the technological solutions being offered. Viewing the city as a marketplace, technology companies often failed to understand the complex, dynamic environment they were intervening in, but merely saw it as a platform on which to site their technology. The challenges and culture of Silicon Valley are not the same as in Kansas City, which are not the same as in Toronto.

No matter the reason, the results can be similar: cities greenlight and adopt technology as a solution for its own sake, skipping over the first step of policy-making: defining the problem. This is not new. As Laimer (2013, 5) put it, "The fundamental problem of the smart city concept is its emphasis on the possibilities of technology rather than the actually existing problems or needs of urban societies. The degree of uncritical faith in technology is strikingly reminiscent of the 1950s/60s. Even the visualisations used by smart city proponents resemble the futuristic urban visions you would find in popular science magazines during the first post-war decade."

The heart of the problem is that technological fixes have been taking precedence over people-centred policy solutions (Lyon 2003). Vanolo (2013) continues with this line of argument, highlighting the role of smart cities in shifting the traditional function of urban government away from democratically elected politicians and public policy-makers and towards data scientists, technicians, private companies, and global consultants. This has led to calls for smart cities to give more credence to "the place of the public" (Joss 2018) in order to move beyond top-down, corporatist visions of what a city needs and towards more citizen-centric considerations. However, even bottom-up smart city approaches come with risks. For example, online participatory planning processes could be subverted by automated bots (Hollander et al.

2020). Green (2019) warns that there are appropriate uses for smart city technology, but policy-makers should not get carried away by it. Technology is no panacea to all that ails cities, and in many cases, could make the situation worse, whether intentionally or consequentially. "There appears to be little or no recognition that smart developments might contribute negatively to social polarisation in cities" (Hollands 2014, 77). Increasingly questions are being asked about whom the smart city is for, with early critics having argued that the smart city too often fails to consider the needs and desires of its most vulnerable residents while instead seeking to provide services and innovations to its wealthier, privileged, and more mobile residents (Graham 2002).

As discussed earlier in this volume, platform economy services have worsened – not improved – historical employment inequities, as the unintentional largest benefactors of jobs have been highly educated white males at the expense of marginalized communities. Hollands (2008, 312) advances this debate further, contending that the impact of the smart city amplifies not only inequalities of work, housing, and neighbourhood, but also the gentrification of city space and even entertainment provision. He argues that smart urban development is generally deaf to class inequality, inclusivity, and social justice. Much of the business-driven emphasis of smart cities is predicated on attracting and retaining an educated "creative" workforce. In doing so, smart city initiatives may help the middle and upper classes move further ahead, but increasingly smart provisions may leave portions of the local population further behind. Instead of a rising tide lifting all boats, smart cities may deepen socio-economic inequalities and advance the propagation of highly gentrified neighbourhoods.

A study of smart city initiatives in Dublin found that smart urban regeneration projects were particularly prone to gentrification and displacement (Cardullo and Kitchin 2017). Social objectives were largely tokenistic, while the real ambition was to create a vibrant digital economy. Cardullo and Kitchin (2017, 12) conclude that living labs and digital hubs were key sites "where local authorities purposively seek gentrification as an ideal policy solution for urban change." Even though some grassroots living lab initiatives may have minimal impact on the gentrification of cities, they all risk being co-opted into the creative economy and, as a result, displacing residents. "Issues concerning the splintering effects of the informational city, the limits of urban entrepreneurialism, problems created by the creative classes for local communities, including deepening social inequality and urban gentrification, not to mention the conflict between environment sustainability and economic growth, loom in the background behind the smart city label" (Hollands 2008, 313).

Though it might be societally bearable for private companies to use technology to deepen inequities, voters may not long tolerate public officials doing so under the pretence of "becoming smart." If government is not for the well-being of its residents, then whom is it for? "Smart for whom?" will become an imperative question as we progress through each stage of technological advancement in years, and decades, to come. We explore a disheartening answer in the next section.

PROFIT-DRIVEN URBANISM

The global techno-centric discourse owes a great deal to IBM's extremely well-crafted marketing campaign developed in 2008 (Söderström, et al. 2014). As noted earlier, IBM pushed the idea of smart cities as a method to sell a new line of services to municipal governments. Drawing on their early experiences in Masdar City and Rio de Janeiro, the marketing team at IBM constructed a global competition, the Smarter Cities Challenge. Twenty-four cities were selected during the initial round of the competition in 2010, but surprisingly IBM initially failed to understand that the reason for the extremely positive response to the challenge had less to do with the actual technological solutions the company was selling and more to do with the prestige that came with it. As Wiig (2015, 262) noted, when asked why so many cities applied to the Smarter Cities Challenge, the IBM director said, "[The Smarter Cities Challenge] generated huge interest from cities all over the world, even though we hadn't really begun to explain what the business case was for these things, what the return on investment was going to be, how much money could we help you save ... It took us a long time to understand that what was really driving this sort of thing is economic development."

This suggests that the IBM Smarter Cities Challenge had greater value as a branding tool to attract international investment than as a means to solve specific urban problems. Cities alone do not have the technical skill capacity or fiscal resources to become smart alone; they need their private sector counterparts. Though the marketplace may be much more crowded now, the general dynamic of vendors pushing their products has not changed much, and that raises serious questions about whether municipalities are turning governance over to for-profit corporations. Hollands (2014, 63) argues, "Too much of the smart city agenda so far has been led by producers; competing corporations offering their own technology to cities as an ostensibly comprehensive solution to every urban problem."

As a case in point, Eric Schmidt, CEO of Alphabet Inc., has had a long-running dream for "someone to give us a city and put us in charge" (Balsille 2018). With the support of Waterfront Toronto, he finally got his wish. Chapter 12 discusses the Sidewalk Labs case study in more detail, but the criticism of the project can be summarized as such: "Sidewalk Toronto has only one beneficiary, and it is not Toronto." These are the words of Jim Balsillie (2018), former CEO of Blackberry and founder of the Centre for International Governance Innovation. He goes on to point out, "The National Research Council warned that Canada was at risk of becoming a nation of 'data cows' leaking our most valuable national resource to companies such as Amazon, Google and others." Toronto joins the ranks of dozens of global cities who, with the support of national governments and international businesses, are eager to re-take control of the smart city narrative. In doing so, many of these global cities have "seized the opportunity to place themselves at the heart of the evolving smart city agenda, using it concurrently to promote urban renewal to their domestic audiences and to signal their global ambitions to foreign audiences, and in doing so frequently engaging in mutual cross-referencing" (Joss et al. 2019, 23). But at what fiscal and opportunity costs?

It is possible to identify cases where smart cities have been embraced, yet the outcomes have resulted in unintended consequences. In Genoa, a smart city visioning project quickly became dominated by business interests, leading to a lack of long-term planning while simultaneously reducing public accountability (Grossi and Pianezzi 2017). Similarly, in India, the 100 Smart City Mission initiative has seen smart city governance diminish the role of democratically elected urban institutions through the imposition of national guidance and a lack of integration and consideration of existing policies across different levels of government (Praharaj et al. 2018). And in the United Kingdom, there is evidence of how a national desire to generate urban innovations for international export through the Future Cities Demonstrator Competition has resulted in, among other issues, conflicts between the needs of the city and the product being produced (Buck and While 2017).

The inherent emphasis on the private sector in the delivery of smart cities means that there is a serious risk of corporate path dependencies and technological lock-ins that tie cities to particular vendors and platforms over a long period of time (Hill 2013; Kitchin 2016). Technology companies could then hold monopoly over municipalities, allowing them to dictate prices and service levels because the barriers to switching platforms may be too high, whether for reasons of proprietary infrastructure, data ownership, technical expertise, or others. Governmental oversight in this scenario becomes nearly impossible. A further concern is that current services offered at current prices may not be financially sustainable. So if a municipality were reliant on a particular private-sector service provider and that business (or the whole model that supports is) files bankruptcy, what then? With the waves of investment and disinvestment in the tech industry (e.g., early 2000s dot-com bubble), this is not a far-fetched scenario.

Some cities have begun to consider this question. There are now instances of smart city initiatives that emphasize local needs over wider corporate interests. Barcelona stands as an example of a pioneering city that aims to integrate public participation, societal concerns, and returns on public investment through a more citizen-centric design to develop and protect residents' "digital sovereignty" (March and Ribera-Fumaz 2018). Amsterdam has also taken a more local strategic approach to its smart city development by thoughtfully drawing on the technological innovations that smart cities offer and linking them to a wide range of non-technological factors through a strategic urban planning framework that prioritizes collaboration and inclusivity (Mora and Bolici 2017). On the other side of the globe, Newcastle in Australia sought to maintain government ownership over key smart city infrastructure while drawing on community engagement to identify priorities for smart city policies (Dowling et al. 2018). Even in the case of Sidewalk Labs in Toronto, we can see the re-emergence of the public interest within the smart city narrative, following the rejection of Sidewalk Labs' full proposal and capitulation to the demands of the public organization vested with regenerating the city's waterfront (Morgan and Webb 2020). Although there is greater public interest in the Sidewalk Labs project, it is by far not the only concern. It may not even be the most important, as we explore in the next section.

PANOPTIC SURVEILLANCE

Jeremy Bentham, the eighteenth-century English philosopher, conceived of the panopticon – derived from Greek for "all seeing" – intended to describe the use of surveillance in institutional settings (e.g., prisons). The panoptic model would allow a single warden to see any and all inmates at once, whereas the inmates would not be aware of whom they were being watched by, or when they were being watched at all. The ruthless efficiency of this system would be that prisoners would be motivated to act as if they were always being watched. It did not take long for this idea to jump from institutional settings to private industry. Frederick Taylor, the nineteenth-century industrial engineer, created "scientific management," also known as "Taylorism," to increase productivity. This management process, originally applied to manufacturing and heavy industry, tracks and studies every physical motion a worker makes in order to improve efficiency by minimizing wasted movements. Observation, standardization, and continual improvement became instrumental, whereas empathy, craftsmanship, and tradition were deemed perfunctory.

Under these same auspices, smart cities necessitate the tracking of every aspect of people's lives. According to Stephen Brobst, CTO of Teradata, "The bottom line is ... we get a view of the whole city across these different domains of the life of the city as it's captured in the sensor data" (Ismail 2018). Smart city technologies create digital panopticons in which every motion can be tracked and counted (e.g., how many people are crossing the street). Like inmates, people never know when they are being watched. Lyon (1994, 5) writes, "They know things about us, but we often don't know what they know, or with whom else they might share their knowledge. What does this mean for our sense of identity, our life-chances, our human rights, our privacy? What are the implications for political power, social control, freedom and democracy?"

This raises the question of how much privacy citizens ought to surrender in the name of efficient government service delivery, enhanced urban mobility, and other government objectives. Are residents aware of that they are trading away their privacy? Do they trust that their data are safe and will only be used altruistically, especially when data-usage and sharing parameters are firmly in the hands of private authorities? Or do citizens even realize they have a right to privacy at all?

Most worrisome, if this surveillance were conducted directly by public agencies, would it be any better? "Smart-city technologies mesh particularly well with an authoritarian government's interest in monitoring dissenters, anticipating likely sources of resistance and forestalling or suppressing acts (or actors) perceived as challenging the government's claim to legitimacy" (Greenfield 2013, 72). Many of the technologies currently used to improve service delivery in the West are finding a second home in China, turning the country into a surveillance state, with a heavy stress on subduing religious and ethnic minorities (Buckley and Mozor 2019). Critics argue that algorithms allow for the automation of dehumanization.

Ultimately, we need to ask even more fundamental questions: What kind of society do we want to live in? What trade-offs are we willing to make? Is efficiency inherently good? As the pace of the public sector's embrace of technology in all facets of policy and governance is only accelerating, this makes the open question of societal values more imperative than ever before. Sennett (2012) argues that urban complexity, chaos, and dissonance are fundamental to city success. The unpredictability of cities creates economic opportunities, the lack of coherent control promotes personal liberty, the disarray creates a rich multi-layered experience. "A city is not a machine ... this version of the city can deaden and stupefy the people who live in its all-efficient embrace. We want cities that work well enough, but are open to the shifts, uncertainties, and mess which are real life" 25).

As much of the debate about smart cities is polarized into two camps of utopian optimism and dystopian servitude, it is increasingly important to unpack and critically examine the changes happening all around us. Some of us are pulled in by the promise of convenience, novelty, and efficiency, while others are repelled by the surveillance, commodification, and perpetuated inequalities. However, we expect that most people feel as we do: somewhere in between. Seeing the promise, but also the peril.

One thing is certain: smart cities and their associated technologies are not a fad that will pass any time soon. Therefore, we must continue to navigate the opportunities and challenges of smart city development critically and, more importantly, collectively. Just as a city is defined by the people who live there not its built environment, technology alone does not make a city smart. Truly smart cities that have the potential to create a better world require engaged, informed, and empowered residents. As Frank Kresin (2013, 91) notes, and is cited in the introduction, they require smart citizens.

REFERENCES

American Planning Association. 2002. *Growing Smart Legislative Guidebook: Model Statutes for Planning and the Management of Change*. Chicago: American Planning Association.

Balsillie, J. 2018. "Sidewalk Toronto Has Only One Beneficiary, and It Is Not Toronto." *Globe and Mail*, 5 October. https://www.theglobeandmail.com/opinion/article-sidewalk-toronto-is-not-a-smart-city/.

Bibri, S. 2019. *Big Data Science and Analytics for Smart Sustainable Urbanism: Unprecedented Paradigmatic Shifts and Practical Advancements*. Cham, Switzerland: Springer.

Buck, N., and A. While. 2017. "Competitive Urbanism and the Limits to Smart City Innovation: The UK Future Cities initiative." *Urban Studies* 54, no. 2: 501–19.

Buckley, C., and P. Mozor. 2019. "How China Uses High-Tech Surveillance to Subdue Minorities." *New York Times*, 22 May. https://www.nytimes.com/2019/05/22/world/asia/china-surveillance-xinjiang.html.

Caragliu, A., C. Del Bo, and P. Nijkamp. 2009. "Smart Cities in Europe." Series Research Memoranda 0048, VU University Amsterdam, Faculty of Economics, Business Administration and Econometrics.

Cardullo, P., and R. Kitchin. 2017. "Living Labs, Vacancy, and Gentrification." Programmable City, working paper 28.

Datta, A., and N. Odendaal. 2019. "Smart Cities and the Banality of Power." *Environment and Planning D: Society and Space* 37, no. 3: 387–92.

Dowling, R., P. McGuirk, and S. Maalsen. 2018. "Realising Smart Cities: Partnerships and Economic Development in the Emergence and Practices of Smart in Newcastle, Australia." In *Inside Smart Cities: Place, Politics and Urban Innovation*, edited by A. Karvonen, F. Cugurullo, and F. Caprotti, 15–29. London: Routledge.

Galdon-Clavell, G. 2013. "(Not So) Smart Cities?: The Drivers, Impact and Risks of Surveillance-Enabled Smart Environments." *Science and Public Policy* 40, no. 6: 717–72.

Graham, S. 2002. "Bridging Urban Digital Divides? Urban Polarisation and Information and Communication Technologies (ICTs)." *Urban Studies* 39, no. 1: 33–56.

Green, B. 2019. *The Smart Enough City*. Cambridge, MA: MIT Press.

Greenfield, A. 2013. *Against the Smart City*. New York City: Do Projects.

Grossi, G., and D. Pianezzi. 2017. "Smart Cities: Utopia or Neoliberal Ideology? *Cities* 69: 79–85.

Hall, R., B. Bowerman, J. Braverman, J. Taylor, H. Todosow, and U. von Wimmersperg. 2000. "The Vision of a Smart City." Report no. BNL-67902; 04042. Brookhaven National Lab, Upton, NY.

Herzberg, C. 2017. *Smart Cities, Digital Nations: Building Smart Cities in Emerging Countries and Beyond.* Petaluma, CA: Roundtree.

Hill, D. 2013. "On the Smart City; Or, a 'Manifesto' for Smart Citizens Instead." Medium, 1 February. https://medium.com/butwhatwas thequestion/on-the-smart-city-or-a-manifesto-for-smart-citizens-instead-7e0c6425f909.

Hollander, J.B., R. Potts, M. Hartt, and M. Situ. 2020. "The Role of Artificial Intelligence in Community Planning." *International Journal of Community Well-Being* 3: 507–21. https://doi.org/10.1007/s42413-020-00090-7.

Hollands, R. 2008. "Will the Real Smart City Please Stand Up? Intelligent, Progressive or Entrepreneurial?" *City* 12, no. 3: 303–20.

– 2014. "Critical Interventions into the Corporate Smart City." *Cambridge Journal of Regions, Economy and Society*, 8: 61–77.

Ismail, N. 2018. "Smart City Technology: It's All about the Internet of Things." Information Age, 14 August. https://www.information-age. com/smart-city-technology-123473905/.

Joss, S. 2018. "Future Cities: Asserting Public Governance." *Palgrave Communications* 4, no. 36: 1–4.

Joss, S., F, Sengers, D. Schraven, F. Caprotti, and Y. Dayot. 2019. "The Smart City as Global Discourse: Storylines and Critical Junctures across 27 Cities." *Journal of Urban Technology* 26, no. 1: 3–34.

Kitchin, R. 2016. "The Ethics of Smart Cities and Urban Science." *Philosophical Transactions of the Royal Society A: Mathematical, Physical and Engineering Sciences* 374: 20160115. http://doi.org/10.1098/rsta.2016.0115.

Kitchin, R., T. Lauriault, and G. McArdle. 2015. "Knowing and Governing Cities through Urban Indicators, City Benchmarking and Real-Time Dashboards." *Regional Studies, Regional Science* 2, no. 1: 6–28.

Kresin, F. 2013. "A Manifesto for Smart Citizens." Waag Society, 12 September. https://web.archive.org/web/20140113213325/http:/ waag.org/nl/blog/manifesto-smart-citizens.

Laimer, C. 2013. "Smart Cities: Back to the Future." *Dérive* 56: 4–9.

Levinson, D. 2016. "On 'Smart Cities' and 'Smart Growth.'" Transportationist, 8 December. https://transportist.org/2016/12/08/ on-smart-cities-and-smart-growth/.

Lim, C., K. Kim, and P. Maglio. 2018. "Smart Cities with Big Data: Reference Models, Challenges, and Considerations." *Cities* 82: 86–99.

Lyon, D. 1994. *The Electronic Eye: The Rise of the Surveillance State.* Minneapolis: University of Minneapolis Press.

– 2003. *Surveillance after September 11.* Cambridge: Policy.

March, H., and R. Ribera-Fumaz. 2018. "Smart Contradictions: The Politics of Making Barcelona a Self-Sufficient City." *European Urban and Regional Studies* 23, no. 4: 816–30.

McNeill, D. 2015. "Global Firms and Smart Technologies: IBM and the Reduction of Cities." *Transactions of the Institute of British Geographers* 40, no. 4: 562–74.

Moir, E., T. Moonen, and G. Clark. 2014. *What Are Future Cities? Origins, Meanings, Uses.* London: Future Cities Catapult. https://www.gov.uk/government/uploads/system/uploads/attachment_data/file/337549/14-820-what-are-future-cities.pdf.

Mora, L., and R. Bolici. 2017. "How to Become a Smart City: Learning from Amsterdam." In *Smart and Sustainable Planning for Cities and Regions*, edited by A. Bisello, D. Vettorato, P. Laconte, and S. Costa, 251–66. Berlin: Springer.

Morgan, K., and B. Webb. 2020. "Googling the City: In Search of the Public Interest on Toronto's 'Smart' Waterfront," *Urban Planning* 5, no. 1: 84–95.

Morozov, E. 2013. *To Save Everything, Click Here: The Folly of Technological Solutionism.* New York: Public Affairs.

Paroutis S., M. Bennett, and L. Heracleous. 2014. "A Strategic View on Smart City Technology: The Case of IBM Smarter Cities during a Recession." *Technological Forecasting & Social Change* 89: 262–72.

Praharaj, S., J. Han, and S. Hawken. 2018. "Urban Innovation through Policy Integration." *City Culture and Society* 12: 35–43.

Sennett, R. 2012. "No One Likes a City That's Too Smart." *Guardian*, 4 December. https://www.theguardian.com/commentisfree/2012/dec/04/smart-city-rio-songdo-masdar.

Söderström, O., T. Paasche, and F. Klauser. 2014. "Smart Cities as Corporate Storytelling." *City* 18, no. 3: 307–20.

Spicer, Z., G. Eidelman, and A. Zwick. 2019. "Patterns of Local Policy Disruption: Municipal and State Regulatory Responses to Uber." *Review of Policy Research.* https://doi.org/10.1111/ropr.12325.

Townsend, A.M. 2013. *Smart Cities: Big Data, Civic Hackers, and the Quest for a New Utopia.* New York: W.W. Norton.

Vanolo, A. 2013. "Smartmentality: The Smart City as Disciplinary Strategy." *Urban Studies* 51, no. 5: 883–98.

Viitanen, J., and R. Kingston. 2014. "Smart Cities and Green Growth: Outsourcing Democratic and Environmental Resilience to the Global Technology Sector." *EPA: Economy and Space* 46, no. 4: 803–19.

Wiig, A. 2015. "IBM's Smart City as Techno-Utopian Policy Mobility." *City* 19, nos. 2–3: 258–73.

Seeing the City as a Platform:
Is Canada's Smart Cities Challenge
a Good Step in That Direction?

Pamela Robinson and Jeff Biggar

- This chapter discusses the conceptual and practical history of the concept of "smart cities," then defines the term in a manner that encapsulates its inherent nebulousness.
- We detail three common critiques of smart city developments: technological solution-ism, profits-driven urbanism, and panoptic surveillance.
- These themes are derived from a multitude of international smart city examples and experiences from academics and policy-makers alike.

INTRODUCTION

In the beginning of the smart city movement, the first projects unfolded in places such as Dubai, Songdo, and Shanghai. Barcelona, London, Moscow, and Amsterdam also have myriad projects underway. More recently, smart city projects are starting to take shape in North America. Toronto has received significant media attention since the October 2017 announcement that Google's sister firm Alphabet Sidewalk Labs was named the preferred development partner on a 4.8 hectare parcel of land on the waterfront. Their $50 million investment in the project has overshadowed a much bigger smart city investment in Canada. In its 2017 budget, the Government of Canada announced the Infrastructure Canada Smart Cities Challenge (SCC). Its $300 million in prize money would be awarded over eleven years and three rounds of funding. In May 2019 the first-round prize-winners were announced with funded projects in four Canadian cities of varying sizes.

These significant financial investments indicate the hope and potential that government and private-sector firms see in new urban technologies. More broadly, the emergence of the platform urbanism movement is considered as transformative as the Industrial Revolution. Though most cities are just beginning to work towards being "smart," growth and innovation in platform technology sector is creating momentum and diversification in cities big and small. For example, single-issue technologies such as Uber, Lyft, and Airbnb, which are deployed at the city scale, are found in metropolises and small cities, unlike the sweeping, precinct-wide, multiple-technology platforms such as Sidewalk Labs "city-as-platform" projects like Sidewalk Lab's project in Toronto, as discussed in chapter 12, which are less common. Although these urban technologies vary in focus and scale, one common thread is that their vendors are seeking to sell their wares to municipal governments. The Canadian Smart Cities Challenge stands in contrast to this paradigm with its government driven-approach. This chapter explores how the Canadian Smart Cities Challenge differs from vendor-driven smart city efforts of the private sector and considers how government-driven platform urbanism is exploring new ground in the smart city landscape.

DEFINING THE SMART CITY:
MORE THAN BIG DATA AND APPS

Early writing about smart cities often starts with an overview of the varied definitions that comprise smart city work, including those questioning what "smart" actually means (see Giffinger and Gudrun 2010; Halpern et al. 2013). Another theme is the benefits that applying new technology solutions to urban problems might yield. Some common positive goals include efficiencies in energy and water use, reductions in waste, more effective and varied mobility options that blend public transit with new private-operator services (e.g., e-scooters, rideshare services, driverless small bus fleets), better economic outcomes, and more accountable, transparent, and inclusive government (Hollands 2008; Townsend 2013; Kitchin 2015; Luque-Ayala and Marvin 2015; Puron-Cid et al. 2015; Lauriault et al. 2018). Detractors, on the other hand, cite robust challenges that smart city platforms present, including: the rise of surveillance capitalism (Zuboff 2019), data governance, ownership, and privacy concerns (Scassa 2014; Pasquale 2015), and economic and social exclusion (Eubanks 2018), among others. These concerns span across and beyond the typical legal, governance, and participation responsibilities that local governments hold. The evolving nature of the technology and the breadth and rapidity of its changes make these barriers significant and challenging to address.

As our experience with actual smart city projects grows, so too do the questions and concerns people raise about future smart city projects. The very premise of smartness is challenged in work by Green (2019), whose "smart enough city" subverts the techno-centric advocacy of technology firms by challenging communities to consider more specific and circumscribed roles for technology. Instead of defaulting to the assumption that technology solutions will make urban issues better, he carefully considers when and if technology tools might advance change in communities. This approach contrasts with the first expressed desire of Sidewalk Labs to build a city "from the internet up" (Wylie 2017; Crawford 2018; Rattan 2018).

Of recent interest is the rise of the "Open Smart City" movement (table 11.1), which frames the characteristics of an Open Smart City (Lauriault et al. 2018; Sunlight Foundation 2018). The focus on open, accessible, inclusive, and participatory smart city planning differs from broader smart city efforts, which tend to emphasize efficiency and innovation above these other values. The Open Smart City framework is being presented to Canadian municipalities engaged in smart city efforts through the jointly offered Community Solutions Network (CSN) run by the organizations Evergreen and Open North. The CSN is designed to help communities build internal capacity to work with emerging technologies. In its first iteration the network is supporting municipalities that participated in the Smart Cities Challenge, but the intention is to grow the network's reach to support a wider range of communities. This positioning stands in stark contrast to the closed, proprietary nature of the majority of smart city projects. As more municipalities purchase and use these technologies, additional questions are raised about data ownership, control access, and possession.

Concerns that the smart city movement is accelerating neoliberal agendas are longstanding (see Kummitha 2018). McFarlane and Söderström (2017) note that the rise of alternative smart city thinking may capture the public desire for innovative approaches to city

Table 11.1
Open Smart Cities characteristics

An Open Smart City includes the following five characteristics:

---

1 Governance in an Open Smart City is ethical, accountable, and transparent. These principles apply to the governance of social and technical platforms which includes data, algorithms, skills, infrastructure, and knowledge.

2 An Open Smart City is participatory, collaborative and responsive. It is a city where government, civil society, private sector, the media, academia and residents meaningfully participate in the governance of the city and have shared rights and responsibilities. This entails a culture of trust and critical thinking and fair, just, inclusive and informed approaches.

3 An Open Smart City uses data and technologies that are fit for purpose, can be repaired and queried, their source code are open, adhere to open standards, are interoperable, durable, secure, and where possible locally procured and scalable. Data and technology are used and acquired in such a way as to reduce harm and bias, increase sustainability and enhance flexibility. An Open Smart City may defer when warranted to automated decision-making and therefore designs these systems to be legible, responsive, adaptive and accountable.

4 In an Open Smart City, data management is the norm and custody and control over data generated by smart technologies is held and exercised in the public interest. Data governance includes sovereignty, residency, open by default, security, individual and social privacy, and grants people authority over their personal data.

5 In an Open Smart City, it is recognized that data and technology are not the solution to many of the systemic issues cities face, nor are there always quick fixes. These problems require innovative, sometimes long term, social, organizational, economic, and political processes and solutions.

Source: Canadian Internet Policy and Public Interest Clinic, https://cippic.ca/en/Open_Smart_Cities.

building that deliver public good outcomes over profit-driven ones. Robinson and Coutts (2019) point to the potential rise of a new variant of smart city effort: government-centred ones.

WHAT HAPPENS WHEN GOVERNMENTS
TRY TO BRIDGE THE TECH-URBANISM DIVIDE?

Government digital services, worldwide, talk about embracing lean policy-making and reiterating policy changes in real time. Organizations such as Code for America, Code for Canada, and Civic Hall (both the New York and Toronto iterations) focus on bringing the best of technology culture inside government to help them benefit from the processes that technology firms use. The goal generally is to make government services easier to access, more efficient to deliver, and more responsive. Beyond the hype around these approaches, there have been actual success stories from such partnerships, such as one of the most celebrated civic technology examples: Code for America's GetCalFresh (Code for America 2019). This app tries to make it easier for potential food stamp recipients to access and navigate the complex application process by presenting an interface that is written in plain language and easy to navigate. GetCalFresh, Expunge.io – which helps people expunge their youth criminal records – and myriad municipal transit and council budget apps are all implemented examples of how technology partnerships with government are workable. They focus on improvements to delivery of government service. We do not yet see a similar proliferation or success with civic technology in land-use planning. Perhaps it is easier to build apps that draw from a narrow range of data sets to tackle a specific issue. Urban planning is multi-faceted and informed by complex and numerous data sets. This is the kind of "technology-urbanism" divide that the Sidewalk Labs Quayside project seeks to address.

Rhetorical slogans shape the narrative of the smart city. Silicon Valley's mantra, "Move fast and break things," has gained pop culture awareness. While the agile, lean, permanent beta, experimental, entre-preneurial mindset has emerged from a culture that spawned an technology economy with impact, its transferability to city building is questionable. On 28 February 2019, the head of product at Sidewalk Labs made a presentation to the Digital Strategy Advisory Panel at Waterfront Toronto about the "double diamond of product develop-ment" (figure 11.1) as part of their technology development update. It emphasizes iteration, ideation, and prototyping works in a technology development space, but its translation to real spaces and places with residents presents a city-building-meets-technology challenge. In city

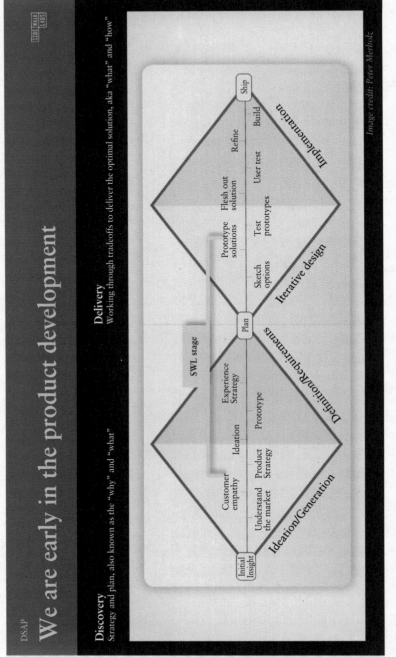

DSAP

We are early in the product development

Discovery
Strategy and plan, also known as the "why" and "what"

Delivery
Working through tradeoffs to deliver the optimal solution, aka "what" and "how"

Image credit: Peter Merholz

Figure 11.1 Sidewalk Labs double diamond of product development.

planning, with civic engagement and big infrastructure budgets, iteration is challenging, expensive, and perhaps legally fraught in liability and investor obligations on large-scale development projects. And these differences signal that city building is not product development.

Smart city vendors use a common narrative that government is broken, ineffective, and/or stuck, and that a partnership with a technology firm can help create innovative solutions (Robinson 2019). But does this simplistic narrative that government can't innovate apply today?

THE MYTH OF THE PRIVATE-SECTOR INNOVATOR: CAN GOVERNMENT INNOVATE?

A larger, more recent narrative questions the capacity of governments to innovate in light of rapid technological change. As mentioned earlier, the prevailing attitude is that governments impede technological progress, and the best thing they can do is step aside and stick to what they know, while the tech experts make the innovations. Research on public-sector innovation and entrepreneurship emphasizes the public sector as a facilitator of the private sector, not an innovator of its own accord (Leyden and Link 2015). The understanding is that the public sector is inflexible, avoids market-based competition, and is inherently risk-averse supports the position that innovation can flourish better and faster when the private sector works alone, not in partnership with government (Sørensen and Torfing 2011). In the city, procurement laws and data privacy standards are considered barriers to business development. City agencies themselves are often perceived as a "black box" whose organizational dynamic does not foster innovative activity, let alone contain the talent to innovate (d'Almeida 2018). Even if governments do innovate, they are seen to mimic a private sector approach. Dominant narratives from political-economy perspectives confirm that innovation in the public sector is mostly market and profit driven. But alternative views suggest innovation and entrepreneurship are not always inherently market oriented. Non-market innovation – solving problems in the name of the public good – may help improve service provision for civil society, such as the creation of new service, or change to an existing one (i.e., mobile health-care delivery), to improve the quality of life for certain populations (Mulgan et al. 2007). As mentioned, open government technology solutions fit this non-market perspective on innovation.

Amidst these debates, it is important to remember the pivotal role the public sector has played in developing innovations. In her seminal work, Mazzucato (2015) debunks the idea that government systems are best suited to facilitate private-sector innovation, instead arguing that governments make high-risk investments, creating the conditions for the private sector to benefit from early economic activity to launch their enterprise. For example, key technologies such as the internet, nano-technology, touch-screen technology, and GPS were developed in laboratories funded by government programs. Such risk capital minimized the risks the private sector found too unmanageable in the early days of prototyping. In places like the United States, private-sector innovation has benefited from an active state making the right investments. But before going further, it is important to define our terms, especially one like "innovation," which is often discussed casually more than it is explained thoroughly. Bringing a conceptual lens to innovation and government requires some context.

Governments around the world acknowledge that innovation is crucial to address wicked problems in urban environments such fast flooding, mobility, and housing shortages, with a view to improving service delivery (European Commission 2013; Mulgan 2007). Innovation, broadly speaking, can is the creation of new practices or approaches or ideas, concepts, products, or programs – a process of change that disrupts procedures to improve institutional processes incrementally or over the long term (Sørensen and Torfing 2011). While definitions abound, we have picked one from the urban innovation and policy literatures that captures what scholars in the field understand public section innovation to be: "a more or less intentional effort to design, realize, and diffuse new public policies, services, organizations, and procedures that disrupt established practices and conventional thinking in a particular domain" (Sørensen and Torfing 2016, 3, in Li 2019, 2). In other words, innovations can help governments understand goals and tasks in a new light, including ways of realizing them.

Innovation in the public sector often emerges in response to changes in laws and regulations, when crises occur, or when new technologies emerge in the absence of a planned response (Osborne and Brown 2011). Early theories of public-sector innovation saw entrepreneurialism and competition as driving public innovations (Osborne and Gaebler 1993). Informed by private-sector innovation theory, "new public management" theory suggests that competition creates incentive for public service providers to innovate, such as to find deficiencies, do more with less (Sørensen and Torfing 2012). Most scholars now agree that collaboration, not competition, is the key driver of public-sector innovations – the view being that the private sector cannot innovate alone, and instead it depends on public-private collaboration and the contributions of all actors (Hartley et al. 2013). Thus, collaboration is considered the underlying force of public innovation. The more current theory used by some scholars is "collaborative innovation" to best describe how governments innovate effectively (Osborne and Brown 2011; Torfing 2019). This theory argues that if you open up the process of innovation to a larger group of actors or users – often in a network format with a mix of public and private actors, citizens, experts, and interest groups – that mix will create the conditions for collaborative innovation to occur. The idea is that the eyes and minds of many can bring diverse experiences and knowledge to pinpoint inefficiencies and shortcomings across the domains of government (Agger and Sørensen 2016).

But the success of innovation in the public sector depends highly on the degree to which innovation is governed, often in a networked context (Sørensen and Torfing 2016). Cities that have strong governance networks have created an institutional foundation ready for public-sector innovation. For example, Rich and Stoker's (2014) empirical study of urban revitalization in Atlanta and Baltimore emphasizes the key role of partnerships in realizing success. But the how-to of network governance is much harder to operationalize, let alone conceptualize. Li (2019) observes a significant gap in understanding of public innovation: "There is no theoretical framework to explicitly tell us how innovation networks can be governed to spur innovations" (11). The conditions required for civic actors and municipal officials to cooperate and innovate are not well documented, leaving much room for future research.

Writing about urban innovation, Shearmur (2016) argues that normative ideas of innovation are inherently biased towards all things private sector. Given the advances that arose from synthesis of public innovation and urban systems, it is time to expand thinking beyond the private-sector bias. Innovations need to be understood as neutral, collaborative efforts between public and private sectors and not a "winner-take-all-contest" but praised for distributional effects of sharing rewards. Of course this requires taking a hard look at innovations and doing away with the techno-optimism rhetoric that controls much of the narrative in the digital economy and the smart city.

GOVERNANCE, INNOVATION, AND THE SMART CITY:
AN EMERGING LITERATURE

Studies on governance in smart city scholarship are nascent yet growing. Despite the efforts of some scholars (see Nam and Pardo's [2011] typology of smart city innovation) to clarify smart city governance, Ruhlandt (2018) observes that few studies on governance outcomes (e.g., procedural changes, substantive outputs) use a consistent taxonomy to describe how change in governance processes occurs. Even so, some studies help paint a picture of how governance dynamics become intertwined with smart city development. Pierce and Anderson's (2017) governance study notes the key challenges faced by municipal staff when rolling out smart city initiatives. Government administrators perceived non-technical challenges such as collaboration, governance, learning, and awareness as greater than technical ones such as security, interoperability, and privacy in smart city development. These challenges aren't necessarily unique to smart city initiatives, but they persist across the operations of municipal departments. So in tackling governance of smart cities, municipal staff may see opportunity to transfer lessons learned to improve general operations. Similarly, lack of collaboration that results from limited trust and understanding among internal and external stakeholders was a predominant challenge in some European mid-size cities developing smart city plans, a dynamic likely present in other cities and governments (Nesti 2018).

When considering the fluidity of urban technology, the experiential nature of proposed smart city intervention, and the changing nature of partnerships, these concepts defy rigid categorization. This fluidity and the rapid pace of adoption also mean scholarship has not kept up with the advance of smart city interventions, resulting in few empirical studies relative to the number of smart city programs underway worldwide (Ruhlandt 2018). Thus researchers are in the early stages of understanding how governance may drive smart city initiatives.

Innovation is often implied in the smart city, given the inevitable adoption of new processes and change that occur. Scholars refer to innovation as an essential element of smart city development, but few studies address the scope, function, and associated outcomes (Nilssen 2019). Broader studies on municipal innovation competitions and urban technology situate the Smart Cities Challenge within current academic debates. Shearmur and Poirier's (2017) case study of

Mérite-Ovation municipal – an annual innovation competition that rewards Quebec municipalities who develop technologies to improve city life – found competitions enabled municipalities to contribute knowledge and expertise towards urban technology, such as the creation of software to optimize the routing and usage of snow-clearing vehicles. Taylor Buck and While's (2017) study of the UK innovation competition (TSB Future Cities Demonstrator Competition) found that competition accelerated strategies and ideas from extra resources to expand thinking and leverage partnerships. Conversely, the competition structure hamstrung collaboration between participating cities and set out unrealistic time constraints to achieve goals, and the capacity for smart city innovation was limited because similar plans/ideas were produced by the same consultants. Consistent with the studies on governance described above, the parameters of the competition saw bids overestimate technology development and underestimate decision-making, building strong relationships, and social innovation.

These insights from an emerging literature draw attention to the invisible, behind-the-scenes work that is instrumental for smart city projects to achieve the scale and impact that is so ambitiously desired. Early research suggests that the potential to realize the purported benefits of new urban technology to improve city life requires a combined tech-driven and people/citizen-driven approach to smart city planning. The literature on smart city governance demonstrates a shift in conceptual emphasis from technology to governance as a central driver of the smarty city, particularly in light of the shift from tech-oriented to people-oriented smart city innovation. More research is needed to develop perspectives on the governance small-scale, people-oriented innovation behind smart city development in cities. As will be shown, Infrastructure Canada's Smart Cities Challenge provides a unique vantage point to address the question of how government-centred smart city approaches in governance and innovation vary or mimic those of the private sector.

CASE: INFC'S SMART CITIES CHALLENGE (SCC)

Infrastructure Canada's Smart Cities Challenge is a $300 million, eleven-year effort to spark innovation in the technology and urbanism space across Canadian communities coast to coast to coast. The Challenge seeks to "give communities a platform for implementing bold ideas to address priorities using innovation, data and connected technology" (Infrastructure Canada 2017). The first round of this competition ran from early winter 2018 through the spring of 2019 in two stages. First, in April 2018 130 applicants from 199 communities made submissions. Next a jury selected twenty finalists who each received $200,000 to develop full proposals. In May 2019 the four winning projects were selected. Research on Innovation Challenges tends to focus on the nature of the innovations themselves. Infrastructure Canada's website provides background information about the applicants, their projects, and further details about the winners. Beyond the projects themselves, what is noteworthy is the Challenge's process design. This approach of Infrastructure Canada distinguishes it from other, more common private-sector methods for smart cities.

First, unlike other smart city projects that are vendor driven, the Smart Cities Challenge submissions came from local governments themselves. The focus within the s c c was for governments to generate innovative ideas first, fostering innovation within government, and to remove the emphasis from technology firms, whether or not they would be a necessary part of implementation. By having units of government apply, Infrastructure Canada created a milieu in which public authorities were deciding which issues to prioritize, what kinds of technology would align with their priorities, and from whom they would source the technology. The starting point for this Challenge differs from other projects. Smart city trade fairs abound with technology firms telling governments what kinds of problems they need to solve. If they pursue vendor-driven approaches, there is the risk that local officials will view technology as the only solution, where technology is purchased and implemented as if one size fits all, without considering actual needs.

Second, first-round applicants were required to engage their communities to identify priorities and then find technology and data solutions that would help address them. The types of public consultation and engagement varied widely. Some communities used Twitter and other social media to generate ideas, some hosted workshops, some used community brainstorming sessions. Though the approaches to community involvement differed, the expectation of all applicants was consistent and clear: local government applications should be fundamentally tied to community needs and priorities, and the technology sought must serve these goals.

Third, Infrastructure Canada designed the competition in a novel way. Applicants in both rounds were required to post their submissions on their websites as part of the application. This decision was innovative because it first provided a check-and-balance opportunity between the application and community goals and process. If a local government had oversold its community consultation and engagement in its application, the community itself could challenge the application before it was adjudicated. This open approach also provided another check-in with the community, allowing community members to ensure their goals and priorities were actually reflected in the application.

Fourth, in the fall of 2018, Infrastructure Canada issued an request for proposals for a community solutions network (CSN) provider to provide support to Smart Cities Challenge applicants from that point onward. Evergreen and Open North were the successful bidders. The CSN offers one-to-one technical advice through Open North and one-to-many workshops and support through Evergreen's Future Cities Group. This network embedded in an innovation competition mediates the ruthless competition spirit reflected in other technology-urbanism examples, including the most recent Amazon HQ2 headquarters siting process. Instead of having municipalities fight it out to outbid each other in incentives and concessions, the Challenge supported applicants as they chose which issues and technologies they hoped the prize money could help them address. By encouraging municipal governments to learn from each other and by seeking to gather municipal partners with similar goals and interests, the intent of the network was to positively disrupt excessive competition and to distribute support and resources as widely as possible.

To further understand how learning, innovation, and governance were spurred by the INFC SSC, we examined the fifteen proposals of the top-tier finalists ($50 million and $10 million categories).[1] The objective was to identify emergent signs of innovation – changes to practices, new ideas or approaches – potentially initiated by the competition. The overarching question of what innovation is happening and where guided the inquiry. This preliminary scoping set the stage for further in-depth research (i.e., survey, interviews). At this stage, we were merely observing signs of emergent innovation (not diffusion or generation) as proposed by communities in their applications, when proposed programs had yet to be implemented (Berry and Berry 2007). Proposals were coded and categorized by theme (see table 11.2).

Table 11.2
Typology of smart city governance and innovation based on theme analysis
of Smart Cities Challenge

Themes	Description
1 Intragovernmental collaboration	Many municipalities prioritized integration or silo management as part of their smart city governance structure. But not just rhetorically. Some municipalities created divisional working groups and committees solely for the scc, whereas most drew on committees and groups already in place.
2 Establishing new partnerships	Most municipalities established some level of new partnership, inside or across government, or with outside individuals and groups in the private and non-profit sectors. Most outside partners were selected for their specialized knowledge of smart cities and their ability to help municipalities to develop new competencies in project management and innovation. For example, innovation challenges run as part of scc in Victoria created lasting relationships between tech entrepreneurs and IBM.
3 Catalyzing existing initiatives	Most municipalities saw the scc as an opportunity to leverage existing goals, plans, strategies, collaborations with a view to better alignment. The Challenge galvanized previous work or attached a tangible direction to implement current and future priorities.
4 Driver for operational or policy change	While too early to assess, some municipalities committed to new open data practices, including related policy and legal changes. One municipality (Vancouver) has changed their procurement policy to be more flexible – a direct outcome of the scc process.
5 New governance structures	The scale of collaboration required for the Challenge led some municipalities to formalize this collaboration as part of their governance goals. Some municipalities created memoranda of understanding or related agreements to provide accountability and structure to a partnership. In some cases, agreements are between governments only, whereas others involved private sector and community groups. For example, the City of Guelph has stated they will create a "circular food economy secretariat" comprising multiple city divisions.
6 Emphasis on openness	The structure of the mechanics of the Challenge itself, the positioning of the Community Solutions Network, and the emphasis in the competition on open data and open government approaches collectively distinguish the Challenge and its finalist submissions from other innovation challenges focused on smart cities elsewhere.

In the innovation literature, competition and collaboration are seen as independent drivers of innovation, each creating a different dynamic and incentive structure (Sørensen and Torfing 2012). So how could one make sense of a municipal competition that asked cities to collaborate with their communities to drive collective changes by adopting new technology? An initiative like the scc was initiated by non-local factors – a federal government competition encouraging municipal innovation and policy transformation. Municipalities played the role of both convener and innovator. Additionally, governance was multi-layered, with vertical governance aspects (interaction with upper-level governments) and horizontal (municipalities, local groups, civil society, etc.). The complexity of proposed governance arrangements through the ssc appeared to defy the norms of categorizing governmental collaboration, moving in one direction horizontally or vertically, or not occurring at all. That said, a closer look at the scc submissions revealed governance outcomes in procedural change. Some municipalities adapted private-sector approaches to project management techniques, such as design thinking, lean management, the stage-gate model, and agile thinking. Vancouver and Surrey, bc, changed their procurement policy to be more flexible, as a direct influence of the roundtables with public and private stakeholders during the competition.

The submissions themselves, therefore, provide a preliminary basis to classify innovation. They also provide fresh insights into how municipalities may be using policy innovation – processes, tools, and practices used to better solve complex issues – to change their approach to policy development and server delivery (see table 11.2). Given the broader implications of smart city work, future research is needed to explore how, if at all, these municipal actors see their roles in these terms.

DISCUSSION AND CONCLUSION

The Smart Cities Challenge has obvious and notable distinguishing features. The structure of the competition itself, with its focus on open and transparent sharing of applications, is innovative. The opportunity for municipalities to team up to apply along with the Community Solutions Network hard-wire cooperation in a competitive environment. And the Challenge's requirement to have local governments apply instead of technology firms contradicts the narrative that governments are broken and technology can fix all that ails.

And the Challenge sparked a new, inward-looking opportunity for municipalities to solve problems and think through new solutions to challenges. Much of the emphasis on public sector innovation faces outward: search for new markets, products, and technologies or to attract new talent. But analysis of the scc reaffirms that innovation emerges in different guises. Changes may be incremental, rather than transformational, or widespread, as governments experiment with new approaches across policy and operational functions. For instance, the interdivisional collaboration in the City of Guelph to form a food secretariat proposes a new governance structure. The ability to build and sustain internal capacity will be the driving internal force of this potential innovation to meet the outward-facing response to food waste and security. Ultimately, success will be based on the problem or issue solved and the response of the local population.

While in early stages, a look at scc leaves us with more questions than answers as municipalities prepare for their next steps and future rounds of the scc. Do new governance contexts marginalize or enhance established planning and decision-making processes? And as norms of engagement change with smart city models, are institutional channels being used or circumvented? Further research on the motivations and barriers in municipal innovation would expand upon this exploratory, preliminary analysis of the scc.

As the four Challenge winners begin to spend their prize money in pursuit of the smart city projects they planned, we have a research opportunity to explore how government-centred smart city efforts unfold. Because these projects, in contrast to other vendor-driven ones, originate inside the city halls of small, medium, and large communities, their implementation will have an impact on the politics and governance of those four cities. The extent to which these municipalities move beyond the purchase or arrival of platform economy technology from vendors to a city-as-platform model remains to be seen. But the Smart Cities Challenge is a different intervention in the smart city landscape, poised to challenge our thinking about the future smart city.

NOTES

1   City of Montreal, Edmonton, Vancouver/Surrey, Ville De Quebec, Waterloo Region, Greater Victoria, Saskatoon, Richmond, Guelph and Wellington County, Town of the Pas, Opakapaka Cree Nation, Rural Municipality of Kelsey, City of Fredericton and Saint Mary's First Nation, Airdrie and area, Parkland County, Brazeau County, Lac Ste Anne County, Yellowhead County, Nunavut Association of Municipalities, and Ville de Côte Saint-Luc.

REFERENCES

Agger, A., and E. Sørensen. 2018. "Managing Collaborative Innovation in Public Bureaucracies." *Planning Theory* 17, no. 1: 53–73.

Berry, F.S., and W.D. Berry. 2018. "Innovation and Diffusion Models in Policy Research." In *Theories of the Policy Process*, edited by C.M. Weible and P.A. Sabatier, 253–300. New York: Routledge.

Code for America. 2019. "GetCalFresh Supports Applicants through the CalFresh (SNAP) Enrollment Process." https://www.codeforamerica.org/programs/getcalfresh.

Crawford, S. 2018. "Beware of Google's Intentions." *Wired*, 1 February. https://www.wired.com/story/sidewalk-labs-toronto-google-risks/.

d'Almeida, A.C., ed. 2018. *Smarter New York City: How City Agencies Innovate*. New York: Columbia University Press.

Eubanks, V. 2018. *Automating Inequality: How High-Tech Tools Profile, Police, and Punish the Poor*. New York: St. Martin's.

European Commission. 2013. "European Public Sector Innovation." Scoreboard. Brussels: European Commission.

Giffinger, R., and H. Gudrun. 2010. "Smart Cities Ranking: An Effective Instrument for the Positioning of the Cities?" *ACE: Architecture, City and Environment* 4, no. 12: 7–26. http://hdl.handle.net/2099/8550.

Green, B. 2019. *The Smart Enough City: Putting Technology in Its Place to Reclaim Our Urban Future*. Cambridge, MA: MIT Press.

Halpern, O., J. LeCavalier, and N. Calvillo. 2013. "Test-Bed Urbanism." *Public Culture* 25, no. 2: 272–306.

Hartley, J., E. Sørensen, E., and J. Torfing. 2013. "Collaborative Innovation: A Viable Alternative to Market Competition and Organizational Entrepreneurship." *Public Administration Review* 73, no. 6: 821–30.

Hollands, R.G. 2008. "Will the Real Smart City Please Stand Up?" *City* 12, no. 3: 303–20.

Infrastructure Canada. 2017. *Smart Cities Challenge*. https://www.infrastructure.gc.ca/cities-villes/index-eng.html.

Kitchin, R. 2015. "The Promise and Perils of Smart Cities." Society for Computers and Law, 8 June. https://www.scl.org/articles/3385-the-promise-and-perils-of-smart-cities.

Kummitha, R.K.R. 2018. "Entrepreneurial Urbanism and Technological Panacea: Why Smart City Planning Needs to Go beyond Corporate Visioning?" *Technological Forecasting and Social Change* 137: 330–9.

Kummitha, R.K.R., and N. Crutzen. 2017. "How Do We Understand Smart Cities? An Evolutionary Perspective." *Cities* 67: 43–52.

Lauriault, T.P., R. Bloom, and J.N. Landry. 2018. *Open Smart Cities Guide.* https://opennorth.ca/publicationdetail?id=3Ptq7I6gVIfzBfl2ZAYoNs.

Leyden, D., and A. Link. 2015. *Public Sector Entrepreneurship: U.S. Technology and Innovation Policy.* New York: Oxford University Press.

Li, Y. 2019. "A Framework in Analyzing the Strategies for Governing Innovation Networks for Public Innovation." *Policy Studies.* https://doi.org/10.1080/01442872.2019.1618809.

Luque-Ayala, A., and S. Marvin. 2015. "Developing a Critical Understanding of Smart Urbanism?" *Urban Studies* 52, no. 12: 2,105–16.

Mazzucato, M. 2015. *The Entrepreneurial State: Debunking Public vs. Private Sector Myths.* Vol. 1. New York: Anthem.

McFarlane, C., and O. Söderström. 2017. "On Alternative Smart Cities: From a Technology-Intensive to a Knowledge-Intensive Smart Urbanism." *City* 21, nos. 3–4: 312–28.

Mulgan, G., S. Tucker, and R. Ali. 2007. "Social Innovation: What It Is, Why It Matters and How It Can Be Accelerated." Working Paper. Oxford Said Business School and the Young Foundation. London.

Nam, T., and T.A. Pardo. 2011. "Smart City as Urban Innovation: Focusing on Management, Policy, and Context." In *Proceedings of the 5th International Conference on Theory and Practice of Electronic Governance,* 185–94.

Nesti, G. 2018. "Defining and Assessing the Transformational Nature of Smart City Governance: Insights from Four European Cases." *International Review of Administrative Sciences,* https://doi.org/10.1177/0020852318757063.

Nilssen, M. 2019. "To the Smart City and Beyond? Developing a Typology of Smart Urban Innovation." *Technological Forecasting and Social Change* 42: 98–104.

Osborne, D., and T. Gaebler, T. (1993). Reinventing Government: How the Entrepreneurial Spirit Is Transforming the Public Sector. London, UK: Plume/Penguin.

Osborne, S., and L. Brown. 2011. "Innovation in Public Services: Engaging with Risk." *Public Money & Management* 31, no. 1: 4–6.

Pasquale, F. 2015. *The Black Box Society: The Secret Algorithms That Control Money and Information.* Cambridge, MA: Harvard University Press.

Pierce, P., and B. Andersson. 2017. "Challenges with Smart Cities Initiatives: A Municipal Decision Makers' Perspective." In *Proceedings*

of the 50th Hawaii International Conference on System Sciences.
University of Hawaii at Manoa, 4–7 January.

Puron-Cid, G., J.R. Gil-Garcia, and J. Zhang. 2015. "Smart Cities, Smart Governments and Smart Citizens: A Brief Introduction." *International Journal of E-Planning Research* 4, no. 2: iv–vii.

Rattan, C. 2018. "Torontonians Should Take Control of Their Data." *NOW Toronto*, 23 May. https://nowtoronto.com/news/owns-data-toronto-smart-city.

Rich, M.J., and R.P. Stoker. 2014. *Collaborative Governance for Urban Revitalization: Lessons from Empowerment Zones.* Ithaca, NY: Cornell University Press.

Robinson, P. 2019. "How Does Government Fit into Smart City Plans?" *Spacing Toronto*, 26 June. https://spacing.ca/toronto/2019/06/26/robinson-how-does-government-fit-into-smart-city-plans.

Robinson, P., and S. Coutts. 2019. "The Case of Quayside, Toronto, Canada." In *Smart City Emergence: Cases from around the World*, edited by L. Anthopoulos, 330–50. Cambridge, MA: Elsevier.

Ruhlandt, R.W.S. 2018. "The Governance of Smart Cities: A Systematic Literature Review." *Cities* 81: 1–23.

Scassa, T. 2014. "Privacy and Open Government." *Future Internet* 6, no. 2: 397–413.

Shearmur, R. 2016. "Debating Urban Technology: Technophiles, Luddites and Citizens." *Urban Geography* 37, no. 6: 807–9. https://doi.org/10.10 80/02723638.2016.1207914.

Shearmur, R., and V. Poirier. 2017. "Conceptualizing Nonmarket Municipal Entrepreneurship: Everyday Municipal Innovation and the Roles of Metropolitan Context, Internal Resources, and Learning." *Urban Affairs Review* 53, no. 4: 718–51.

Sørensen, E., and J. Torfing. 2011. "Enhancing Collaborative Innovation in the Public Sector." *Administration & Society* 43, no. 8: 842–68. https://doi.org/10.1177/0095399711418768.

– 2012. "Introduction: Collaborative Innovation in the Public Sector." *Innovation Journal* 17, no. 1: 1–10.

– 2016. "Introduction: Governance Network Research: Towards a Second Generation." In *Theories of Democratic Network Governance*, edited by Sørensen and Torfing, 1–20. New York: Palgrave Macmillan.

Sunlight Foundation. 2018. "Smart Cities: Best Practices for Transparency." https://sunlightfoundation.com/policy/open-cities/smart-cities/best-practices.

Taylor Buck, N., and A. While, A. 2017. "Competitive Urbanism and
the Limits to Smart City Innovation: The UK Future Cities Initiative."
Urban Studies 54, no. 2: 501–19. https://doi.org/10.1177/
0042098015597162.

Torfing, J. 2019. "Collaborative Innovation in the Public Sector: The
Argument." *Public Management Review* 21, no. 1: 1–11.

Townsend, A. 2013. *Smart Cities: Big Data, Civic Hackers, and the Quest
for a New Utopia.* New York: W.W. Norton.

Wylie, B. 2017. "Think Hard before Handing Tech Firms the Rights to
Our Cities' Data." *Huffington Post*, 8 November 8, 2017. http://www.
huffingtonpost.ca/bianca-wylie/think-hard-before-handing-tech-firms-
the-rights-to-our-cities-data_a_23270793.

Zuboff, Shoshana. 2019. *The Age of Surveillance Capitalism: The Fight
for a Human Future at the New Frontier of Power.* New York: Hatchett.

A Smart City for Toronto:
What Does Quayside Tell Us about
the State of Smart City Building?

Zachary Spicer and Austin Zwick

- This chapter walks through the development history of and the relationship between Waterfront Toronto and the Quayside project of Sidewalk Labs.
- The potential benefits and common critiques of this project are viewed through exploratory questions on community building, data privacy, and governance.
- The authors argue for the need for national governments to play a greater role in smart city development projects to address data use and privacy.

INTRODUCTION

The age of smart cities is here. The key to creating a smart city lies in harnessing the connectivity of the Internet of Things and establishing a digital layer that coordinates physical and cloud-based infrastructure. A smart city is intended to effectively build networks and platforms that connect citizens with the services they need and make physical services more efficient to bolster policy goals. A smart city is designed to use data to be responsive to residents and, most importantly, learn. Using great amounts of data, smart cities gather intelligence about people and processes in order to constantly refine and monitor servicing and resources (Hashem et al. 2016).

In October 2017, Waterfront Toronto, the tri-level agency responsible for the Toronto waterfront, announced that Sidewalk Labs had won the right to pilot their vision at Quayside, a five-hectare parcel of land along the city's waterfront. The land in question, once used for industrial purposes, had sat idle for many years and Waterfront Toronto had long wanted to breathe new life into the area. In a city with no shortage of skyline-busting condominiums, Waterfront Toronto wanted something different, something worthy of the prized lakefront land the development was bound to grace. Sidewalk Labs offered a vision of creating one of the world's first purposefully designed "smart" communities, one with sensors and technology embedded throughout. In May 2020, that vision fell to pieces when Sidewalk Labs announced it was cancelling its project and leaving Toronto. Although the project will no longer come to fruition, the inter-jurisdictional and inter-governmental interplay between the private and public sector is informative about the future of the global smart city sector.

Smart cities developments are not new: they occur all over the world. For example, large-scale, state-run smart city developments are under construction in South Korea and Masada (Shwayri 2013; Cugurullo 2013; Yigitcanlar 2016). However, unlike all other global projects, the Quayside project was proposed as an offshoot of one of the world's largest private data firms: Alphabet. Critics argued that the Sidewalk Labs Quayside project was being imposed upon Toronto because the process to approve has been so quick, especially given the scale and scope of the vision Sidewalk Labs has presented, that a competitive bidding process could not have possibly occurred. The project had also been a lightning rod, with some describing it merely as "paving the way for tech billionaires to fulfill their dreams of ruling over cities" (Sadowski 2017). However, the project also had prominent public supporters, including urbanist Richard Florida, former Toronto mayors Art Eggleton and Barbara Hall, and a host of leaders from the city's philanthropic sector such as Sharon Avery from the Toronto Foundation, and Daniele Zanotti from the United Way of Greater Toronto (Vincent 2019).

While Quayside did not ultimately move ahead, it is important to take stock of the project and the process to implement a privately constructed smart city. Specifically, in this chapter we overview the unique potential contributions of Quayside's Sidewalk Labs proposal while invoking questions about community building, data privacy, and governance. We argue that there is a governance mismatch: munic-ipal governments are responsible for local development, but only the national government has the power and authority to create rules for data privacy. This dilemma can be solved only by national governments working with cities to create "smart city development" guidelines.

ALPHABET'S NEXT PRODUCT: THE CITY

Waterfront Toronto sought a very different type of developer for Quayside. The Eastern Waterfront was a "unique opportunity for governments, private enterprise, technology providers, investors and academic institutions ... to create a new global benchmark for sustainable, inclusive and accessible urban development" (Waterfront Toronto 2017, 6). Waterfront Toronto sought an "innovation and funding partner" for the initial site, making it clear that a typical urban development firm would not be successful in responding to the request for proposals (RFP) (Waterfront Toronto 2017), as explained below. In fact, the phrase "innovation and funding partner" not only appears several times in the RFP, it also graces its title as well. The community that Waterfront Toronto envisioned was technology enabled, leaving only a very narrow list of potential applications able to bid.

Founded in 2015, as a subsidiary of Alphabet Inc., Sidewalk Labs describes itself as an urban innovation organization, headed by Daniel L. Doctoroff, the former deputy mayor of New York City for economic development, who facilitated the analogous Hudson Yards development in New York City (Schwab 2017). Sidewalk Labs argues that it aims to improve physical and digital infrastructure in urban spaces by harnessing the connectivity of the platform economy to create a blueprint for the "neighborhood of the future" (D'Onfro 2019). As a result, Sidewalk Labs markets itself as a firm applying technology and digital thinking to land development, conceptualizing what a city would look like if it were built "from the internet up" (Hawkins 2019).

Sidewalk Labs promised to achieve or surpass all of Waterfront Toronto RFP's three major objectives. The first was sustainability, resiliency, and urban innovation. Waterfront Toronto is a member of the C40 Climate Development Program, a sustainability-focused urban development institution leading collaboration of more than ninety cities. Its goal is to meet Paris Agreement standards by 2030 and reach carbon net zero by 2050 through delineated participation standards and policy goals. Participating cities "must a) set a measurable target for reducing greenhouse gas emissions, b) develop a climate action plan with concrete initiatives to meet the target, and c) actively share best practice examples with other cities through the C40 network" (C40 Cities 2017). Cities should focus on "decarbonizing the electric grid, optimizing energy efficiency in buildings, enabling next-generation mobility, and improving waste management" (C40 Cities 2017). Sidewalk Labs Toronto advocated that. Through use of its data-gathering and -processing prowess, it had a unique ability to achieve this framework.

The second objective of the RFP was to build complete communities. Waterfront Toronto defined "complete communities" as mixed-income and mixed-use housing connected by efficient transit, constructed to integrate cultural and social amenities. Waterfront Toronto mandated that at least 20 per cent of constructed rental units be set aside as affordable housing. Like many large cities, Toronto is the midst of a housing crisis, with average rents and home prices soaring out of reach of many middle-class residents (Mauracher and Zettler 2020). In their RFP, Waterfront Toronto sought to pilot a mixed-income housing development and was seeking a partner to identify financing strategies. Sidewalk Labs promised to not only offer over 40 per cent of its units below market rent – which is double the minimum standard – but also to do so by creating mixed-use neighbourhoods that integrate residential, commercial, and social services for residents.

The third objective of the RFP was economic development and prosperity. To compete with other large and prosperous marketplace cities in North America, it was believed that Toronto must provide economic and business amenities to attract investors, companies, and talent to move to the city. The City of Toronto has hopes to use the eastern waterfront project as a "testbed for Canada's clean tech and innovation clusters" (Waterfront Toronto 2017). Waterfront Toronto hoped to find long-term partners in this mission, create a catalyst fund for emerging businesses, and partner with tech companies developing projects that would assist in the growth of Waterfront's Smart Cities concept. Alphabet Inc., with the potential jobs and innovation eco-system that surrounds it, embodies this vision. Sidewalk Labs devoted US$50 million in planning alone, with a bonus of sister company Google intending to relocate its Canadian headquarters in the new neighbourhood (Garfield 2018).

Sidewalk Lab's response to the RFP included technology-driven solutions for the delineated policy areas, with the approach of "viewing [the city] as a platform that integrates the physical environment with digital technology" (Sidewalk Labs 2017). Sidewalk Labs identified four key components to the physical layer: "flexible buildings, people-first streets, an adaptable public realm, and open utility infrastructure," which would weave into its platform of digital infrastructure (Sidewalk Labs 2017). The project itself would encompass at least 3.3 million square feet of residential, office, and commercial space, including Google Canada's new headquarters – all of which would be built around information technology and use environmental data to guide the community's operations and adjust service levels for residents (Bozikovic 2017). Ultimately Sidewalk Labs aimed to balance elements of progressive urbanism, such as multi-modal roadways, walkable streets, and green space, with information and communication technology, such as self-driving taxis and busses, cloud-assistant parking, and garbage robots (Bozikovic 2017).

Despite a practically non-existent record of completed projects, in the summer of 2018, Waterfront Toronto's board unanimously selected Sidewalk Labs to head the development of Quayside after a selection process that lasted only six weeks. That led to a year-long consultation phase, which concluded with the firm releasing a 1,524-page draft Master Innovation and Development Plan (MIDP) in June 2019, titled "Toronto Tomorrow: A New Approach for Inclusive Growth." Sidewalk's total planned investment had risen to US$1 billion, as the new proposed development went well beyond the original five hectares of Quayside. Sidewalk Labs had unveiled a second and third phase of the project to create the Innovative Development and Economic Activation (IDEA) District, which expanded to districts adjacent to Quayside and would cover an additional 150 hectares. This addition meant that another 50,000 residents would be added to Quayside's already planned 5,000. Quayside was therefore positioned, not as *the* development project, but the catalyst for a much larger vision. A much larger proposal was introduced because, as Doctoroff said, "a number of these systems require a greater scale to be proven or make economic sense" (Bicks 2019).

The MIDP was ambitious and controversial, incorporating not only elements of traditional urban design and planning, but also vast amounts of technology, which raised issues about who would collect, store, and own the equally vast amount of data created by the project. Smart cities run on data; in fact, data are best conceived as the life-blood of smart cities. This rightfully raises questions about how well Sidewalk Labs could achieve the key aspects of Waterfront Toronto's RFP and quell a chorus of criticism that believed the firm was poised to grossly violate privacy and run roughshod over governance standards. As mentioned above, we aim to take stock of the Quayside project, and by extension smart city development writ large, by asking probing questions in three key areas:

- *Community building*: How affordable and accessible could a community like Quayside be, given the background of Sidewalk Labs? Could a technology firm, with roots planted firmly in a business model designed to acquire and commercialize data, build a neighbourhood with a sense of community?
- *Data use and privacy*: How robust were the measures being proposed to gather, use, and store data collected from the public for the Quayside project? Could Torontonians feel safe knowing that a firm like Sidewalk Labs intended to build a community that required the constant collection of data to perform optimally?
- *Governance*: Waterfront Toronto was intended to be temporary and focused on development. Did this agency have the capacity and scale to properly govern a smart city project of this magnitude? Could reign in a firm backed by a global titan of the technology industry?

CAN A TECHNOLOGY COMPANY BE A COMMUNITY BUILDER?

On the surface, Sidewalk Labs seemed an odd lead for a development project. Before the recent creation of Sidewalk Labs, Alphabet never had an interest or a stake in real estate or land development of any kind. Nevertheless, Sidewalk Labs responded and won an RFP that placed building "complete communities" as a central objective. How well was the firm placed to meet that objective?

Sidewalk Labs aimed to build a mixed-income, mixed-use community that married affordability with economic opportunity. Maintaining a long-term income-diverse population is crucial to developing a feeling of community and a sense of belonging in a neighbourhood, making housing affordability to be one of the most pressing policy challenges in Toronto.

As space for real estate development dwindles, construction costs annually increase, and as Toronto's population continues to grow, residents are increasingly feeling squeezed out. In Ontario, 34.6 per cent of households earning $40,000–$60,000 are classified as "rent burdened," defined as spending over 30 per cent of income on rent, with even higher percentages at lower income groups (Advocacy Centre for Tenants Ontario 2018). High-priced condominiums has comprised 77 per cent of all new construction in Toronto over the last twenty years, largely in response to a loophole in legislation passed in the 1990s that exempted rental properties constructed after 1991 from rent control (Sienkiewicz 2017). In 2017, the Province of Ontario passed the Fair Housing Plan in an attempt to mitigate rising housing costs. The sixteen-point policy targeted myriad housing concerns, including inflated market prices due to foreign speculation and lack of adequate rent control (Sienkiewicz 2017). Though effective in cooling the low-rise marketplace, the policy has had a detrimental effect on affordability for renters. Since the plan was passed, condominium construction has continued to rise, while development of rent-controlled apartments has stagnated. Lack of diversity in financing options and construction technology has pigeonholed the market in the city.

Sidewalk Labs committed to the city that Quayside would not become an elite housing enclave, despite sitting on some of the potentially most valuable land in Toronto. It had planned to accomplish this by pairing innovations in construction technology with a prototypical affordable housing financing system to design a new kind of community. Sidewalk Labs planned to offer 40 per cent of all its units under market rate – double the provincial required 20 per cent in this area (Mathieu 2019). To make this possible, the strategy of Sidewalk Labs was to lower production costs in the private sector to alleviate the cost burden of affordable housing units for developers. It intended to target efficiency in building technology and the supply chain – a strategy Sidewalk Labs dubbed "strategy by design," which they believed could create up to $475 million in value through 2048 (Sidewalk Labs 2019) for private-sector actors in the construction supply chain, rendering affordable housing units affordable to private developers. The units that fell in the 40 per cent group of affordable housing would have also been eligible for the $77 million available in government affordable-housing programs from the City of Toronto (Mathieu 2019).

The first innovative building technology meant to bring down costs was to build a first-of-its-kind entirely mass-timber neighbourhood. Mass timber has been compressed and laminated in a processing plant. The beams are lighter, cheaper, and more environmentally friendly than steel, and can support a building up to thirty stories tall. Sidewalk

Labs planned to stimulate the mass timber industry by constructing a factory based in Ontario to provide Quayside's building materials.

The second innovative technology involved uses flexible, loft-style buildings with modular construction. Modular construction units are manufactured in advance and off-site, then constructed Lego-style on site in significantly less time than traditional construction. The process is cheaper, faster, and less intrusive than current building methods (Huber et al. 2019). These plans were designed to produce a flexible building style with a strong shell and minimal interior, making it easy to convert the space for multiple uses. The idea was that the spaces could be navigated and redesigned to meet the changing needs of Quayside residents. For example, one-bedroom apartments could be reorganized into multi-bedroom units to adapt to a growing family, demonstrating adaptability that was likely impossible to find elsewhere in the city. Similarly, Sidewalk Labs was pulling inspiration from Ancient Greek open markets – *stoa* – to create adaptable ground-floor commercial spaces. This had multiple functions. Making interior renovation more efficient protected residents from dramatic rent increases. Expensive renovations are a common impetus for landlords to raise rent – the term "renovictions" had arisen in Toronto to describe landlords who used expensive renovations as a legal means to evict tenants, as a means to sidestep rent-control laws (Vincent 2020).

Finally, to make the community "smart," Quayside housing would also have been connected to the digital layer. Apartments would have smart utilities that automatically adjusted themselves to optimal efficiency and create monthly analytic reports for dwellers to see their current and forecast utility costs. Sensors would be embedded in the units to monitor a multitude of living quality indicators, including noise levels, air pollutants, and code violations. These base-level data would be digitized and uploaded to a cloud-based data platform, where they would be subject to algorithms that determined the scope of, and required response to, housing issues. Apartments would effectively communicate with each other to create working evaluations of Quayside's housing ecosystem – all of which was intended to better manage resources throughout the community and ultimately increase liveability.

Although the "strategy by design" plans of Sidewalk Labs were impressive and potentially path-breaking, nothing was ultimately built, so we cannot evaluate the results. While there may have been strong reason to believe that Quayside would be much more sustainable than many developments throughout Toronto, there is also strong reason to believe it may have had a weakened sense of community and the potential to widen the digital divide. Technology – and especially platform technology – has a well-documented likelihood to actually lead to increased isolation (Parigi 2014; Turkle 2017). A community with platform technology as its base is unlikely to build the kind of intimate connections that one would expect in a traditional neighbourhood. Additionally, some fear that smart neighbourhoods such as Quayside may be digitally gated, as the community's operating system distinguishes between insiders and outsiders and adjusts the community experience accordingly (Sterling 2018).

While the commitment of Sidewalk Labs to pass down cost savings into affordable housing may be admirable, it is worth remembering that Sidewalk Labs is not a development company, and its parent company, Alphabet, makes money primarily from the capture, control, and sale of data. Many have long insisted that the real value in the community comes from the data it will generate (Vincent 2019), meaning that the value of the real estate is not a driving factor to the parent corporation of Sidewalk Labs. Next we explore in detail the question of who collects, controls, and profits from the data collected in Quayside.

CAN A TECHNOLOGY COMPANY ADEQUATELY PROTECT DATA AND PRIVACY?

As Quayside progressed, key questions about how Sidewalk Labs would collect and use data remained unanswered. Sidewalk Labs described their use of open digital infrastructures as a layer that "provides ubiquitous connectivity for all, offers new insights on the urban environment" amongst other opportunities (Sidewalk Labs 2019). However, critics argued that collection, processing, and governing of the data produced from digital infrastructure does not appear to be as well planned – or perhaps, not as publicly disclosed – as other components of Quayside (Fussell 2018).

A key component of the Quayside community was a "digital layer," which was described as akin to the operating system on a smartphone. As mentioned earlier, data are the fuel for a smart city. A community like Quayside was designed to be responsive to user needs, meaning that there must be a continuous collection and analysis of data. The "digital layer" as designed by Sidewalk Labs was to include a network of sensors that would collect "real time data" about the surrounding environment (Sidewalk Labs 2019, 6–7). The sensors, the MIDP argued, would be necessary to "measure the data needed to craft the outcome-based code system" that would run the community (Sidewalk Labs 2017, 17). There was no mention about what data would specifically be collected and how those data would be stored or used. Critics were concerned that there were no de facto data protections at all. Jim Balsillie, co-founder of BlackBerry-maker Research in Motion, called the project "a colonizing experiment in surveillance capitalism attempting to bulldoze important urban, civic and political issues" (Cecco 2019).

Sidewalk attempted, unsuccessfully, to lay criticism to rest in its MIDP in June 2019, where they pledged to set up an independent, government-approved board to set oversee data collection and set guidelines on its use (Warren and Mathieu 2019). The firm pledged to adhere to Responsible Data Use guidelines, which is a framework of self-imposed regulations that mandates transparency about the kind of data collected on individuals, limiting the amount of data collected, and making it practical for people to control their own data. Sidewalk Labs claimed that personal data gleaned from sensors across the community would be de-identified at the source and uploaded to a proposed independent data trust. The overarching commitments made by Alphabet in the MIDP were: no selling personal information, no using personal information for advertising, and no disclosing personal information to third parties without explicit consent (Sidewalk Labs 2019).

However, although a step up from the response to the original RFP, there was still ambiguity about how data capture, storage, and use would work in practice – along with an open question of whether the government would have an enforcement mechanism to hold Alphabet accountable to the original MIDP, as a common issue with data-protection on digital platforms occurs when firms later decide to unilaterally modify their "terms of services" and their only legal requirement is to merely disclose the changes. The data collected would still be property of Sidewalk Labs, leading some to argue that the data generated by Quayside ought to be considered government information and, where possible, public information (Wylie and Murakami Wood 2018). Sidewalk Labs claimed that data would never be sold, but again there are not rigorous governance mechanisms to ensure compliance. For instance, Sidewalk Labs pledged to create a panel to oversee its data collection but did not discuss penalties for contravening their earlier policies. While the panel would have provided oversight, there were no meaningful sanctions that could be placed upon them by government if they sold data. The MIDP was also silent on how data would be used by any of Sidewalk Labs sister firms. Granted Sidewalk Labs pledged not to sell data, but did the same standards apply to sharing data internally within the Alphabet family of companies? Or to their third-party partners and subcontractors?

Sidewalk Labs pledged that data would never be disclosed to third parties without consent. However, in their own documents Sidewalk Labs indicated the "digital layer" over Quayside would include a robust set of APIs (application programming interface), which would provide a "well-designed canvas" for developers to build applications into the community (2017, 70). The document compared the set of APIs to Apple's App Store, the Google Play Store, or Amazon Web Services, presenting the "digital layer" as an evolving platform that could be added to by a series of actors (70). One comes away from the document with an appreciation that the "digital layer" was more of a commercial platform. Presumably, all of these developers would have access to the data stored in the "digital layer" and would be paying some type of licensing fee for such access. This aspect of the Quayside proposal had yet to resolved.

Even internally within Sidewalk Labs, employees found that their data privacy policies were problematic. In late October 2018, the privacy advisor of Sidewalk Labs, Ann Cavoukian, resigned from her role, citing "concerns over personal data security" policies the firm had in place (O'Shea 2018). According to Cavoukian, the proposed plan addressing privacy was unacceptable, given that there was very little regulation to protect personal identifiable information collected in new smart cities projects. This resignation provoked an avalanche of criticism about data collection and security in this project. Other board members, such as Saadia Muzaffar, also resigned, citing several concerns, including transparency (Deschamps 2018).

Although the MIDP framework promised creation of an external advisory board that would determine policy on data stewardship, access, and data privacy, it only vaguely described the logistics of how the community would be involved throughout the project. Considering the business model of Alphabet, as well as its continued controversies surrounding data privacy, one wonders whether this board would have a meaningful oversight role.

WHAT IS THE RIGHT GOVERNANCE MODEL FOR THE SMART CITY?

Overseeing the Quayside R F P, the selection and proposed development of the community was Waterfront Toronto. Waterfront Toronto was formed in 2002 as a partnership of the three layers of government to lead revitalization projects for a 1,150-hectare stretch along Lake Ontario. At the time, Toronto was planning to bid on the right to host the 2008 Olympic Games, and organizers saw the city's waterfront as an ideal location for Olympic facilities (Eidelman 2013). As part of the bid process, the governments of Canada, Ontario, and Toronto established a task force to develop a business plan to kick-start redevelopment along the strategically located, but underdeveloped stretch of land across the city's lakefront (Eidelman 2013). Headed by investment banker Robert Fung, the task force recommended creation of a joint federal, provincial, and municipal enterprise that was modelled on successful waterfront development agencies in London and New York City (Eidelman 2013). Waterfront Toronto was established through special legislation in December 2002 and, while given a broad mandate to develop land along the lakeshore and $500 million in funding from each level government, it was expressly prohibited from borrowing money, mortgaging assets, raising revenues, or establishing subsidiaries without tri-government consent (Eidelman 2013).

As a tri-governmental agency, Waterfront Toronto comprises twelve board members, four representatives each nominated from federal, provincial, and local government. The board acts as a steward of the Toronto waterfront, but has long had a mandate rooted in property and economic development. Waterfront Toronto has a twenty-five-year mandate to transform 800 hectares of brownfield lands on the waterfront into useable, mixed public space. Needless to say, smart city design is uncharted territory, as are thorny issues such as data governance and privacy. This, of course, raises questions about whether Waterfront Toronto is up to the task of properly regulating a data firm like Alphabet. It is ironic that the role to regulate and govern the mass collection of data has fallen to an agency with the least capacity to work through such issues and does not have the direct authority to confront data governance challenges.

Truthfully, local governments, agencies, or boards are not in a position to regulate a firm like Alphabet, or design and enforce robust data governance rules to protect the public. The role to regulate should fall to the federal government. However, the Canadian federal government has yet to act. The European Union's General Data Protection Regional is the only global law that fits the bill, and it has been criticized as its coverage and enforcement are still not up to the task it is expected to fill (Thornhill 2018). In the absence of any strong government direction, agencies such as Waterfront Toronto will continue to be unable to properly regulate large data infrastructure projects, such as Quayside.

This absence of strong, standardized rules regulating data firms, means that all technology firms, including Sidewalk Labs, take on a large self-regulatory role. The level of authority that Sidewalk Labs would have had over development of the Quayside neighbourhood had been the subject of scrutiny from all sides of this debate. Questions of governance, profit-sharing, and ownership of intellectual property were raised by critics wary of private interests commandeering a piece of Toronto. After Sidewalk Labs released the MIDP in June 2019, it received public backlash in response to the expansion of its self-delineated development powers. For example, the firm asked for governance and taxation powers well beyond what Ontario grants to municipalities. As such, the overwhelmingly negative public reaction should not have come as a surprise.

CONCLUSION

Waterfront Toronto attempted to create an innovation partnership to turn Quayside, an underutilized formerly industrial parcel on the waterfront property, into a model smart city by fulfilling the objectives of (1) sustainability, resiliency, and urban innovation, (2) complete communities, and (3) economic development and urban innovation. With the help of Alphabet's subsidiaries, Sidewalk Labs proposed to accomplish these goals and much more; its ambitions to improve the public realm went well beyond the initial guidelines, towards an overhaul of almost every facet of daily urban life. Housing in their Quayside community was designed to be mixed-use, mixed-income, and affordable, thanks to modular construction and passive heating and cooling, monitored dutifully by algorithmic schedulers. Pedestrian life would have been prioritized, with place-making theory guiding the allocation of space to local businesses, parks, and open spaces for residents to enjoy. A swath of transportation options would have been made available to improve mobility efficiency and remove the need for car ownership in Quayside. Renewable energy sources would have convened in the district energy system to power buildings and support a carbon-neutral, if not positive, footprint. Across all of these benefits rested the digital layer – the people-programmed algorithms that would collect, process, and respond to a constant flow of data.

On paper, the vision that Sidewalk Labs produced sounded ideal. What's not to like? However, handing over responsibility to build a community from the ground up on some of Toronto's most coveted real estate proved controversial. Concerns were raised early about the affordability of housing in the community and the relationship between Sidewalk Labs and Waterfront Toronto, but quickly shifted to privacy and data governance. Critics of the projects pointed out flaws, slowed approvals, and made the city constantly renegotiate terms with the firm. Although Sidewalk Labs cited COVID-19 as the official reason for its withdrawal, ultimately it was the inability of Sidewalk Labs to win over the public that led to the demise of the project. In this chapter, we looked at three main questions about the Quayside project:

- Can a technology company be a community builder?
- Can a technology company adequately protect data and privacy?
- What is the right governance model for the smart city?

On the first question, the promise of smart technology can facilitate affordable housing and more efficiently manage resources. The literature has shown this, and Sidewalk Labs appeared to have realistic and positive physical design plans prior to cancellation of the project. Quayside, however, was never truly about the land. Instead, the project rested on data and ultimately we argue that segregation across the digital divide remains a central concern. Quayside held the very real possibility to digitally segregate the community.

On the second question, complex issues remained, involving data privacy and governance. While Sidewalk Labs promised to abide by Responsible Data Use frameworks, details were short on how this this goal would be accomplished. The MIDP was far too ambiguous in its treatment of data governance mechanisms, and oversight seemed uncertain.

On the third question, the answer is clearer: the governance model set up in Quayside is ill-suited for the task at hand. As discussed earlier, Waterfront Toronto has no track record in data governance or management and insufficient expertise to manage the data and privacy practices of a global data firm such as Alphabet. In fact, few municipalities do. The ironic aspect of smart city development is that the complex task of regulation is falling to the level of government least equipped to handle it.

What does Quayside tell us about the state of smart city building? Quayside was never realized, but the process to bring Quayside to life has been instructive for those studying the smart city space globally. The main conclusion is that we need to collectively think about the right governance structure for data-intensive public infrastructure projects. It is high time for national governments to become involved in smart city development projects, like Quayside, to help municipal and provincial or state governments work through complex data governance issues. Though it is not the traditional role of national governments to be involved in local building projects, Quayside shows that municipalities can no longer go it alone.

REFERENCES

Advocacy Centre for Tenants Ontario. 2018. *Where Will We Live? Ontario's Affordable Housing Crisis.* ACTO Report, May 2018.
Bickis, I. 2019. "Sidewalk Releases Grand Vision for Controversial Toronto Development." *National Post,* 24 June.
Bozikovic, A. 2017. "Google's Sidewalk Labs Signs Deal for 'Smart City' Makeover of Toronto's Waterfront." *Globe and Mail,* 17 October.
C40 Cities. 2017. *Annual Report.* New York: C40 Cities.
Cecco, L. 2019. "'Surveillance Capitalism': Critic Urges Toronto to Abandon Smart City Project." *Guardian,* 9 June.
Cugurullo, F. 2013. "How to Build a Sandcastle: An Analysis of the Genesis and Development of Masdar City." *Journal of Urban Technology* 20, no. 1: 23–37.
Deschamps, T. 2018. "Saadia Muzaffar Resigns from Google's Sidewalk Labs Advisory Panel on Toronto Waterfront Project." Global News, 5 October.
D'Onfro, J. 2019. "Google Sibling Sidewalk Labs Unveils 'Smart City' Plans for Toronto Waterfront." *Forbes,* 24 June.
Eidelman, G. 2013. *Three's Company: A Review of Waterfront Toronto's Tri-Government Approach to Revitalization.* Toronto: Mowat Centre, University of Toronto.

Fussell, S. 2018. "Privacy Advocates Are Criticizing Google Sidewalk Labs." *Atlantic*, 21 November.

Garfield, L. 2018. "Google's Parent Company Just Reached an Agreement with Toronto to Plan a $50 million High-Tech Neighbourhood." *Business Insider*, 31 July.

Hashem, I., A. Targio, V. Chang, N.B. Anuar, K. Adewole, I. Yaqoob, A. Gani, E. Ahmed, and H. Chiroma. 2016. "The Role of Big Data in Smart Cities." *International Journal of Information Management* 36, no. 5: 748–58.

Hawkins, Andrew J. 2019. "Alphabet's Sidewalk Labs Unveils Its High-Tech 'City-within-a-City' Plan for Toronto." *Verge*, 24 June. https://www.theverge.com/2019/6/24/18715486/alphabet-sidewalk-labs-toronto-high-tech-city-within-a-city-plan.

Huber, J.A.J., M. Ekevad, U.A. Girhammar, and S. Berg. 2019. "Structural Robustness and Timber Buildings: A Review." *Wood Material Science & Engineering* 2: 107–28.

Mathieu, E. 2019. "Sidewalk Labs Says It Needs Discounted Land for Its Affordable Housing Plan." *Toronto Star*, 24 June.

Mauracher, J., and M. Zettler. 2020. "Toronto's Affordability Crisis: How Residents Are Being Forced Out of the City They Love." Global News, 9 March.

O'Shea, S. 2018. "Ann Covoukian, Former Ontario Privacy Commissioner, Resigns from Sidewalk Labs." Global News, 21 October.

Parigi, P. 2014. "Disenchanting the World: The Impact of Technology on Relationships." In *Social Informatics*, edited by Luca Maria Aiello and Daniel McFarland, 166–82. New York: Springer.

Sadowski, J. 2017. "Google Wants to Run Cities without Being Elected. Don't Let It." *Guardian*, 24 October.

Schwab, K. 2017. "How the Chief Architect of 21st Century New York Envisions the Future of Cities." *Fast Company*, 12 September.

Shwayri, S.T. 2013. "A Model Korean Ubiquitous Eco-City? The Politics of Making Songdo." *Journal of Urban Technology* 20, no. 1: 39–55.

Sidewalk Labs. 2017. *Response to Waterfront Toronto RFP*. New York: Sidewalk Labs.

– 2019. *Master Innovation Development Plan*. New York: Sidewalk Labs.

Sienkiewicz, A. 2017. "Bye Bye 1991 Loophole: Rent Control to Expand to All Rental Units in Ontario." CBC News, 20 April.

Sterling, B. 2018. "Stop Saying 'Smart Cities.'" *Atlantic*, 12 February.

Thornhill, J. 2018. " GDPR Is a Start, but Not Enough to Protect Privacy on Its Own." *Financial Times*, 25 May.

Turkle, S. 2017. *Alone Together: Why We Expect More from Technology and Less from Each Other.* London: Hackette, UK.

Vincent, D. 2019. "30 Influential Toronto Leaders Pen Letter Supporting Controversial Sidewalk Labs Plan." *Toronto Star*, 4 July.

– 2020. "Ontario Unveils Plan to Combat 'Renovictions.' Critics Say the Rules Will Make It Easier to Evict." *Toronto Star*, 12 March.

Warren, M., and E. Mathieu. 2019. "Sidewalk Labs Is Pledging to Protect 'Urban Data.' Critics Question If Their 'Untested' Plan Is Worth the Risk." *Toronto Star,* 24 June.

Waterfront Toronto. 2017. "Request for Proposals: Innovation and Funding Partner for the Quayside Development Opportunity – RFP: 2017-13." Toronto: Waterfront Toronto.

Wylie, B., and D. Murakami Wood. 2018. "Is Sidewalk Labs Doing Enough to Protect Privacy? No." Centre for International Governance Innovation, 28 August.

Yigitcanlar, T. 2016. *Technology and the City: Systems, Applications and Implications.* London: Routledge.

13

From Processors to Platforms: Innovation and the Changing Nature of Space

Nathan Stewart, Austin Zwick, and Eamonn Dundon

- Local politicians and policy-makers, under the marketing banner of creating smart cities, have long called for public investment in innovative industries, along with growth of human capital, to attract the jobs of the future.
- This chapter offers a truncated yet detailed understanding of how theories of innovation are understood and discussed within contemporary economic geography, helping us think about the connections between space, innovation, and public investments.
- We conclude by advocating for a stronger connection between urban planning and innovation-based industrial policy to focus on the revitalization of distressed neighbourhoods with the goal of creating more equitable and effective urban policy.

INTRODUCTION: INNOVATION AND INDUSTRIAL POLICY

Mayors push their cities to become smart because they want the jobs of the future, and to take the political credit for bringing them home. Full stop. But the question remains: Will innovation-based industrial policy bring economic growth? Will tech-sector jobs be spatially located within cities/regions to improve distressed neighbourhoods? Will "smart city" investment policies improve quality of life in their cities for all residents? This chapter reviews the economic geography literature as it applies to the platform economy and smart cities, concluding with a case study of Silicon Valley, to try to answer these questions. The results are not promising.

With the transition to the post-Fordist economy that has characterized much of the developed world over the last sixty years, a new orthodoxy has emerged amongst urban economic policy-makers. Today, it is widely held that the key driver of a competitive urban economy is its people. Supported by the work of economists and economic geographers such as Edward Glaeser, Enrico Moretti, and Richard Florida, the axiom upon which this orthodoxy stands is that creativity and human capital are the economic fuel that drive sustained growth in the innovation economy.

In recognition of this belief, politicians and regional policy-makers have supported the development and capitalization of human capital – often under a banner of "becoming smart" – by providing subsidies for education and employment in high-skill, creative industries (Oliveira 2016). Examples of such industries include software development, industrial and manufacturing design, law, and advanced manufacturing. Informed by the research on "innovation systems," these policies often focus on creating, promoting, and supporting innovative institutions such as universities, colleges, start-up incubators, and established corporations. Epitomized by the 238 bids submitted to Amazon by North American cities hoping to secure the company's promised "HQ2" bounty of US$5 billion in local investment and 50,000 "creative" jobs, the primacy of innovation systems thinking is a glaring feature of contemporary regional development policy.

Despite the popularity of these innovation-based regional development policies with politicians, the results of this "big push" towards developing and maintaining regional innovation systems have fallen short of their promises. Even when successful at attracting industry, innovation-based industrial policy has a diverse landscape of regional winners and losers. On one side of the balance there are success stories like that of Pittsburgh, Pennsylvania. Regional planning and revitalization strategies to attract, generate, and support entrepreneurial talent, capital, and young, innovative labour have launched this formerly declining city into a globally competitive place of innovation and growth. However, those benefits that have accrued to a small fraction of the population introduced questions of how equitable such investments were (Dietrich-Ward 2017). On the other side of the balance are cities like Rochester, New York, and Youngstown, Ohio, where such strategies have failed to stall the post-industrial decline that has blighted these once prosperous cities, stimulating questions of whether these public investments were not only wasteful, but also inhumane at a time when residents desperately needed basic necessities and services.

After reviewing the concepts and literature and elucidating them through a case study, we advocate for a more geographically sensitive approach to innovation-based industrial policy. The novelty of this approach is the transformation of turning the phrase "becoming smart" from a meaningless catchphrase to a specific orientation of place-based investment and urban planning to stimulate the creation of innovation jobs in specific, distressed neighbourhoods.

CONCEPTS OF INNOVATION

Innovation has long been regarded as a central factor in economic competitiveness and growth under capitalism. According to modern scholars of innovation, to begin to understand innovation, it is first crucial to recognize that innovation is at once a manifestation of human labour and a fundamental driver of capitalist competition (Gertler 2003; Wolfe 2014; Sardana 2016; Silve and Plekhanov 2018). Beyond this fundamental description, however, innovation can be understood as more than the outcome of a black box process. Instead, contemporary scholarship posits that the process of generating and commercializing new ideas can be broken down into its composite parts. In pursuit of such an analytical understanding, innovation scholars have generated a typology of innovation based on the novelty and impact of new ideas and identified the key inputs associated with this process.

Within this typology, *incremental innovation* refers to small changes made to a product or process. Examples could include adding a new feature to product (such as integrating Bluetooth technology into motor vehicles), or slightly altering the way a popular commodity or service is produced (such as switching from cast moulding to injection moulding). Alternatively, *radical innovation* refers to instances where a profoundly new idea reaches the market. In radical innovation, an idea is often so new that it can disrupt markets and create space for new social, economic, political, and commercial possibilities (Christensen et al. 2018). In contrast to the relative frequency with which incremental innovations are produced, radical innovations have occurred only rarely. Examples of disruptively radical innovations include the automobile and the internet – both of which reshaped the world.

To identify key drivers of innovation, scholars have found it helpful to compare the modern geography of innovation to the "flat world" hypothesis of the 1990s and early 2000s (Rodriguez-Pose and Crescenzi 2008). It argued that the advancement of globalization would create a world in which access to all mobile factors of production (labour, capital, technology, and knowledge) would become perfectly even across space (O'Brien 1992; Cairncross 1997; Friedman 2005). Referred to as "ubiquitization" by Maskell and Malmberg (1999),[1] the "flat world" theory posited that this new geography of access would enable a decentralization of economic production and the emergence of a new, more equal global space-economy.[2]

While some "flattening" did take place alongside the advancements in transportation and communication technologies that have helped drive globalization, the landscape of this "new" space-economy remains characterized by "mountains in a flat world" (Rodriguez-Pose and Crescenzi 2008). Representing the concentrations of wealth, economic activity, and *innovative capacity* that constitute the world's largest and most competitive urban spaces, these "mountains" opposed the utopian idealism of "flat world" theorists. The continued presence of these mountains in the era of ubiquitization provided compelling evidence that, even under conditions of near-perfect access to economic inputs, space – and geographical proximity in particular – continues to be important in production, competition, capital accumulation, and economic growth.

With these paradoxical results being observed all over the globe, scholars have turned to economic geography to help them understand how and why space and proximity matter so much in the "flat world." The consensus is that while there is now a global abundance of *codified knowledge* (knowledge that can be easily transported across long distances), access to such knowledge is only one ingredient in innovation. In addition to access to codified knowledge, scholars have found that successful innovation relies *crucially* on the ability of economic actors to access and mobilize stocks of *tacit knowledge*. Defined as embodied or implicit knowledge (knowledge that requires experiential learning), tacit knowledge is an *essential* input to innovation, as it is *this* form of knowledge that enables, is produced by, and circulates through collaborative problem solving and novelty generation. It is in this regard that tacit knowledge, much more than codified knowledge, is the primary driver of successful innovation (Polanyi 1958; Lundvall 1992).

Because the generation and transmission of tacit knowledge are embodied and collaborative, tacit knowledge is stubbornly resistant to being transmitted over long distances (Gertler 2003; Bathelt et al. 2004; Simmie 2005). So the transmission of tacit knowledge – and thereby, the successful (re)generation of innovation – requires that knowledge exchange takes place face-to-face[3] between individuals who have a diverse but complementary capacity to communicate, interact, and interrelate (Polanyi 1958; Storper and Venables 2004). Understanding the role and the scarcity of tacit knowledge stocks is therefore key to understanding the key driver of the innovative process as well as the globally uneven geography of innovation (Polanyi 1958; Howells 2002; Gertler 2003).

The mass codification of information has accompanied the communications technology revolution, so the *innovative capacity* of actors and places now hinges on the diverse networks of individuals that have and can continuously generate and circulate complex knowledge with each other within a spatially bounded social context (Howells 2002). Such a constant flow of tacit information facilitates recombination of these knowledges into viable new ideas, thus generating new innovations (Howells 2002; Asheim et al. 2016). This is what makes tacit knowledge – much more so than codified knowledge – the "glue" that holds concentrations of wealth and economic activity together. So the concentration of innovation within many of the world's most diverse, dense, and dynamic "mountains" has provided the clue to understanding its secret ingredient. That is, in order for a collection of economic actors to continuously generate new and successful innovations, they must exist within a social context that facilitates – if not *encourages* – face-to-face interaction, collaboration, and the creation and dissemination of tacit knowledge. It is this aspect of innovation that is most important for understanding the "stickiness," and therefore the geography, of innovation.

TYPOLOGY FOR UNDERSTANDING THE GEOGRAPHY OF INNOVATION

To delineate different approaches to understanding the geography of innovation, a simple typology is presented below. This typology distinguishes these different theories on the geography of innovation based on their scalar focus (small, medium, large), functional focus (causality, productivity, and description), and actor focus (individuals, firms, and institutions) (see table 1). Although often overlapping

Table 13.1
Typology for understanding geography of innovation

Line of thought	Scalar focus	Functional focus	Entity focus
Proximities and institutions	Small- to medium-scale	Causality	Individuals and firms
Innovation systems	Large-scale	Description	Firms and institutional actors*
Externalities	Medium- to large-scale	Productivity	Firms

* Institutional actors are formal/legal institutions that interact with other economic actors to support innovation.

and inter-referential, these three lines of thought can be classified as (1) *proximities and institutions*, (2) *innovation systems*, and (3) *externalities*. This typology is intended to be used for understanding the different ways that scholars make sense of the geography of innovation.

Proximities and Institutions

The stimulation of innovation requires that *geographical proximity* be augmented and complemented by the presence of other, more socially determined 'proximities' (Gilly and Torre 2000; Boschma 2005). Termed "proximities" because of the word's capacity to convey notions of "closeness" and "alignment," these common understandings have been broken down into four major categories: cognitive proximity, organizational proximity, social proximity, and institutional proximity.

1 *Cognitive proximity*: The degree to which actors share a common knowledge base and outlook in relation to a given problem. While cognitive proximity can be created to some degree via a transfer of codified knowledge (i.e., a similar educational background), tacit knowledge also plays a key role in its formation where actors must share a common understanding of new, uncodified knowledge as well as corporate routines/ways of doing things. Related to the idea of "absorptive capacity" (Boschma 2005), cognitive proximity enables actors to effectively share and receive complicated information.

2 *Organizational proximity*: The degree to which actors are affiliated with and informed by the same organization/ organizational structure. Intimately connected to the concepts of command and control and the division of labour (Mann 1986),

organizational proximity recognizes that information sharing between actors requires direction and management to be effective in a competitive environment (Boschma 2005). Stated simply, organizational proximity refers to the degree to which organizationally affiliated, knowledge-imbued actors are strategically organized and oriented towards the completion of a common agenda.

3 *Social proximity*: The degree to which actors have mutual trust, friendship/kinship, and reciprocity. More so than any other proximity, social proximity draws on the idea of social embeddedness[4] to argue that the strength of social relations that exists between actors represents a key determinant of their willingness and capacity to share and receive complex and valuable information.

4 *Institutional proximity*: The degree to which actors exist within similar macro-institutional contexts. Inclusive of common habits, routines, practices, laws, regulations, and rules, the idea of a "macro-institutional" context refers to the overarching ways that socially interconnected actors govern individual and collective behaviour via formal and informal institutions. Highly related to the notion of social contexts, actors can be considered institutionally proximate on the basis of how well their understandings of these rules and norms align.

While geographical proximity alone is insufficient to stimulate information transfer and innovation, the physical closeness of individuals can be a vehicle for the development and operation of these other proximities (Balland et al. 2015; Broekel 2015; Bouba-Olga et al. 2015). In social proximity, geographical proximity is important because it reduces uncertainty and increases communicative efficacy of individuals as they repeatedly interact with one another face-to-face, forming common understandings and "languages."[5] Alternatively, in organizational proximity, the ability to manage and direct teamwork and knowledge transfer amongst individuals who have large endowments of tacit knowledge requires that they frequently and repeatedly interact face-to-face (Nelson and Winter 1982; Mann 1986). Similar arguments can also be made for cognitive proximity, particularly in the development of idiosyncratic corporate routines and "ways of doing" between geographically proximate groups operating inside firms (Nelson and Winter 1982). Finally, in institutional proximity, the geography of macro-institutional contexts is perhaps the easiest to understand. Particularly in formal institutions, the emergence and solidification of rules and norms requires that social expectations amongst individuals be built up and legitimated over time via experience and trust building. As a result, the stability required for their emergence and reproduction places a premium on the geographical proximity of the actors involved, as this enables a form of collective learning and legitimation between proximate actors. In sum, proximities and institutions are subject to positive feedback.

Innovation Systems

First developed by the Organization for Economic Cooperation and Development (OECD) in the 1980s, the idea of "innovation systems" (IS) arose from a renewed interest in Alfred Marshall's concept of industrial districts. Originally conceptualized at the national scale, the IS concept takes a systems-level view of a territorially bounded economy to identify and study the formal actors and institutions that participate in and enable the circulation of knowledge across space. Examples of institutions that make up an IS include those that provide research outputs, such as universities and think tanks, as well as those that exploit this knowledge such as firms, entrepreneurs, and at times governments (Asheim et al. 2016).

The focus of IS on the role of formal institutions does not mean that the idea ignores the insights of other relevant approaches, such as those of the *institutions and proximities* line of thought. The IS approach places great importance on these considerations – proponents of the framework recognize that the actors who operate within innovation systems must be capable of generating and sharing complex new ideas within and between their institutions in order to facilitate the circulation of knowledge. Iammarino (2005) notes that the operation of regional innovation systems (RSIS) is heavily influenced by the local actors operating within the region, as well as the region's historical development. She further argues that RSIS exist within a hierarchy of geographies and institutions, each with a history that informs and mediates the operation of a given RSI. The importance of context and history is due to the formation of local communication patterns, localized invention and learning patterns, localized network integration, and historical path dependency. Such interrelations are exemplified by the Silicon Valley case study outlined in the next section.

The IS approach also takes into account insights from the *externalities* approach, detailed next, by considering the levels of industrial specialization (MAR externalities) and diversity (Jacobs externalities) found within a region (Martin and Simmie 2008).[6] Nevertheless, it is important to recognize that the IS approach should not be understood as a simple amalgam of these two lines of thought. In addition to its unique prioritization of systems thinking, the IS concept also considers insights developed outside the previously mentioned approaches. These include the tolerance level of an IS, the level of technical sophistication amongst producers and consumers, economies of scale, and access to international knowledge spillovers (Iammarino 2005; Asheim et al. 2016).

Regarding the geography of the IS approach, its orientation around description and policy development indicates the way space is treated by its proponents. The IS approach views space in an absolute sense – as a measurable container of actors separated by distance – rather than in the socially constructed and relational sense prioritized by the *institutions and proximities* approach (Smith 1984). This view of space as a container of economic activity is useful for policy-makers because it is viewed as something concrete that can be acted upon, rather than an individually variant and fluid construct (Scott 1994).[7]

Externalities

In contrast to *proximities and institutions*, the *externalities* line of thought pays less attention to the causal factors that undergird the capacity of actors/firms to generate innovation. Unlike the IS approach, the *externalities* approach gives more weight to local interaction instead of international knowledge flows. This line of thought is more concerned with understanding theoretical and empirical relationships between industrial ecosystems and innovation. The *externalities* approach brings together insights from scholars such as Alfred Marshall (industrial districts) and Jane Jacobs ("new work") to theorize how the industrial make-up of productive spaces affects their innovative output.[8]

Regarding the distinctions between Marshall-Arrow-Romer (MAR) externalities and Jacobs externalities, the primary point of divergence can be found in the underlying urban economic theory that informed their development. In the former, it is believed that a series of potential impacts can accrue from the co-location of firms that are specialized in the same or similar industries, and that these impacts can generate important competitive outcomes for regional economies (Krugman 1991; Glaeser et al. 1992; Feldman and Audretsch 1999). Originally theorized by Alfred Marshall in his *Principles of Economics* (1890), most conceptual and empirical work that has been directed at understanding MAR externalities has revolved around providing a mechanistic understanding of how the co-location of firms can drive down the costs of production and increase the rate at which firms produce incremental innovations.

In Marshall's original conception of externalities, the key factors assumed to generate these benefits include (1) the formation of a thick, localized market of specialized labour that can be drawn on by firms within the region; (2) the creation of highly efficient forward and backward linkages between related firms; and (3) the emergence of knowledge and technology spillovers between firms. This line of thinking was later added to by economists Kenneth Arrow (1962) and Paul Romer (1986), who merged their insights about localized benefits accruing to firms through learning-by-doing with the original ideas put forward by Marshall (Glaeser et al. 1992).[9]

In Jacobs's conception of externalities, her key argument is that a large amount of industrial diversity within a regional economy increases the likelihood that diverse industrial knowledges will "collide." These impacts have the potential to drive high levels of incremental and radical innovation in firms located in highly diverse regional economies. More specifically, Jacobs (1969) discusses the process by which diverse production knowledges and technologies can recombine within regions as a result of the co-location of diversely specialized firms and their agents. If this results in a "cross-fertilization" of knowledge, communication between actors and knowledge spillovers can create "knock-on" effects within regional economies that can lead to the formation of "new work." Ideally, the creation of "new work" will drive an injection of economic dynamism into regional economies, with the result that firms become more capable of producing highly innovated products and processes (Acs 2002; Audretsch 2003; Ejermo 2005).

The entirety of the *externalities* approach depends on the assumption that spatial proximity *begets* economic and social interaction. Rather than simply enabling economic growth, space thereby becomes the most important factor underlying competitiveness and dynamism in regional economies.[10] In this regard, the *externalities* approach concerns itself less with theorizing how or why this interaction takes place and is instead dedicated to understanding the implications of these interactions for growth and competitiveness. Of course, this means that the *externalities* approach relies heavily (implicitly or otherwise) on the operation of *proximities and institutions*.

FROM PROCESSORS TO PLATFORMS: THE CONSOLIDATION OF INNOVATION IN SILICON VALLEY

Home to thousands of small, medium, and large firms specialized in the production of high-technology goods and services, the economic output of Silicon Valley ranges from the mass-appeal consumer content offered by Netflix to the infrastructural supports provided by Cisco Systems. Also playing home to other modern tech giants such as Facebook, Intel, Hewlett-Packard, and Tesla, Silicon Valley is now one of – if not *the* – most technologically sophisticated and innovative economic clusters in the world (Engel 2015; Pique et al. 2018).

The economic success and dynamism of the Valley was not bestowed upon Northern California from on high, however. Rather, the development of Silicon Valley's famous "innovation cluster" offers a prime case study of the interactions and impacts generated by the three "geographies of innovation" discussed in this chapter. Summarized in brief, the most common explanation offered for the rise of Silicon Valley has been that the dynamic evolution of the region over time can be attributed to its economic heritage and the ways in which the actors, institutions, and environment that constitute "the Valley" have interacted throughout its history (Saxenian 1996; Storper et al. 2015). Marked by periods of growth, decline, rebirth, and consolidation, the history of the Valley has also been one of perpetual reinvention and migration (Henton and Held 2013). Beginning with the establishment of sophisticated regional assets, technological expertise, and the propensity to encourage – not to tolerate, but to *actually encourage* – the circulation of people and ideas between regionally embedded institutions and firms, the success of Silicon Valley can be traced to provide empirical support for the importance of multi-scalar and nuanced innovation policy. The remainder of this chapter divides the history of Silicon Valley into three consecutive eras – processor, software, and platform – where production shifted to a new type of product, while the innovative milieu warped to reflect an increasingly interwoven economic geography of the Valley.

THE PROCESSOR ERA: NASCENT INNOVATION AND THE LEGACY OF FREDERICK TERMAN

The technological legacy of Palo Alto and Silicon Valley was first seeded as a result of the decisions made by early electrical equipment innovators to settle in the area between 1909 and 1934 (Storper et al. 2015; Adams 2017). Specialized in the production of radio transmission technologies, pioneering firms such as the Federal Telegraph Company (FTC), Eitel McCullough (EM), and Litton Engineering Laboratories (LEL, later Litton Industries) chose to call the Bay Area home during the emergent decades of the computing technology era. Led by prominent figures such as Cyril Frank Elwell and Lee De Forest (FTC), William Eitel and Jack McCullough (EM), and Charles Litton Sr (LEL), the engineering teams at these first-mover firms made substantial advances in the nascent field of vacuum tube production. An early predecessor of the modern semi-conductor, the increasingly prominent production of vacuum tubes in the Bay Area provided the first step in the virtuous cycle of growth and rebirth that has marked the history of Silicon Valley.

The coalescence of vacuum tube innovators during the early 1900s was not an accident, however. As noted in numerous historical studies of the Valley, many of these technological forefathers shared a common connection through their education in electrical engineering. Split between the local education offered by Stanford University and sources of knowledge further afield such as Yale (Connecticut) and Bell Labs (New Jersey), this common education combined with a keen interest in pursuing the development of vacuum tube technologies served as a unifying beacon for the innovators.[11] The result was the emergence of a new concentration of vacuum tube production and innovation that relied on the generation and translation of new knowledge by and between actors in the space. As the region's productive capacity grew, the settlement and development of engineering talent away from the traditional heartland of vacuum tube research (Bell Labs and the Northeast) was apparent, and by the dawn of the Second World War, the United States had produced a second regional economy that was now attracting skilled labour and threatening to compete for primacy in the nascent industry.

The continued growth and coalescence of the Palo Alto tech industry was not sustained solely by the efforts of these early inventors, however. By 1925, the region saw the arrival of a new force in electrical engineering: enter Frederick Terman. Widely dubbed "the father of Silicon Valley," Terman took up a faculty position in the Department of Engineering at Stanford University. Having received his doctorate in electrical engineering from the Massachusetts Institute of Technology[12] one year prior, Terman immediately began assembling and directing a research and learning lab focused on vacuum tube technology, electrical circuits, and instrumentation. Often referred to as a "robust actor" in academic literature, Terman used his knowledge, passion, and persistence in the field of electrical engineering to further stimulate innovation and growth in the region.

During Terman's pre-war tenure at the university, he was responsible for recruiting, training, and/or directly funding a series of early computing technology entrepreneurs. Most notably, some of Terman's students and beneficiaries included Russel and Sigurd Varian (Varian Industries), William Hewlett and David Packard (HP), and even Charles Litton Sr Interrupted by a brief war-time stint spent at an Ally-linked research lab at Harvard, Terman returned to Stanford in 1945, this time as dean of the Faculty of Engineering. From this position, Terman made his greatest impacts on Silicon Valley's innovation geography.

Terman's three most impactful acts as dean of the faculty included the establishment of the university's Honours Co-op Program, the founding of the Stanford Research Institute (SRI), and the creation of the Stanford Industrial Park (Ferrary and Granovetter 2009; Storper et al. 2015). In each instance, Terman's unique contribution was to focus on forging linkages with local, high-tech industries and promoting the circulation of knowledge between academia and commercial research. In doing so, Terman laid the groundwork for strong ties to develop between Stanford's Engineering Department and the growing technical expertise in the Valley (Williams 1998). Built up through the rotation of students through local industry, the hosting and incubating of start-ups in the Stanford Industrial Park, and the co-development of innovative products and solutions at the SRI, these strong ties remain a hallmark of Stanford's elite technical education.

With Terman's lineage firmly etched in the institutional makeup of the region's fledgling innovation system, the stage was set for the next phase in the Valley's ascent to hardware dominance. As an intimation of this next phase, it is germane to note that despite Terman and Co.'s early successes in the field of vacuum tube technologies, San Francisco and the Bay Area region are not known today as "Stanford Valley" or "Vacuum Tube Valley." Of course, it is known as *Silicon* Valley ... But why?

To answer this, it is necessary to contextualize the growth of the Valley in the wider scheme of the US economy. While Silicon Valley *was* growing as a node of electrical engineering and innovative technology production, the region was showing few signs that it would become the technological powerhouse it is today. This position was still reserved for the Northeast – the original home of American techno-innovation. This is well evidenced by the fact that by the dawn of the Second World War, the "Silicon Valley tech cluster" was largely centred upon vacuum tube production, employing fewer than 100 researchers and scientists (Adams 2011). By 2010, however, the region had expanded its specialization(s) to encapsulate a wide diversity of high-tech products and services, with the number of scientists and researchers employed in the cluster having reached about 100,000.

While part of this growth can be attributed to the investment in branch plants by technology firms elsewhere around the United States (Ferrary and Granovetter 2009; Adams 2011), it was the transition away from vacuum tubes and towards their successor that really drove change in region. Specifically, Silicon Valley's international brand as a technology powerhouse can be traced back to the growth and development of the semiconductor industry, as well as its eventual transition towards the integrated circuit (Klepper 2010; Henton and Held 2013; Cheyre et al. 2015). But how did these technologies end up in Northern California?

As one of the three inventors of the transistor at Bell Labs in New Jersey in 1947, William Shockley was a Nobel Prize–winning scientist who was well recognized and respected for his intelligence and innovation within the engineering community (Brock 2012). In 1956 (shortly before winning the Nobel Prize), Shockley relocated himself from the East Coast to Palo Alto, California, purportedly to be closer to his ill and aging mother (Saxenian, 1996; Adams 2011; Storper et al. 2015). Always the entrepreneur, Shockley then formed a financial agreement with Arnold Beckman to open Shockley Semiconductors as a division of Beckman Instruments (Brock 2012). Intent on capitalizing on the growing popularity of semiconductors as a replacement for vacuum tubes, Shockley began to manufacture silicon semiconductors, as opposed to earlier germanium models, with great financial success.

By bringing in substantial profits and enabling growth of the regional industry, Shockley's transition to the use of silicon further energized the technological heart of the Valley and enabled it to grow beyond the small-scale production that characterized its settlement period.

By 1957, however, Shockley's notoriously crass management style had left many of his top engineers upset and frustrated with their working conditions. After an unsuccessful attempt by Beckman to reconcile the situation, Shockley's failure to adjust his style resulted in the high-visibility exodus of eight of his best employees – the "Traitorous Eight' – who went on to found Fairchild Semiconductor (Klepper 2010; Storper et al. 2015). Placed in direct competition with Shockley, Fairchild Semiconductor soon found success in the marketplace.

The result of this initial success became legend throughout the Valley. Riding the wave of its initial success, Fairchild Semiconductor then spun off companies at an almost unthinkable rate – not only more than any other in Silicon Valley between 1957 and 1986 (twenty-four in total, fifteen more than the next-highest firm), but also more successful on average than any other firms in the Valley (Adams 2011).

THE SOFTWARE ERA: BRINGING THE INTERNET INTO THE VALLEY

By the mid-1970s, the original hardware focus of the Valley began to give way to a new wave of dynamic software providers. Emergent from the technical skill base and training associated with the region's hardware-based firms, institutions, and personal networks, the entry of this new group of companies marked a shift in the industrial mix of the Valley. Driven by the advent of the personal computer (and eventually the internet), the diversification of Silicon Valley's competitive base saw the region become the home of some of the most innovative firms of the twentieth and twenty-first centuries. Founded between the late 1970s and the 1990s, prominent examples of software firms that established themselves in Silicon Valley include Apple, Oracle, Adobe, and Google.

The first of these companies to build a bridge between Silicon Valley's mature specialization in component design and manufacturing with the novel skillsets associated with the software era was Apple. Starting with the invention of the Apple II computer in 1977, Apple launched a revolution that unleashed the market for ready-to-use,

Table 13.2
Major companies in Silicon Valley

Company	Year founded	Location
Processor era		
Hewlett Packard	1939	Palo Alto
Fairchild Semiconductor	1957	San Jose
National Semiconductor	1959	Santa Clara
Intel	1968	Santa Clara
Apple	1976	Cupertino
Oracle	1977	Santa Clara
Adobe	1982	San Jose
Cisco Systems	1984	San Jose
Software era		
Yahoo	1994	Sunnyvale
Netflix	1997	Los Gatos
Google	1998	Mountain View
LinkedIn	2002	Sunnyvale
Tesla	2003	Palo Alto
Facebook	2004	Menlo Park
Yelp	2004	San Francisco
YouTube	2005	San Bruno
Twitter	2006	San Francisco
Platform era		
Airbnb	2008	San Francisco
TaskRabbit	2008	San Francisco
Square	2009	San Francisco
Slack Technologies	2009	San Francisco
Uber	2009	San Francisco
Pinterest	2010	San Francisco
Postmates	2011	San Francisco
Instacart	2012	San Francisco
Lyft	2012	San Francisco

out-of-the-box personal computers. Led by Steve Jobs and Steve Wozniak, this breakthrough in computing technology brought the power of computer processing and software to the masses in the form of a personal device. Inspired and informed by the founders' experiences at Atari and Hewlett-Packard, as well as by tests and feedback at the influential Homebrew Computer Club, this personalization of technological power disrupted the economic and social dynamics of the world before the end of the century (Williams and Moore 1984).

Apple's product continued to develop through the late 1970s, culminating yearly revenues of around US$117 million and the company's valuation hitting US$1 billion at its initial public offering in December 1980 (Morgan Stanley 1980). Though Apple had significant business and leadership difficulties throughout the 1980s and 1990s with the exit of founders Jobs and Wozniak, the company continued to bring iconic personal computing products to the marketplace. During this time, Apple cemented its status as a premier Silicon Valley company, building a sprawling corporate campus known as Apple Campus in Cupertino in 1993 with over 850,000 square feet of office and research and development space (Simonson 2005). The allure of Apple's campus was heighted further with the 2017 debut of its Apple Park headquarters, also in Cupertino, totalling 2.8 million square feet and anchored by a massive circular building that Jobs envisioned as "the best office building in the world" (Vanhemert 2013).

Apple was not alone in creating a new economic culture in the Valley, however. Whereas Apple brought personal computing abilities to the wider consumer marketplace, Google brought the vast recesses of the internet to the fingertips of web surfers the world over. Born in 1995 from a dorm-room partnership of Larry Page and Sergey Brin at Stanford University (Google 2019), Google is typical of the many Silicon Valley companies that grew from entrenched institutions like Stanford into the massive, publicly traded technology company it is today. With $100,000 in venture capital funding in 1998 Google was officially established and grew quickly from a leased garage to the type of suburban corporate campus now synonymous with tech companies of the era (Google 2019). Based in Mountainview, California, Google's main campus was purposefully built on the site of the former home of Silicon Graphics. Such a blatant act of repurposed space provides a tangible example of the gravitational shift taking place in the Valley that saw the region's silicon-based enterprises yield the reins to a host of internet-based companies that have come to symbolize the Valley's predominant image in media and popular culture.

Google has since grown into much more than a search engine. Since its founding, the company has used its base as the undeniable leader in search engine technology ("Just Google it") to expand into a broad suite of new technological capabilities. Eventually listed under their parent company, Alphabet Inc. (founded 2015), examples of Google's forays into new technological frontiers include the founding of Google Fiber, an internet service provider much like Cisco Systems, and Waymo, a producer of autonomous vehicle technologies. This expansion has not been limited solely to the company's holdings and ventures, however. Google has also chosen to grow its Silicon Valley–based corporate campus through the addition of the "Bay View" buildings in 2013 (Goldberger 2013).

Building upon Google's initial success, in the early 2000s new social networking sites began to emerge in the Valley in the hopes of taking advantage of the region's status as a hub of technological capability, social connectivity, and internet know-how. Despite coming after formidable social networking enterprises such as Myspace and Friendster, Facebook is perhaps most emblematic of this phase of innovation in Silicon Valley. With a founding story now memorialized by the film *The Social Network* (2010), Facebook was established by Harvard University student Mark Zuckerberg as a social networking site for college students (Hoffman 2008). Early on, Zuckerberg and his team were pulled from the Boston area towards its eventual home in Menlo Park by the impressive tide of venture capital funding that flowed its way in the mid-2000s. This funding first came in the form of a $500,000 investment from PayPal founded Peter Thiel, followed by more conventional venture capital funding from the likes of Accel Partners and Greylock Partners (both located within Silicon Valley). This move to Silicon Valley was further strengthened with the impressive human capital Facebook attracted through their hiring of top developers and engineers sourced from companies such as eBay and Yahoo. As mapped in figure 13.1, other notable companies established in Silicon Valley during this time include Yahoo in Sunnyvale in 1994, Netflix in Los Gatos in 1997, LinkedIn in Sunnyvale in 2002, Tesla in Palo Alto in 2003, Yelp in San Francisco in 2004, and YouTube in San Bruno in 2005.

THE PLATFORM ERA

Today, the trend of increased concentration of technological innovation in the Valley has manifested in the proliferation of "platform" companies. Used to denote companies such as Airbnb, Uber, and Taskrabbit, these "platform" companies have moved beyond the Google model of providing a portal for consumers to connect, interact, and exchange online, and instead connect consumers to goods and

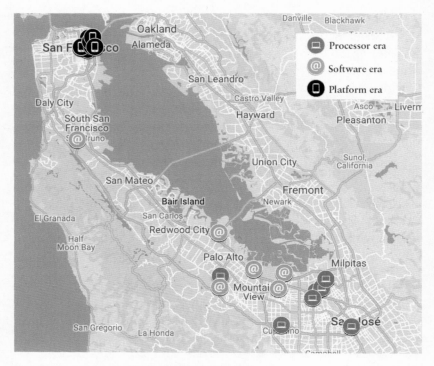

Figure 13.1 Location of Silicon Valley headquarters.

services in the offline world. While bearing only little resemblance to the early processor companies that started off in Silicon Valley, these platform companies are a natural product of the perpetual cascading of technological innovation that distinctly marks the productive and innovative character of the Valley. Attracted by the abundant flows of venture funding and institutional knowledge transfers that became an established feature of the Valley in earlier years, this new platform frontier has overwhelmingly called Silicon Valley's neighbour city to the north, San Francisco, its home (see figure 13.1). This has solidified the San Francisco Bay Area's status as the most dynamic, capital-rich tech environment in the world, with the forty-four platform-based companies in San Francisco producing over half the value of the global platform industry (Wladawsky-Berger 2016).

First out of the platform-gate in 2009, Airbnb began as a simple solution to its founders' problem: making extra money to pay their rent. Inspired by the rapidly rising housing values in the Valley, the solution of Airbnb's founders to this problem was to design a website that enabled them to rent floor space in their San Francisco apartment to attendees of a design conference. With the success of their first rental, the company was officially launched in 2008, although it would require much more support before it achieved it current valuation of $31 billion.

Initially, Airbnb had little more than an unproven business model and no financing. The company's fortunes reversed after moving through the renowned Y Combinator incubator program in San Francisco, however (Brown 2016). Now recognized as a San Francisco institution, the Y Combinator program instructs young companies on how to succeed in the competitive tech environment, creates networks of talent and capital for them, and offers an initial seed investment of $20,000 in exchange for 6 percent equity in participant companies (Gallagher 2017). While Airbnb is certainly one of the most recognized firms to emerge from this elite start-up bootcamp, other prominent names have also emerged from the program, including Stripe, Cruise, Dropbox, Instacart, and DoorDash (Y Combinator 2019).

Airbnb's model of conquering the once indomitable hotel industry has led it to higher valuations than traditional hotel giants. Similarly Uber, and other ride-hailing platforms that followed, has changed the game of urban mobility, while also moving into other facets of the platform economy such as food delivery, bringing it into direct competition with many platform players in the Bay Area. Having grown rapidly from $495 million in revenue in 2014 to over $11.2 billion in 2018, Uber is seeking to extend their platform of simple ridesharing into a global mobility powerhouse, uniting ride hailing, autonomous vehicles, and mobile delivery (Farrell and Brown 2019). Uber is inspiring a new revolution in mobility, causing entrenched automakers such as Ford, General Motors, and Toyota to rethink their approaches to car ownership and move towards Uber's vision for shared mobility fleets. As mapped in figure 13.1, other big-name platform businesses calling San Francisco home include Task Rabbit in 2008, Square in 2009, Slack Technologies in 2009, Pinterest in 2010, Postmates in 2011, and Instacart in 2012. As the map shows, the start-up scene has expanded from being centred in the "old" Silicon Valley to within a radius of a few blocks in downtown San Francisco.

The evolution of Silicon Valley's innovation prowess can be traced by changes in its industrial mix and its geography of innovation. Beginning in the era of hardware design and manufacturing, the connection between the Valley's geography and its innovative output is clearly defined. As mentioned above, the initial seeding of "innovative space" in the region was the result of the interactions enabled by the proximities and institutions developed between the similarly educated and like-minded founders of the Valley's first vacuum tube manufacturers. Facilitated by geographical proximity, the convergence of the likes of De Forest, Litton Sr, Eitel, McCullough, and Elwell in Northern California enabled these early creators to generate and exchange complex, new information between each other effectively and efficiently. An early example of what is now called an "innovative milieu," the spaces of information exchange and co-learning enjoyed by the founding engineers of Silicon Valley perfectly reflect the catalyzing role played by geographical and social proximities and common institutions in the stimulation of growth and development of the region.

The systemic embedding of the Valley's proximities and institutions could not have taken place without the deliberate actions of Frederick Terman, however. As both founder of Stanford's vacuum tube research and learning lab and dean of engineering, Terman made the explicit decision to bring together talented, like-minded thinkers in a formal institutional setting. In doing so, he not only enabled the reproduction of essential proximities and institutions between engineers, he also sketched out the initial structure of the region's formal innovation system. This action – likely more so than the natural evolution of proximities and institutions – was the essential catalyst that sparked the tremendous growth of Silicon Valley as an innovation mecca.

Most importantly, Terman's decision to recruit and integrate new engineers such as William Hewlett and David Packard into the innovative milieu forming around the initial founders in the Valley created a space where new knowledge could be translated, circulated, and reproduced between differently endowed, yet like-minded actors. Further still, Terman's later decision to integrate Stanford's knowledge-producing prowess with that of the region's private sector through his co-op program, the Stanford Research Institute, and the Stanford Industrial Park further formalized the circulation of labour and new ideas across the region. In a sense, it was these actions by Terman that first outlined the geographical extent of knowledge circulation that now takes place between Silicon Valley's private producers and Stanford's engineering program.

With such infrastructure playing an integral role in the supply of skilled labour to later innovators such as William Schockley and the Traitorous Eight (as well as the firms of the software and platform eras), it is arguable that without these formal institutions (i.e., the regional innovation system), it would have been exceedingly more difficult for the innovators of the hardware, software, *and* platform eras to seed and circulate the knowledge necessary to allow the region to leap into its next phases of development.

The early geography of innovation in Silicon Valley thus portrays the innovative potential that can arise when a nexus of proximities and institutions, innovation systems, and externalities (i.e., the diversification brought by Hewlett and Packard and Shockley) is allowed and encouraged to emerge. Clearly, however, while the hardware era offers evidence of the value of this nexus, the era also illustrates that it was Terman's institutional decision-making that was most essential in transforming an already innovative space into a hotbed of knowledge generation, circulation, recombination and learning. It must be recognized, however, that it was not Silicon Valley's innovation system alone that drove these outcomes. As illustrated and discussed throughout the remainder of this chapter, this stands as an important lesson for modern policy-makers.

With its innovative nexus firmly established, Silicon Valley was primed for the double movement of specialization and diversification that would mark the software era of production and innovation. Regarding the former, the unbridled success of the Traitorous Eight and their spinoffs allowed hardware production in the valley to grow their markets, reap economies of scale, and continue to generate targeted innovation in an in-demand industry.[13] In doing so, the region became today's spatially interconnected powerhouse of computer technology design and manufacturing. Regarding the latter, the injection of software engineering and entrepreneurial talent that characterized the transition to the Valley's software era further enabled a recombination of technological capabilities that spurred the evolution and growth of the region's computer design and manufacturing industry.

With these increases in the specialization and diversity of production, the geography of innovation in the Valley made its first movements towards galvanization and consolidation. Still enabled by the scaffolding of proximities, institutions, and the region's innovation system (which as this point included venture capital firms), the generation of positive externalities created an environment of directed R&D and knowledge recombination (i.e., Jacobs externalities) as well as learning-by-doing (i.e., Marshallian externalities). As evidenced by the corporate geography displayed in figure 13.1, the geography of innovation associated with the increased specialization and diversity of the software era demonstrates a dense clustering of industrial activity around the established innovative spaces of the hardware era. As per the original theorizations of Jacobs and Marshall, the prescribed benefits associated with increases in industrial specialization and diversity depend *fundamentally* on such geographical concentration.

The consolidation of Silicon Valley's geography of innovation cannot be better evidenced than by the intense clustering demonstrated by the new industrial actors of the platform era. Displayed again in figure 13.1, the co-location of the most recent wave of new innovators within a few city blocks indicates the necessity of proximity that governs innovation within and between these firms. Disincentivized by the famously high rental prices in San Francisco, the co-location of these firms in one of the world's most expensive cities demonstrates the degree to which these firms depend on geographical proximity to stimulate innovation. Still benefitting from the Valley's regional innovation system and its high levels of technological specialization and diversity, it seems apparent that the innovating firms of the platform era are now trying to harness the power of geographical proximity to help (re)produce the necessary social proximities and common informal institutions that first seeded the innovative potential of Silicon Valley. In doing so, these firms are recreating the conditions necessary to perpetuate a territorial nexus of innovative spaces that will help to propel San Francisco and the Valley into the next phase of technological dominance.

DISCUSSION II: THE ROLE OF POLICY

Cities become "smart" because their people do. The IESE Cities in Motion Index (2019) consistently ranks London and New York City as the smartest cities in the world, not because they have the newest infrastructure and the best data integration into government-decision making (they don't), but because they have the highest accumulation of human capital. Glaeser (2019) says, "Rise in returns to skill, a rise in returns to innovation, a rise in returns to being smart. And at our heart we are a social species that gets smart by being around other smart people." What does this mean for policy-makers?

Enrico Moretti's *The New Geography of Jobs* (2012) proves that, accelerated by high economic multiplier effects of high-paying jobs in the technology industry, innovative jobs are clustering in a handful of regions across the country. His unit of analysis in the metropolitan statistical area (MSA), more commonly known as the region. Likewise, industrial policy-makers have historically focused on supporting business development and job growth, regardless of geographic location within a region. We believe this thinking is outdated because it does not consider the changing nature of space. As a result, we believe that it is no surprise that industrial policy, especially around innovative industries, has a poor track record of accomplishing its stated objectives (Brown et al. 2016).

By studying the geography of innovation and applying it to a case study of Silicon Valley, it becomes apparent that innovative milieux are becoming geographically denser. As noted above, the neighbourhood has taken on a new role of importance that was once held by the region. During the processor era, it was simple enough to be located somewhere in the Valley, with most choosing nearby Stanford Research Park. The sprawl of the region was still close enough to share the spillover benefits of proximities and institutions – university resources, suppliers, customers, and technological spillovers. Moving into the software era, in relatively similar organization structures, companies began placing all of their workers together in large-scale facilities, geographically north of San Jose in Silicon Valley, that could stimulate knowledge and idea sharing within a firm. These firms then fiercely competed against each other while ideas spilled over between firms – akin to the IS approach. Finally, in the platform era, firms and their employees need to be in as close contact with each other as possible to facilitate communication, ideation, and cross-germination. All firms in the platform economy are now merely blocks away from each other in San Francisco – externalities are now what matters most. What is clear is that companies in each era manipulated space to increase their competitive advantage by enhancing knowledge flows between individuals.

At the same time, urban planners have long advocated for place-making investments to attract new residents – from "new urbanism" starting in the 1970s to "landscape architecture" in the 2010s. Municipal policy-makers have obliged: building new museums and cultural centres, tearing down abandoned homes and factories, redoing streetscapes to make room for trees and bicycle lanes, subsidizing sports stadiums and recreational activities, and offering tax abatements to turn dilapidated warehouses into new-age condominiums. To build these investments, cities use tactics to unlock eminent domains, open up federal subsidies, and create new taxation paradigms (Gordon

2004; Mallach and Vey 2011; Coates and Humphreys 2014). However, these investments are rarely part of any grander strategy other than to eliminate blight and/or increase long-run property tax revenue. As Moretti (2012) points out, such place-making investments have a mixed track record, at best, of starting new innovative clusters and creating long-term growth, calling these investments "necessary, but insufficient." Though he offers his own policy prescriptions, we believe he is missing a different piece of the puzzle: the place.

The missing puzzle piece is simple: the co-location of where cities make their industrial policy investments *and* cities make their place-making investments. We speculate that the successful cases of place-making investments leading to innovative job creation are spatially in proximity to where new jobs are being created, allowing for the flow of tacit knowledge through informal exchanges. In response, place-making and industrial policy ought to be jointly focused on creating spaces where innovation is most likely to occur, creating places where human capital can densify. Therefore, cities ought to be strategically investing where the built form is already designed for density to accrue: often distressed downtowns, university neighbourhoods, and other low-income urban communities.

The traditional approach to industrial policy is to allow mega-projects to be built on green fields or grey sites on the urban fringe; mirroring the IS approach in the software era. This creates exclusive enclaves (e.g., Apple Park in Cupertino) that capture and internalize knowledge accumulation inside a company. By focusing industrial policy on urban place-making in distressed neighbourhoods, knowledge spillover benefits through physical and social proximity can spread to the surrounding community (Balland et al. 2015; Broekel 2015; Bouba-Olga et al. 2015) and can benefit a wider – and perhaps disadvantaged – population. Even if knowledge does not, low-income populations will have easier access to the service jobs within the area, no longer excluded by the long, expensive commutes to distant suburbs. Policy-makers need to embrace this new reality of spatial proximity when considering giving subsidies to public firms in order to make their cities "smart" in more efficiently and equitably. To accomplish this, the Project for Public Spaces (2017) identified four key attributes:

1   They are accessible and well connected to other important places in the area.

2   They are comfortable and project a good image.
3   They attract people to participate in activities there.
4   They are sociable environments in which people want to gather and visit again and again.

CONCLUSION

Mayors want jobs of the future, so they use "smart cities" as a buzz-word for accumulation of human capital that creates jobs. By examining three approaches to innovation – proximities and institutions, innovation systems, and externalities – in the context of Silicon Valley's transformation from processors to software to platforms, it becomes apparent that the nature of space is changing accordingly. As a result, traditional regional industrial policy has lost its effectiveness as the economic geography of innovation has changed with it; externalities through proximity matter more than ever. We argue that to make industrial policy-making more effective and equitable, it must be paired with effective place-making strategies in order to match the externality approach of innovation that has taken hold. Not only will this allow local knowledge transfers, it will also allow for the improvement of distressed neighbourhoods and the livelihoods of their residents. This innovation in strategy is necessary because, in this era of Schumpeterian capitalism, there is no other choice; cities, like the innovative firms they wish to be home to, must continuously innovate or disappear into obsolescence.

NOTES

1   In their use of the term "ubiquitization," Maskell and Malmberg (1999) were not advancing the flat world hypothesis. On the contrary, they used this term to help explain the importance of knowledge and learning in a post-Fordist economy.
2   This aligns with/is derived from the assumptions of neoclassical growth theory.
3   While exceptions have been observed (see Bathelt et al., 2004), this is often possible only after extended periods of face-to-face interaction have taken place.
4   The idea that social interactions and networks constitute social institutions.

5 For a more exhaustive discussion of this concept, the literature of "communities of practice" is a helpful starting point.

6 Martin and Simmie (2008) also point out that the presence of Porterian clusters within RSIS are important for understanding the system-level dynamics.

7 It should be remembered that the IS approach relies heavily on the work of the institutions and proximities approach to inform its assumptions. Therefore, while the IS approach may be absolutist in its spatial orientation, the framework and its proponents are not ignorant about the constructivist view of space and its importance for explaining the building blocks of innovation.

8 The externalities approach is sometimes referred to as the "production function" approach due the tendency for adherents to employ complicated econometric models with the aim of measuring the specific impact of different socio-industrial variables on the capacity of regions to "produce" innovation (Feldman 2000).

9 This idea is now referred to as "Marshall-Arrow-Romer" externalities.

10 Such a reification of space and geography can be similarly seen in the popular cluster literature based on the work of Michael Porter and his competitive diamond, although Porter makes strides to theorize the basis of these interactions at the level of the firm.

11 While Elwell and Litton Sr both received an education in electrical engineering at Stanford, it is unclear whether Eitel and McCullough shared this education. It is well documented, however, that they had earlier worked alongside Litton Sr on vacuum tube–related projects prior to Litton Sr leaving the radio manufacturer Heintz and Kaufman to found his own company in 1932.

12 Terman received both his bachelor's and his master's from Stanford.

13 In addition to their competitive market position, many of the Valley's hardware firms were further bolstered by securing procurement and R&D contracts from the US military.

REFERENCES

Acs, Z. 2002. *Innovation and the Growth of Cities.* Cheltenham, UK: Edward Elgar Publishing.

Adams, S.B. 2011. "Growing Where You Are Planted: Exogenous Firms and the Seeding of Silicon Valley." *Research Policy* 40: 368–79.

– 2017. "Arc of Empire: The Federal Telegraph Company, the U.S. Navy, and the Beginnings of Silicon Valley." *Business History Review* 91: 329–59.

Arrow, K.J. 1962. "The Economic Implications of Learning by Doing." *Review of Economic Studies* 29: 155–73.

Asheim, B., M. Grillitsch, and M. Trippl. 2016. "Regional Innovation Systems: Past, Present, Future." In *Handbook on the Geographies of Innovation*, edited by R. Shearmur, C. Carrincazeaux, and D. Doloreux, 45–62. Cheltenham, UK: Edward Elgar Publishing.

Audretsch, D.B. 2003. "Innovation and Spatial Externalities." *International Regional Science* Review 26, no. 2: 167–74.

Balland, P.-A., R. Boschma, and K. Frenken. 2015. "Proximity and Innovation: From Statics to Dynamics." *Regional Studies,* 49, no. 6: 907–20.

Bathelt, H., A. Malmberg, and P. Maskell. 2004. "Clusters and Knowledge: Local Buzz, Global Pipelines and the Process of Knowledge Creation." *Progress in Human Geography* 28, no. 1: 31–56.

Boschma, R. 2005. "Proximity and Innovation: A Critical Assessment." *Regional Studies* 39, no. 1: 61–74.

Bouba-Olga, O., C. Carrincazeaux, and M. Coris. 2015. "Proximity Dynamics, Social Networks and Innovation." *Regional Studies* 49, no. 6: 901–6.

Brock, D.C. 2012. "From Automation to Silicon Valley: The Automation Movement of the 1950s, Arnold Beckman, and William Shockley." *History and Technology* 28, no. 4: 375–401.

Broekel, T. 2015. "The Co-evolution of Proximities: A Network Level Study." *Regional Studies* 49, no. 6: 921–35.

Brown, M. 2016. "The Making of Airbnb." *Boston Hospitality Review* 4, no. 1: 1–9.

Brown, R., G. Gregson, and C. Mason. 2016. "A Post-mortem of Regional Innovation Policy Failure: Scotland's Intermediate Technology Initiative (ITI)." *Regional Studies* 50, no. 7: 1,260–72.

Cairncross, F. 1997. *The Death of Distance: How the Communications Revolution Is Changing Our Lives.* Cambridge, MA: Harvard Business School Press.

Cheyre, C., J. Kowalski, J., and F.M. Veloso. 2015. "Spinoffs and the Ascension of Silicon Valley." *Industrial and Corporate Change* 24, no. 4: 837–58.

Christensen, C.M., R. McDonald, and E.J. Altman. 2018. "Disruptive Innovation: An Intellectual History and Directions for Future Research." *Journal of Management Studies* 55, no. 7: 1,043–78.

Coates, D., and B. Humphreys. 2014. "Professional Sports Facilities, Franchises and Urban Economic Development." UMBC Economics Department Working Paper 03-103.

Dietrich-Ward, A. 2017. *Beyond Rust: Metropolitan Pittsburgh and the Fate of Industrial America.* Philadelphia: Penn.

Ejermo, O. 2005. "Technological Diversity and Jacobs' Externality Hypothesis Revisited." *Growth and Change* 36, no. 2: 167–95.

Engel, J.S. 2015. "Global Clusters of Innovation: Lesson from Silicon Valley." *California Management Review* 57, no. 2: 36–65.

Farrell, M., and E. Brown. 2019. "Uber IPO Filing Shows Growth Leveling Off." *Wall Street Journal*, 12 April. https://www.wsj.com/articles/uber-discloses-ipo-filing-11555015305.

Feldman, M.P. 2000. "Location and Innovation: The New Economic Geography of Innovation, Spillovers, and Agglomeration." In *The Oxford Handbook of Economic Geography*, edited by G.L. Clark, M.P. Feldman, and M.S. Gertler, 5–25. Oxford: Oxford University Press.

Feldman M.P., and D. Audretsch. 1999. "Innovation in Cities: Science-Based Diversity, Specialisation and Localised Competition." *European Economic Review* 43: 409–29.

Ferrary, M., and M. Granovetter. 2009. "The Role of Venture Capital Firms in Silicon Valley's Complex Innovation Network." *Economics and Society* 38, no. 2: 326–59.

Friedman, T. 2005. *The World Is Flat: A Brief History of the Twenty-First Century.* New York: Farrar, Straus, and Giroux.

Gallagher, L. 2017. "Airbnb's Surprising Path to Y Combinator." *Wired*, 21 February. https://www.wired.com/2017/02/airbnbs-surprising-path-to-y-combinator/.

Gertler, M.S. 2003. "Tacit Knowledge and the Economic Geography of Context, or the Undefinable Tacitness of Being (There)." *Journal of Economic Geography* 3: 75–99.

Gilly, J., and A. Torre. 2000. "Proximity Relations: Elements for an Analytical Framework." In *Industrial Networks and Proximity*, edited by M.B. Green and R.B. McNaughton, 1–17. Aldershot, UK: Ashgate Publishing.

Glaeser, E. 2019. "Edward Glaeser: Should We All Be Living in Cities?" *Harvard Magazine*, 30 September. https://www.harvardmagazine.com/2019/podcast/edward-glaeser.

Glaeser, E., H.D. Kallal, and J.A. Sheinkman. 1992. "Growth in Cities." *Journal of Political Economy* 100: 1,126–52.

Goldberger, P. 2013. "Exclusive Preview: Google's New Built-from-Scratch Googleplex." *Vanity Fair*, 22 February. https://www.vanityfair.com/news/tech/2013/02/exclusive-preview-googleplex.

Google. 2019. "From the Garage to the Googleplex." https://about.google/our-story.

Gordon, C. 2004. "Blighting the Way: Urban Renewal, Economic Development, and the Elusive Definition of Blight." *Fordham Urban Law Journal* 31, no. 2: 305–37.

Henton, D., and K. Held. 2013. "The Dynamics of Silicon Valley: Creative Destruction and the Evolution of the Innovation Habitat." *Social Science Information* 52, no. 4: 539–57.

Hoffman, C. 2008. "The Battle for Facebook." *Rolling Stone*, 26 June. https://www.rollingstone.com/culture/culture-news/the-battle-for-facebook-242989.

Howells, J.R. 2002. "Tacit Knowledge, Innovation and Economic Geography." *Urban Studies* 39, nos. 5–6: 871–84.

Iammarino, S. 2005. "An Evolutionary Integrated View of Regional Systems of Innovation: Concepts, Measures, and Historical Perspectives." *European Planning Studies* 13, no. 4: 497–519.

IESE. 2019. "Cities in Motion Index 2019." https://blog.iese.edu/cities-challenges-and-management/2019/05/10/iese-cities-in-motion-index-2019.

Jacobs, J. 1969. *The Economy of Cities.* New York: Random House.

Klepper, S. 2010. "The Origin and Growth of Industry Clusters: The Making of Silicon Valley and Detroit." *Journal of Urban Economics* 67: 15–32.

Krugman, P. 1991. "Increasing Returns and Economic Geography." *Journal of Political Economy* 99: 483–99.

Mallach, A., and J. Vey. 2011. "Recapturing Land for Economic and Fiscal Growth." Brookings-Rockefeller, Project on State and Metropolitan Innovation, May 2011.

Mann, M. 1986. "Societies as Organized Power Networks." In *The Sources of Social Power.* Vol. 1, *A History of Power from the Beginning to AD 1760*, edited by M. Mann, 1–33. Cambridge: Cambridge University Press.

Martin, R., and J. Simmie. 2008. "Path Dependence and Local Innovation Systems in City-Regions." *Innovation: Management, Policy and Practice* 10: 183–96.

Maskell, P., and A. Malmberg. 1999. "Localised Learning and Industrial Competitiveness." *Cambridge Journal of Economics* 23, no. 1: 167–85.

Moretti, E. 2012. *The New Geography of Jobs.* Boston: Houghton Mifflin Harcourt.

Morgan Stanley. 1980. "Apple Computer, Inc. Common Stock Prospectus." Retrieved 20 August 2019. http://www.swtpcemu.com/mholley/Apple/Apple_IPO.pdf.

Nelson, R.R., and S.G. Winter. 1982. "Forces Generating and Limiting Concentration under Schumpeterian Competition." In *An Evolutionary Theory of Economic Change*, edited by R.R. Nelson and S. Winter, 308–28. Cambridge, MA: Harvard University Press.

O'Brien, R. 1992. *Global Financial Integration: The End of Geography*. London: Royal Institute of International Affairs.

Oliveira, A.D. 2016. "The Human Smart Cities Manifesto: A Global Perspective." In *Human Smart Cities*, edited by G. Concilio, and F. Rizzo, 197–202. London: Springer International Publishing.

Pique, J.M., J. Berbegal-Mirabent, and H. Etzkowitz. 2018. "Triple Helix and the Evolution of Ecosystems of Innovation: The Case of Silicon Valley." *Triple Helix* 5, no. 11: 1–21.

Polanyi, M. 1958. *Personal Knowledge: Towards a Post-Critical Philosophy*. Chicago: University of Chicago Press.

Project for Public Spaces. 2017. "What Makes a Successful Place?" https://www.pps.org/article/grplacefeat.

Rodriguez-Pose, A., and R. Crescenzi. 2008. "Mountains in a Flat World: Why Proximity Still Matters for the Location of Economic Activity." *Cambridge Journal of Regions, Economy, and Society* 1: 371–88.

Romer, P. 1986. "Increasing Returns and Long-Run Growth." *Journal of Political Economy* 94: 1,002–37.

Sardana, G.D. 2016. "Innovation and Growth." *South Asian Journal of Business and Management Cases* 5, no. 1: vii–xi.

Saxenian, A. 1996. *Regional Advantage: Culture and Competition in Silicon Valley and Route 128*. Boston, MA: Harvard University Press.

Scott, A.J. 2007. "Capitalism and Urbanization in a New Key? The Cognitive-Cultural Dimension." *Social Forces* 85, no. 4: 1,465–82.

Scott, J.C. 1994. *Seeing like a State: How Certain Schemes to Improve the Human Condition Have Failed*. New Haven, CT: Yale University Press.

Silve, F., and A. Plekhanov. 2018. "Institutions, Innovation and Growth: Evidence from Industry Data." *Economics of Transition* 26, no. 3: 335–62.

Simmie, J. 2005. "Innovation and Space: A Critical Review of the Literature." *Regional Studies* 39, no. 6: 789–804.

Simonson, S. 2005. "Apple Gobbles Up Cupertino Office Space." *Silicon Valley Business Journal*, 2 October. https://www.bizjournals.com/sanjose/stories/2005/10/03/story4.html.

Smith, N. 1984. *Uneven Development: Nature, Capital, and the Production of Space*. Athens: University of Georgia Press.

Storper, M., T. Kemeny, and N. Makarem. 2015. *The Rise and Fall of Urban Economies: Lessons from San Francisco and Los Angeles.* Stanford, CA: Stanford University Press.

Storper, M., and A.J. Venables. 2004. "Buzz: Face-to-Face Contact and the Urban Economy." *Journal of Economic Geography* 4, no. 4: 351–70.

Vanhemert, K. 2013. "Look Inside Apple's Spaceship Headquarters with 24 All-New Renderings." *Wired*, 11 November. https://www.wired.com/2013/11/a-glimpse-into-apples-crazy-new-spaceship-headquarters/.

Wladawsky-Berger, I. 2016. "The Rise of the Platform Economy." *Wall Street Journal*, 12 February. https://blogs.wsj.com/cio/2016/02/12/the-rise-of-the-platform-economy.

Williams, G., and R. Moore. 1984. "The Apple Story. Part I: Early History." *Byte Magazine*, December. https://archive.org/stream/byte-magazine-1984-12/1984_12_BYTE_09-13_Communications#page/n461/mode/2up.

Williams, J.C. 1998. "Frederick E. Terman and the Rise of Silicon Valley." *International Journal of Technology Management* 16, no. 8: 751–60.

Wolfe, D.A. 2014. *Innovating in Urban Economies: Economic Transformation in Canadian City Regions.* Toronto: University of Toronto Press.

Y Combinator. 2019. "Top Companies List: 2018." https://www.ycombinator.com/topcompanies.

14

Conclusion

Zachary Spicer and Austin Zwick

Throughout 2020, our lives were consumed by the COVID-19 pandemic. Urban areas around the world felt the effects of the virus deeply. Density and the close interaction of work and play were initially pinned as key culprits for the more rapid spread in cities. While the virus disproportionately affected urban over rural municipalities, it also disproportionately affected certain groups within urban areas: racialized and poor communities who did not have the luxury of being able to practise social distancing while maintaining their livelihoods and community bonds. Those in precarious work found themselves more exposed to the virus than those able to work comfortably from home and maintain distance from others. In the process, our relationship with the platform economy changed – platform services became an essential lifeline for many families to safely get food and supplies, while platform operators were left potentially exposed to the virus daily. Those who could not access these digital spaces were even more disadvantaged. The inequities of the platform economy have never been so clear.

Similarly, government marshalled all available resources to keep the public safe, including the deployment of new technology – much of this smart city technology used for mapping and tracking individuals. New apps emerged to self-assess for COVID symptoms, track and maintain social distance between individuals and monitor compliance with local by-laws began to quickly emerge. For instance, the small town of Orangeville, Ontario, used an AI-enabled video application to alert staff when the number of residents in a particular park exceeded the locally imposed limit (Halliday 2020). Similar technology was deployed rapidly, with the intended purpose of easily enforcing local by-laws on social distancing, but little forethought was given to the types of people who would be disproportionately punished through this tool: lower-income groups who live in housing without backyards. The wealthy, of course, continue to use their large private outdoor spaces, while the poor are quietly detoured out of shared public outdoor spaces. This is just one example, but it highlights the need to thoroughly consider the social consequences of smart city technology.

This volume delved into the developing relationship between evolving technology and the city. The COVID-19 outbreak confirmed that this technology is now omnipresent in our cities, deployed widely and intersecting our lives in important and critical ways. Beyond just delivering food and ferrying people around the city, platforms mediate our relationships with others, regulate labour conditions, and create societal boundaries. The density of tech firms has increased, as new start-ups compete with scale-ups and global platform behemoths like Uber and Airbnb. As firms big and small spread their reach, smart city technology has been slowly permeating the urban landscape, creating not just cities with new platforms but also smarter cities. As the COVID-19 crisis revealed, technology's role in facilitating our relationships with each other, our communities, and our government is becoming increasingly central to contemporary life.

The authors in this book covered important terrain: labour precarity, mobility, regulatory policy, privatization, affordability, power, data governance, privacy, job creation, and the excesses of capitalism. It is clear throughout this work that the platform economy is ubiquitous, and because of the reach and density of platforms that surround us, we ignore them at our peril. Platforms not only warrant continuous study from an academic perspective, but present complex policy problems for urban decision-makers as the economic and societal consequences of unfettered platform capitalism rapidly mount. This final chapter explores the transition of the platform economy into the smart city, asking what it means not only for our lives, but also for urban policy and governance of cities and regions.

FROM THE PLATFORM ECONOMY TO THE SMART CITY

The organization of this volume is deliberate. We present our authors' work in three sections: Managing Platforms (chapters 2–5), Governing Platforms (chapters 6–9), and Cities as Platforms (chapters 10–13).

This organization mirrors the rapid transition that we have seen over the past decade, as platforms morphed from an emerging feature of urban economies, to disruptors of industries and labour markets, and finally to the hard infrastructure and social architecture of our cities themselves. How did we get to this point?

The platform economy was presented initially as innovative and novel. Platforms offered exciting new options to connect with others and form new social bonds. Many marvelled at our newfound ability to find a home to stay while traveling in foreign countries; others revelled in lower-cost options to travel around the city. These potential efficiency gains prompted some to urge restraint from policy-makers. As Brail demonstrates in chapter 6, these firms entered a "legal grey zone," where they did not look or act like a traditional firm, but were similar enough to draw the ire of those in established industries, such as taxi drivers. Profits for investors and convenience for consumers were enough to create quick acceptance of firms such as Uber and Airbnb, but soon questions emerged about who was really profiting from the platform economy (Kenney and Zysman 2016).

A series of these questions were asked about the relationships between the operators and the platform. As Grisdale demonstrates in chapter 2, many platform firms feigned communitarian values, wrapping themselves in the notion of the community. In reality, however, these firms embraced neoliberal values and began to siphon money from the communities they purported to serve to off-share tax havens. Despite empowering many individuals to earn extra money, Grisdale argues, these firms actually devolved risk and responsibility to those same communities, absolving themselves of any responsibility.

Serious questions also emerged about those using platform services. At first, consumers were attracted to platform businesses and their generally lower costs than traditional businesses. Firms attributed the lower costs of their services to their technology, but subsidies from mountains of venture capital were, in reality, the real cause (Dean 2019). Further, in chapter 4 Young and Farber argue that many low-income individuals are prevented from accessing platform services because the technology that guides the platforms is simply out of economic reach for them.

Further questions followed about the health of the platform firms themselves. As Woudsma demonstrates in chapter 5, the evolving desire for certain on-demand goods is not strong enough to support the business model of many "sharing" economy firms. Although he looks specifically at goods movement, Woudsma's argument that challenges in labour, security, and services undermine the viability of the business model of platform delivery services can be seen in a number of sectors – namely food delivery, where platform firms struggle to find a sustainable business model amidst a changing urban economic landscape.

With increased scrutiny of the benefits of the platform economy, governments began to step in with regulatory regimes once the uneven nature of the platform economy began to reveal itself. As Brail describes in chapter 6, the regulatory process was slow, but it included a significant amount of policy learning from other jurisdictions, as regulators tested new policy approaches. Regulatory approaches were confronted with unique institutional and market design features, as Donald, Sage, and Moroz detailed in Kingston, in chapter 7.

It is not just city services, but also governance functions and social relations that are increasingly pulled from the physical realm into the digital (Grech 2015). These digital and physical elements intersect, but with the increased use of smart city technology, we are inviting digital elements of city life into our personal lives at an alarming rate. Combined with these elements are a host of glaring data governance concerns (see Stucke 2018; Batty 2013; Ruppert et al. 2017) and it is clear the platformization of the urban space poses real governance challenges for local governments and urban residents alike. Spicer and Zwick argue the same in chapter 12, highlighting the inability of smart city projects, such as the Quayside project in Toronto, to solve challenges with social inequities. In fact, they argue that smart city projects will likely exacerbate them, compounding a host of other data governance and privacy challenges. However, as Robinson and Biggar demonstrate in chapter 11, the government can and likely should play a greater role in the creation and motivation of smart city projects that are designed with public benefit in mind.

Regulation was too slow to emerge in some sectors, as the platform economy permeated urban life, manifesting in more insidious forms of development. In chapter 3, Wolf details much of the malignancy that platform firms brought into urban life. Technologically mediated work splintered urban labour markets, with insidious forms of control, such as "gamification" forcing contractors to work longer and for less pay. Other research has shown that platforms increase precarious labour (Zwick and Spicer 2018; Theodore and Peck 2013), compromises safety standards (Zwick 2017), and facilitates service discrimination by race (Schor and Attwood-Charles 2017; Leong and

Belzer 2016; Edelman et al. 2017). The transactions between consumers, contractors, and platforms are not entirely fair. The exchange of labour or resources or material for money is not entered into equally. The platform economy, we slowly learned, was fundamentally weighted in favour of platform firms – consumers, contractors, transportation markets, and government all lost ground to private tech firms.

Why did policy-makers embrace technology then? Several factors have brought us to this point. Chief among them is the desire of politicians and policy-makers to bring the jobs of the future to their home communities. If you believe that technological progress is inevitable, cities need to get their cut of the pie before they are left out. As Stewart, Zwick, and Dundon discuss in chapter 13, innovative industries are at the forefront of contemporary industrial policy. However, benefits and consequences are not always what they are cut out to be, and such public investments may not be successful, while others may not be spatially located where policy-makers want them. They advocate for a closer alignment between public investment and urban planning to promote equity and help distressed neighbourhoods.

Furthermore, mayors understood that publicly supporting the integration of technology into urban life is a form of signalling that the city is a truly global city and open for business. But the opposite also holds true, for no city wants to be seen as a Luddite or hostile to entrepreneurship (Spicer et al. 2019). This is a type of long-standing local boosterism that views gains in the local economy as inherently good for the community (Boorstin 1965; Logan and Molotch 1987). It also draws on a natural competitive instinct, which often pits cities and regions against each other (Asworth and Voogd 1990; Gold and Ward 1994). The same platform actors that upended urban economies have now set their sights on doing the same to urban space and governance. As discussed by Robinson and Biggar in chapter 11, the city is now widely regarded as a platform in and unto itself, with smart cities and smart city technology becoming ubiquitous in more urban centres (see Bollier 2016; Goldsmith and Kleinman 2017).

Accompanying the desire for economic growth is a belief of many urban policy-makers that technology and innovation are inherently good – a kind of technological utopianism that views new and unique uses of technology as valuable in and of themselves, without casting a critical eye to potential social or economic consequences (Segal 2005). These narratives focus on the possibility that technology will unlock human potential or economic gain, focusing on the transformation of the material environment of human existence and of human nature itself (Dickel and Schrape 2017). This thinking views the efficiency gains promoted by platforms by advocating the commercial value in underused assets (cars, homes, etc.) as serving the greater social good without negative consequences (Kenny and Zysman 2016). As criticized throughout this volume, this is dangerous thinking.

If you walk away, feeling that the smart city is still a nebulous concept, you are not alone. In chapter 10, Hartt, Zwick, and Webb attempt to grasp this purposefully vague term by surveying the criticisms directed at them in the academic literature. Smart cities are not inherently good or bad, but fall between what they call "utopian optimism and dystopian servitude"; different models of potential technology governance – drawing from the platform economy to apply to autonomous vehicles – are weighed by Zwick and Dundon in chapter 12.

The editors of this volume argue that it is, therefore, increasingly important to gain a greater understanding of individual projects and processes. Overall, we implore readers to keep in mind that it is citizens who make a city "smart," that it is ultimately in their interest that we harness technology. As we started off in the introduction, we conclude the same way: a citizen-centred smart city ought to be the real goal.

CHARTING A NEW PATH: WHERE DO WE GO FROM HERE?

The density of platforms has scaled the concept of platforms in everyday life. Smart cities and their associated technology now envelop large swaths of urban terrain. Sensors are now commonplace in the urban core of nearly every city in North America, making data the new currency of urban governance. Municipalities now have more information than ever available about how people use and move about their city. Private vendors of this technology now have access to the same data. Technology permeates the urban landscape in dozens of cities around the world.

The city is now very much also a platform. Platforms are conceived as open and accessible – as many advocates had long hoped (Bollier 2016). Platforms should encourage co-creation, where democracy is more accessible, individuals take ownership of the space and collaborate to improve their communities (Bollier 2016). This promise has not materialized in large-scale, internationally recognized smart city projects, which place the platform firmly at the centre of community life (see Shwayri 2013; Ko et al. 2011; Cugurullo 2013). Without meaningful policy intervention, we risk the hollowing out of cities, just as platforms have done to vast swaths of our economy.

Platforms individualize and compartmentalize our lives. The platform experience is generally conceptualized as one-to-one transactions between individuals are mediated by the platform, whether they are rides, accommodation, or even social interaction. It is this feature of the platform economy that creates the mentality of favouring a solo trip in a ride-hailing vehicle rather than taking a bus or subway with others, or eating at home by ourselves with a meal delivered by Uber Eats rather than enjoying time at a restaurant with others.

Discourse about platforms tends to avoid the tensions between the growing number of public acts now taken into the private realm. The transactional nature of the platform economy privileges efficiency (Goodman and Powles 2019). The platform is seen as inherently good and well-intentioned, even beautiful in its simplicity – it wants nothing more than to provide a ride, or food, or create a relationships, while also providing labour and value. The quantity of these transactions is often valued above the quality, in that, for instance, the number of connections on a platform is more meaningful than quality of the connection. Once the transaction is complete, the connection ends and the cycle begins anew. The speed of the transaction often reduces the time between impulse and consumption (Greenfield 2017), with the human element lost along the way.

The nature of these transactions devalues the role of the public in urban governance, meaning we tend to avoid the tensions between the public and private interests by focusing on the efficiency of the platform (Goodman and Powles 2019). Platforms are not inherently bad – the efficiency gains inherent in platform life cannot be dismissed, but without meaningfully dissecting the effect private platforms have on public interests, values, and institutions, we are turning a blind eye to the potentially damaging by-products of unchecked techno-capitalism. As Van Dijck, Poell, and De Wall (2018, 23) argue, the interests of the platform become the public interest, at least in the mind of platform architects: "In the platform society, the creation of public value toward the common good is often confused with the creation of economic value serving a nondescript amalgam of private and public interests." Platforms unchecked will not produce social good, for that is the role of government. Here is a key lesson for policy-makers and the central message running throughout this volume: recognize the value of and distinction between public good and private efficiency, and govern accordingly.

Regulators were caught off-guard by platform firms. As numerous authors in this volume describe (see Brail; Donald, Sage, and Moroz; Spicer; Wolf; Grisdale), regulators failed to distinguish between the good of the platform and the good of the public, seeing both as intertwined. Innovation, as we are told, is inherently good. Platform firms, therefore, were simply using technology to improve traditional services, squeezing efficiency gains from app-based computing. What was the problem? If we accept this premise, we regulate more promiscuously, allowing platform firms to take liberties with regulatory structures out of a fear that any evenly applied regulation would stifle the creativity and efficiency of firms and producers. Along the way, regulators lost sight of their role in protecting the public, labour markets, and local economies.

The regulators' dilemma when approaching technology is to create a balanced marketplace, where platform firms are responsible citizens, held to account, and properly taxed and regulated with clear policy goals that serve the public interest. There should be no special treatment for innovative firms, but at the same time, nor should they be singled out by regulatory overreach or punitive taxation. How to maximize the benefits, minimize the costs, and to ensure an equitable distribution of both is – and has always been – the of role of urban policy and governance; from the platform economy to the smart city, there are no exceptions.

FINAL THOUGHTS

We reached out to some of the most active and prominent thinkers on the platform economy and the smart city and asked them to contribute to a volume critically examining their connection. The authors took their task seriously and delved deeply into pressing issues in the platform age. A number of points became clear throughout this work. The first is that unchecked platformism has profound consequences for urban economies and urban populations. In this volume, a number of authors highlighted the potential damage, ranging from the hollowing out to local labour markets, inequities in platform access for certain users, unequal gains for certain cities and populations, and abuse of contractors. COVID-19 exasperated many of these challenges and reinforced the need to reconsider the inequity inherent in unchecked platformism.

Despite the clear consequences of providing platform firms with unfettered access to urban economies, regulators – much like many of us at the time – conflated private value with public value and missed an early opportunity to regulate the platform economy in the public interest. Once the regulatory field had tilted towards platform firms, it was difficult to move it back; the industry saw slight changes as major concessions, as regulatory leeway became baked into the platform economy (Young 2019).

Over time, platform firms gave way to platform cities, as smart cities came to be constructed on the same value set: data-intensive undertakings that privatize swaths of the public realm. The platform city individualized transactions, creating connections between users and the platform, rather than with peers. A devaluation of community occurred in lockstep, as weak oversight created weakened data governance measures, virtually assuring private gain of public interests. The transition to the smart city has been abrupt, but we risk making the same mistakes again that we made with the platform economy. We are again missing an opportunity for early regulatory victories to ensure public interests dominate smart city construction. Toronto's Quayside project is just one example: we are at the precipice of major governance reforms in the life of the smart city. The regulatory and governance regime put in place in Toronto will be replicated elsewhere. The pressure is on to find the right model – one that emphasizes public benefit, while allowing a culture of innovation to flourish.

As governments transition from the platform economy to the smart city, what kind of city will we choose?

REFERENCES

Asworth, G.J., and H. Voogd. 1990. *Selling the City: Marketing Approaches in Public Sector Urban Planning*. London: Bellhaven.

Batty, M. 2013. "Big Data, Smart Cities and City Planning." *Dialogues in Human Geography* 3, no. 3: 274–9.

Bollier, D. 2016. *The City as Platform: How Digital Networks Are Changing Urban Life and Governance*. Washington, DC: Aspen Institute.

Boorstin, D. 1965. *The Americans: The National Experience*. New York: Random House.

Cugurullo, F. 2013. "How to Build a Sandcastle: An Analysis of the Genesis and Development of Masdar City." *Journal of Urban Technology* 20, no. 1: 23–37.

Dean, S. 2019. "Uber Fares Are Cheap Thanks to Venture Capital. but Is That Free Ride Ending?" *Los Angeles Times*, 11 May.

Dickel, S., and J.-F. Schrape. 2017. "The Logic of Digital Utopianism." *Nanoethics* 11, no. 1: 47–58.

Edelman, B., M. Luca, and D. Svirsky. 2017. "Racial Discrimination in the Sharing Economy: Evidence from a Field Experiment." *American Economic Journal: Applied Economics* 9, no. 12: 1–22.

Gold, J.R.. and S.V. Ward. 1994. *Place Promotion: The Use of Publicity and Marketing to Sell Small Towns and Regions*. Chichester, UK: Wiley.

Goldsmith, S., and N. Kleinman. 2017. *A New City O/S: The Power of Open, Collaborative and Distributed Governance*. Washington, DC: Brookings Institution.

Goodman, E.P., and J. Powles. 2019. "Urbanism under Google: Lessons from Sidewalk Toronto." *Fordham Law Review* 88: 457–63.

Grech, Gerard. 2015. "Cities as Platforms." Tech Crunch, 7 August https://techcrunch.com/2015/08/07/cities-as-platforms.

Greenfield, A. 2017. *Radical Technologies: The Design of Everyday Life*. Brooklyn: Verso.

Halliday, Chris. 2020. "'We're Watching You': Orangeville Will Use Smart Cameras with AI to Monitor COVID-19 Crowds in Public Spaces." *Orangeville Banner*, 15 July.

Kenney, M., and J. Zysman. 2016. "The Rise of the Platform Economy." *Issues in Science and Technology* (Spring), 61–9.

Ko, Y., D.K. Schubert, and R.T. Hester. 2011. "A Conflict of Greens: Green Development Versus Habitat Preservation: The Case of Incheon, South Korea." *Environment* 53, no. 3: 3–17.

Leong, N., and A. Belzer. 2016. "The New Public Accommodations: Race Discrimination in the Platform Economy." *Georgetown Law Journal* 105: 1,271–87.

Logan, J.R., and H.L. Molotch. 1987. *Urban Fortunes: The Political Economy of Place*. Berkley: University of California Press.

Rupert, E., E. Isin, and D. Bigo. 2017. "Data Politics." *Big Data & Society* (July–December), 1–7.

Schor, J.B., and W. Attwood-Charles. 2017. "The 'Sharing' Economy: Labor, Inequality and Social Connection on for-Profit Platforms." *Sociology Compass* 11, no. 8: 1–16.

Segal, H.P. 2005. *Technological Utopianism in American Culture.*
  Syracuse, NY: Syracuse University Press.
Shwayri, S.T. 2013. "A Model Korean Ubiquitous Eco-City? The Politics
  of Making Songdo." *Journal of Urban Technology* 20, no. 1: 39–55.
Spicer, Z., G. Eidelman, and A. Zwick. 2019. "Patterns of Local Policy
  Disruption: Regulatory Responses to Uber in Ten North American
  Cities." *Review of Policy Research* 36, no. 2: 146–67.
Stucke, M.E. 2018. "Should We Be Concerned about Data-Opolies?"
  Georgetown Law Technology Review 2, no. 2: 275–324.
Theodore, N., and J. Peck. 2013. "Selling Flexibility: Temporary Staffing in
  a Volatile Economy." In *Temporary Work, Agencies and Unfree Labour,*
  edited by K. Strauss, 26–47. London: Routledge.
Van Dijck, J., T. Poell, and M. De Waal. 2018. *The Platform Society:
  Public Values in a Connective World.* Oxford: Oxford University Press.
Young, M. 2019. "Ride-Hailing's Impact on Canadian Cities: Now Let's
  Consider the Long Game." *Canadian Geographer* 63, no. 1: 171–5.
Zwick, A. 2017. "Welcome to the Gig Economy: Neoliberal Industrial
  Relations and the Case of Uber." *Geojournal* 83: 679–91.
Zwick, A., and Z. Spicer. 2018. "Good or Bad? Ridesharing's Impact
  on Canadian Cities." *Canadian Geographer* 62, no. 4: 430–6.

Contributors

KATE ALEXIS ABOGADO works as a tech-sector business consultant in New York City. She holds a BA in policy studies from Syracuse University. Her work centres on smart city strategies and real-world applications with specific focus on blockchain and AI.

JEFF BIGGAR is a planning professional and independent researcher. His research focuses on community planning and urban governance in Canadian cities. He was recently a part-time faculty member with the Department of Human Geography Program in City Studies at the University of Toronto Scarborough and a post-doctoral fellow at Ryerson University's School of Urban and Regional Planning. He holds a PhD in planning from the University of Toronto.

SHAUNA BRAIL is an associate professor at the Institute for Management & Innovation, University of Toronto Mississauga. Brail is a senior associate at the Innovation Policy Lab in the Munk School of Global Affairs & Public Policy and a faculty affiliate at the University of Toronto Transportation Research Institute and at the School of Cities. As an economic geographer and urban planner, her research focuses on the transformation of cities as a result of economic, social, and cultural change.

BETSY DONALD is a professor in the Department of Geography and Planning at Queen's University.

EAMONN DUNDON is a financial analyst in Boston. He has a bachelor's in policy studies from the Maxwell School of Public Affairs and

Citizenship, Syracuse University. He has conducted research on affordable housing policy in Hong Kong and worked on development projects for the Syracuse Housing Authority.

STEVEN FARBER is an associate professor in human geography at the University of Toronto Scarborough. His research focuses on the social and economic implications of transportation planning and travel behaviour.

SEAN GRISDALE is a PhD student in human geography at the University of Toronto. His research on the political economy of urban development focuses on how digital technologies and platforms are increasingly centred as solutions to problems of sustainability and affordable housing, particularly in post-industrial, global city contexts like Toronto. His most recent projects have considered the politics of short-term rental platforms and the "smart city" as expressions of the ongoing but shifting dynamics of urban planning and governance under capitalism.

MAXWELL HARTT is an assistant professor in the Department of Geography and Planning at Queen's University. He is a former Fulbright Scholar (Tufts University) and holds a PhD in planning from the University of Waterloo. His research focuses on the intersection of demographic change and planning policy, specifically shrinking cities and age-friendly communities.

ANNA MOROZ is a recent graduate of the master's program in geography at Queen's University.

PAMELA ROBINSON is a professor at the School of Urban and Regional Planning, Ryerson University (Toronto). She is also a registered professional urban planner in the province of Ontario. Throughout her career Pamela's research and practice have focused on complex, emergent challenges that Canadian communities face. Since 2010, Pamela has written a regular column for *Spacing Magazine*, where she writes about sustainability, technology, and civic engagement in Canadian cities.

MORGAN SAGE is a recent graduate of the master's program in geography at Queen's University.

ZACHARY SPICER is the director of research and outreach with the Institute of Public Administration of Canada, a lecturer with the local government program at the University of Western Ontario, and an associate with the University of Toronto's Innovation Policy Lab. He obtained his PhD from the University of Western Ontario and held post-doctoral fellowships with the Laurier Institute of Public Opinion and Policy at Wilfrid Laurier University and the Institute on Municipal Finance and Governance at the University of Toronto's Munk School of Global Affairs. His research focuses on urban public policy and governance of Canadian cities.

NATHAN STEWART is a PhD candidate in economic geography at the University of Toronto. His work looks at the relationship between technological change and organizational innovation within the marketing services industry. Nathan also works as a research consultant for the Asia Pacific Foundation of Canada, where he conducts research into Asian innovation ecosystems.

BRIAN WEBB is a senior lecturer in spatial planning in the School of Geography and Planning, Cardiff University. He has over ten years of experience in planning practice and research and has been involved in policy-focused research for public, private, and non-profit organizations. He obtained his PhD from the University of Manchester in planning and landscape and has undertaken research on the governance and implementation of smart cities, national planning policy, strategic planning, infrastructure planning, and housing and neighbourhood dynamics.

ANDREW WOLF is a PhD Candidate in the Department of Sociology at the University of Wisconsin–Madison. He previously worked as a research analyst for the Service Employees International Union Local 32BJ. He researches the intersection of law, work, and social movements. In particular, he studies how labour movements and governments are responding to emerging phenomena like the gig economy and international trade, with a particular focus on the impacts for immigrant populations. He is working on a book project about immigrant worker and union response to the gig economy in New York City.

CLARENCE WOUDSMA is an associate professor in the University of Waterloo's School of Planning where he was also director from 2008 to 2020. He is a past president of the Canadian Transportation Research Forum and obtained his PhD from McMaster University. His research experience includes transport market deregulation, climate change impacts and adaptation, GHG emissions, freight sprawl, and a recent emphasis on new mobility and last-mile delivery.

MISCHA YOUNG is a post-doctoral research fellow in the Institute of Transportation Studies at the University of California, Davis. He obtained a PhD from the University of Toronto in planning and has a background in economics and urban studies. His research focuses on emerging transportation technologies and the future of personal mobility. He is especially interested in the transport equity concerns that these new modes may engender, and the ways in which transportation policies may be used to modulate travel behaviours.

AUSTIN ZWICK is an assistant teaching professor and assistant director of the Policy Studies Undergraduate Program at the Maxwell School of Public Affairs and Citizenship, Syracuse University. He obtained a PhD from the University of Toronto in planning and an MPA in public finance and fiscal policy from Cornell University. He previously worked as a planner for the Ontario Ministry of Transportation on plans and regulations for autonomous vehicles and other mobility technologies. His research focuses on urban policy and governance challenges arising from emerging industries with an emphasis on transportation and economic development.

Index